ROUTLEDGE LIBRARY EDITIONS:
DEMOGRAPHY

Volume 10

THE GROWTH AND DISTRIBUTION OF POPULATION

THE GROWTH AND DISTRIBUTION OF POPULATION

S. VERE PEARSON

Routledge
Taylor & Francis Group

LONDON AND NEW YORK

First published in 1935 by George Allen & Unwin Ltd

This edition first published in 2024
by Routledge
4 Park Square, Milton Park, Abingdon, Oxon OX14 4RN

and by Routledge
605 Third Avenue, New York, NY 10158

Routledge is an imprint of the Taylor & Francis Group, an informa business

British Library Cataloguing in Publication Data
A catalogue record for this book is available from the British Library

ISBN: 978-1-032-53819-8 (Set)
ISBN: 978-1-032-55332-0 (Volume 10) (hbk)
ISBN: 978-1-032-55335-1 (Volume 10) (pbk)
ISBN: 978-1-003-43016-2 (Volume 10) (ebk)

DOI: 10.4324/9781003430162

Publisher's Note
The publisher has gone to great lengths to ensure the quality of this reprint but points out that some imperfections in the original copies may be apparent.

Disclaimer
The publisher has made every effort to trace copyright holders and would welcome correspondence from those they have been unable to trace.

A HUMAN BEEHIVE, NEW YORK

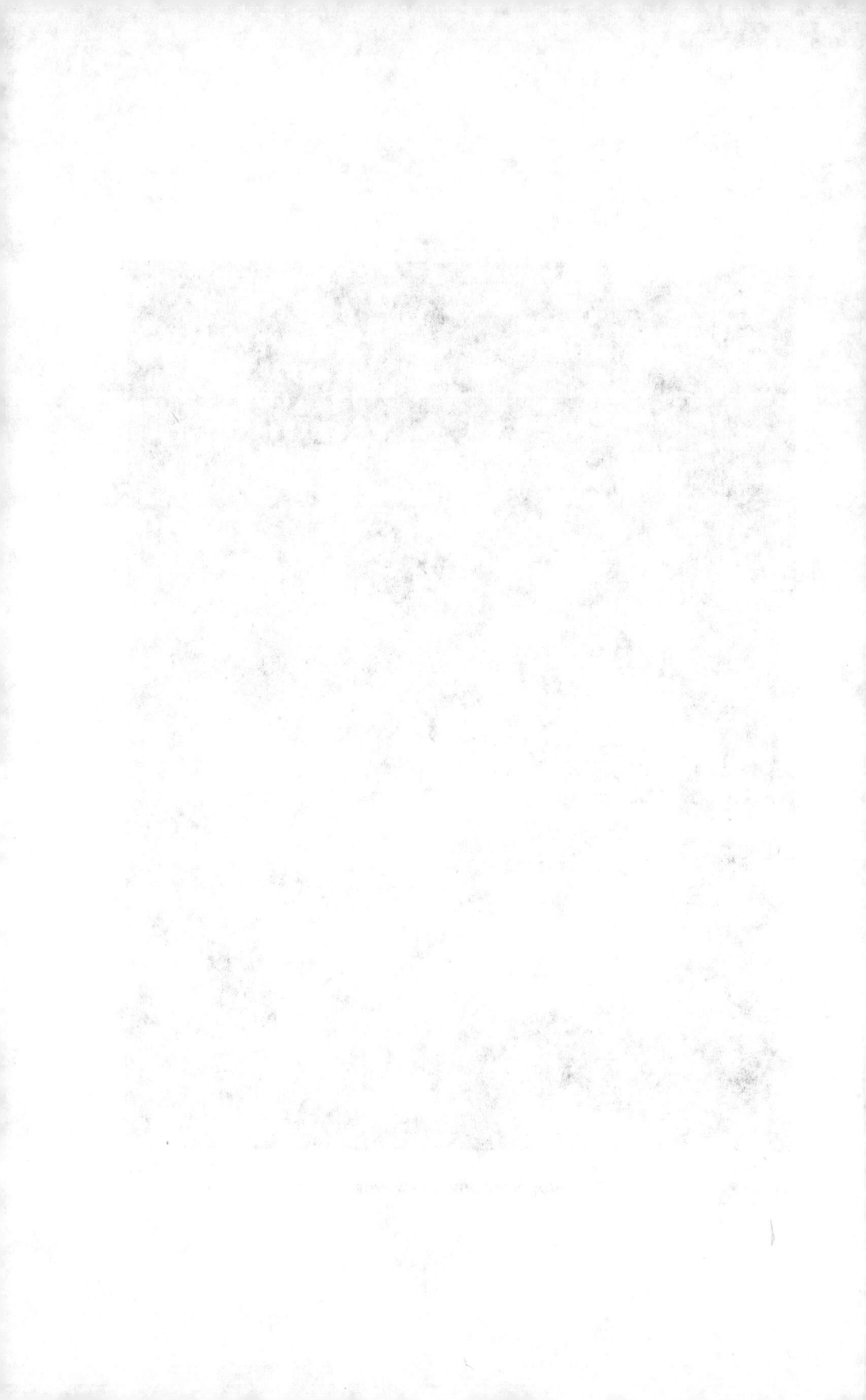

The Growth and Distribution of Population

by

S. VERE PEARSON

M.A., M.D. (*Cambridge*)
M.R.C.P. (*London*)

LONDON

George Allen & Unwin Ltd

MUSEUM STREET

FIRST PUBLISHED IN 1935

PRINTED IN GREAT BRITAIN BY
UNWIN BROTHERS LTD., WOKING

CONTENTS

LIST OF ILLUSTRATIONS

A*

PREFACE

AN understanding of the problems connected with the growth and distribution of population requires a knowledge of economics and psychology, two sciences which I have studied for more than thirty years. I do not refer so much to the economics and psychology of the textbooks as to the elementary common-sense forms a knowledge of which an average man or woman acquires from life's experience and from nowhere else. These require neither instruments nor laboratories.

As regards economics: anyone able to travel even a short distance sees open spaces which appear to be quite capable of supporting life easily, yet he is told the world is over-populated. The economists, he finds, hardly seem able to understand what "employment" is, and are coming to look upon a certain amount of unemployment as a normal state. He hears talk of over-production, of a surplus of goods, and of prices being too high. Yet he knows plenty of people who want goods, who could produce more if given a chance, and he feels sure most people would like low prices. He cannot be persuaded that killing people off by wars, or by famine or disease, can ever be good; and he believes these evils are much more controllable than they were in former times. Yet the economists do not show clearly how they can be prevented.

The conclusions I set down in the following pages differ in many particulars from the conclusions arrived at by those who write on the subject of population. I have attempted to set them forth in an orderly manner, despite the size and complexity of the subject, by evolving certain principles which I believe under-lie the growth and distribution of populations. It is because these principles have been too often ignored that wrong ideas have sprung up, ideas on such matters as over-population; conflict between classes, races, and nations; restricted emigration; differential birth-rates; rural depopulation; town planning; slum clearances, etc.

As regards psychology: this science has only come into line with the lessons of life during recent years. When reliance was placed upon laboratory experiments and too close a respect for the influences of heredity, everyday happenings in the home and in the city appeared essentially aloof from this science, and even at variance with it. To-day human behaviour and human illnesses both individual and in the mass can be better understood because psychology has had a new birth. Basic causes of domestic disharmonies, of childhood phobias, of complexes having a familial origin, of the actions of the crowd, are coming to be recognized. Their influence, however, upon the growth of population is but little appreciated.

The writing of a Preface gives me the opportunity of thanking the many friends who have helped me, two of whom in particular I wish to mention specially, Mr. Mervyn J. Stewart for his unfailing inspiration, and Mr. G. J. Hornsby-Wright for his indefatigable patience in reading the manuscript.

S. VERE PEARSON

MUNDESLEY
November 1934

THE GROWTH AND DISTRIBUTION
OF POPULATION

CHAPTER I

INTRODUCTION

THIS is a book on human geography, on the relationship of
man to his environment. It deals with the way people are
distributed over the land surface of the globe, and how they have
grown and are growing. Population problems are becoming
increasingly popular. They have often fascinated the minds of
past generations. Their study has been advanced a great deal in
recent decades. Many researches have been made, many observations have been collected to elucidate them. In the days of
Nebuchadnezzar, of Cicero, of Queen Elizabeth, of Malthus, the
increase of population, its distribution, the tendency city-wards,
the effect of pressure of population on the means of subsistence
were subjects of special attention. But it is really only within the
last fifty years that reliable data for appraising and judging these
matters have been collected and have made it possible to arrive
at scientific conclusions. Even now, knowledge is incomplete;
many conclusions must be considered tentative. Several excellent
books have been published on these topics in the last few years,
yet some of the most important influences governing the distribution of population in the past, in the present, and in the
future still remain inadequately appreciated and elaborated.

Population is distributed over the face of the globe according
to circumstances which primarily depended upon geographical
conditions. The nature and degree of fertility of the soil, the contour of the surface, the climatic conditions, the accessibility to
other human beings are all factors of first importance. But these
primary influences are less important than they were. This is due
to increased knowledge, mostly acquired in the last sixty or
seventy years, facilitating the production of food, clothing, and
other commodities, and in the science of transport and of com-

bating climatic peculiarities of various regions formerly adverse
to humans. In surveying the whole subject of the distribution of
population it is necessary to study each of these influences in
detail and to weigh their relative importance. Many other factors,
possibly affecting populations even more than the primary ones,
must be reviewed.

Throughout the ages old laws and customs, more especially as
to the rights of property and of families and tribes, have important
bearings on how individuals were grouped on the earth. Ancient
law knew next to nothing of individuals. The personal relationship
of one individual to another has been and still is inextricably associated with the proprietary rights of human beings. Such factors are
perhaps more important to-day than ever before, yet they usually
receive rather scant attention in writings on population. If they
are more important to-day than ever it is expedient to examine
them fully in order that the knowledge acquired by such study
may help to guide the trend of events in the future. It is especially
desirable to discover, if possible, what modern tendencies in
population distribution are undesirable, how such tendencies
arise, and how they can be overcome. In doing this it will, of
course, be necessary to probe into the past which is living in us
in order to find out how the present state of affairs has arisen.

The distribution of population is not only dependent upon such
influences as have already been mentioned, but must also obviously depend on actual numbers. Thus a survey is necessary of
all the facts, so far as they have been ascertained, regarding the
numbers of individuals in one place and another, their rate of
increase or decrease in various countries and under varying circumstances, both through past ages and to-day. This involves
some study of birth, death, and marriage rates, as well as the
means and reasons which control these rates, subjects about
which it is only in comparatively recent years that any knowledge
has been acquired. It also involves an examination of the complicated economic and political institutions of to-day in so far as
these have an effect upon population. Under this head must be
included especially, because rightly falling more under it than
under any other division of the subject, rural depopulation, emigration, and the effects of recent changes in industrial and
trading habits.

Since the days of Rousseau no inquiry of this kind can neglect an examination of Natural Laws. Not only is it necessary to recognize that nature ordains an adjustment between life and its inorganic environment, but the modern science of ecology shows how nature insists, too, on a nice balance between any animal and its organic environment. This science is defined as the science of the economy of animals and plants, as that branch of biology which deals with the relations of living organisms to their surroundings, their habits and modes of life, etc. Furthermore, in the sphere of sociology it is only in comparatively recent times that man has learnt at all clearly his inability to prosper if his man-made customs are at variance with natural laws. Habits in organized society must conform to these laws. No human ordinance, however long established, which defies God (which is one way of putting it) can stand without doing harm to the human community. It is only now becoming at all widely acknowledged that economic laws are as irrefutable as the laws of physics, astronomy, chemistry, etc., and that if nations transgress them in their methods of providing for the management of the common fund, in their administration of justice, or in other ways they can but do hurt to their own peoples.

There is an idea coming to be very prevalent which assumes that the larger part of the earth's habitable surface supports about as many people as it can under the prevailing types of culture and standards of living. It is true that there is a growing tendency for the great mass of the poorer people who swarm in the industrial cities to drop to a standard of living which is lower than that of corresponding people at an earlier age. Especially is this so when account is taken of the enormous advances which have been made in the means of production due to the many inventions and discoveries of the last hundred years. Coincident with the wide adoption of this idea and somewhat naturally springing from it there are alarms about the future. The pages of this book will examine this idea. They will attempt to refute it, and to dispel such fears.

The magic touchstone for establishing a just and beneficial distribution of population should be freedom. Though this century has seen a serious relapse to coercion and a curtailment of liberty here and there, it should shine out as one in which a greater freedom reigns than ever before. The people of Great Britain at all events can pride themselves upon having attained by degrees a wider freedom compared with previous centuries. They have, perhaps largely through the long-established institution of parliamentary government, of which they are so rightly proud, established a large measure of liberty in the religious and political spheres as well as in the administration of justice. There is freedom of speech, too, and freedom of the Press. Economic freedom is still far to seek, and this fact involves many of the most important matters which to-day, more than ever before, affect the distribution of population. When man has got, not a stupid communism, not an impossible levelling, but equality of opportunity to life, health, and the pursuit of happiness, then will disappear all those unnatural hindrances to changes in the number of persons and interferences with their distribution which are so rife to-day. A different outlook will automatically arise on the problems of population which now interest, not to say excite, those who discuss these things. A proper exercise of the sexual instinct if based on free love (in its purest and widest sense), combined with a happier and less harassed state of family life due to economic freedom, would throw an entirely new light on many of the suggestions put forward to-day. Under the head of eugenics, doctrines are preached which find their real origin in a combination of the fears referred to above and the sense of superiority and desire for a continuance of the prestige which under the present conduct of society belongs to certain privileged classes.

CHAPTER II

SOIL FERTILITY, CLIMATE, ACCESSIBILITY: ORIGIN OF VILLAGES AND TOWNS

NATURALLY man will tend to congregate more closely where land is most fertile because there he can more easily produce the food he needs. This is true only in that stage of society into which agriculture has been introduced. Before man learnt to grow foods he was a hunter and a shepherd. He therefore dwelt in those parts of the globe which were suitable for the grazing of animals, and, because pastures tended to want resting, he was frequently a nomad. Therefore pastoral tribes spread over more surface than those which engaged in agriculture. They required more land. The degree of skill in production is one of the important factors governing man's numbers. This was especially so in his early days when to scratch a subsistence from nature's resources was so much more difficult than in modern times. The advance in knowledge makes it much easier to earn a living in the present day. The following estimate—conjectures, perhaps, would be a better word—of population in prehistoric times gives an indication of this: When the earliest Danes were only developed up to a stage comparable to that of the aboriginal Australians when first discovered, their 15,000 square miles contained only about 500 people. When they had reached a state comparable to the original natives of Patagonia their land could support about double this number. Later, when they became pastoral (? about 5000–4000 B.C.), one farm required 300 cattle or 2,000 acres. At that time France could support 50,000 and Europe had less than 1,000,000 people. In A.D. 500 Europe had about 40,000,000, in 1500 70,000,000, and could not support 170,000,000 until A.D. 1800. The north with hunters was thinly, and the south with agriculturists thickly, populated. Agricultural production was easiest where flat lands of good fertility, free from growths of forests or weeds, were found in warm or moderately warm climates. Thus it comes about that treeless flood plains in fairly warm regions with long, dry seasons have been the main centres of early civilization, namely, the plains of the Nile, Euphrates, Tigris, Indus, and Huang in the Old World, and a series of smaller streams in Peru and Mexico. But before the advent of agriculture ancient Egypt and Mesopotamia were probably able to support less than one hunter for every square mile. Yet a few generations later, when agricultural pursuits were being developed, even though primitively, these regions were able most likely to support twenty or more times as many people.

The nature and fertility of the soil, because so closely related to the means and methods of sustenance, are factors of primary importance, influencing not only the amount but also the distribution of population. The character of a soil depends partly upon the character of the underlying rocks, upon the contour or relief of the land, and upon climate. Soil, which may be of a fertile kind arising from satisfactory underlying strata, may be washed away by rain and storm from the sides of steep mountains. On the other hand, beautifully fertile soil may grow nothing at all if it is situated in an arid desert, or it may be so water-logged as to be useless to human beings. Methods of supplying water to rich desert soils are improving rapidly. This, taken in conjunction with the fact that the soils of many vast desert areas are really amongst the most fertile of all, will tend to make fertility of less importance than before in its effect upon the distribution of population. Some of these areas, too, are in warm climates where vegetable life will grow quickly if given other suitable conditions. A rich soil requires the retention in it of a fertilizing humus. Such a humus arises from the decay of vegetable material. Again, a rich soil depends upon a due supply of certain mineral salts, and these are generally best got from the decay of animal material. The animal and vegetable kingdoms perpetually play into one another's hands, and conserve each from exhaustion. Hence an everlasting cycle of life. These things are now well understood. The management both of the vegetably originating humus and of fertility produced from animal manures or certain other mineral sources are well under the control of man. Consequently a given fertility of soil can be produced on a certain site in a way which was quite impossible a generation or two ago. None the less, population still tends to become dense where the character of the soil, and its position regarding water content, are such that food can be easily produced. Large numbers are found in such regions. For example, in the Nile Valley there are 11,000 persons to every square mile, but adjoining part of it is the Egyptian desert where there is scarcely one person in three thousand times as much territory. Nowadays, however, this influence of soil fertility on how peoples are aggregated is less than it was. This is not only because fertility is more readily controlled but also because food-stuffs are so much more easily transported from place to place than was possible before the inventions of the last hundred years revolutionized transport. The very character of the food of thickly inhabited countries in temperate climes, such as England where there are 700 people per square mile, has become quite altered in living memory through this factor. Oranges and lemons are now cheap and plentiful in England, and bananas, almost unknown about a generation ago, are a common article of diet. In spite of the inhabitants of London, who are as thick as 58·7 to the acre,[1] being almost completely unable to grow any vegetables or catch any fish, there is always an abundance of fresh vegetables and fish to be procured, and cheaply too, in her markets. Much labour in shipbuilding, in rail and motor traffic manufacture, even in road repairing, in the work of transporters and of clerks and insurance brokers, etc., might be spared from the secondary industries if more labour were spent in the primary industry of agriculture through a more even spread of population. And civilized man would be both healthier and happier for such a change. Charles Kingsley in 1859 wrote (*Miscellanies*, Vol. II, p. 339), "If you cannot bring the country into the city, the city must go into the country"; and he pointed out that the enormous amount of vested interests in the value of city lands seems to make it impossible to contemplate any attempt to rebuild our cities so as to incorporate garden production in them. He therefore advocated "to build better things than cities. They will issue in a complete interpenetration of city and of country, a complete

---

[1] This is the density in the 74,850 acres of the Administrative County of London. The density in the 443,455 acres of Greater London (containing a population of 8,203,942 persons) is 18·5: see *London Statistics*, Vol. XXXVI, 1931–32, L.C.C.

fusion of their different modes of life, and a combination of the advantages of both." Ten years previously James Silk Buckingham, too, made suggestions similar to those of Kingsley. He adumbrated most of the reforms for healthy and pleasing town planning which are apt to be considered as of quite modern innovation, and in his *Model-Town: Victoria* the inhabitants were to be in "such due proportions between the agricultural and manufacturing classes . . . as to produce the highest degree of abundance in every necessary of life . . . with the lightest amount of labour."

It has been said that fertile soil can be manufactured. It can even be transported. In the Channel Isles, for example, there are many sites originally more or less bare rock to which good soil has been taken where plentiful crops are now growing year after year, and on some of them two or three crops within the year. The use of glass as garden frames, as cloches, or in greenhouses has, of course, brought about profound changes in cultivation. These followed long after those effects upon the distribution of population which resulted from its first introduction for windows. Glass windows permitted window openings to be enlarged so as to enable indoor dwellers to work better than formerly at sedentary occupations because in ampler light and with warmer hands. Glass did not become common until after 1600, by which date there was less time wasted in the winter because those unable to find work out of doors could more easily work indoors. Still more important in influencing the distribution of population was the introduction of glass into horticulture and agriculture. Prince Kropotkin, the great Russian philosophical anarchist, when imprisoned in Paris at the behest of Czarism, asked leave to be allowed access to a small patch of land in the prison grounds. His studies at that time, about the year 1884, gave a great impetus to the intensive system of agriculture which came to be practised subsequently so extensively round about Paris, and which for a long time was one of the chief sources of supply for early salads and tender spring table vegetables for the London luxury markets. Where population is thick many mouths can be fed from smaller areas of land if intensive cultivation is practised. Four or five crops are grown from one patch in less than twelve months, sometimes in less than six months. This is being increasingly done in England on hotbeds whose sole heat is obtained from the spontaneous heat of manure, generally horse manure, though difficulties now arise through the increasing scarcity of this commodity. But greenhouse heating appliances are improving and glass should gradually become cheaper.

Intensive cultivation employs more human labour howsoever the land is used. There is an area of eight acres, for example, known to the writer which used to produce, at the outside, about £100 worth of foodstuffs per annum when it was used as ordinary farm land. The average number of "hands" required on such a farm was three and a half men per hundred acres. Nowadays that same land used as a poultry farm for the production of eggs and table birds produces not less than £1,500 worth of foodstuffs per annum, and provides occupation for two full-timers and part-time occupation for a third person. Progress is slow. Changes from one kind of cultivation to a more intensive kind do not take place in a day. While there are many parts of the world where such changes are occurring, there are other regions where more extensive forms of cultivation are the suitable modification from old-fashioned practice. These use more machinery, more tractors, etc., and fewer "hands" per acre. Decisions as to where to encourage the one and where the other kind of change are not always wisely made. Political influences and wrong notions frequently influence such decisions rather than sound reasons based upon the common weal. If general welfare alone were heeded, the distribution of population would be more sensible. People would be dispersed more widely, but not too far apart for human health and convenience.

The length of time during which the soil of a given district has been under cultivation is an important consideration. This is wrapt up with the method of keeping up soil fertility, with the numbers cultivating it, and with the climate of the region. Compare the United States of America with China. The former is as yet a nation of but few people widely scattered over a broad virgin land with more than twenty acres to the support of every man, woman, and child, while the people of China are toiling in fields tilled for more than three thousand years. They have barely one acre *per capita*, for more than half of China is uncultivable mountain land. The question of the maintenance of soil pro-

ductivity for the support of the increasing population of the world
was debated in Athens and Rome over two thousand years ago.
Cato answered the question very emphatically by saying: no, the
soil does not die as man dies, but will respond but little to a
shiftless and unintelligent care of ignorant people. In Japan the
soils which have been longest in cultivation, possibly in some
places for as long as five thousand to six thousand years, are
most prized because they are under more perfect control and
are considered surer and more productive. Some holdings have
been in the occupation of the same family for hundreds of
years. Since the days of Liebig, from 1840, and of Sir John
Lawes, who established the famous agricultural research plots
at Rothamsted in 1844, empirical knowledge gained by practice
has become augmented by a whole body of scientific researches
into the chemistry and bacteriology of soil fertility. Although
some tentative practices in intensive cultivation were made
in ancient times in countries as far apart as China and Italy,
real intensive methods have only become well understood
within the last eighty years. So much has been learnt in the last
twenty years or so about these things that at length agriculture
is developing in a way which is more comparable with the
development of industry. Consequently, increasing crop yields
can meet the needs of the increasing population of the world.
Professor East, of Harvard, said a few years ago that the cultivable acreage of the world is about 13,000,000,000 and two and
a half acres are required to feed each human being. Since the
present population of the globe is estimated to be rather less than
2,000,000,000 and the rate of increase to be 0·8 per cent per
annum, the people of the world are not likely to starve yet a
while from reaching the limit of the possibilities of food production
even on this basis. But the calculations are probably inaccurate,
and the rate of increase is conjectural. Certain it is that food
in greater abundance than ever can be produced now that so
much more is known about how to make and keep soils more
fertile, how to produce food of all kinds from smaller areas, and
how to transport easily the foodstuffs produced.

Soil fertility has been altered by moving chemical substances,
often great distances, to increase the soil's content of certain
mineral salts which add to its productivity; and this method of

influencing fertility has only been practised to any appreciable
extent during the last one hundred years of the world's history.
The production and transportation of these so-called artificial
fertilizers is a big business nowadays. They affect the dispersal
or agglomeration of population in a way which was unthought
of a generation or two ago. Not only so, but some authorities think
they actually affect numbers. Here is a quotation from Sir Charles
Fielding's *Food* (Hurst & Blackett, 1923, p. 224): "The normal
increase of our population will, twenty-five years hence, require
an amount of food necessitating the consumption of nearly
4,000,000 tons of phosphates, and a similar ratio of need will
exist all over the world. Within the next three or four decades the
scramble for phosphate rock will be so severe that those countries
not obtaining it will be compelled to keep down its population."
Or perhaps the world will develop such intrigues amongst politicians and financial magnates as Hilaire Belloc so amusingly
depicts in his story of the year 1979 entitled *Shadowed!*

The other geographical conditions of primary importance in
determining how population is distributed, besides the fertility of
the soil, have to do with the contour or relief of the land, and the
climate. These have direct or indirect influences upon soil fertility,
as they undoubtedly have upon the growth and welfare of life,
both vegetable and animal. The richest soil which is always
frozen cannot support life; nor can earth which is devoid of
water. Soils are usually of mixed origin from materials which
sometimes are carried by storm or river from great distances. A
mixing of ingredients usually makes for fertility. The nature of the
rocks from which the ingredients originally come is an important
element affecting the value of the soil. These factors depend
upon the steepness or otherwise of the land from which the
ingredients are derived and on which the soils are found.

The question of temperature and altitude naturally affect
population directly through the associated climatic conditions.
Coldness affects the soil, which must be looked upon as something
living. The earth is always eating, building up, and decaying,
breaking down, and if these processes are too slow through low-
ness of temperature the soil will be poor. They are partly
dependent upon the growth of bacteria, which are minute organisms belonging to the vegetable kingdom. They are aided by a

due amount of moisture in the soil, and by a soil atmosphere. The gaseous pores of the soil commonly take up from 10 to 20 per cent of its volume. The soil atmosphere is slightly altered air (richer in carbon dioxide gas, for example). It is for the most part in close contact with the roots of plants growing in the soil or with the bacteria. If the processes of life of a soil are too quick, as may happen in hot climates, fertility is interfered with. Such variations due to climate largely account for the kind of things that grow best at different altitudes and in varying climates, and upon what the earth can naturally produce depends, to a considerable extent, the density of the human population of a district. Take Japan as an illustration. This is a somewhat densely inhabited country with more than 400 people to the square mile, but its population is unevenly distributed, a fact partly due to the comparative smallness of the area in crops. It is estimated that but 14 per cent of the area of Japan is arable land, there being 63 per cent in forest, and 11 per cent that is possible of reclamation. Of the total area of Japan, 12 per cent is not susceptible of use for agriculture of forestry, being utilized for cities, town lots, and roads, and including among other areas the rough mountain tops not in forest. Forty per cent of the inhabitants are engaged in agricultural pursuits. Japan had a total population of 64,500,000 in 1931, i.e. in Japan proper and not including oversea populations. If these are included there is a population of about 90,000,000 in the whole of the Japanese Empire, Korea possessing 20,000,000 and Formosa 4,000,000 inhabitants. The average density of population per square mile of agricultural and industrial areas in Japan is about 720 persons, and the rate of increase of population is more than 750,000 every year. About one-half of the country is mountains and lakes; and much of her soil is rather barren. Though mountainous, every little valley in Japan is tilled, and so are the slopes, except where they become so steep that the farms cannot cling to them, or are so high up that the temperature becomes too low. Agrarian and political unrest and a steady drift to industrial centres are marked characteristics of the Japanese of to-day. Small-holdings of about eight acres are a general rule in Japan. But in recent years the farmers of Japan have fallen heavily into debt, to the extent it is said of 5,000,000,000 yen in 1932. What with a big fall in the price of rice and silk, and much unemployment and food shortage, it is not surprising that Japanese workers have fallen an easy prey to her own military jingoists. Thus an indirect connection can be traced between climate, land surface contours, soil fertility, and war, which again through the destruction of human life influences the numbers of individuals on the earth. The interweaving of influences affecting population is close.

Climatic conditions alone chiefly account for the fact that half the earth's surface has less than one inhabitant per square mile. These regions include 12,000,000 square miles which are too dry for agriculture, 5,000,000 in Africa, 4,000,000 in Asia, and 2,000,000 in Australasia. There are another 13,500,000 square miles with less than one person per square mile because the districts are too cold for agriculture, either through high latitude or through high altitude. There are smaller areas also included in these sparsely populated regions which are too warm and wet for agriculture. But increase of scientific knowledge makes steady strides, and an interesting question is whether, if it seems necessary so to do, the climatic handicaps of some of these regions can be overcome so that they will become moderately densely populated. The main areas where the inhabitants number more than 120 per square mile are either located in warm, moist regions where mostly sugar and rice are raised, or in temperate lands where rain storms at most times of the year are not scarce. The rice regions support approximately 700,000,000 people in about 2,250,000 square miles—one person for every two acres compared with one for every twelve hundred or more in the sparsely settled half of the world. When the two kinds of thickly settled regions are combined it is found that nearly two-thirds of the people of the earth are crowded into 7 per cent of the lands. The point of importance to note is that a rich soil is easier to create than artificial water-courses or an artificial climate. For example, parts of Florida now possess productive soils through fertilizers, energy, and brains where formerly there were poor, sandy, unproductive earths. In some places water is all that is needed to make thinly populated regions with good soil more productive. Much has been done in various parts of the world to fill this want in the last fifty years. Yet the ravages of wars of long ago resulting in an abandonment of good

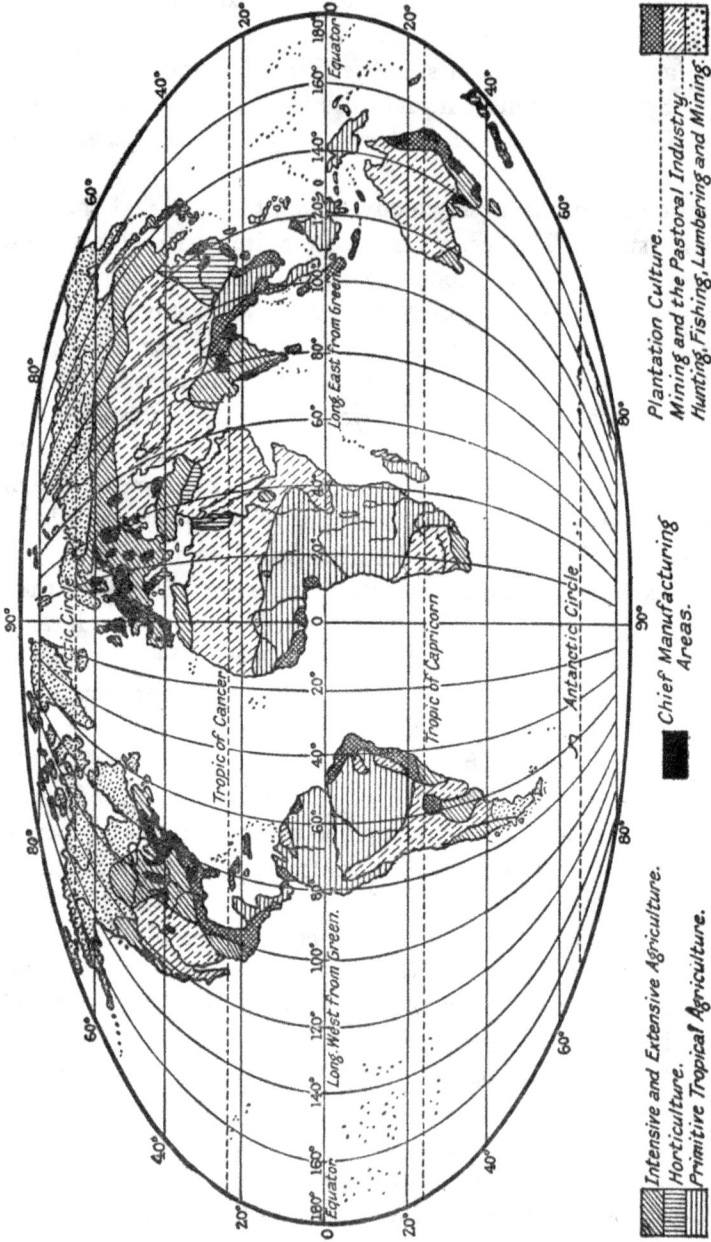

OCCUPATIONS OF MANKIND

By kind permission of Messrs. Sir Isaac Pitman & Sons, Ltd.

agriculture and the destruction of irrigation works[1] have scarcely been made good by all the great engineering feats of modern construction which carry water to rich and desirable but parched types of soil (in such places as Egypt, India, and Burma). Furthermore, recent developments have frequently been carried out in countries other than those formerly pursuing a prosperous agriculture, countries often having also thriving industries and a thick population. Asia Minor, for example, for centuries up to about a thousand years ago was rich and prosperous. From about A.D. 1070 the prosperity and peace of the previous centuries came to an end, and the country was for long years the prey of Turkish nomad tribes, who wandered through it, caring nothing for any agriculture or for urban pursuits. They left the land bare behind them. Sir William Ramsay (*National Geographical Magazine*, November 1922) gave a graphic description suggestive of a vast irrigation and water control system which had been built up in past ages but which is now totally destroyed. He mentions also that Asia Minor once boasted two hundred and thirty independent cities. Before the Seljuk Turks desolated Asia Minor the devastation was started by the Crusaders, who cut down olive and fruit trees ruthlessly and eventually forests for purposes of war. The death of agriculture in these regions was not due to a deterioration of the soils but to political changes.[2]

When official efforts are made to control population either directly, from political or racial motives, or indirectly as a result of warfare, ill results generally accrue. Take the case of Spain in the Middle Ages. Her autocratic and bigoted Governments expelled the Moors, who were some of the most industrious and enlightened elements of her population. Industry and agriculture suffered for generations. She expelled the Jews to the serious detriment of her business and commercial prosperity. And, in the interests of a decadent religious orthodoxy, she tortured and killed, again, of course, to her hurt, many of her most intellectual citizens. Religious and sectarian intolerance and racial jealousies throve in former times and often caused great interference with

[1] See the author's article on "Man and Mosquito in Ceylon" in *Discovery*, January 1935.

[2] See Milton Whitney's *Soil and Civilization*, pp. 188 et seq. (Library of Modern Science: Chapman & Hall, 1926).

the growth and distribution of population. The desire for power, and spirit of animosity born out of lack of knowledge about and hence of sympathy for people of a different race, a scramble for adequate sustenance amongst competing individuals and classes have been common influences affecting the growth and aggregation of various groups of human beings throughout the centuries. Though tolerance has grown, jealousies are less rife, and freedom is greater in many ways nowadays, it must unfortunately be admitted that these influences have not been banished.

To return to the question of relief, to the amount of flatness or slope of the land and how this affects the number of inhabitants. Man needs level land for prosperity and high numbers closely congregated. The world's greatest populations are all located in regions of gentle relief; but usually these places are where good climates are to be found. Often mountainous regions are bad climatically for agriculture and other kinds of production as well as for human beings. Yet mountains in themselves do not necessarily preclude large numbers thickly congregated, as is exemplified by Java, a mountainous country but very thickly populated. There the mountainous sides are terraced for agriculture very carefully, and the climate is favourable. Were it otherwise good soil would be washed from the slopes. This naturally occurs more readily when man has cleared away forests. This is but one of the many connections between deforestation, and afforestation, and population, some of which will be referred to in later pages.

The earliest settlements in Europe of peoples who had learned something of agriculture occurred in regions where it was possible to practice the newly acquired art on suitable sites not covered by trees. Evidence has come to light in recent years that these sites were to begin with chiefly along the basin of the Danube. At first small patches of land were cultivated until these were exhausted and then abandoned.[1] There was hardly any knowledge about manures. In out of the way parts of the world primitive peoples are still to be found who have not advanced beyond this stage. Their villages are unlikely to be found closely settled and permanently built. When villages came to be more permanent and fixed a system of cultivation which includes

[1] See *Report on Types of Village Settlements.* 1928 (Union Géographique Internationale).

periodical rest, or fallowing for the land, is generally found. With this system evidences are sometimes to be discovered of both rotation in cropping and the communal ownership of the land. Knowledge about these things in as remote times as the Bronze Age in England and on the continent of Europe is slowly being accumulated. Whether, therefore, population dwelt in olden times in concentrated villages or in a dispersed fashion is seen to depend upon soil, relief, climate, and upon methods of obtaining a livelihood. An enclosed field system, which usually comes at a later stage in history, tends to go with a dispersed habitat and less obvious arrangements of a tribal nature in the use of the land. Even to-day, when agriculture is aided by all that modern science gives, these influences on the distribution of population are not absent. Various parts of Italy of differing fertility, contour, and methods of land tenure are instructive regions in which to make a study of these matters both as to conditions extant in the past and in the present. Russia is another part of the world to watch. Here big-scale experiments in the organization of agricultural production, in systems of land tenure, and in the relationship of the individual to the State are being made. An antagonism often arises between town and country, between rural and industrial workers; and this antagonism, it would seem, is difficult to allay in the Soviet Republic. Persons of diverse tastes and capabilities should be able to follow the vocation to which they incline. This, with change and variety in occupation and recreation, is conducive to the health and happiness of individuals and of the community. A better knowledge of political economy will lead to this and to the overcoming of class antagonisms. Present leaders in Russia have not yet acquired this better knowledge. Hence freedom and plenty do not reign there, nor a sound distribution of population so that none feel overcrowded and none too isolated.

Besides methods of agricultural culture and property rights, more especially in respect of land, the following influences affect the distribution of population in agricultural communities: abundance or scarcity of water; the needs of defence; the requirements of stock farming; and ethnic traditions. How different are the causes which lead to the agglomeration of large groups of peoples at the present day, in thickly populated industrialized countries at all events! But to understand the present it is necessary to know how things have developed. Professor Huntingdon has said: "In the long run, though accessibility counts, soil, relief, and especially climate are the main determinants of where people dwell."[1] That is true for the world at large. But for most of the inhabitants of closely populated countries in the temperate cyclonic regions it is economic influences which now largely determine the distribution of population. These are, more than ever before, leading people to migrate from rural districts and pursuits into the cities.

The precise time and the exact method of the introduction of the idea of private property in land varies from country to country and from age to age. In some places it occurred through a modification of a feudal system added to a fundamental change in the methods financing public services. In other places or at other times it was associated with wholesale "enclosure Acts." Customs which are apparently different, however, are sometimes found, upon examination, to be in essentials the same as, or at all events very similar to, those found in widely separated places.

For many ages the way in which dwellings were dispersed or placed close together depended quite clearly and to a big extent upon the customs followed in the community in regard to property rights. In the present age the same is true, though not so apparent. When man advanced beyond the stage when husbandry was almost the sole means of livelihood, the grouping of dwellings depended less and less upon the methods of husbandry, and the vesting in the community of property rights to land became more and more necessary, but more and more complicated and difficult. The study of these further developments of society and how they affected the growth and distribution of population is best grouped around the idea expressed by the word "accessibility."

As the science and art of living becomes developed, man's need for getting into touch with human beings other than just his own family or small tribal group increases. This has been so throughout the ages, and necessitates a study from this new point of view of the advantages of site and of means of transport. What may be called nodal points, i.e. sites of importance as

[1] E. Huntingdon's *The Human Habitat*, p. 33 (Chapman & Hall).

crossings of two trackways, or spots where rivers were fordable, came to be places where towns grew up. The introduction of the cultivation of root crops on a large scale brought about an increase of live stock. Indirectly this led to a development of roadway communications unknown before. So villages grew up sometimes from new causes. They appeared at bridge-heads, or fords, around smithies, or at favourable spots along roadsides. Rather later towns were established favourable of access to groups

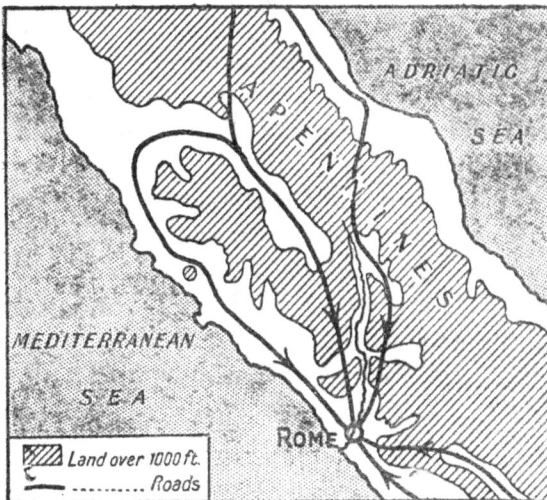

SKETCH TO SHOW THE SITE OF ROME
By kind permission of Messrs. Sir Isaac Pitman & Sons, Ltd.

of agriculturists around. In these the church was built, meeting the religious aspirations of man which have been conspicuous throughout the ages. Even in prehistoric times many of the nodal points, where population was in all probability most congregated, were places where the temple for worship and the centre for common council were to be found. Avebury, in Wiltshire, for example, was a meeting place of this kind, and had got trackways leading to it from far distant parts of England. Amongst the first to dwell in towns which sprang up at such points of ready accessibility were administrators of native law, and merchants to aid in the exchange of goods with their shops, storehouses, or offices. To-day market towns, as they may be called generically, have most of the following buildings in them: schools, hotels, and a post office. These are followed by the dwellings and offices of doctors, science inspectors and workers, insurance and banking clerks, transport workers; to be followed later generally by various kinds of industrial works such as milling, brewing, leather and furniture factories, and a host more. It is an upset of a due balance between what may be called the primary industrial pursuits of food, unfinished fuel, clothing, and building materials production on the one hand, and all the host of secondary pursuits which have multiplied so greatly in the last century that has, above all other things, altered the balance between town and country occupations and habitations.

This is a subject which will be treated much more fully later in this book. A detailed examination of the causes of the disbalance will be undertaken, and of the means it is necessary to take to eradicate any ill effects producing unsound population growth and distribution. The enormous improvements which have been made in recent times in transport and communications account for many of the blessings man now enjoys. But these improvements have also contributed indirectly to the evils associated with the depopulation of the countryside. Their interplay with climate and soil fertility and the effect of this interplay on the density of population is well illustrated by making a few comparisons between Nova Scotia and the State of Massachusetts, and between New Zealand and England. To take the former pair first. The soil of Nova Scotia in its natural state is about as fertile as that of the State of Massachusetts. The summers, however, are rather cooler and the winters are longer in the former country; but there is not sufficient difference in these particulars to explain the contrast between populations of 25 and 500 per square mile. "Only when modern communication enabled food to be brought from the Western United States did Nova Scotia fall much behind southern New England. As soon as food could be brought from Ohio and farther west, where the soil is very rich, it was distinctly cheaper to bring it to southern New England than to Nova Scotia. In the same way, as soon as the cotton gin raised the textile industry to high importance, southern New England had an advantage because it was nearer to the cotton fields, and also to the market for manufactured goods afforded by the farmers, who raised food on the western plains and cotton in the South."[1] Similarly, the importance of accessibility is impressively illustrated by looking at the position of New Zealand and comparing it with that of England or Japan. New Zealand, with an excellent climate, has but 12 persons whereas England has nearly 700 people per square mile. The main islands of Japan, which are warmer and moister than New Zealand, have about 400 persons per square mile. But it is remoteness rather than climate which seems likely still to hinder New Zealand from becoming either a highly populous or a great manufacturing country. How can people become frightened, however, that the world will soon be over-populated when there is a country so well circumstanced as New Zealand, so sparsely inhabited?

Accessibility becomes increasingly important as numbers grow and population becomes denser, and as industrial production is augmented and improved. Rural industry flourished best when the village and the country town were, so to speak, self-contained. To-day, with machinery and mass production, the old-fashioned village industries are hard to revive. Generally it is impossible to retrace steps. Yet more sensible use might be made of the great modern increase in facilities of production and transport. It is absurd that it costs two or three times as much to get a cabbage to the market of one of our big cities as it does to grow it; and that to retail a side of beef costs about as much as it does to rear or feed the animal for three years. The connection between food production and commerce historically considered is fascinating, but can only be lightly touched upon here. When commerce arose in Western Europe about the twelfth century the population of the whole of Europe was only about 40,000,000. At that time the nobility and the clergy alone were powerful, for they alone controlled landownership. Yet landowners had no wide markets, or big ones, and so had no incentive to cultivate well and in improved fashion. As G. C. Coulton has shown in his *The Medieval Village*, the peasant throughout Europe for the greater part of the Middle Ages was very, very poor, and his tenure very insecure. The increase of commerce gave an economic impetus to the rural classes through the gradual appearance of a new rich class not entirely dependent upon landownership, which hitherto

[1] E. Huntingdon's *The Human Habitat*, p. 30 (Chapman & Hall).

had ensured to the owners personal liberty, riches, and social prestige. Liquid capital in contradistinction to wealth in real estate came into being. There was a speeding up, too, of the circulation of money about the same time. Money came to be more used; there was consequently a drop in its value. All these changes were potent factors in the growth of medieval cities, and naturally such cities flourished on sites which were favourably

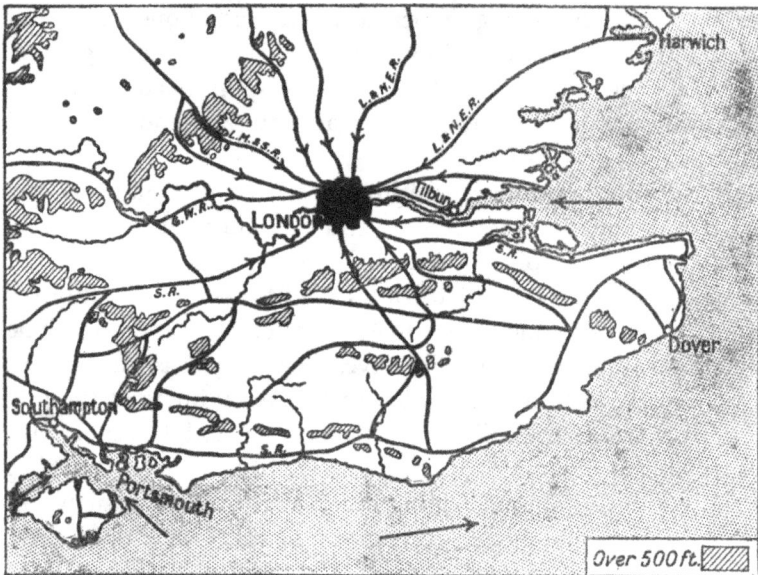

SKETCH SHOWING ACCESSIBILITY OF LONDON'S SITE
By kind permission of Messrs. Sir Isaac Pitman & Sons, Ltd.

situated for transportations to them of persons and merchandise. Again to-day, it is an intensive exploitation of land of exceeding accessibility through an extensive use of land brought about by improvements in transportation that in modern times has made possible the multi-storied buildings of the densely inhabited cities. But to-day other factors, and some new ones, count more than they did.

One further point about accessibility: There are densely populated regions where to-day the inhabitants are mainly vegetarians; for example, the rice-eaters of China. Some of these regions are subject to crop failures from floods, unfavourable climatic conditions, or what not. Severe famines arise and decimate the people. To-day many of these regions enjoy an accessibility which should ensure supplies of food reaching them in time to avert disaster and death, especially when the ease of rapid communications is taken into account. Yet as often as not thousands or even millions of human beings perish from hunger in this world of the twentieth century where knowledge is so advanced and widespread. What is wrong with civilization? Abundance of foodstuffs, often in very transportable and concentrated form, can nowadays be easily produced. Why are the economic conditions of the famished so bad, why are they so poor that they cannot get the food even to save their very lives? And has this state of affairs anything to do with the density of population or with any other condition pertaining to actual numbers or the distribution of people? These questions require investigation.

CHAPTER III

BREAD TO EAT AND SPACE TO LIVE IN

THROUGHOUT discussions on population problems there runs the assumption that a tendency exists for the multiplication of numbers to proceed faster than the increase in the powers of production. Malthus, rather over a hundred years ago, was perhaps the man more than any other who gave impetus to this idea that population tends to increase faster than subsistence. With this idea goes the theory that beyond a certain point the application of capital and labour to land yields a diminishing return. It is a comfortable view to hold in this world of poverty in the midst of plenty in these times when the ingenuity and inventiveness of man has increased the facilities for production so manifoldly. It relieves the mind of those who might otherwise think that man might yet discover, and banish, the causes of poverty if ignorance and stupidity could be dispelled. It is so easy to say, with John Stuart Mill: "The niggardliness of nature, not the injustice of society, is the cause of the penalty attached to over-population." And, on the face of it, it does seem reasonable to believe "a greater number of people cannot, in any given state of civilization, be collectively so well provided for as a smaller." Though each additional mouth is provided with a pair of hands and a fertile brain, there is some satisfaction, amongst the well provided for at all events, in believing that the additional "hands do not produce as much." The law of diminishing returns, as this assumption has been labelled, is supposed to apply especially to agriculture. That is probably due to the fact that living things in their growth and expansion require more space than inanimate things. In all modes of production the things produced, and man the producer, want a certain amount of space. As a general rule, up to a point it spells economy in production to diminish the space occupied, but beyond that point, varying from one kind of production to another, it does not do to overcrowd things. That is all there is to it.

People are very apt to lose sight of the importance of this matter of space. That the use of land is largely a question of space is a fundamental perception, yet it is one which in its manifold ramifications is apt to be overlooked. Furthermore, a fundamental perception is not usually a first perception. For example, weight is a fundamental perception of air, but men have lived without ever realizing that air has weight. Early man looked upon land merely from the point of view of a hunter, according to its capacity to provide him with wild animals. Later man viewed land largely from the angle of its capacity to yield rich crops to the grower. It is only in later days still that land has become valued, more highly than elsewhere and than ever before, according to its use in centres of exchange and commerce. And even to this day, if "the land question" is raised in political circles the thoughts of most persons immediately fly to land's rural uses.

It is only in this century that a realization of some of the laws of progress is coming about. When these laws are better appreciated the development of society will be more orderly, and will produce a more even distribution of wealth. Qualms about food shortage will vanish, and panics lest over-population wreck us. One of these laws is that *the natural and numerical progress of human beings entails access to areas of natural opportunity progressively smaller.* Access to areas of natural opportunity means access to the earth. The development of human skill coincidently with the increase in numbers of human beings enables man to exist comfortably upon smaller and smaller areas of land. There is a regular progression in these developments. First of all there is the nomadic hunter requiring wide areas. Then the nomadic pastoral, with domesticated or semi-domesticated animals. Later, the pastoral within fixed frontiers, as in birds' nesting areas. Next, the pastoral-agricultural, some tending more one way, some more the other, in one place or another, or at one age or another. Seasonal shortage is made good by saved hay and, later in the world's history, by the introduction of root crops. Grain culture is followed by orchard cultivation and dairying. Then comes spade culture on small-holdings, intensive production of truck crops, by which time factories and shops are plentiful. All these varying methods of producing the commodities required to meet human needs involve successively the more intensive use of smaller areas. They also involve displacement of the earlier systems as numbers increase. A means can be found by which these changes can take place without discord, without coercion, and without injustice.

Since all must eat to live, questions of food production are of primary importance in connection with population problems. As society advances, however, the more close settlement and use of sites, the increased skill of man, and the greater subdivision of labour enable more persons to expend their labour profitably in producing other things than food, which things they exchange for the food they require. The old conundrum arises then as to whether those who are particularly skilled so as to be able to get plenty of goods for their sustenance and comfort are those most likely to be prolific, or whether, on the other hand, those who are prolific become skilled through the force of circumstances. Amongst the French about forty years ago it was a widely held opinion that the English and the Germans were prosperous because they were prolific.

There are many apparently sound reasons for believing that increase of population depends on increase of food and not on a profusion of babies. Take as an illustration a comparison between Canada and New England at a certain stage in their development last century. At a time when the birth-rate was decidedly higher in Canada than it was in New England (and was not associated with an unduly high death-rate), population increased far more rapidly in the latter place than in the former (apart from immigration), and this would seem to be dependent upon the fact that New England devoted herself to food production while Canada was depending on the fur trade. Again, in Babylonia of old, and in Egypt, food production has depended largely upon an efficient system of irrigation. After this system broke down in Babylonia population went permanently down. In Egypt, when irrigation was disorganized, the population fell from 12,000,000 to 2,000,000; but rose to 14,000,000 on bettering irrigation and food production again. When the Spaniards first came to the Philippines the population was said to be about 1,000,000. To-day, three centuries later, it is 6,000,000, and Woodruff, in his *Expansion of Races* (p. 18), says, "in each case it is certain that it is the maximum which could be fed." He also illustrates this belief by reference to Java. Java has a population of

28,750,000. In 1825 it was only about 5,000,000. The density in the plains and villages equals 568 persons for every square mile of surface, which is greater than in any province of China, excepting Shantung, where in many places are rich loamy plains of loess. The Chinese very commonly raised three or four crops in the same season on the same ground, and without exhausting the soil. They raise more per acre than is raised in the United States of America, but less per man. There are few food-producing areas in the world more thickly populated than certain regions in Java, China, and Japan. Population rises in these regions to a density of 500 to 600 persons per square mile. When big cities come to be considered it will be found people are crowded so closely together that there are 11,428 persons per square mile in the 700 square miles of Greater London, which roughly has a radius of fifteen miles. In that part of New York which is situated on the Island of Manhattan, i.e. in New York City, the crowding is much worse still (23,178 per square mile), especially during office hours. The City of Peking has in the combined area of the two parts which comprise it, which together have a circumference of 21 miles, a population of 1,280,000.

Since food production is so important in connection with increase of population, since a belief in "the law of diminishing returns in agriculture" is still extant, and since this belief engenders a fear that the world will soon be over-populated, it is expedient to examine man's powers of food production in detail. How much have these powers been increased? When were the main improvements in facilities of agricultural production made? Are they commensurate with the increase in actual numbers in the globe generally, or in special countries where increase of population is known to have been particularly rapid? And are they likely to continue at a sufficiently high rate of augmentation to keep pace with the probable rate of increase of population?

The surprising thing to discover when the increase of facilities in food production comes to be examined is the rapidity and extent in this increase. It has been especially rapid in the last fifty years. Many prophecies of last century have proved to be false. They were not based upon adequate knowledge.

Amongst the prophecies of last century two may be mentioned now because they have to do with food production and population: (1) It was said that if the population of Great Britain and Ireland grew to 40,000,000 all the navies of the world could not bring the inhabitants of these islands food enough. (2) Sir William Crookes prophesied in 1898 that there would be an acute shortage of wheat in the world by 1931. Both these prophecies have proved false, like two others, viz. that there would be a growing scarcity of gold, and that the coal supplies of the world would run out. It was doubtless impossible to foresee the great financial cataclysms, largely connected with wars and tariffs, which have occurred in the last twenty years, and the discovery of more and more oil and of how better to use this fuel. But in the case of food supplies, had the laws of human progress in these matters been better understood no false prophecies as those just mentioned need have been made.

The various stages in man's capacities for food production can be studied not only in the past history of the nations but also by surveying agricultural production to-day in various places. For example, the nomadic pastoral life can be seen amongst primitives in Bakhtian Persia or in Bedouin areas, and in more perfective form in the summer and winter conditions in the Swiss Alps. The somewhat early pastoral-agricultural type of production can be studied in Australia or on Salisbury Plain. The stages in the development of grain production as the science of growing "white crops" develops, in itself forms a fascinating study. Similarly, the progress of the dairy-orchardist can be watched, and the exporting farmer can be compared with the small-holder. The many developments that have taken place in recent years in the production of truck crops, and the ways in which and the places where this form of food production has displaced earlier ones, can be reviewed. In later chapters consideration must be given to the displacement of some of these by the gardener and the house builder. Moreover, to ensure a healthy distribution of population, methods of co-operation in serving others or in producing various commodities, and methods whereby individuals can readily take up more than one occupation must be studied, so as to bring them into vogue. Now that the world is smaller through easier transport and increased intercourse and knowledge, it is necessary to learn precisely where various foodstuffs can be most economically produced, and how exchange can be made most easy for those who can produce other commodities than food.

Bread to eat in sufficiency is the most important question in so many households the world over that a study of grain production will prove a profitable one. Facts about the growing of this kind of foodstuff have been extensively collected, and their influence upon population's growth, and distribution has always been considered as of paramount importance. There are enormous numbers of persons in the world who are not bread-eaters at all. Bread of wheaten flour is of more recent introduction than bread made from other cereals. In 1871 the bread-eaters of the world numbered 371,000,000. In 1881 the number rose to 416,000,000; in 1891 to 472,600,000, and in 1917 they numbered 516,500,000. Bread eating is therefore seen to be increasing rapidly, though in quite recent years the *per capita* consumption of *wheat* has slightly decreased.

Now in Norfolk there is an old ditty which is said to date from the twelfth century. It runs as follows:

> Satan on the road to Hell
> Ruined Norfolk as he fell,
> Stripped it clean of every good,
> Ne'er to eat of wheaten food.
> Bread of Darnel do they munch,
> Darnel in their teeth they crunch,
> If a blade of wheat they see,
> 'Tis the Devil that they flee.

This poem is an indication of an early appreciation of wheaten flour which would, of course, be home-grown and stone-ground. The last two advantages cannot be found to-day. In many parts of Europe to-day, especially in Russia, and in Germany though to a less extent, rye bread is the commonest kind of bread. Now rye compared with wheat is hardier, will grow on poorer land, can be sown later, has fewer pests, is often more profitable, produces more valuable straw, endures acid soil better, and uses less nitrogen. The bread made from it is rather less easily digested, but is eminently suitable in many ways to a rural population which acquires vigour from out-door life and healthy muscular exercise. It is interesting, therefore, to note that the substitution of wheat for rye, which is, amongst other things, a mark of an increased urbanization of the population of a country, may have a physiological basis. Also it may be that more protracted use of rye for bread in Germany as compared with England has directly to do with the fact that Germany has continued much longer than England to be an agricultural country and consequently a much larger proportion of the nation can digest it with comfort. Another aspect of rye versus wheat growing is this: It is found that the medieval customs of land tenure leading to peasant proprietors, mostly on relatively small holdings, have persisted in Germany longer than in England. Where large-scale farming arises and is first developed there the growing of wheat gradually replaces the growing of rye. The agrarian history of Russia seems to bear out this view. For we are told that down to about 1890 rye was the only winter crop of the peasant proprietors, as well as on the smaller noble estates, whereas on the larger estates it was supplemented to a great extent by winter wheat. The production of winter wheat was said to have been especially noticeable on the estates bought by business men who had made fortunes in commerce in the towns, and brought to the land business objects and methods. It will be interesting to learn in due course what happens in such matters in the Russia of to-day and to-morrow.

Wheat is the cereal of most interest and importance to the English-speaking nations. Therefore a brief review of wheat production and consumption is called for. It can be profitably prefaced by a quotation from a speech made by Lord Bledisloe, then Minister of Agriculture in England, at the British Association meeting which was held at Oxford in 1926. He said "that in his early days an early exhaustion of the wheat productivity of the United States was prophesied as a hope for the British agriculturist. First he was a sceptic, then an agnostic, and now he was a convinced unbeliever. Both the wheat area and the population of the United States had roughly trebled in the same period, and the production of wheat, as distinct from acreage, had more than trebled. American wheat exports in the fifty years had quadrupled to 240,000,000 bushels, and the latest increase was at the highest rate measured by quinquennial periods.

"All these figures took no account of Canada. The main increase was due to the extent of the area and only partially to the increase of the yield, though this was higher in America than in Great Britain. Proportionately the consumption per head showed no net increase. Concentrated food for animals was being obtained more and more from tropical and sub-tropical countries, where economic development had barely begun.

"He thought Sir D. Hall had also under-estimated the prospects of research work in finding new wheat lands and new wheat breeds. Fifteen to twenty per cent of the food crops of the world was now lost through the insect and fungoid attacks, so there was room here for a vast improvement through the development of agricultural research. The wheat yield of the world might in his opinion be raised 50 per cent above its present level by the application of fertilizers."

Sir William Crookes said in 1898 that "all civilized nations stood in deadly peril of not having enough to eat" through world food shortage, especially of wheat. He had not grasped the laws which govern human progress affecting numbers and knowledge. Despite much knowledge he was surprised when the increase in the acreage under wheat in the British Empire went up 43·5 per cent in ten years, 1901–11, during which time the population of the British Empire only increased 6·6 per cent. He could not wholly foresee why in England, and some such similarly circumstanced places, the cultivation of wheat would go out because other farming operations became relatively more profitable. The improvements in dairying, the cultivation of barley, and the raising and feeding of stock all tend to displace wheat growing for economic reasons. Besides these farming developments, others have occurred. The science of so-called continuous cropping, with much stress on new types of forage crops, has been increasingly adopted in the last forty years. Beyond that there are replacements of grain growing of all kinds in favour of other agricultural or horticultural uses of land, such as vegetables, salads, and fruit, and poultry and pig farming on an intensive scale, not to mention the use of land for entirely other purposes. All of these uses of sites replace old-fashioned ones because found to be more lucrative. It is the way sites are used that determines the distribution of population. But the natural development of things is being constantly interfered with through human ignorance. But by 1917, when Sir William Crookes' *The Wheat Problem* was revised and republished, he had modified his views considerably, in spite of this year being in the middle of the Great War, when overseas transport arrangements were much hampered and when food scarcity in some countries had become a revived anxiety or an actual grim reality. On the last page of that edition of his book he wrote:

"Although modern agricultural methods have possibly deferred the time when the wheat problem becomes of extreme urgency, the fact still remains that sooner or later a deficit in wheat must arise which will be met only by the more extended manufacture and use of artificial fertilizers of a nitrogenous nature. 'Starvation will be averted through the laboratory,' and the intelligent application of the results obtained by the work of the botanist and chemist will provide an assured future for the millions of bread-eaters in the world."

He would not, perhaps, have been so easily scared in 1898 had he realized, as he did more definitely by 1917, that human skill advances with increased numbers and that this law affects the primary needs of food production especially. In later pages I shall hope to demonstrate that it is neither lack of skill nor over-population that produces any menace of famine, but a heavy weight of removable poverty consequent upon a restricted freedom to produce and to exchange commodities. Under-production and a deplorable maldistribution of wealth result. If man had freedom of access to natural resources he would be able to produce all that is necessary to fulfil his desires.

If the people of the British Isles had had to grow all the wheat they required in 1917 they would have required about 8,250,000 acres of good wheat-growing land, or nearly 13,000 square miles. (This is based on a yield of 29 bushels per acre, the average for the preceding ten years. An increased area of about 100 square miles per annum would have been necessary for the annual increase of population.) This area is about one-fourth the size of England. In 1916 there were rather over 3,000 square miles (producing 56,296,000 bushels) under wheat in the United Kingdom. Sir Henry Rew's estimate of the British requirements in 1917 is slightly higher than the above. He put them down as 34,000,000 qtr. of wheat per annum, which would occupy nearly 9,000,000, acres. He states that, "The largest acreage under wheat of which we have actual record is 3,981,000 acres in 1869"; and that: "The reduction of wheat growing reached its climax in 1904 when the total area under wheat was 1,407,000 acres." As long ago as 1808 the United Kingdom grew more than 3,000,000 acres of wheat a year, and in 1850 probably as much as or slightly more than in the high year of 1869 just mentioned. In 1933 England and Wales had 1,660,360 acres under wheat (29 per cent more acreage than in 1932), and the yield was nearly 31,500,000 cwt. (42 per cent more than in 1932). But the areas under barley and oats went down. The United Kingdom (still a convenient term to use to indicate Great Britain and Ireland) consumes roughly 6 bushels of wheat per head of population, and imports roughly 75 to 80 per cent of her supplies. The French consumed 8·1 bushels in the 1891 to 1900 period, and 7·8 in the 1901 to 1910 period; Germany 2·9 and 3·1 in the two corresponding periods. The percentage of supplies imported into France was 11 in 1891 to 1900 and 3 in 1901 to 1910; into Germany 27 in 1891 to 1900 and 36 in 1901 to 1910. A recent review of "The Wheat Problem" is to be found in the *Westminster Bank Review*, No. 235, September 1933. In this it is shown that while the total consumption of wheat in the world has not gone down in recent years, the *per capita* consumption has (numbers of inhabitants meanwhile increasing). This diminished consumption is due to a gradual rise in the standard of living, causing more meat, fruit, and vegetables to be eaten.

"It is estimated that the United States of America will have a population of 200,000,000 by 1950. Long before then the States will be importing cereals, as they are already sometimes importing meat." So wrote Sir Charles Fielding in his *Food*, published in 1923. But fourteen years previously Woodruff had been able to write (in his *Expansion of Races*, p. 12) that: "In the United States of America recently one State alone added 45,000,000 bushels to her yield of corn without increasing the acreage. . . . It is predicted that these new discoveries will eventually add a billion bushels to our crop, and every year, at least in every decade, there is a discovery which increases the yield of some food." The average yield of wheat per acre in the United States of America for the period 1911 to 1920 varied from State to State considerably. The two States where the yield was highest were Maine, 23·0 bushels per acre, and New York State, where it was 20·6. At the other end of the scale comes Tennessee with 10·8 bushels per acre and Alabama 10·6. It is difficult to make a comparison between yield to-day and yield long ago; but it seems probable that an average yield of wheat per acre in the Southern States of the United States of America of 10 or 11 bushels to-day is about equal to the yield to-day and the yield ages ago on the Roman Campagna. In 1926 Milton Whitney[1] wrote that "in the past forty-one years the average yield of wheat in the United States of America has increased from about 11·5 bushels per acre to somewhere in the neighbourhood of 16 bushels per acre." He also says a recent observer in a very fertile region of China saw a number of fields in different places where, he assures us, the yield of wheat was at least 117 bushels per acre. About one-half of China is too rough and mountainous for agricultural use. The rainfall in South China is about 80 inches a year and mostly falls in summer, that is, in the growing season. In Shantung it is 24 inches a year, and 17 inches of this falls in July and August. It is true still, however, that the greatest enemies to large parts of China are droughts and floods. Mr. King, a well-known authority on agriculture in China, says that the average yield of wheat is about 25 bushels per acre, but that the average yield in Shantung is 42. The average yield in Roumania is said to be 16·7 bushels per acre (1909–13), and it had at that time a surplus in normal years of 40,000,000 bushels of corn (maize), 50,000,000 bushels of wheat, and 11,000,000 bushels of barley for exportation. The average yield from Eastern European countries, i.e. the Danube and Baltic States other than Russia, was 16·6 bushels per acre in the 1905–14 period, 14·7 in 1919–24, 17 in 1925–32, and 13·2 in 1932.

In 1840 Britain grew food for 24,000,000 people, whereas to-day only 15,000,000 are fed from British soil. In 1850 England and Wales employed 1,350,000 people in agriculture, which is the same number as in 1913. On December 17, 1925, Lloyd George declared "that if you had as many men employed on the soil of Great Britain in proportion to the size of the two

[1] *Soil and Civilization*, p. 257.

countries as they have in Denmark, there would be 750,000 more workers on British land than are engaged at this hour; if you take Germany as a basis, 1,100,000 more; if Holland, 1,750,000 more and Belgium 2,000,000. That is, if we had devoted the same care to the possibilities of the soil as they have done, these countries, there would be no unemployment problem of any magnitude." The people of Belgium obtain five times as much foodstuff from 100 acres of land as is obtained in this country. Now the percentage of areas growing bread—not necessarily wheaten, of course—(as given in Sir Charles Fielding's book, *Food*, published in 1923) in the following countries is: 3 per cent in the United Kingdom, 25 per cent in Germany, and 30 per cent in France. The total quarters of bread grain produced was 7,000,000 in the United Kingdom, 58,000,000 in Germany, and 47,000,000 in France. The production of bread grain per head of population was 90 lb. in the United Kingdom, 485 lb. in Germany, and 500 lb. in France. Germany, with a population rather less than double ours, was employing 10,000,000 people permanently in agriculture in 1913; and France 8,000,000 out of a population smaller than our own. Whereas we employ in agriculture only about 2,500,000.

Until ninety years ago Britain produced all her own wheat from her soil to sustain her own people. Now we grow only about one-fifth. If we grew wheat on 8,000,000 acres with a yield of 40 bushels per acre, we should have 320,000,000 bushels; enough to provide the bread-food, at the rate of 6 bushels per adult each year, for 53,000,000 people. When the decline of wheat growing is investigated some remarkable facts emerge. For example, in 1801 there were 32½ acres of wheat per 100 of the population in England and Wales, while in 1914 the acreage per 100 people had been reduced to one-fifth. Thomas Middleton has pointed out that 100 acres of grass of poor or medium quality will provide only enough meat for from 2 to 14 persons; of very good grass, up to even 40 persons; but 100 acres of wheat, average crop, can be reckoned to provide a substantial diet for 200 persons. The whole production of wheat was 1,515,000 tons in 1920 against 6,298,000 tons of imported. In 1929 the corresponding figures were 1,329,000 and 6,262,000. And in 1931 the wheat acreage fell compared to the previous year by 11 per cent to the lowest recorded level (1,200,000 acres). Since then it has risen again (see a few pages back) to 1,600,000 acres.

During the years 1891 to 1921 the population of Great Britain increased by 13,000,000, or about 43 per cent, and during that period the proportion of the occupied population engaged in agriculture fell from over 12 per cent to about 7 per cent. The nation could be self-supporting in wheat if the 5,000,000 acres of land which has gone down to grass since 1870 were put under the plough again. In 1868 we had nearly 4,000,000 acres under wheat. In 1928 and again in 1933 about 1,500,000. We have now about 12,000,000 acres of uncultivated soil.

In 1922 (January, in the *Journal of Statistical Society*) Sir Henry Rew published an article on "The Progress of British Agriculture." He pointed out that about 90 per cent of the 56,000,000 acres of Great Britain is put to productive use, 3,500,000 acres being above an altitude of 1,500 feet. Of this, 31,250,000 acres are under crops or permanent grass, 13,500,000 under rough grazing, 3,500,000 (not including that above 1,500 feet) given to deer forests, 2,750,000 occupied by woods and plantations, and 5,000,000 by urban areas, roads, railways, mines, etc. The shrinkage of the farmed area during the last thirty years is mainly attributable to the demand of urban agglomerations. Towns and urban districts, including London and county boroughs, occupied 4,164,500 acres in 1921. Sir Henry Rew, in his article of 1922, gives the following record of arable cultivation in England and Wales: Comparing 1869–78 with 1905–14, we find 19 per cent as against 12 per cent of the arable land being used for grain crops, especially wheat. The acreage under cabbages increased 100 per cent and under orchards increased by 50 per cent during the period. In four years an acre will grow (taking official average yields) 18 tons of "farm" produce (as to three-quarters turnips or swedes, and assuming the acre cropped successively with wheat, roots, barley, and clover); 25 tons of potatoes; and 120–140 tons of tomatoes under glass. By substituting potatoes for wheat, roughly one-fifth the area will give about as large an output of food.

In the opening chapter of this book it was pointed out that the touchstone for sound human development was freedom. Society has passed through a see-saw of restriction and liberty, but gradually more and more liberty evolves. To-day, however, there is still nothing which militates against the natural laws governing and guiding the distribution of population so much as a lack of freedom here and there, in this way and in that. To keep, for the moment, to wheat growing: big and little restrictions of one sort or another interfere with the free production of this most important of all foodstuffs. Those with a bent for agriculture quite frequently find themselves foredoomed to follow some other occupation through lack of the right kind of opportunities, and vice versa, those who should never have been placed in agriculture, wheat production possibly, find themselves in this vocation. Few town-dwellers' children, however strong their inclinations may be towards agriculture, can follow their bent. Probably no large proportion hanker after growing wheat; but in the aggregate there must be many. Then there is a certain amount of lack of freedom in the family. How often, even to-day, does not a stern father order his son or daughter to adopt, against their own inclinations, this or that mode of life! Again, in the realm of education teachers often have to push children into unsuitable moulds. For example, children in rural districts are not sufficiently prepared at school to follow the vocation they are most likely to take up. On this point the following passage from Professor Thomas Wibberley is worth quoting:

"As far as the agricultural labourer is concerned, no attempt whatever is made to give his early education an agricultural bias. The children in the village school at Crawley receive precisely the same education as the children living in the heart of London. Their little heads are crammed with such facts as that Manchester is famed for its cotton industry, Sheffield for the manufacture of steel, and Liverpool for its shipping. They have to memorize such features as the width of the Ganges and the height of the Himalaya, though they may never have to swim the former nor climb the latter. Did one wish to devise a system of education, with the specific object of enticing rural labour to industrial centres, one could not improve upon the existing system."[1]

Yet in the county of Norfolk inquiry proves that 50 per cent

[1] "The Economic and Social History of an English Village" by Gras, *Harvard Economic Studies*, Vol. XXXIV, p. 692.

of the boys from the elementary schools go into agriculture. [Of the girls 50 per cent go into domestic service.] Even when adult education comes to be considered it is sadly true, except in a few places (Denmark, for example), that the science of agriculture is too divorced from those who are carrying out the operations of practical farming.

Great restrictions upon free production of such a commodity as wheat are imposed by the laws and customs affecting access to land. Tenants are not always free agents. Would-be holders of land for intensive cultivation of grains along modern lines, often shrewd men with experience but poor, are unable to get holdings because of land monopoly. Other monopolies are nearly always edifices founded upon land monopoly. Though there are many advantages in combination and sensible "rationalization," many of these secondary monopolies restrict people's ability for acquiring cheaply machinery to help in such things as the harvesting, thrashing, etc., of wheat crops. Other restrictions on liberty are connected with the distribution of wheat through combines and cartels cornering the market. To this subject alone a whole book has been devoted.

But worst of all are the restrictions which the legislators of the world impose upon freedom of production and exchange; and no commodity could better illustrate this than wheat. It matters not at all whether the legislators belong to a nation whose people have found reasons to be great importers or great exporters of wheat. A truly remarkable set of restrictions have been imposed by both sets. Behind them is a clique of vested interests, landlords, special producers, and merchants, which is apt ever to batten upon the mass of people. The monopolists at the head of combines always emphasize how much in the public interest combinations are. But, as Adam Smith wrote in 1776: "People of the same trade hardly meet together for merriment or diversion, but the conversation ends in a conspiracy against the public, or in some contrivance to raise prices." The manacles on freedom bring about strange results. Prices may here be too low, there too high. Here a reduction of acreage under wheat is arranged. There an increase is encouraged. All regardless of what is the truest economy and the best method of procedure. While many are starving or under-fed for lack of wheat, in another place the grain is being thrown away, eaten by moth or mice, or being used for fuel. The growers of some countries are making sacrifices in order to maintain wheat production, whilst in other countries the low price level obtained for producing almost entirely wipes out the purchasing power of the population. The artificial devices which bring these things about are generally labelled "protection" and include, amongst others, constant increases of Customs duties, quantitative limitation of imports, reduction in the percentage of foreign wheat allowed for bread making, indirect subsidies in the form of credits and preferential rates, and direct financial assistance by the public Treasury. The "Corn Laws" again! Last of all, say Conservatives and Labour alike, the Government must play a part and take a hand themselves. But it matters not a jot whether that plan is enforced by Socialists of the one label or the other; the bureaucrats put in office are unconsciously taken care of and guided by those who are experts—at looking after their own vested interests. No wonder there is now arising the cry, "Back to Adam Smith." He was vehement in his denunciation of the efforts which have been made from time to time to attempt two things which are quite incompatible—trading and governing. The history of India should make that clear if principles are studied and their application to present-day conditions appreciated.

An instructive article appeared recently from the pen of Mr. Arthur Wynn in *The Economic Journal*.[1] He shows that grain tariffs in Germany brought about wide-spread injuries. The high price of grain increased grain production above home requirements and decreased live stock. "For the first time for fifty years Germany had a surplus production of grain."

Year	Wheat Area	Crop
	Million Acres	Million Bushels
1929	3·96	123·1
1930	4·40	139·2
1931	5·36	155·5
1932	5·63	183·8

[1] "A Note on German Agriculture," by Arthur Wynn (Berlin, July 1933), *The Economic Journal*, Vol. XLIII, No. 171, September 1933, p. 518.

The peasant's market produce is live stock as to 70 per cent of it. The peasant was doubly hurt, first by the price of the fodder he wanted going up, secondly by the purchasing power of the industrial population upon which he depended going down. An artificial stimulus, given to grain production by the grain tariffs, coupled as it was in 1932 with exceptionally favourable weather conditions, resulted in a surplus of grain. This brought a fall in grain prices. Meanwhile landlordism had benefited, and because the benefit seemed about to end the landlords recently began to cry out for more help. As Arthur Wynn says, "Some 600,000,000 Rm. had already been swallowd by the landlords without the community obtaining any advantage . . . the whole 'Osthilfe' scheme is an example of far-reaching political corruption." "The Big Landowners" now "demand that the State should buy the whole surplus and stabilize prices. There is no doubt, however, that the State finances will in future be too weak to restore prices to their old level. Any policy of price stabilization must in any case be eventually doomed to failure, for it is clear that it would result in a still further decrease in live stock and increase in grain production, which would only make matters worse. The grain tariffs become almost useless as soon as home supply exceeds demand and thus defeat their own purpose of protecting the large landowner."

"In respect of grain tariffs the German agricultural policy of the last decade is similar to that of Italy, France, and Czecho-slovakia. In the latter countries the effects have been no less disastrous; thus in Italy between 1925 and 1929, in a period of general world prosperity, the number of horses fell by 8 per cent, mules by 18 per cent, donkeys by 13 per cent, cattle by 7 per cent, sheep by 20 per cent, goats by 43 per cent, the direct cause of the decreases being the grain taxes and the consequent change-over from live stock and fruit production to wheat which (considering only the interests of the Italian peasants) it would have been better to import. Further, the importance of the contraction of the European market for grain had played an important part in intensifying the world agricultural crisis. There is little doubt but that if all European countries were content to do without grain duties and quotas and concentrate their attention on other branches of agriculture, North America would have no wheat surplus, but would still be able to increase production at profitable prices. This policy of restricting imports has already led to retaliation by most countries exporting to Germany, e.g. Denmark, Sweden, Holland, Bulgaria, Roumania, etc., which in turn will lead to a diminished German export, diminished purchasing power of the industrial population, and finally further impoverishment of the peasants."

"The conversion of agricultural debts, which is one of the most important schemes promised by the Hitler Government, is also a plan for subsidizing agriculture at the expense of the town and city population, for it implies the partial compensation of creditors from State funds. One hundred million Rm. have already been put aside for this purpose. It is clear that a policy of all-round protection for agriculture is hurtful all round." "Moreover, the following figures illustrate, Firstly, that such an attempt is quite

Year	Net Value of Industrial Production	Net Value of Agricultural Production	German Industrial Export
	Mld. Rm.	Mld. Rm.	Mld. Rm.
1925	26	7·85	10·6
1926	24	8.35	11·8
1927	32	9·00	12·5
1928	34	9·85	14·0
1929	32	10·00	15.1
1930	26	9·30	13·2
1931	19	8·10	10·5
1932	14·5	7·10	6·2

unjustifiable, in that industry has suffered during the crisis much more seriously than agriculture, and secondly, that the prosperity of agriculture is dependent on the prosperity of German industry, and in particular on the ability to export."

Prior to the regime of Hitler, during the Chancellorship of Dr. Brüning, import duties raised the price of foodstuffs in Germany to two and a half times the world price. Yet the inefficient Junker system of cultivation broke down and estates were heavily mortgaged. Herr Hitler, to start with, talked about drastic land reform and schemes for increasing the number on and the use of land. His programme, issued at Munich on March 6, 1930, contained the following "requirements": "The land of Germany . . . must be at the service of the German nation as a home and as a means of livelihood. . . . German land may not become an object of financial speculation, nor may it provide an unearned income for its owner. It may only be acquired by him who is prepared to cultivate it himself." But, as Mr. Wickham Steed showed (*Sunday Times*, August 20, 1933), before very long the Prussian landowning nobles and gentry, or Junkers, in alliance with "big industry" (still the masters of Germany, the two cliques), triumphed over Hitler. Dr. Brüning had proposed to liquidate a portion of the bankrupt Junker estates and to turn them into peasant holdings. Then the great Junkers surrounded the President at Neudeck and denounced Brüning as a "Bolshi." He found himself dismissed like an impertinent lackey. More intrigues and wire-pulling occurred and Hitler was given more power, but only by the sanction of Junkerdom.

It would certainly be wise for England to grow more wheat and, still more, to produce more foodstuffs of other kinds. It would be healthier if more people took up such pursuits. Despite the fact that certain forces are constantly leading persons from purely agricultural occupations to vocations which are more remunerative, it is possible to show that the inhabitants of these islands could grow all the wheat they required on home land and that this might be economically advantageous. But before developing that theme a brief reference to French producers is apposite.

The inhabitants of France have usually grown all the wheat they require, and their numbers are more or less stationary now. Even were the population of France suddenly to become doubled or trebled, it would be possible to grow sufficient wheat (as well as a great abundance of practically all the other foodstuffs they required) from their own soil. Here is an apposite quotation from the pen of the late Prince Kropotkin, a great authority:

"It thus appears that, while the population increased by two-fifths only (by 41 per cent), the chief means of subsistence—i.e. the wheat crop—increased by over three and a half times (355 per cent); that means that if the population of France had trebled within the last one hundred years, and 50,000,000 idlers were added to the population, the average Frenchman would still have more wheat at his disposal than he had before the Revolution.

"But if we take into account the colossal development of market and fruit gardening in France within the last twenty years, its irrigated meadows of recent origin and its green crops, as well as the oily grains and the crops (especially beetroot) which are grown for industrial purposes, we certainly shall be below the truth if we say that the means of subsistence in France have increased, not by 355 per cent, but by at least 600 per cent, and probably more, to say nothing of the food which is or can be

Year	Population	Areas under Wheat in Acres	Yield in Bushels per Acre	Total Crop in Bushels
1789	27,000,000	10,000,000	9	88,000,000
1888*	38,000,000	17,000,000	18	312,000,000
Increase	11,000,000	7,000,000	9	224,000,000

* The acreage under wheat is to-day about the same as fifty years ago. The population of France to-day is 40,744,000, which is equal to about 190 per square mile.

imported in exchange for manufactured produce. What would it have been, however, if only a small part of the interest which is now paid every year on a debt of £1,200,000,000 were applied to the permanency of the soil, or if the above-mentioned obstacles did not exist? There is not one practical or theoretical agriculturist in France who would not answer this last question by saying that the agricultural production of France would have been by this time twenty times, or more, what it was a hundred years ago."[1]

The late William Wright, M.P., in a little book he wrote in 1925 with Mr. A. J. Penty, *Agriculture and the Unemployed* (Labour Publishing Co., London, 1925), made the following comments on the above quotation from Prince Kropotkin's article: "Which means, in fact, that France, on this basis and by these methods, can support a population equal to the population of India, France, and England, or twice the present population of Russia and Germany. No one of any consequence has questioned the facts or conclusions of Kropotkin."

[1] "What Man Can Obtain from the Land," *Co-operative Wholesale Annual,* 1897, pp. 359–60.

But to return to the British Isles and to wheat growing there. The British Isles fortunately possess some of the most fertile land in the world, and have a climate particularly well suited for the cultivation of wheat. The ways to increase a crop of any particular plant can be divided under a few separate heads, particularly (a) manuring; (b) plant breeding; (c) tillage. Wheat takes more nitrogen out of the soil than many other crops. That is one reason why it is often grown in rotation (for example, in the common four-course rotation) after a clover crop, because the roots of the clover, which are afterwards ploughed in, have on them certain bacteria which are able to use the nitrogen of the air and bring it into such a state that it becomes incorporated in the soil and helps to feed the next crop. The processes of a physical and chemical nature which enable the free nitrogen of the air to be manufactured into fixed nitrogenous manurial substances have been greatly improved in recent years. Under the auspices of the Imperial Chemicals combine a big plant for their production now exists in England. Apart from this our knowledge of how to manure land for wheat has increased enormously during the last century. As having a bearing on this point it is worth mentioning that Sir William Crookes forty years ago looked with awe on the levy the world was making annually, for enriching agricultural land, on the then production of nitrate of soda, sulphate of ammonia, and guano; and he considered we were "drawing on the earth's capital." He wisely deplored the waste of "fixed nitrogen to the value of no less than £16,000,000 per annum," which we were "content to hurry down our drains and water-courses." He considered that human ingenuity should be able to convert the waste involved in our methods of sewage disposal so that the land got fed properly from animal excreta, and thus made more productive.

Throughout the history of agriculture the science of feeding the soil has been one of the most important. Nature conserves material and energy, and arranges to have a never ending cycle whereby the animal kingdom by its excretal waste and its dead bodies feeds the soil in which the vegetable kingdom thrives, and the vegetables in turn feed the animals. The earth and life upon it can therefore be counted as indestructible and everlasting. A similar provision preserves the atmosphere from becoming exhausted. Great strides in knowledge about manuring crops, both by animal and chemical fertilizers, have been achieved in the last fifty years and have aided the increase of wheat production. Wonderful advances, too, have been made, mostly in the last thirty years, in the breeding of improved varieties of wheat. Patient work in the field laboratories of Cambridge and elsewhere have created varieties which are more prolific, or able to avoid or overcome the evils of insect pests, rust, frost, drought, and other drawbacks. Hence both acreage and yield have been increased.

In Canada, for example, varieties of wheat have been produced, in the last twenty years or so, which have enabled the acreage to be advanced further north because a sort of wheat has been created which can be sown later and which matures quicker. Sir Rowland Biffen, the most renowned worker at plant breeding, and especially connected with these developments in wheat production, made investigations for the inhabitants of Kenya, where in certain parts there is a possibility of getting two crops yearly. The problem there, in regard to wheat, was whether to attempt to find varieties resistant both to black-stem and yellow-rust, which are the two chief diseases of the country—confined, however, to certain definite altitudes—or whether they should continue to endeavour to produce varieties resistant to one disease only. In 1927 Sir Rowland Biffen expressed himself, after visiting the Colony, strongly in favour of the former plan, but uttered a warning that immediate results must not be expected. The report of the previous year's agricultural census showed that there were 200 additional occupiers of the land, bringing the total to 1,800. Of 4,500,000 acres alienated to Europeans, 460,000 are being cultivated, maize represents 41 per cent, coffee and sisal each 14 per cent, and wheat 9 per cent. About 20,000 tons of maize were exported from the Colony of that season's crop.

But it is especially under the head of tillage, the actual preparation of the ground, combined with the handling of the seed and the seedling, that perhaps the greatest strides have been accomplished. The average yield of wheat, about 30 bushels per acre, in England can be enormously increased, so that on good land, by good farming, double, and on the best treble, the average yield can be grown. Lord Bledisloe, in the year 1929, in the county of Gloucestershire, grew 96 bushels per acre. Men have grown, by the intensive method, from one grain of wheat only, forty to ninety or even more stalks, ears, that is, producing from 1,000 to 8,000 grains. The late Sir Arthur T. Cotton, in his Life (p. 538), wrote about such production; Major Hallett, at the Exeter Meeting of the British Association not many years ago, exhibited such plants; and an Essex farmer, Mr. John Hepburn, originally from Orkney, known to the present writer, also exhibited plants of this kind. He and the late Mr. William Wright, M.P., who grew a few similar plants in his back garden in Balham (in South London), showed these at a big meeting in a committee room of the House of Commons, at which the present writer took the chair in July 1930. At this meeting a non-party Home Agriculture Society was started, but through unfortunate accidents it died in infancy. Plants of wheat with stalks of from forty to sixty-six, grown from one seed, were shown. Mr. Hepburn grew many acres on not very suitable, heavy land in Essex. All such results come from deep cultivation, in Mr. Hepburn's case done by machinery, and from selected seeds and hand-planted seedlings. But in time machinery, to save hand planting, would be invented; and England is specially blessed with the ability to manufacture the most perfect agricultural machinery and labour-saving appliances in any quantity. New farming ways are but slowly adopted—partly because of the hindrances to freedom already referred to. Although these methods have only recently come to the fore, the intensive cultivation of wheat by these methods has been in use in England for one hundred and forty years at least, and it has been in vogue in China and Japan during a far longer period. Mr. George Jacob Holyoake and Mr. Joseph Morland tried setting wheat by hand, instead of sowing it, on a small scale in the year 1789—see the former's *Self-Help One Hundred Years Ago* (p. 122). [Other references to this subject are: (*a*) Alfred Broadbent in *The Co-operative Annual*, 1904, recorded (pp. 288-89) the experiments of Mr. C. Miller, of Cambridge. (*b*) *Daily Express*, January 16, 1928.]

Some say our home production of wheat can be increased by 10 to 15 per cent. What a statement! It could be increased by 200 to 400 per cent. Yet a leading politician, Sir Herbert Samuel, said in the House of Commons (March 13, 1930):

"This small island, which must necessarily import most of its foodstuffs and raw materials, even if every acre of land were cultivated to the highest point, can only purchase them by exporting, and mainly by exporting manufactured goods."

Truly it may be advantageous for the British to import many foodstuffs and to export many manufactured articles, but this is not because they cannot produce far more foodstuffs.

Some indications, partly by inference, have already been given of the possibilities of increased acreage and yield in the United States of America. But the quantity of wheat produced there for the year 1933 (an estimate at the time of writing) seems likely to be almost as low as it has been for about thirty years, and likely to fall somewhere near to the domestic requirements. The average domestic use in the last three years is about 725,000,000 bushels. This fall is being accompanied by a rise in price. It is partly due to the previous slump in prices. The wiseacres of the world are putting their heads together in order to try and stabilize prices and keep them up. Yet the fluctuations and often some measure of artificial cheapness which have occurred in recent years are frequently directly or indirectly due to the manœuvres of these self-same wiseacres. Restrictions and interferences crop up instead of the free play of human intelligence and ability, and they hamper wheat production in this country and that.

These remarks take but little cognizance of the possibilities of educating some growers of other grain stuffs in various parts of the world. The Russian rye producers, and even the Japanese rice growers in certain locations, might change their habits and grow wheat. There are districts in Japan where the warm, damp, and monotonous weather favourable for the growing of rice is not so prevalent as in most regions where rice is cultivated. Russian Marxists would have benefited their fellow-countrymen much more if they had spent all the energy and money they have for years expended upon organizing production in large-scale, State-regulated fashion, upon educating the multitude of peasant producers so that they, working in freedom, had become acquainted with modern methods of cultivation. The leaders of the Soviet Republic are still faced with the antagonism of town versus country, or industrial versus rural workers, and with the problem of taxation, while they have imposed a new bureaucracy and a new kind of dictatorship upon the inhabitants of Russia, which is making many hungry and some miserable.

What has been written about wheat applies also to many another commodity. But wheat has been taken because it is a commodity of such primary importance, because it is one the production of which has been widely studied, because so many fears have been raised from time to time about its possible shortage, and because it is one which, more obviously than many, has a connection with the distribution of population.

The introduction of machinery into agriculture and other industries has been blamed for displacing labour and causing unemployment and poverty. This is a century-old fallacy. On the face of it there appears to be something in the argument. A farm tractor operated by one man can, in the four autumn months, do as much ploughing, stirring, and cultivating of the ground as six horses and three men could do in *double* that time. This is only one illustration. Take the production of beef and milk: in many places hand labour for chopping up the swedes is still employed, truly with the aid of a chopping machine turned by hand. But compare this with the many devices seen on progressive farms where an engine does the chopping, and a machine of a neighbouring sugar-beet factory contributes a big proportion of the bullock or cattle fodder. In some places much more machinery is used; for example, for milking, cooling, separating, pasteurizing, churning, etc. The use of machinery enables more beasts to be turned into beef in a given area. It is to be noted also that in England there is nowadays a quick turnover. This is due to the fashion for "early maturity," i.e. the killing of the animal at three years of age, a comparatively modern introduction. This, by the way, must be borne in mind when comparing the numbers of beasts now and formerly and with those in countries where oxen generally used for draught purposes live to seven or eight. In spite of such facilities in the production of meat of various kinds we in England import 80 per cent of the meat we eat, thereby keeping the price of meat down to a level which enables a bigger proportion of our population to eat it than in most other countries. Improved methods of production and marketing of meat at home are possible and desirable. Yet to be more "self-contained" would not be all benefit and might not lead to an increase in employment. Some believe, without stopping to work it out, that if our meat production from home farms were trebled it would give three times as much employment in our own country. But this reckoning is shallow. Even if no extra machinery were used to cope with the extra work involved, the additional "hands" needed would not be doubled. Moreover, a certain number of workers would be put out of employment who made the goods, or supplied the services which went to the Argentine, to Australia, or elsewhere in exchange for the carcases which came from overseas. Not only so but there are many subsidiary occupations in England which depend upon the overseas meat trade. There are shipbuilders, sailors, marine engineers, shipping clerks, brokers of various kinds, bankers, refrigerator manufacturers, etc. The essence of the matter is to find out—as automatically as possible—where the commodities to meet the various needs of human beings, for example cheap meat, can be most advantageously and economically produced, taking all things, such as transport costs, etc., into account.

Again, nearly all machines not only increase the facility of production but also give occupation to a new collection of workers. Increased facilities of production, in the long run, should make everyone richer, i.e. capable of having more wealth at his or her disposal (wealth being defined as the products of the application of labour to the resources of the earth). Unfortunately, society is now so organized that it is by no means everyone that participates in the results of the easier production of wealth, and, though the reasons for this have been discovered, they are still far from being widely appreciated. When they have become so, then the present wrongs and injustices which are found to harass society can be set right. The new work to another set of workers which results from the adoption of new machinery can be well illustrated by taking almost any machine, say a locomotive steam-engine, or a sewing-machine of one sort or another. To take the case of the locomotive: compare the thousands of workers who now find occupation in connection with these machines with their complete absence a hundred years or so ago. There are the many manufacturers of the locomotive steam-engines themselves and their subsidiary and complementary parts. This has given rise to vast hosts of workers in all the new developments in transport which soon evolve from the discovery of such a piece of machinery. But it is hardly necessary to labour this point further.

Population can be denser where it is possible to grow food in plenty. It is usually found to be denser when and where foodstuffs are produced in greater abundance. Agricultural production must always depend upon suitability of soil, site, and climate as well as upon the intelligence and knowledge of man. But intelligence and knowledge have increased so much in the last hundred years that geographical conditions are not quite so important as they used to be. The production of foodstuffs has been rendered so much easier by the increase of intelligence and knowledge and, given freedom, can now be still further enormously increased, while transport has improved to such an undreamt of extent in the last hundred years that it is absurd to raise any anxiety over shortage of food in the world of to-day, or even in any world containing such increased numbers of people as at present can be conceived as possible. Whilst these changes have occurred in food production, somewhat similar changes have happened in man's capabilities of producing most of the other commodities which he needs to fulfil his desires. It is poverty which stands in the way, poverty in opportunity to produce and exchange the fruits of human labour's application to land, and poverty to find the individual means for procuring such fruits as have been produced.

Coincidentally with an increase in population occurs a decrease in the area of land found necessary for existence and comfort. This is a beneficent provision of God. This is an ever-present, all-pervading principle of nature which should be learnt, accepted, and acted upon without let or hindrance, and without qualm or fear. With increased numbers has come augmented knowledge, accumulated wisdom, higher intelligence; so that man's powers can serve his increased and ever-increasing needs and aspirations. Were such things not so, were these not the laws of nature, human beings would crowd and eventually overcrowd one another and starvation conditions would reign. Because this law governing human development, namely, that larger numbers can do with relatively less space, has not been recognized, fears arise over the possibility of over-population. And because the way to act after recognition of this law is not commonly clear, population is badly distributed. In subsequent chapters of this book a study will be made of the principles which must be followed to avoid over-crowding and poverty. It will be useful to discover how the more remunerative use of land can replace the less remunerative without coercion, and without hardship to anyone. It is quite possible for suitable sites for more intensive occupation, for easier means of obtaining a livelihood to become occupied by a new set of workers quite voluntarily and with due compensation to those displaced.

Such rearrangements of population properly brought about provide improved services out of communal funds, and should lower prices by enhanced facilities of production. When sites can be put to better use goods can be more easily produced and marketed. Marketing schemes to-day too often spell the creation of monopolies in the interest of producers. But under a proper regime improved methods of marketing would reduce the gap between producer and consumer. They would give the producer a better price and the consumer a cheaper supply. The easier distribution of goods may be done partly, often largely, through better means of communication and transport provided out of communal funds. To take just one illustration at this stage: In ancient days some growers of crops by a riverside found their location, as population increased, to be suitable for the setting up of landing-places for the better transportation of goods and persons across the stream. Their sites increased in value through the increase in the numbers of human beings, through the needs of this increased population, and through the progress of human cleverness in devising means of transport, etc. How can such growers of crops get displaced? How can the community's needs be met without hurt or detriment? Obviously if the agriculturist extract compensation (for what?) from the newcomers they receive something for nothing —a bad principle, for they get paid for something which was not really theirs. On the other hand, what principle should be followed to equalize everyone's opportunity in life? How are the newcomers to place themselves in a just position with their displaced fellows? And how these latter with the former? The secret to the answer of these riddles is contained in an understanding of the word "rent." By this term the economists have come to mean: that value which attaches to a site which has nothing to do with what the individual has done, but which is attached to it because of and through the needs of an increased population. Obviously in the case of the illustration taken the river-side site which becomes suitable for transport purposes (near a ford, quay, or bridge, for example) is worth more to rent than the site to which the agriculturists will now have to move. But to whom must this rent, this measure in the difference between one site and another, be paid? It would not be fair to pay it to the agriculturists, as has already been shown, for they never earned it. Nor can it be paid by the payers to themselves! It must therefore be paid into a common pool, so equalizing matters. But how used? Obviously for the common good, for the use of both parties. This can be done by both parties agreeing, as they would readily, to spend it on something in the nature of common services. For example, they might arrange to employ some of their number to build a bridge or a boat to be used by all, thus further facilitating production and exchange, the latter in this instance. Another way whereby the matter of equality of opportunity and justice to all is settled in many primitive, or even sometimes in more advanced, societies is by means of a frictionless and quite voluntary mutual arrangement in this wise: a decision is arrived at to convert a poor all-weather track (to the ford or bridge, for example) into a better one, into something in the nature of a road, by community labour contributed to by the various workers of the community in different amounts according to the value of the sites each occupies. Thus the new river-side dwellers would give more services, or get and supply more of the materials, than the displaced agriculturists. They see the fairness of this arrangement because both parties recognize the superiority of the river-side site now wanted for a new purpose over the other locations, a superiority which enables the new inhabitants more easily to earn a living. They perform duties which earn them fees in goods, or money to obtain goods (if some kind of currency had been invented), while contributing at the same time to the common weal. They can do better in this way in a given time than their agricultural neighbours. This superiority over their neighbours is adjusted equitably to all concerned by such devices.

CHAPTER IV

DEVELOPMENTS IN AGRICULTURE

THE first law of economics is: man seeks to satisfy his desires with the least effort to himself. The earliest agglomerations of population are consequently found in warm, moist regions where treeless alluvial soil is found, for there food, man's first need, can most easily be produced. It is there, too, that he can live without having to make many clothes, or build large and substantial dwelling-houses. Later, regions of thick population are found where other climatic conditions prevail, namely, where the temperature is lower but no great extremes occur, and where variable weather and cyclonic rain storms furnish the conditions which enable man to provide for himself quite easily after his knowledge of agriculture and other kinds of production has advanced to some extent. Man's health and energy are found to be greater in these latter regions and so he comes to develop most of the science and art of living more rapidly in such regions. Later still, and largely not until within the last fifty to one hundred years, man has found the means of overcoming many of the handicaps which are apt to go with the hot climates.

"Does all this mean that mankind is becoming free from geographical control? Not at all. It merely means a change in the geographic factors which exert that control. Here is the whole thing in a nutshell: The lower the stage of human culture, the more inevitably man is compelled to live near his food supply, and to follow only the occupations for which the local environment is favourable. As he advances in culture he becomes able to transport food and raw materials so that he begins to concentrate his industries in places which he finds especially advantageous. At the same time he finds himself more and more able to pursue sedentary industries in cool climates because he learns to utilize clothing, buildings, glass, and heating devices. In addition to this, he unconsciously finds that in fairly cool climates his innate ability increases because he must exercise judgment, economy, thrift, and foresight in preparing for the winter. Those who fail in these respects are likely to be eliminated. Finally, although even yet he scarcely knows it, man discovers that in a certain type of cool, stormy climate with a strong but not overwhelming contrast of seasons, he has better health, greater energy, and more initiative than anywhere else. As a result of these tendencies, the centres of civilization keep moving into the regions where man's stage of progress makes him most efficient."[1]

In no department of science has so much progress been made in the last fifty years as in that of tropical medicine. There are many parts of the globe in which a generation ago white men could hardly live at all, and where the natives had not good health and long lives, but where to-day people of European origin can live in health and the native's bodily condition has improved enormously. Especial mention is always made about the conquering of malaria, yellow fever, trypanosis, and hook-worm diseases. These triumphs are fine illustrations of how it is only possible to banish evils when their true causes are discovered, fully explored, and understood. The triumphs have been over vegetable pests, too (boll weevil, potato blight, smut disease of wheat, etc.). Man's scope for food production has been greatly widened, and he has been able to make a comfortable living through these and other discoveries on smaller areas of land. In modern times the concentration of population has in many places brought about, amongst other disadvantages, a difficulty in obtaining fresh food, despite rapid transport facilities. Though the methods of preserving food without destruction of vital vitamins have made enormous strides in recent times, it is still open to question how far the present generation suffers from not getting more fresh food. One friend of mine goes so far as to believe that one of the chief causes of cancer lies in this direction. Here is a relevant quotation from the pen of G. D. Elsdon:[2]

"Probably the two general aspects of chemistry and its industrial application as applied to food which are attracting most attention at the present time are preservation and vitamins. It seems to be generally agreed that the ideal type of food is that natural product

---

[1] E. Huntingdon's *The Human Habitat*, p. 161 (Chapman & Hall, 1928).

[2] *Reports of the Progress of Applied Chemistry*, issued by Society of Chemical Industries (Vol. XVI, 1931, p. 566).

which is eaten within a few hours of gathering, and this, for a large part of the population collected as it is in large towns, is manifestly impossible. It follows, therefore, that the development of methods which have as their goal the preservation of food in its natural state with all its important biological properties fully retained is obviously a matter of the greatest importance. Such methods, at their best, can only be regarded as temporary measures to be adopted while more satisfactory methods of distribution are being developed."

Many of the food transport and sanitary drawbacks to swollen town agglomerations of population have been overcome nowadays. None the less, reasons abound for refusing to tolerate the present excessive tendency citywards. Many of the curses heaped to-day upon the head of the middle-man would be more appropriately directed towards attempting to get population more dispersed, and to obtaining wiser marketing arrangements. Especially should efforts be made to get more space for markets in thickly populated districts, to decentralize markets more from such centres, and to plan the distribution of goods from rail-head depots arranged at strategic points. Big firms, such as Lyons & Co., Unilevers, and Cadbury-Fry, can work road and railway transport economically and conveniently in combination. Yet in other realms of business absurd rivalry brings discord and heightened freights. Is this due to too much governmental interference? English freight rates are still very anomalous. Why should they in many instances be two to four times higher than Belgian from station to station for approximately 100 miles per ton mile? Again, if home growers of wheat could get their rail freightage rates down to the United States of America levels, with no shipping freight to pay, they would save about twenty shillings a ton as compared with foreign competitors. The production of fruit and vegetables in England is lamentably short of what it might be. The grower is often inadequately rewarded. Rates and taxes, middle-men's costs, unduly high rents, high freight rates, and delay in transport all contribute to this. If such commodities could be produced nearer to the crowds who want them, and if these crowds were not too big, some of these drawbacks would be greatly minimized. Cities of

20,000 to 200,000 possessing spacious and free markets, where stalls would be conducted by practised salesmen selling on commission, would give a big stimulus to production.

Reference has just been made to the fact that rates and taxes detract from the reward a grower gets for his labour. Apart from that simple fact, however, there are other ways in which rates and taxes interfere with production. One of the most effective exposures of the system (still in vogue) of local taxation in England is made by the Duke of Bedford in his book published in 1897, entitled *A Great Agricultural Estate*.[1] The Duke converted an arable field into a fruit garden by the employment of capital and labour in 1894.

"The land was duly planted with a valuable stock of fruit trees and bushes, and after a few months there came up—I confess to my amazement, for I had not foreseen this result of my experiment—the Overseer. Now the Parish Overseer said: 'The employment of capital has wrought a great change in this spot, and it is my duty to report the same and treble (afterwards halved) your rates.' Well I was in search of experience in the matter of fruit farming, and I am now in a position to record an important result, it is this: If you invest capital in a fruit farm, your rates will be trebled before you have any chance of a return for your outlay."[2]

In this book the Duke shows how national taxation penalizes enterprise, decreases employment, and damps down initiative; how it "rewards the starvation and ruin of a property by a light assessment, and reduces the capable owner below the level of him who has squandered his inheritance."

In 1927 the University of Cambridge Department of Agriculture published a report on *The Economy of a Norfolk Fruit Farm*, 1923–26. It appears from this that the value of the net output on an average of two years (1925–26) of this farm is roughly three times that obtained from arable farming, as disclosed in a similar report on fifteen East Anglian arable farms investigated at the same time. Furthermore, the actual profit

[1] Recent so-called "de-rating" Acts have done more harm than good, and have not altered the principle of local taxation.

[2] Duke of Bedford's *A Great Agricultural Estate*, p. 72, etc. (John Murray, London, 1897).

is more than double that per acre of arable farming, and the wages paid to labour are four times as great. In passing it is worthy of note that the adoption of a bonus system in 1926 (freedom to work without trade union or such-like restrictions) had astonishing results in improving the efficiency of both the permanent and the temporary employees. Though fruit farming has increased in England in recent years it is a form of cultivation which fluctuates a good deal. This depends, amongst other things, upon fluctuation in prices. This is illustrated by the average prices realized by the East Norfolk Fruit Growers' Association for its members' fruit in three different years. In 1926 it was £72, in 1928 £52 10s., and in 1930 £27 a ton. A census of the acreage under fruit taken in 1925 showed that the country had nearly 18,000 acres less orchards and bush fruit cultivation than in 1908.

Fruit farming goes with thicker population because it finds occupation for more persons than less intensive and more primitive forms of farming, and it produces, as has already been shown, foodstuffs of greater value per acre than ordinary arable farming. It can often be undertaken on land which is poor from the point of view of general farming. For example, on the Worcester-Gloucestershire borders there is a farm of 130 acres which has only 5 inches of soil on top of limestone. It would be a strain to find employment for four workers on this if it were worked as an arable farm. But since it has been turned into a fruit farm it gives employment to forty men, women, and boys permanently, together with the available population of two villages in picking time. One of the dangers to the proprietor of such a fruit farm is that the middle-men and the retailers will curtail sales in order to make easier profits by handling less first-class fruit at higher prices. Transport and price-drop difficulties also often arise. But it is the poor buying capacity of large numbers of people through low incomes that is, after all, the greatest handicaps to the producer of sound, high-class food of this kind. Were there more persons in the enviable state of the well-to-do classes, would there be so ready a market for cheap jams made from foreign fruit pulps? Some second-quality jams have only about 20 per cent of fruit in them, whereas good-quality home-made jams usually have 55 to 80 per cent of fruit.

Do not all really prefer the best quality they can get? Again, would not more co-operation amongst growers, better organization for advertising and salesmanship do much to help the markets for home fruit? Home canning, and not only canning, factories should receive more commendation and encouragement, though here again the poverty of consumers not only in means but in room—room to live and move in overcrowded towns—stands in the way. Undoubtedly, competition from abroad helps to keep prices down, and this is advantageous to the mass of workers, besides helping employment by enabling our industrialists to send their manufactured goods abroad in exchange. In 1930 Great Britain imported 27,000 cwt. of gooseberries, 122,000 cwt. of currants, and 233,500 cwt. of plums from Italy, France, and Spain. This refers to fresh fruit only. Several thousands of hundredweights of the currants came from Holland, a country almost more dependent upon its soil than any other country in Europe, because it imports most of its manufactured articles and raw materials. The transaction over the currants is closed by the products of English factories in nine cases out of ten, though the steps taken are not always easy to follow.

The English *could* grow all the wheat they wanted, as has already been shown. It would be a healthier situation if they produced many other of the foodstuffs they require. But at the present moment, at all events, no similarly circumstanced country is actually self-supporting in her food supply. France, with a population density of 190 per square mile, comes nearest to this condition. Denmark which, outside the cities of over 20,000 people, has a population of more than 130 to the square mile, imports many foodstuffs. Germany, with a population density of 345 persons to the square mile, has never produced more than 80 per cent of her food. Belgium has 635 to the square mile and imports at least half her food. Holland, too, imports a large proportion: she has 580 people to the square mile. (England and Wales have 650 per square mile.) Furthermore, though most authorities agree that we should all be the better for eating bread much nearer in quality to that of our grandfathers, the use to which home-grown wheat is now put must not be forgotten. The bread of our grandfathers usually had a much bigger proportion of wholemeal stone-ground flour in it, made from home-grown wheat. To-day, home-grown wheat is used to feed poultry. Our poultry farms have in recent decades gradually produced an increasing proportion of our home requirements of eggs and table-birds. To-day nearly two-thirds are produced from home land. Associated with this is the fact that one-third of the wheat grown at home, up to 1932 at all events, was used for poultry feeding direct as grain, and of the remaining two-thirds, one-third is manufactured into miller's offals. Furthermore, of the 7 per cent of our population engaged in farming only a small proportion is concerned with wheat or grain; the rest is more concerned with cheap food for stock (and for themselves). Again, the mechanization of wheat growing by the introduction of the tractor and the harvester and thrasher has revolutionized the growing of wheat so completely, according to some, that its success can only now be permanent on the great plains of the world, such as North America, Argentina, Australia, and Russia. Such authorities consider the surface of Great Britain is too undulating, farming is conducted on too small a scale, and the harvesting climate is too uncertain for wheat growing ever again to attain its old importance if left alone. There is much to be said for these views. None the less they do not take sufficiently into account modern intensive methods, outlined above, nor the desirability of combining various kinds of culture together, according to local conditions of soil, site, and transport, and the ability and education of the agriculturists, and nearness to dense population. The production of more truck crops is *the* development of agriculture in England which, above all others should proceed more rapidly than it has done. It is true that by comparing the years 1905 to 1914 with the years 1869 to 1878 it is found that the acreage in England and Wales under cabbage increased 100 per cent and under orchards by 50 per cent during the period; and again, that in 1920 it is recorded there were 4,270 acres of celery in England and Wales, 5,541 of rhubarb, 1,625 of brussel sprouts, 8,823 of cauliflower, and 4,450 of onions. At this time the acreage of orchards was 222,000, and of small fruit 58,000. But considering the increase of population during these periods in England and Wales and the needs of that population these figures are poor.

In agriculture it is not easy to find the true balance between an economic use of horses and of machines, and the relationship between these and the man power; and these vary from country to country, from district to district, and also according to the agriculture which is being pursued. A few facts regarding Canada, for example, will be of interest: In 1830, with hand-labour production methods, 32 hours of man-labour were required to produce 10 bushels of wheat. In Montana an acre of land has been summer fallowed and a crop removed the following year with 2·5 hours of man-labour. The labour in one ton of hay in bales was reduced between 1860 and 1894 from 35½ hours to 11½ hours. Canada still has over 3,250,000 horses, and the United States of America over 13,000,000, in spite of the increasing use of machinery and electric power in agriculture. As a consequence of such increased use a larger acreage operated per worker has naturally resulted. The average acres of improved land per worker in the United States has steadily increased from 30 in 1850 to 49 in 1925. In Canada, between 1881 and 1891, the increase per worker was 95 per cent for farm land, 105 per cent for improved land, and 109 per cent for crop acres. In Canada, whereas in 1901 the average value of goods produced by each farm worker amounted to barely £102, twenty years later it increased to £268, or by 163 per cent. In Canada the percentage of population engaged in agriculture was 48·1 in 1881, while in 1921 it was only 32·8; yet during this period the surplus of farm exports over imports increased by 600 per cent.

On the subject of the connection between agriculture and the town life of to-day and its associationship with a more mechanized form of production the following quotation is apposite. It relates to farming in America.

"Farming is still idyllic and pastoral in journalism and popular thought. The world of letters reveals scant comprehension of the kind of agriculture which makes possible the city and town life of to-day. Even in economic literature the urban industrial revolution which followed the introduction of the steam engine is not often correlated adequately with the equally revolutionary changes in agriculture which took place in the nineteenth century.

"The industrial revolution in the cities, which came from the extraction of energy from age-old coal beds, would have been stillborn if it had not been for the contemporary agrarian revolution founded on the transformation of energy from grain and forage crops into the work of animals. At the climax of the era of animal-powered agriculture before the World War, the average agricultural worker in the United States was cultivating 24·4 acres against 16·6 for the Scottish farm worker (including a considerable percentage of shepherds on grazing lands), 9·5 acres for the English farm worker, 8·3 acres for the Frenchman, 6·2 acres for the German, and 4·2 acres for the Italian. The average number of horses per farm worker in the United States was 2·05, but only 0·88 in Great Britain, 0·55 in Germany, 0·37 in France, and 0·19 in Italy, where more than five men are engaged in farm work for every animal employed.

"As agriculture moved into the era of mechanical power and approached present conditions, when only 61 per cent of the power output on farms in 1924—and it is less to-day—was by animals, the rate of power installation on farms kept pace with that of manufacturing. At the beginning of this century the total installed power per farm worker was 2·2 horse-power. It rose to 4·5 horse-power in the first quarter of the century, while the horse-power per person engaged in manufacturing increased from 1·9 to 3·6.

"From 1850 to the beginning of the present century, American agriculture increased its power resources from 6,597,000 to 23,519,000 horse-power. From the beginning of the century to the advent of mechanical field-power on a considerable scale in 1910, the increase was from 23,519,000 to 31,107,000 horse-power. When the peak of animal-power on farms was reached at the close of 1918, the total of all kinds of power equipment installed on farms was in capacity equivalent to 43,722,000 horse-power. From 1919 to 1923 in the period of declining animal-power, farm-power installations increased to a capacity of 47,420,000 horse-power, and to-day the total capacity is undoubtedly in excess of 50,000,000 horse-power."[1]

When certain places where agricultural production supports dense population are surveyed—for example, China—there are

[1] *Harvest and Highlines*, pp. 2–6 (Middle West Utility Co., Chicago, 1930. Gratis).

several important points to note. There is not a fat living to be found for the multitude. Increase of population is generally going on at a rapid rate. The size of agricultural holdings is for the most part small. Human labour is cheap and hard work has to be done to make a livelihood. The amount produced per man is low. It is much higher in places like England, which probably comes near to the United States of America which is highest of all, largely because more mechanical aid and electrical power are used there than anywhere else. But the yield per acre is generally highest where human hand-labour is most, partly because with hand-labour often goes the production of three or four crops within the year. To-day the American farm hand produces three times as much as do similar workers in important European countries, but, compared to the Chinaman, less.

The agricultural workers of China, comprising not less than 70 per cent of a population of over 400,000,000, could produce far more had they more help from modern aids to cultivation. The land-holding peasant in China is held up to admiration by Western observers for his individual skill and industry, but it is largely unaided by organized knowledge. As R. H. Tawney, a recent English visitor to China, points out,[1] Chinese farming is intensive in its use of labour, but is unintensive in the inadequacy of the equipment by which it is assisted. "It produces an output per acre which, in the case of one crop, is surprisingly high, but its output per worker is invariably low. . . . Neither biology and chemistry, nor mechanical transport, nor enclosure and consolidation, nor the reform of land tenure, nor co-operative marketing and credit have as yet, save in a few exceptional areas, begun to affect it." In a few districts there are as many as 2,000 persons per square mile of cultivated land. About half the holdings are only 1½ to 4½ acres in extent. Animals are scarce so that considerations of pastures, common or otherwise, do not arise. There is no landed aristocracy, none the less serious questions connected with land tenure are to the fore in many parts; and the poorer peasants at all events are in a dire state of permanent debt. Interest rates of 25 to 50 per cent, or even higher, are not uncommon. The famines which devastate whole districts of China from time to

[1] *Manchester Guardian*, April 20, 1931.

time, sometimes contributed to by drought or flood, are often really merely the last stage of a disease which is always present, the precarious state of the peasants due to the various causes just indicated. What is wanted more than anything else is better means of communication, and more education, especially elementary education. But both these advances are seriously hampered by public debts and taxation. China has not even got tariff autonomy. Her military expenditure in 1928 accounted for over $130,000,000 out of a revenue of $148,000,000. Several prominent persons who desire to see more and better roads and railways in China move no finger to get them built because they hold that at present these improvements would merely play into the hands of the militarists. China is a boundless country practically without roads. It is partly on this account, because the public forces are unable to move quickly in the interior of the country, that banditry is still rife, though the amount of it reported—for political purposes—in the European Press is 'much exaggerated. The collection of taxes, still in part directed by foreigners, is difficult, again partly for the reason of poor means of communication. And when they are collected they do not fructify production, but are used up too much for the meagre pay of numerous soldiers, who are really State paid out-of-works unable through paucity of public funds to get adequate military equipment. This apparent paradox consequently arises: the military forces are inadequate because they are excessive in man-power. But perhaps these conditions are transitory. If only Japan would leave China alone! Or, to put it more accurately, if only a few of the Japanese with grandiose ideas and with greed after obtaining material concessions for their own advantage would stop interference and cease placing obstacles in the way of the reconstruction of China! The portion of the Chinese revenue which came from Manchuria, an item of about $55,000,000 a year, together with the cost of the war that Japan forced on the Chinese, make up an annual figure of at least $200,000,000, which equals roughly one-third of the Chinese Budget to-day. Further borrowing is difficult nowadays and might precipitate China's financial collapse, or delay the most essential reforms, constructive works. The League of Nations apparently does not find it possible to intervene helpfully. The teeming multitudes of China, the masses of peasants who might lead a less precarious existence, who might be more mobile and able, in times of distress especially, to be distributed on the surface of the earth to their better advantage, are really very dependent on reforms along the above lines if genuine improvements are to be accomplished.

CHAPTER V

REGIMES OF PROPERTY IN ASIA

IN all the ancient empires the system of land tenure and the system of land assessment for purposes of taxation were the two main factors in good government. Most of the great administrators of antiquity and of the Middle Ages owe their fame to the fact that they identified themselves with the reform of land tenure and land revenue assessment. The Gracchi brothers in ancient Rome, and Julius Caesar and his nephew Augustus in Imperial Rome, were great land reformers. Later on we find Naushirwan in pre-Moslem Persia. His name is a household word in the East; it is symbolical of justice. He was the first to fix the standard of measure based on that of Caesar which was to be applied in valuing land, and also the State share of the produce which was to be exacted from the holder of this land. The renowned Khalif Omar was identified with land reform. Later on Akbar the Great owed his name and fame in India largely to the just and far-reaching land reforms which he inaugurated there. In China the greatest Emperors were those who imposed or improved the best systems of land tenure and taxation. When the empires of antiquity failed it was mainly due to the fact that they did not handle properly the two great problems of land tenure and land assessment. An indication of weak government is often a bad system of farming out the taxes, especially so when the revenue is based on the land. The revenue systems of the Empires of both Rome and Turkey of old tended to a recurrence of this weakness. This undoubtedly helped to bring about their decline. So, too, with the Mogul Empire: the State delegated its responsibilities for land revenue collection to tax-farmers, and these, as often happens, developed into territorial magnates.

Again, the whole history of China hangs upon the system of land tenure and assessment of land revenue. The Chinese have been a nation of agricultural producers since time immemorial. Agriculture in China is recorded as beginning with Shonnung (2737 B.C.), the ruler to whom is credited the teaching of farming to the Chinese people. But there is evidence that it dates back even beyond his time. The productivity of their soil has clearly depended not only upon their wonderful skill as cultivators, upon the advantages of their climate, and their methods of conserving soil fertility, but also upon the various changes of policy in regard to land tenure and land revenue assessment. The history of Chinese agricultural administration "coincides with the history of the Tsing Tien System, for it started with this system of land tenure. Its vicissitudes, its crises and epochs were timed by the abolition or re-establishment of the system."[1] Tsing Tien means fields laid out like the character tsing ⊞. Each tsing consisted of a square divided into nine plots. This system acknowledged public ownership of land with private possession for family use. Land was distributed to families in groups of eight and was practically rented from the Government, rent being paid by labour on the central plot with reservation to the Government on death or disability. A study of agriculture through the ages in China is complicated and difficult, because the measures of length and area were altered from time to time. These changes had direct relationship with the systems of land tenure and assessment. During the time of the pre-Chow and the Chow Dynasties (1110 to 250 B.C.) the Government had a free hand with all the land in the Empire and the people owned no land at all. There were no great changes in measure throughout nearly the whole of that period. Spasmodic efforts after the Chow Dynasty towards private ownership sprang up, but for the most part without success right down to A.D. 780, though it is correct to say that for about five hundred years prior to this date the Governments followed a system of land equalization rather than one of an absolute land distribution. About 780 Yang Yen did away with the old system and opened a new era with the establishment of the biennial tax system. To this day a land-tax revenue is collected, though not based on a good system of assessment, and much corrupted from the system and methods of old times, as well as perverted in its use, and mixed with other kinds of taxes. In ancient times census returns were very inaccurate, partly because of taxes being based, in an endeavour

[1] Mabel Ping-Hua Lee's *The Economic History of China*—with special reference to agriculture—p. 33 (Columbia University, New York. 1921).

to assess the amount of land held, upon the number of doors (families) and mouths (heads). The number of doors and mouths were concealed in order to escape the taxation based upon them.

Ancient law concerns itself hardly at all with individuals, but with families or tribal groups. The customs of to-day in most parts of Asia and Africa show their connection with ancient law far more than is the case in most other parts of the world. Turning to India, for example, the influence of Village Communes holds sway throughout the greater part of this peninsula right up to the present day.

"The Village Community in India, known to be of immense antiquity, is at once an organized patriarchal society and an assemblage of co-proprietors. The personal relations to each other of the men who compose it are indistinguishably confounded with their property rights, and to the attempts of English functionaries to separate the two may be assigned some of the most formidable miscarriages of Anglo-Indian administration. . . . Conquests and revolutions have swept over the institution of the Village Community without disturbing or displacing it, and the most beneficent systems of government in India have always been those which have recognized it as the basis of administration."[1]

As has been pointed out by Sir Evelyn Howell and Sir Michael O'Dwyer[2] the growth of society in India, in spite of many upheavals and difficulties, has proceeded better than in Mesopotamia, largely because more respect has usually been shown, in the former than in the latter place, to ancient forms and age-long customs. And this is so, even though in both countries the people have frequently pushed new civil laws aside calmly in favour of regard to old local custom. Such action is especially likely to occur in the rural districts where the people are closely associated with the land. For example, ask a Syed what custom is followed as to the inheritance of land—whether that of the Sheriat, which gives a share to women, or that of the country, which denies all share to women—he will say at once that he follows the custom of the country, in other words that he

---

[1] Sir Henry Maine's *Ancient Law*, p. 153 (Everyman's Edition).
[2] *Journal of the Central Asian Society*, Vol. IX, 1922, pp. 21 and 81.

disregards the Sheriat ordinances laid down for his observance by his Government. It would have been interesting to see what system of land tenure and assessment would have been developed had the native tribes been left in freedom to evolve their own. Sir M. O'Dwyer believes they would have evolved along similar lines, suiting their own local needs, as in the system which holds good amongst the nomadic tribes in North-western India. Unfortunately a well-meaning doctrinaire, Midhat Pasha, intervened with laws based not on what the people wanted but what it was thought they should want, and thrust upon the inhabitants of 'Iraq from above an unsuitable and unworkable system devised largely in the interests of the bureaucracy of Constantinople. In India, on the other hand, though many mistakes have been made, the old system of land revenue assessment and tenures has been accepted as the basis of any further changes, and the authorities have worked not from above downwards but from below upwards. Land records are based on inquiries made locally. Maps and records are prepared locally, in the village, by the expert local agency, and in the presence of and after inquiry from the people whose rights are in question. They are tested, also on the spot, by higher officials. In the end they are quite often a miracle of accuracy. The system in India is largely based on the reforms introduced by Akbar the Great, who knowing the value of old authority, in the first place took Naushirwan as his model and as his support in what he did. He set up a fixed standard of measurement and laid down as the State's share of the produce one-third, following Naushirwan and Omar.

Revenue is often raised, concurrently with that levied on the basis of land holding assessments, by forms of taxation which in most cases are arbitrary, burdensome, and which impose hindrances on production and trade. Furthermore, if the levies assessed on land holdings are not scrupulously fair between one party and another, revenue collection may be vexatious to the people and destructive to good government and a sound state of society. Unfairness may arise in one or other of several ways. If assessments are based on area they generally take quite insufficient account of quality. A measured area, bearing the same levy to an occupier as another one of the same size, may be more or less fertile than the neighbouring piece; or it may be better situated, having better accessibility to other groups of people; or it may be flatter and easier to work agriculturally. Or the levy may be unfair between district and district through fluctuations in the amount of the crop produced, which varies, of course, from season to season too, and in the cash value of the crops. Such difficulties are not hard to deal with in countries where for generations a more or less fixed and stable system of agriculture is followed. But they become great just when and so far as society becomes more complicated and the interests of the community, as well as of individuals, become more varied. Yet these things are just as important from the point of view of the effects they have on the distribution of population in the more advanced as in the primitive stages of society. The introduction of money payments adds another complication, but one which ought to tend to greater ease and fairness in administration. That is one of the functions of money. Akbar, after acquiring ten years' experience of collecting each year according to crop and prices, fixed a regular assessment on the average assessment of the ten years and took that as the amount that each village should pay. His practice is the origin of the system of land revenue administration which is being followed in India to-day.

"Akbar's equitable system died away after him as the country fell into anarchy; but the roots were there; the tradition survived. It was not difficult to revive it. The system we derive from Akbar was derived by him from Omar, who derived it from Naushirwan, and has much in common with, even if not directly based on, the old Roman assessment and survey. For it is quite possible that the Persians and Arabs copied the Roman system.

"The two things which have done most to justify our rule in India up to date are: Firstly, we have made just distribution of the rights in the land, and have prepared an extremely accurate record of those rights. In the next place, we have placed on the land an assessment which is just and equitable, and the pitch of which in my experience has yearly been getting lower and lower. Akbar, the great reformer, took one-third of the produce and prided himself on his moderation; roughly we take one-eighth or one-tenth. The Native States of India take about double what the

British Government takes. We hope that 'Iraq, under the Government which has now been established there, will be able to obtain and enjoy those two main elements of prosperity—that is, an equitable distribution of rights in the land with a good record of such rights and moderate assessments. For such work knowledge, experience, and sympathy are essential. If the new Government of 'Iraq are able to do this work well, they will be very well repaid by the increased prosperity and contentment of the people."[1]

It is necessary to make sure that the machinery of land assessments for public revenue are not too cumbersome, whether it is in places like India, China, or 'Iraq, or in other countries; that antagonism between the needs of central and local administration, and between peaceful and war-like expenditures are not subversive; that the officers employed to carry them out are honest and competent; and that the revisions of the assessments are made sufficiently frequently. In order to bring all these things about the only safe antidotes against the corruptions, waste, and incompetence which are so liable to creep in are ever and only the identifying of the interests of the community with the best interests of individuals. This identification again depends upon a proper education and knowledge. In most places in the world to-day, as has already been hinted in previous pages of this book and as will be elaborated again further on, a clash of the various business, political, and class interests is far too rife, so that a true identification of community and personal interests is obscured and but poorly attained. The influences which lead to a natural and sound distribution of population cannot work freely so long as this is the case. In many ways the inhabitants of some countries of old and many of the more primitive peoples of to-day were in and are in a better state in this respect than the more advanced and highly organized nations. The officers of a State cannot be expected to be and are not found to be prudent, truly honest, moderate, sober, painstaking, and competent unless this identification which is so very difficult to establish can be maintained. But, as Herbert Spencer wrote years ago: "The co-heirship to the soil is consistent with the

[1] Sir Michael O'Dwyer, *Journal of the Central Asian Society* (Vol. IX, 1922, p. 85).

highest civilization. . . . However difficult it may be to embody that theory in fact, equity sternly commands it to be done." And in *Social Statics* (pp. 130–31) he writes as follows:

"When we regard the history of land tenure in England in the light of such propositions as these, we are forced into a humiliating confession, very painful to those who have indulged a belief in the progressive development of civilization. Our direction of movement has not, we learn, been progressive, but retrogressive. The custom of land tenure in primitive times started out by recognizing the ownership of land to be in the whole community, not in individuals, and it gave substantially equal rights to all. From this starting point we have not, as we fondly fancied, risen to loftier heights, but have despicably fallen."

The profound effect on population distribution of customs of land tenure is more obvious in places where agriculture is the chief occupation, but is equally true for other places and nations. Invariably systems of land holding are wrapt up with the equal and fair treatment of individuals and families in the matter of the raising of revenue for public services. "The desire for equal and fair treatment is the most powerful and unquenchable in human nature, but it is not the only one. Very strong and deep is the desire of men to find the easiest way of doing things, and if a plan intended to secure fair play does not also secure economy and efficiency it is bound to fail.

"The progress of agriculture depends (1) on man's knowledge of the nature of soils and seeds, and of the proper way in which to handle them, and (2) on his knowledge of human nature, and of the way in which men should treat each other in order, as the German chiefs said, 'to preserve their contentment,' their loyalty to each other in their pursuit of a common enterprise. For hundreds of years there are few achievements to record on either of these possible lines of progress."[1]

Contentment rests upon the pursuit of a common enterprise. But so long as the common inheritance, the earth and all that therein is, is treated as rightfully the private property of indi-

[1] John Orr's *A Short History of British Agriculture*, p. 19 (Oxford University Press, 1922).

viduals, and burdensome taxation has as a consequence to be imposed, then just so long will the commonweal conflict with the interests and welfare of many individuals. Contentment can reign only when the common enterprise can be shown to be perfectly consistent with the welfare of individuals and their families.

In early agricultural communities the compact village form of rural settlement had its basis in a system of intensive cultivation with communal tendencies. This variety of population distribution is seen to-day in many parts of China. The connection between regimes of property in early days and the forms of rural settlements can be followed by studying the plans adopted in former days in the Island of Alderney,[1] and in the Highland Open-field System described by Miss I. F. Grant.[2] In Italy, too, to-day, as Professor O. Marinelli[3] points out, rural settlements vary, and depend more upon the regime of property system than upon the agrarian system; for he has shown that they vary according as to whether the *podere* unit and the *mezzadria* regime on the *contadini* system based on the contract of rent be adopted. Similarly in Denmark at the present day the density of the farming population is by no means everywhere proportional to the fertility of the soil. The population is thinner in rural districts in Denmark where the estates are large, even in those parts of the country where the soil is boulder clay and the fertility only varies within narrow limits. Denmark is the one country in Europe where the majority of land *owners* is opposed to the private ownership of land, and favours a reversion to the natural conditions of property regime in an agricultural community. The small-holder is re-colonizing his home land there with holdings of only moderate extent, while fighting steadily for lower taxes and the collection for the common use of the communal values (land rent).

Away from agricultural communities a distinction between the possession for use and the ownership of land is rather more difficult to appreciate. But it should be made, because unless made, many difficulties arise leading to unhealthy agglomerations of

[1] *Report of the Commission on Types of Rural Settlement* (Union Géographique Internationale), No. 1, 1928, Miss Harris, pp. 25–38.
[2] Ibid., pp. 102–13.　　　　　　　　　　　　　　[3] Ibid., pp. 4–6.

inhabitants into overcrowded centres of population. Because it becomes necessary to enclose land to protect crops, or to mark off sites to be held exclusively for other purposes than agriculture, people lose sight of the essential wrongness of private ownership of land; and it is not obvious how to make exclusive possession secure while continuing to honour public ownership. This is accomplished if it is realized that no injury to others can come about in holding land for exclusive possession provided that the value of such loss of access *to* others be paid them for the common benefit and such share be taken *from* others in common services. In other words, land rent must be used for the communal services, thereby placing a man in a fair and proper position to his neighbours for having exclusive possession; just as when, for example, three brothers own a horse, all are quite fairly treated if the use of the horse is given exclusively to that brother who bids the highest for such use, provided that the rent paid for the horse (if it can be called "rent" for a moment) is used first for the fodder and insurance of the horse, and any balance divided equally amongst the three owners.

There is not really any basic antagonism between individual and community rights in a well-ordered and free society. It is because this is only now becoming very slowly recognized that for generations the science of political economy has generally appeared to be a description of a struggle between the competing interests of individuals, of sections and groups of individuals, and often between individuals and the State. Even religious tenets are tinged with a perverted outlook, moral values are built on wrong foundations, and politics have come to shape a condition of society which makes privation and poverty more rife in a world of plenty than could have been dreamt of even a generation ago had the much greater facilities of production now existing been foreseen.

Sectional economic selfishness is a grave problem that perplexes every statesman in every large country, and it indirectly hampers not only freedom to produce and exchange the commodities needed for life, comfort, health, and happiness, but also a natural and sound development of society as reflected by the distribution of population. The only way to bring about a better state of affairs is to gain a full understanding of the causes which have given rise to such selfishness and such conflicts, and to discover how to eliminate them. One reason why considerable space has been given to a study of China and India and the effect of ancient customs there, still surviving to some extent, more especially those dealing with property rights, is because they undoubtedly throw light upon the problems of to-day. Many traditions and ideas, especially those based on very ancient laws and customs regarding property rights, are of Aryan descent. They permeate a large part of Europe. They have descended through hundreds of generations. They die hard. Ancient Europe survives in India. Therefore India repays study.

In India the ancient land revenue system has been handed down to the present day. Through the good fortune and good management which has often distinguished British rule in this and other parts it still forms the basis of our administration. A line of great rulers there were frequently wise enough to appreciate its importance and to study closely its application. It behoves us, however, to find out how far ancient customs have been departed from and what effects such departures have had upon the growth and distribution of the population. Obviously if private ownership of land occurs in any parts of India and land-lords can extract higher rents into their own pockets without contributing anything in return, producers are discouraged from increased production. Moreover, land users, in whatsoever way they may be using their locations, do not get that return which they would obtain from their rent payments if these went to finance services, of one sort or another, for the community's welfare. For they, as members of the community, would participate in those services and to an extent fairly closely commensurate with the rent payments they had made. The minds of a great many of the inhabitants of India, it must be remembered, are prone to discouragement, and the climate does not stimulate to a busy industriousness. These are two important influences which are sometimes overlooked when the low standard of living amongst the masses as compared with some other parts of the world is under consideration. The expectation of life in India is still only about half that in England. There can be no doubt, however, that the material condition of the peasants in India, compared with even one hundred years ago, has gone up a good deal, in some parts a great deal. In some of the cities of India great squalor and poverty continue to be prevalent (97 per cent of the working classes in Bombay City were accommodated in one-roomed tenements ten years ago), and amongst rural workers, who constitute about 85 per cent of the population of India, the improvement is nothing to what it might be if Western ideas had permeated India thoroughly.

In the days of the East India Company and subsequently there were unfortunately some prominent British administrators whose minds were too inelastic, too much influenced by the ideas they brought to India from England. They were drawn from the landlord class, and the present system of land tenure and revenue is, unfortunately, far too much tinged by their outlook. The British landlord theory found expression in that disastrous blunder, the "Permanent Settlement" of land revenue in nearly all Bengal and large portions of other provinces.

"In the kindness of their hearts Lord Cornwallis and his advisers desired to extend to India the blessings of the landlord system of the British Isles. The Zemindars, who were mostly hereditary local State officials, were regarded as owners of the land, liable to pay only a definite quit-rent to the East India Company. When the amount of that rent was fixed, in 1793, it may have been as much as nine-tenths of the economic rent of the land. Since then population and land values have grown greatly, and the real value of the rupee has also very greatly diminished. Over vast areas, in Bengal and elsewhere, by this permanent settlement the East India Company in the first place, and the Imperial Government subsequently, have handed over the power of taxing the community by extorting rent, in ever-increasing sums, to a small, favoured section of the population, without demanding any public service in return. Lord Cornwallis no doubt hoped that the Zemindars would voluntarily render services to agricultural progress which would be an equivalent to the privileges conferred upon them; but this expectation was not justified in the result. The enormous increase in the incomes of the Zemindars has been almost unmitigated unearned increment."[1]

[1] Article by Gilbert Slater in *Land Values*, No. 281, October 1917, p. 601.

Partly owing to this disastrous blunder the land revenue under British rule is much smaller in proportion either to the produce of the land or to the total revenue than it was under the Governments that preceded ours, and in both ratios it is steadily declining. Yet some still think that the rights of proprietors *and cultivators* were assured and protected by the Permanent Settlement of the Land Revenue and the Tenancy Acts respectively, 1793 and 1859. In some places rents have been increased by landlords as soon as mission teachers showed cultivators how to increase their crops. Cultivators even come to ask not to be taught better farming methods because they do not receive any benefits from their knowledge. Yet these same peasants are following much the same methods as their forefathers did four or five thousand years ago. It is reckoned that had they the tools and machinery equivalent to those a British workman uses the Indian could attain to an efficiency of about 45 per cent of his European rival, and often perhaps more, for in India nature, though cruel at times, is extraordinarily bounteous.

India contains 1,819,000 square miles, of which about half is under British rule. The cultivable area occupied and used in British India is just over 1,000,000 square miles of crops. Of this area about one-tenth was subject to the error of the Permanent Settlement. In the whole of India, which has a population of 351,000,000, an increase of 32,000,000 in ten years, something like nine out of every ten persons are found inhabiting villages of less than 5,000 souls. The increase of population is not being absorbed by the cities or by industry. The thirty-six largest cities in India include every town as large as Reading and every important industrial centre, except Tata's steel-works at Jamshedpur and a few mining areas. The total population of these cities is under 10,000,000, and has increased very little more than the average throughout India; it is about 10 per cent increase every ten years, against about 8 per cent throughout India. The proportion of added persons which the cities and industries absorb is but a small fraction of the increased numbers the growth of population in the agricultural districts produces. India is to-day supporting over 54,000,000 more human beings than it did fifty years ago. It is calculated that India has but 300,000,000 acres fit for cultivation, and some of this is poor land. The only practical means of adding to this area is by irrigation, by which means perhaps another 50,000,000 acres may be added during the next twenty-five years or so. There is

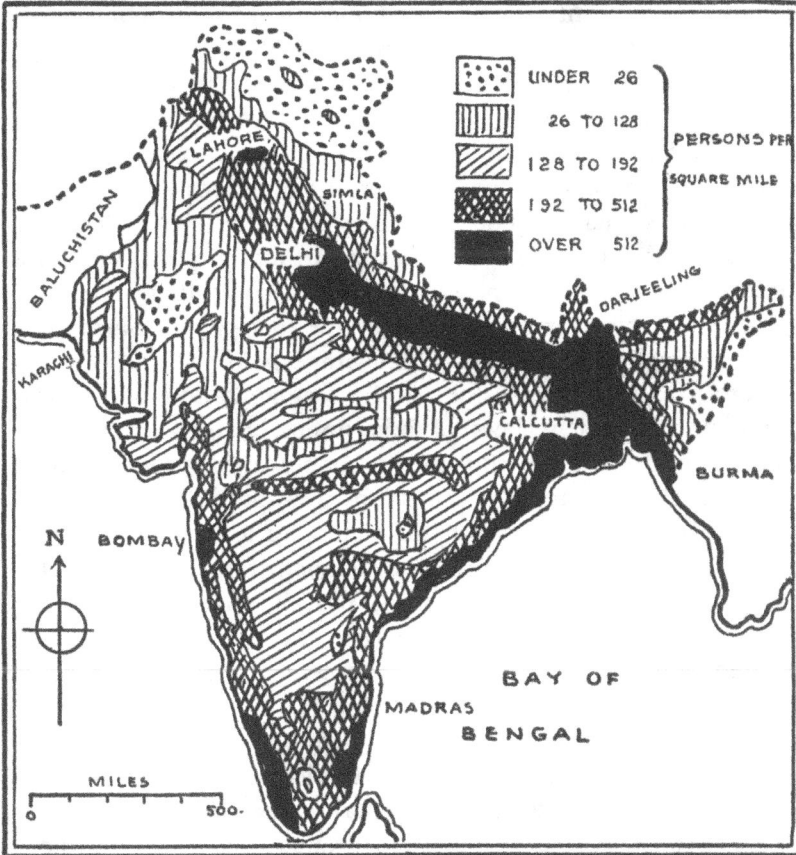

THE DENSITY OF POPULATION IN INDIA

The total population of India is 320,000,000. 72,500,000 of these are in Indian State territory, and only 33,000,000 of the total live in towns. The increase in the population in the last fifty years is about 20 per cent

little movement of population from one part of India to another, though in the north-east there is available fertile land for closer settlement. Most of the new irrigation work is being done in the Punjab.

The population density in Bengal is just over 500 persons to the square mile, and stretching right away from Calcutta to

Lahore in the north-west is a broad belt of India which possesses from 192 to 512 persons to the square mile.

India is not as heavily taxed as some people try to make out. Even including the rent revenue paid, taxation only amounts to about 6 per cent of the average income, against about 20 per cent in Japan and 30 per cent in Great Britain. The total *per capita* tax (including land revenue) paid by the inhabitants of British India in 1923–24 was 5½ rupees, say 6s. 5d., or nearly $1.32 in U.S.A. currency at the then rate of exchange. Antiquated farming operations and certain obligations imposed upon Brahmins by their religious teachings are subversive of improvements in the living of the masses in many parts of India. Brahminism forbids a peasant to kill a cow; that is bad for farming. Precious manure is burnt for fuel—again harmful to good cultivation of the soil. The average holding is a little over 4 acres. This is partly due to the fragmentation of property through the ancient laws of inheritance. Sometimes a man's holding is so split up into absurd shapes and widely scattered splinters that its useful cultivation is impossible. The priests demand high fees; for example, sometimes a wedding may cost two or more years' income. Moneylenders are resorted to. The debt becomes unpayable, and the peasant's land is foreclosed. A majority of the land of India (like that of England and the United States of America at the moment of writing this!) is in the hands of the moneylenders.

The land assessment to-day averages 4s. per head, or about 2s. 3d. per acre, in the Bombay Presidency, and takes about one-third of the unimproved rental value of the land. The Western Presidency of Bombay has 33,000,000 cultivated acres under British administration (in England and Wales there are 13,750,000 cultivated acres), and for every 100 acres there are 57 human beings and 34 cattle to be fed. In the Bombay Presidency the land to-day is fully occupied, and taking into account the fact that since 1850 the total area in cultivation has increased from 12,690,000 to 33,290,000 acres, and that during the thirty years or so before 1850 there is evidence that then, too, a considerable addition was made to the areas under crops, agricultural production has increased about five times in the last hundred years. According to one authority, Mr. F. G. H. Anderson, British rule brought an improvement in this part of India both in land assessment and, consequently as he maintains, in the material prosperity of the peasant. He says that before the British administration poverty was extreme because the land revenue was assessed on the *gross* produce and little was left for the producer; whereas after British rule had started the assessment was levied on the *net* produce and on all land claimed by anyone as privately occupied whether used or not, and it was made on the natural qualities of the soil, excluding any improvement made by the holder after the land was measured and mapped. He holds that this practice was a break with all past history in India and that it was due partly to the teaching of Ricardo, who had about that time established for the first time the theory and definition of rent as accepted by the economists since his day. It is important to note that 1793, the date of the introduction of the Permanent Settlement, was a generation before the Indian Civil Service had been formed and before Ricardo had formulated his theory of rent.

Unfortunately for a continuance of prosperity in India and a continuance of a satisfactory distribution of a contented populace before long "a new factor, or social element never before seen or comprehended in India, made its appearance. That is the *landlord*, who could let his land to a worker and, after paying the revenue demand, still enjoy a surplus rental without working. This class . . . has done what in every other country it has done and would always do—it has induced the Government . . . to whittle down and surrender the right to apply the true principles"[1] of a sound land revenue system. Together with this mistake another one was made, namely, through the Governments assuming that rental values would not vary for long periods, the valuations on which the land revenue assessments were based were not made sufficiently often. Thirty years was fixed as the period. Not only so, but through the influence of a variety of factors producing fluctuations in land values which were not foreseen, but which on the whole tended usually to be ever upward, the landlords came to gain at the expense of land users and of public administration. Hence, through this increase of rentals due to increase of population and of

[1] F. G. H. Anderson's *Indian Land Revenue Systems* (1929).

facilities of production and exchange, which increase did not flow into the Government's coffers, there arose an ever-increasing margin going into the landlords' pockets, who consequently grew more and more powerful. Another consequence was that the public services, all those reforms which otherwise might have found money to finance them (education, sanitation, better communications, etc.), were starved. At least half the land in Western India is now leased by landlords who do nothing for tenants. The cultivator is slipping back, according to Mr. Anderson, into the pre-British economic bondage, not to the State this time, but to the new landlord who has squeezed in between the State and the worker. Under the old system of assessing land revenue on the crop-share tenure, when an occupier learnt how so to improve his holding and produce more crops the revenue went up. Progress was not encouraged. So, too, under landlordism the producer is robbed of his first reward by having taken from him that which should be his alone, the true products of his own enterprise and labour. But when the tenure is fixed and all improvements made by the landholder himself are exempted from levy, enterprise and industry encourage bigger production. It appears to have been the intention of those officers who conducted the survey at the outset of the British rule thus to encourage production, and where they succeeded population increased and thrived. But, as has been shown already, success was by no means universal and was balked in various unforeseen ways. This became especially true of urban districts, small and relatively unimportant at the beginning of the British administration. Hence slumdom, privation, and poverty to-day in the cities of India. When and where the proper scheme of land assessment was put and kept in force there a different story can be told. Even recently a successful effort to revert to the proper method has produced a wonderful result in a few years. For example, in a well-defined tract in Gogho (Ahmedabad) no fewer than 14,620 acres of cultivable land were desolate and lying waste in 1925. Then the new terms of tenure and assessment were offered. By 1928 no less than 12,281 acres were taken up and a population of nearly 10,000 was living on 20 square miles of crops.

A few figures will give an idea of the effects of the mistake of the Permanent Settlement in Bengal. The East India Company found the land revenue of Bengal in the hands of revenue "farmers" who were collecting 91 per cent for the Government of the Mogul and keeping 9 per cent, not an unreasonable proportion, for their trouble. In error the Company looked upon the "farmers," who are now the Zemindars, as owners of the land; it erroneously supposed, too, that the revenue was justly calculated, and that there was no likelihood of any material change in rental value. In the year of the settlement, with interest at about 10 per cent, the value of the rights of a Zemindar or revenue "farmer" was about ten years' purchase of one-eleventh of the assessed revenue, or, more shortly, one year's revenue. In 1796–98 the "farm right" over land assessed at Rs. 3,693,632 was put up for sale and realized Rs. 3,937,996, that is a trifle over one year's purchase. But less than twenty years later, land assessed at Rs. 83,485 was sold for Rs. 233,451; that is, twenty-eight years' purchase. Such happenings came as a shock which, fortunately, saved the rest of India from the error of a permanent settlement. Bengal cultivators pay 11d. per head per year as their tax to the Government, while in Bombay 47d. is due; but the average rental value of Bengal is much higher, and the cultivator has to pay this full rent to the Zemindar.

From causes already indicated the revenue of the Government of India expands insufficiently. The increases in the nominal amount of the revenues that take place are chiefly due to irrigation works carried out by the Government, or to the rise of prices —which means the shrinking in the real value of the rupee. While the true economic rent of the land of India has been increasing greatly in consequence of increased population, improved means of communication, and increased demand among industrial nations for tropical produce, the revenue drawn from land by the Government has decreased. Two consequences of all this follow: the Government is impoverished, every department is starved (agricultural improvement, education, roads, etc.), and on the other hand the landlord class gets a continually larger share of the expanding economic rent which is all the time really a community-created fund and should be used solely for the public services.

The inhabitants of India are debt-ridden because the expanding rental values go to individuals. This increases their credit and tends to make a crowd of speculators, big and small, really speculators in land values, though not always quite obviously. This kind of scramble for gain, ill-gotten gain because not earned by individuals, inevitably leads to the rich gaining at the expense of the poor, the idle at the expense of the industrious, and the unscrupulous at the expense of the ignorant and confiding.

The Permanent Settlement affects not only Bengal (not exactly the area now so labelled), but also Bihar, Orissa, and a part of Assam. The Indian population that is plundered by this direct historic interference with Indian law numbers 89,000,000 out of 320,000,000. But it is not only the Permanent Settlement which injures the inhabitants of India. Taxes of various kinds, for example the salt tax, are burdening them. Moreover, the land revenue is assessed on rural land only, and on what is produced, and includes improvements made by the occupier. If such a levy were swept away, the pledge not to increase the land revenue in the "Settled" regions would become extinguished. The way would be open, too, to bring in revivifying influences on production, and a prosperous population well distributed, by means of levying all assessments (for "duties" to be paid into the public coffers) on the true value of the land whether used fully or under-used, and whether in rural or urban districts. Then also would taxes on the improvements due to an individual's own exertions be abolished.

I have spent many pages on a consideration of some aspects of the condition of affairs in India, because many believe the pressure of population in this great peninsula is one of the most pressing of population problems and because an historical and fiscal survey of these regions of the world affords a good opportunity of showing the connection which exists between the laws and customs of a country in respect of land holding and the raising of public revenue and the growth and distribution of population. These things are paramount in trying to guide the destinies and improve the welfare of peoples. Yet to-day, too, little attention is given to them, while all the time in most countries of the world—India, Ireland, Spain, Germany, etc.— matters of far less importance, such as forms of government and methods of bolstering up ill-starred financial legacies from wars and what-not, are agitating the minds of men. In India, next in importance to the subjects of land tenure and land assessment comes a recognition of the status of the Village Commune. Local government cannot be vital if merely organized from above. It will but form a clog upon the development of the people unless it is in some way grafted on to the spontaneous groupings of the people themselves. As Sidney Webb wrote: "The Indian village, like the Russian Mir, may remind us that vote by ballot and party government are only two among several expedients for bringing administration under public control."[1]

In the India of the future it may be the Village Councils "which will be found exercising actually the larger part of all the functions of government, expending the greater part of that share of the people's income which is administered collectively, appointing and controlling the majority of all the salaried servants of the community, and even enacting . . . the greater volume of the laws that the people obey."[2]

Truly such an arrangement would save money. Furthermore, the life and health of the people of India depend to a large extent upon sanitation, water supply, and elementary medical aid, all matters to be attended to in the villages where about 90 per cent of the population live. In so far as there has been a breakdown of the Village Councils since the British rule started, the rural population has been left worse off in some respects than they were in ancient times, in spite of all that which has been done by the British in the way of improved medical organization and the prevention of disease (plague, smallpox, and cholera particularly). In the old days, when private ownership of land was not dreamt of and when its common ownership was recognized through land assessments for the public's purse, the Village Commune held almost complete control over the people's destinies. There did not exist in those days any signs of conflict between central and local administrations, or very little. That was before taxation as the present generation knows it was invented. To-day taxes are the hall-mark of civilization! And perpetual squabbles arise between conflicting interests as to how they should be raised and how spent.

[1] Preface (p. xii) to John Matthais' *Village Government in British India* (Fisher Unwin, 1915). [2] Ibid., p. xviii.

It is only during the last sixty years or so that the population of India has increased rapidly. It is difficult to get accurate figures of the number of inhabitants of India in past ages; but good authorities have formed the following conclusions, namely, that the population of India in 1650 was 80,000,000; in 1750, 130,000,000; and in 1850, 190,000,000. To-day the population is 353,000,000. The density is 196 persons per square mile as against 177 in 1921. The birth-rate in India has been very steady at about 36 per thousand of the population ever since 1885. The death-rate in that year and again quite recently stands at 26 per thousand of the population, but in the interval between these two dates the death-rate has varied considerably. It was as high as 30 in 1914. The exceptional rise to 62 in the year 1918 was entirely due to the influenza epidemic. This killed off about 12,000,000 people in India. Previous writers on these questions have usually paid attention to the question of food production and supplies. Undoubtedly, much depends on that, as goes without saying, and within modern times big augmentations of population have occurred as a result of creating new facilities for food production, e.g. by great irrigation works such as the Sukk Barrage and the Sutlej Projects in the Punjab. The unusual increase of persons in Bikaner since the 1921 census, which is 42 per cent, is an illustration of the increase of population which occurs from such undertakings. It is accounted for almost entirely by the increased areas available for cultivation under the recent scheme of irrigation undertaken by that State. Not only is the area extended, however, but better seed and farming have also had some effect. In this connection it may be mentioned that better types of wheat ("Pusa 12" and "Pusa 4" especially) and of cotton have helped in the United and Central Provinces of India. Nearly one-sixth of the total acreage under cotton is now cultivating improved varieties. If only animal husbandry could progress similarly agriculture in India would go forward as never before. In fact, it may be said "there are in India no limits to agricultural improvement with the advance of science."[1] But the population of India increased most in the second half of the nineteenth century and was associated perhaps,

[1] "The Population Problem in India," by Professor G. F. Shirras, in *The Economic Journal*, Vol. XLIII, March 1933.

more than anything else, not with agricultural progress but with general productiveness due to better communications, increase of knowledge, and better government. There was an unusual economic development, especially in the third quarter of the nineteenth century, brought about by the extension of railways, irrigation, and increase of commerce and industry. A fact which must never be forgotten in regard to India is that nine-tenths of the population live in villages. There is 65 per cent of the area of India available for cultivation, but the net area actually sown with crops during 1928 to 1929 was only 34 per cent of the area available. The growth of population coincidentally with the increase in production and wealth is shown in the two tables which Professor Shirras[1] publishes:

GROWTH OF POPULATION AND PRODUCTION IN INDIA
(Quinquennial Averages)

	1900-1 to 1904-5	1910-11 to 1914-15	1920-21 to 1924-25	1926-27 to 1930-31
Population*	100	107	108	120
Production:				
1. Area under crops—				
Unweighted	100	124	119	132
Weighted	100	131	134	150
2. Out-turn—				
Unweighted	100	129	125	137
Weighted	100	134	137	141

* The figures refer to the censuses of 1901, 1911, 1921, and 1931.

Year	Population	Per Capital National Income*
1871	100	100
1881	123	130
1901	142	123†
1911	153	270
1921	156	230
1931	171	273‡

* Allowing for the change in prices.   † Severe famine, 1900.   ‡ 1929-30.

[1] "The Population Problem in India," by Professor G. F. Shirras, in *The Economic Journal*, Vol. XLIII, March 1933.

P.S.—I think Professor Shirras' figures are somewhat misleading.—AUTHOR.

The name of Malthus is usually associated with his views regarding birth-control. These probably have had very little real influence on the growth and distribution of population. On the other hand, what did profoundly influence these things were the opinions he taught at Haileybury in the East India College. He was professor of political economy there for twenty-nine years. He had discovered the law of rent even before Ricardo, although it was the latter who elaborated it. Malthus, however, was very keen on impressing the importance of this law upon the whole succession of students who passed through his hands on their way to help rule India during the years 1805 to 1834. It seems likely that the impress of his teaching moulded the whole policy of our government in India, more particularly in regard to land tenure and public revenue, as has already been explained in this chapter. A writer in 1836 (Sir William Sleeman) has said: "Of all the instruction which the servants of the Honourable East India Company have ever brought with them from their parent land to India, that which they derived from the lectures of that truly amiable man, Dr. Malthus, on Political Economy, has been perhaps the most substantially useful to the Country."

The influence of right government, more especially as it affects matters of land tenure and taxation, is illustrated by British rule in another part of the world at the same period, namely, in the early part of the nineteenth century, if we look at Ireland. There the object of the Home Government was to cripple industrialism in Ireland which about that time had begun to spring up. This was done, supposedly, for the benefit of the industries in Great Britain. At the same time grave interference with home rule and systems of land tenure and taxation were carried through. Landlordism had, of course, been planted on the Irish by the British, who were looked upon as aliens in previous generations. Nevertheless, the bad results of landlordism were particularly obvious in Ireland during the first half of the nineteenth century. Famine and want were very rife particularly in the years of the potato famine. Mrs. J. R. Green's history says that "from 1846 to 1848 over 1,000,000 lay dead of hunger. Yet £17,000,000 worth of foodstuffs were sent to England in 1848; and English soldiers guarded from the starving, fields of corn and wagons that carried it to the ports to pay rent and taxes in England." In 1840 Ireland had a population of over 8,000,000. To-day it is 4,250,000. Had its natural increase been allowed to continue, and its resources developed, it might now have been 12,000,000 or more. Ireland has over 5,000,000 acres of arable land and 9,000,000 acres of permanent pasturage. The total number of emigrants from Ireland between May 1851 and December 1910 was 4,187,442.

Before leaving this part of the subject a few paragraphs must be devoted to the subject of irrigation. Ancient civilizations have broken down, thickly populated parts of the globe have lost most of their population entirely from the fact that irrigation works have fallen into decay. This has generally happened as a result of war. The late Sir William Willcocks, one of the foremost authorities on irrigation, has stated that "the ancient irrigation of Bengal combated malaria, provided an abundant harvest of fish, enriched the soil, and made congestion of the rivers impossible."[1]

The systems of irrigation employed in different places are somewhat different in their nature. Sir William Willcocks maintained that the ancient system in Bengal, which had such beneficial results before the break up of the Mogul Empire and the long continued fight between the Mahrattas and Afghans, was an "overflow irrigation." This is worked by canals which are broad and shallow, carrying the crest waters of the river floods rich in fine clay and free from coarse sand. Though the war just referred to had upset the irrigation of the Ganges the earlier irrigation of Damodar had held its own, and as late as 1860 it is said to have been working fairly well. This overflow irrigation differs from the "basin irrigation" as practised in Egypt and from the "perennial irrigation" suited to the needs of Babylonia. About 1855 the Government, acting on the recommendations of a committee to remove the banks of the Damodar, took over the embankments and made them watertight. Shortly after this date poverty and malaria became rife, and according to Sir William Willcocks, Bengal irrigation went from bad to worse till 1928, because "the irrigation department tried its hand at every kind of project it could imagine except overflow irrigation." Bengal is handicapped, too, by having a system which arranges an

[1] Sir William Willcocks' *Irrigation in Bengal* (Calcutta University Press, 1930).

annual measurement of irrigated fields and payment for individual irrigation, instead, as in Egypt, of combining a charge for irrigation with the land revenue levy. The Egyptian system has lasted six thousand years and is working well to-day; the combined levy is applied to the whole area of each block of the land and allows every land-holder to look on land and irrigation as one, and encourages him to irrigate his fields when they need water. It does not encourage him to put off irrigation to the last moment and often lose no small part of his harvest. Irrigation means insurance against drought and the vagaries of rainfall; and a fixed combined land and irrigation tax, to be paid year in and year out, insures against the worries of watching wind and cloud and seeing if one cannot evade part of the tax; while all the time crops are losing value. It protects a man against himself.

In Bengal the unsatisfactory state of land tenure and the imperfections connected with the irrigation system lead to the private appropriation of more and more of the public domain. Not only so, but the intensive agriculture in which way much rich land might be used is not practised. Two or three or even more crops in one year could often be grown with better skill in cultivation and irrigation; and there is a big market for many of the crops through the proximity of Calcutta.

In other parts of India extensive and wonderful irrigation systems are working, on the whole, successfully. India, like China, has about 50,000,000 acres of irrigated land in cultivation. In Sind 80 per cent, and in the North-West Provinces 32 per cent, of the cultivable land is irrigated. The United States of America now ranks third with over 20,000,000 acres in the irrigation countries of the world. When most of the rain-watered lands of the United States had been taken up by settlers, the problem of the so-called arid lands came into prominence, and now in many of these parts, formerly sterile though with rich but parched soil, magnificent crops are grown. The engineering works, also often supplying electric power as well as water, the new agriculture, fresh roads, market towns, etc., brought into being a big population to districts previously but very sparsely inhabited. Altogether $800,000,000, of which one quarter comes from Government funds, have been spent in the United States on irrigation projects. But a big proportion of the added values to land resulting from public expenditure has gone into private pockets.

The effect of good irrigation works on the value of land is well seen by reference to Egypt. More extensive areas of land were irrigated in Lower Egypt than ever before by the construction of the dam at Assiut in 1902. But water failed in very dry seasons. The difficulty was partly met by raising the height of the barrage so as to hold back the waters, but as further areas came into cultivation it became necessary to construct a feeding lake. This was successfully done in Lord Cromer's time, though Egypt's public coffers were empty, through the aid of Sir Ernest Cassel the financier. The Assuan Dam was constructed in 1898 to 1902 at a cost of £3,000,000, and thus created a reserve of 1,000,000,000 tons of water. Rents of irrigated land varied in direct proportion with the quantity of mud carried on to it by the water. The first time the effects were felt of the early low flood waters of the Nile being made to flow (in 1902 by the finishing of the Assiut Dam) over 550,000 acres of high-lying ground, the rents of the land went up 10 rupees per acre. Within six months of the completion of the Assuan Barrage the price of land in Egypt rose from fourteen years' purchase to twenty years' purchase, or by 40 per cent. In forty years the value of agricultural land in Egypt rose from £150,000,000 to £550,000,000 and it is to-day worth £700,000,000. To show the influence on rent of new irrigation machinery it may be mentioned that the late Sir William Willcocks replaced four powerful old pumps on the Nile by four absolutely up-to-date ones which lifted twice as much water at half the cost; £100,000 was spent on the work, and it added £470,000 to the value of the estate.

CHAPTER VI

LAW AND CUSTOM IN AFRICA: THE MAGIC INSTRUMENT

AS population grows and knowledge increases smaller areas per family furnish the most profitable and beneficial way of using land. What economic instrument is there for simplifying this change in quantity and usage at the proper time? In the last chapter something has been said about the more intensive use of land in agriculture through better knowledge of how to cultivate, and how to fructify land by irrigation. Relatively small holdings worked chiefly by hand labour in good climates and locations, where several crops can be grown within the year, associated with some markets and shops go with this progress in knowledge; and with these changes progressively smaller areas for use and increase in the numbers of human beings are found. Inevitably involved in this closer density of population and this enhanced facility to provide for human needs through better knowledge there comes about spontaneously a greater skill in co-operation by better communications, etc. This, again, is reflected in more use being made of services for the common-weal which are generally called "communal," and in a rise in the value of the better placed pieces of land. Coincidently with these developments a lowering of prices occurs through more specialization in the processes of production and exchange and through the direct effect of increase of customers. In ancient times, and to-day amongst many primitive races, such developments are inured by custom and hallowed by usages which are instructive. Communal services were performed in old times by a fixed amount of each worker's time being spent, voluntarily, or sometimes more or less compulsorily, in performing services for the common good. In Indian villages, for example, water carrying, scavenging, and other sanitary procedures were thus performed. Or one plot of several of the public domain, that is of all the land, was worked solely to produce the funds for the communal services, which were generally also contributed to by a proportion of a man's earnings being willingly given up to this fund in return for the share of the services he individually received. If he held a particularly good piece of land, better irrigated with muddy waters than his neighbours, he did not mind paying a rather bigger amount, when compared to an area of similar extent, than his neighbours. Thus he squared himself with them for exclusive possession of that piece. As society developed, as skill advanced, as numbers increased, then still, in many places for many ages, no difficulties arose, for such contributions to the common pool for superior sites went on being paid without demur. This plan was the magical instrument which enabled the gradual increased density of population in certain locations to occur without hindrance and without bother. But a day came, in some parts of the world sooner than in others, when peoples lost the instrument, and having lost it in some places friction and trouble came thick and fast. And the more difficulties arise the heavier and harder seems to be the task of discovering it again. Amongst those difficulties are all, or nearly all, the evils which can be put under the head of maldistribution of population—under-cultivation of agricultural land with poverty of many rural workers, the suck to the towns and the overcrowding in city slums, the greater fertility of the poor and ill-educated compared with the well-to-do and trained, the ill-regulation of emigration at many times and in many places in the world's history, the apparent impossibility of black (or red) and white working side by side in certain parts of the globe without the gradual extinction of the former, etc. To take the last difficulty, since the first has already been dealt with and the others will be fully considered in subsequent chapters.

What has been the history of the Red Indians in America, of the Blackfellows in Australasia, of many tribes in Africa when Europeans have got into touch with them? First of all be it noted these human beings were generally found originally to be fine stock. They were in a somewhat primitive stage of society, for the most part hunters, and therefore few in number and sparsely scattered. Their adaptability for gaining a quite new accession of knowledge was probably much greater than they were generally given credit for, but the Europeans they met for a generation or more when first they "came into touch with civilization" were keener than anything else on acquiring the best pieces of their land, and on trying to turn them away from their long established religious beliefs and towards others they found difficult to grasp. An old Maori once said, "Oh, yes, I know your ways; you get me turn my eyes to the skies, so you can take the ground from under my feet." Unfortunately, too, they were introduced to new diseases and new habits. Unquestionably the sale of alcohol for the profit of European traders has worked terrible havoc amongst these primitive peoples. Undoubtedly measles, tuberculosis, and syphilis were new diseases to some of these races, and again, largely because new and not counterbalanced by any acquired immunity, they decimated them. But whichever of these people is considered, the question of paramount importance so far as the growth (or diminution) and distribution of population is concerned, is the question of land tenure.

Whole books and columns and columns in the newspapers have been written about land tenure in Kenya. Comparisons which are odious to those responsible for the administration of this territory can be heaped up when other colonies in Africa, and under British suzerainty, too, are considered; Northern Nigeria and Tanganyika for example. And when eyes are turned further afield, to the Malay States particularly, it can be seen how easy it is to do things better. But more of the latter places anon.

The black and the squatter could co-operate well if the black had assured access to water and some beef and mutton as "dividend" against game no longer procurable by him or against pasturage (for his cattle) from which he has been displaced in certain areas. But no; the squatter wants to acquire good land for coffee planting or maize growing, or discovers gold reefs, and if he herds the natives into reserves he gets what land he wants while he creates a "landless proletariat" which he can draw upon for cheap labour. Read E. D. Morel's *The Black Man's Burden*, one of the finest books ever written. Read Norman Ley's *Kenya*; or the long report published by the South African Institute for Medical Research on "Tuberculosis in South African Natives with Special Reference to the Disease Amongst the Mine Labourers on the Witwatersrand." In these books is traced very clearly the dire results for mankind through having lost the magical instrument whereby the more profitable use of land in smaller areas with increased population can be brought about without hurt to anyone, white or black (for the white man is injured, too), hunter, grazier, farmer, merchant, or gold miner. The displaced black would willingly give up certain localities if in so doing the newcomer were called upon to pay into the common pool (according to the rule of economic rent) some levy which he too would be quite willing to pay. That pool would be used to finance such communal services as would be of use to both, and the black could be assured of obtaining the milk and meat he wanted. He would get these commodities easily if fair dealings all round had marked the new contacts through enhanced facilities of production and exchange due to increased knowledge and co-operation. The distribution of population in Africa would, indeed, become altered, but in a natural and healthy way. The aboriginal natives of Africa, a fine race for the most part, would increase and thrive, and at the same time Africa would be all the more easily "opened up" for humans of European and Asiatic stock. There would not be trouble over "indentured labour," over health in "compounds," over squalor in "locations"—the native quarters in some of the cities—over detribalization, over hut and poll taxes, and over water rights. To-day the natives of South Africa and Kenya are in a sorry plight, because the people who came to Africa from without (except—fortunately—in some parts under British rule where the history of recent events is very different) did not see how to apply the law of the land which all natives recognized from time immemorial, and because they came imbued with ideas about landlordism, about taxation, about inequality amongst humans. According to Lord Olivier, one among other ominous findings of the Native Economic Commission which reported in 1932 to the Government of the South Africa Union runs as follows: "We have now throughout the Native Reserves a state of affairs which unless soon remedied will within one or at least two decades create in the Union an appalling state of Native poverty." It is further stated in the latest Economic Commission Report that, "In about ten years' time the Native population will begin to suffer starvation."

In Lord Olivier's article (page 286) he says: "If the Basuto and the Bechuana had not been placed under British Protectorates they would have been eaten up. . . . If they had been annexed by the Crown their societies might have been disturbed by Mining Concessions as the Native Communities of Kenya are at this moment being disturbed."[1] But before proceeding further a few bald facts about areas and population in Africa are worth setting down.

The area of Africa, including Madagascar and the other adjacent islands, is nearly 12,000,000 square miles, or three times that of Europe. The population is estimated at 143,000,000. The most thickly populated regions are the Nile Delta, the Lower Nile Valley, and the basins of the Congo and Niger. The original natives consist of Negroes, Hottentots (in south-west coastal districts), Bantu (Zulus and Kaffirs), Bushmen (west of Cape Colony), and several dwarf tribes. The Negroes dwell mostly in the Senegal and Gambia districts, the Guinea Coast, and the Soudan. The Union of South Africa, together with all the other parts under British administration, have a combined area of 4,652,000 square miles and an estimated population of about 50,000,000. Johannesburg, founded by the Uitlanders in 1886, grew quickly after the development of the Witwatersrand gold-fields, and now has a population of about 290,000. Cape Town with its suburbs had a white population of 130,568 in 1926. In the same year the total white population of Cape Colony was 706,137, and the coloured population in 1921, 2,132,110. The Bushmen and Hottentots have become gradually much reduced in number. The increase of the white population in Cape Colony is about half that of the coloured in the ten years to 1921. The latter increase amounted to 8 per cent, and 17 per cent in the Union.

The area of Egypt is 383,000 square miles and its population 14,166,756; and the Egyptian Soudan has an area of 1,008,100 square miles and a population of 5,500,000. Cairo was founded in A.D. 968 by Jaurel Kaid, though there existed a Roman fortress, a mile away where Old Cairo now is, more than fourteen centuries before this date. Almost its only commercial importance is that it is a depot for the transit of goods of every variety from all over the world. After the British occupation in

[1] Lord Olivier's article in *Contemporary Review*, March 1933, on "Native Poverty in South Africa."

1882 its new water supply and better sanitation greatly improved the health of Cairo's inhabitants. Within the nineteenth century its population, including all the suburbs, more than trebled itself. The total in 1907 was 654,476, of which some 40,000 only were Europeans. In 1927 the population was 1,064,567.

British East Africa, which includes Kenya Colony and Protectorate, and Uganda, has a total area of approximately 320,300 square miles, including 15,000 square miles of water in Uganda, and a population of about 6,090,000, of whom about 14,600 are Europeans and 54,000 Asiatics. Kenya has three times as many European settlers as all the rest of the territories together. The area of Kenya Colony and Protectorate is 224,000 square miles, and the population in 1926 was 2,891,691, of which 12,529 were Europeans and 41,140 Asiatics.

The British Colony and Protectorate of Nigeria is approximately 373,078 square miles. The coloured population is estimated at 19,308,688 and the number of Europeans, on an average, is 5,900. The total area of the Colony and Protectorate of Sierra Leone is 27,250 square miles; its total population 1,541,311 in 1921; all except 85,000 in the Protectorate and nearly all in the Colony are Africans—only 900 British and 600 Asiatics.

When "the dark continent" first began to be extensively "penetrated" by white people the outlook of the natives on all sorts of subjects was difficult for Europeans to learn. For example, the habits of the Basuto, Embu, and Kikuyu tribes were appreciated only after years of study started by a few enterprising and noble-hearted missionaries. As Major Orde Browne has pointed out,[1] the general Bantu law that the land should be held for the good of the community was modified by a variety of customs. The peoples of these primitive tribes called upon the men to clear the land for cultivation, but when this had been done it was the women who did most of the work. Inheritance rights and the habit of polygamy produce complications. It was difficult for a native to conceive of absolute and perpetual occupation of a piece of land. His wasteful method of cultivation, if an agriculturist at all, necessitated letting his plantation revert to bush after it had been worked for a few years, while the flimsy

[1] G. St. J. Orde Browne's *The Vanishing Tribes of Kenya*.

nature of his hut precluded any conception of permanence. He could, therefore, hardly contemplate such complete and permanent loss of land as is entailed by the erection upon it of a railway station or a church. It was this outlook which made the native fatally ready to dispose of what a European regards as permanent land rights. In this way a native community willingly parts with a large portion of land, only to realize later it is cramped for space. A feeling of resentment then springs up. Nevertheless, natives in many parts of Africa have full justification for resentment. Many of them have been rendered people without a job by the intervention of Europeans. They were a pastoral and military community. The Bantu who exterminated the earlier Bushmen races are pastoral steppe-people, as they still are in Bechuanaland. Europeans have driven them off the best pasture land and better watered districts in which by degrees agriculture might have been developed by them.

South African land does not lend itself to continuous production of food; but in addition to keeping cattle, maize and millet are crops which in some places can be snatched through the bounty of rain. Native cattle have increased but pastures have not. Although in the largest native territory (Transkei) before the Union a certain amount of sincere attention had been given to the development of native polity and productive economy, since the Union such attention has been for the most part conspicuously absent. When the lands that were available to the native tribes of Southern Africa were taken away from them to a considerable extent, and they had less grazing for their cattle, they lost half their occupation, and, incidentally, their vitamin intake through having less sour milk to consume was diminished. In the second place they were given peace. Now to such the giving of peace was like introducing oil fuel amongst a community of coal miners. The consequence of these alterations in the life of many of these natives was that without the gold mines to which to resort starvation faced them. The only alternative employment from mining to give them enough money to get cattle wherewith to buy wives and live comfortably in the kraals of their native reservations is the terrible one of the drift to the locations. These are the native districts in urban centres where the wretched natives live in the most horrible hovels, mostly of rusted corrugated iron, for which they often pay the extortionate rent of 25s. a month. Yet the urban native's average wage is only about two and a half times this amount. In these districts they work either as domestic servants, as prostitutes, or participate in the trade of illicit sellers of drink, generally beverages of the most poisonous kind dispensed by Jews and Arabs at enormously high prices. If the natives serve for a period in the mines on the Rand (it generally covers only 12–24 months) there is no doubt but that they benefit in health, apart from an unfortunately rather large proportion who contract or develop bacterial disease, and return home fitter as well as richer. Some of them only present themselves to the mine recruiter when driven to do so by sheer hunger. They return to their kraals and their tribe. Be it remembered, however, they work underground (there are 250,000 of them) for wages which are less than one-tenth of those earned by the white man for shorter hours, and that they are a cheery, contented, and honest lot of men, as well as docile under trying conditions. The conditions of life in the compounds on the Rand are not all that can be desired, though the mine magnates expend much money and effort to render them as good in many ways as necessity demands and opportunity allows. Nevertheless, the compound is in some ways preferable to the idle life of the kraals, now that wars have ceased and tribal wanderings have come to an end. But if the natives drift to the locations they become detribalized even if in touch with missionaries. These, who are a fine lot of men and women, are looked up to by the natives. They are tremendously devoted to one another, and the native especially reveres the head missionary as a sort of new chief, as "Jesus Christ," indeed, in many cases. But away from the missionaries they sink, especially if they get into the liquor-selling trade.

There are other influences besides the earning of money to attract native Kaffirs to the mines. With many tribes the ex-miner alone is considered a man of consequence. He is spoken of as one "acquainted with the deeds of men." A girl who is in a position to choose a husband will choose a miner, and this not only because he may make a better home for her, but because he has accomplished the present-day equivalent of "wetting his spear." The European may not approve of polygamy, but the native does. The dignity of a man is increased by the number of his wives, and the wife or wives encourage him to take more. It is like showing the neighbours that one's husband can keep more than one car. Few natives other than those who have been employed on the gold mines can run to more than one *lobola*. As an illustration of the dependence for prosperity on mine earnings, in spite of the low wages earned there, the following saying from the reserves of the Ciskei and Transkei tribes can be quoted. They assert, "we could not carry on for a twelvemonth without the remittance from the miners." The report on tuberculosis in South African Natives[1] states that "when, in 1850, Sir Harry Smith exacted a fine of 50,000 head of cattle out of the Ciskei this loss made little or no difference, so numerous were the cattle then. Now (in 1928) it would be difficult or impossible to find 50,000 head of cattle in the same district. The custom of making and using *amasi* (sour milk) has almost ceased for want of milk." Again, on the next page of this report occurs the following passage:

"While the natives of the Ciskei and Transkei still present, to the eye of the visitor, the appearance of good health and good humour so characteristic of African Natives in general, . . . it seems that all is not well with them. Their number continues to increase without any corresponding increase in territory; and the lands they now occupy are very much less in extent than those over which they roamed with their flocks and herds before they encountered the advance of the White man from the Cape and from Natal. . . . The men have lost the hard discipline of warriors and hunters, and the women, with all the attractions of the trader's store close at hand, dream of short frocks and silk stockings and see the monetary advantages of tinned fruit and tinned milk over wild berries and herbs and the calabash of *amasi*. As for the children, they are under-nourished; and in seasons of drought many of the natives, both adults and children, approach starvation line."

The gold and diamond mines of Africa have also some link with the mine magnates, the richest of whom, like Cecil Rhodes

[1] The South African Institute for Medical Research, No. XXX; Report on Tuberculosis in South African Natives, pp. 262–64.

"the empire builder," Barney Barnato, and Otto Beit, had their palaces in Park Lane and elsewhere. They founded scholarships, endowed colleges and museums, built hospitals and magnificent racing stables, etc., out of their superfluity of wealth. A proper growth and distribution of population does not occur in Africa, or anywhere else, and a maldistribution of wealth does occur, if the instrument for avoiding all friction between individuals and classes is not used. That magic instrument gives no sanction to the idea of private property in land, whether containing gold or whether used for grazing cattle or growing maize. Nature ordains that when the instrument is lost or wilfully set aside, disaster and distress follow. What if the native reserves could not produce an adequate supply of fit workers for the mines! There is a high rate of rejection on account of unfitness for industrial work amongst the Bantu population of the Union, and restrictions have been placed on the numbers of recruits for the Transvaal mines from Portuguese territory. Hitherto the mines have obtained more than half their complement of native labour from the neighbouring Portuguese colony. But from 1933 onwards only 80,000 of these natives will be employed instead of the 100,000 that were employed up to four years previously.

The relative allocation of land between black and white in the Union of South Africa is:

	Morgen per Head	
	White	Black
Province of the Cape	108·1	4·3
Province of Natal	47·2	2·6
Province of Transvaal	45·0	3·7
Province of Orange Free State	73·6	0·3

Yet the 1926 census statistics showed the relative population to be: whites 1,672,000; blacks 4,905,000. Furthermore, in proportion to his income, the native (for example in the Transvaal) is more highly taxed than the European, and the native feels that much of his taxes goes in the provision of public services for the white community. In Kenya the total area of land reserved to the 2,500,000 natives is less than a quarter of the area of the colony. Their "trustees," the 14,000 Europeans of the colony, own some, and are some day to acquire the rest of the remaining three-quarters. In Kenya the native population is decreasing. But the native population is increasing in similar parts of Africa under British rule—in Basutoland and Uganda, for example, where a different system of land tenure and taxation holds good.

The natives of every country should be able to gain easy access to land. The blacks of Africa might by now have learnt much more about modern agricultural methods had they received more education. Useful production of this and that commodity associated with a natural development and distribution of population might have come about by now had there been no departure from that principle which all the aboriginal peoples of Africa understood so well, namely, that effective useful occupation alone justified individual possession of land. With the blessings of peace really established, instead of the abolition of war being turned into a curse, and with full advantage from contact with the white man, the native Africans should now be far more prosperous everywhere than is the case. They should be free producers. Why should not labour be freely available for tobacco, maize, or coffee farming, for gold mining, or what-not from men living with their wives and families, and well housed? Why should so many be isolated in compounds or dwelling in squalid locations? Indentures or "contracted" labour might be done away with under a proper system of habitation, under a proper distribution of population. Labour should be freely attracted by good conditions. The present arrangements are definitely inimical to the moral welfare of native communities now in process of abandoning polygamy and adopting monogamy. It should be possible to change them however difficult it may be to get mining populations nicely distributed and properly housed, as witness such regions in Wales and Scotland as the Rhondda Valley and the Lanarkshire coal mining districts. Though the gold-mining industry in South Africa pursues its own existence on the Rand far from the life of the farming population (as unfortunately is the case in most other mining districts in the world), there are no unsurmountable obstacles why this should always be so. In other parts of Africa the indigenous population have found a great measure of independence. There are many parts of British West Africa, for example, where tropical agriculture progresses without the evils of indentured and contract labour and without sweated labour, so that even if gold mines were discovered there freer conditions of employment would probably prevail. But then in those places crops and the land they grow upon belong to the people of the soil. In Nigeria (at all events in Northern Nigeria) British administration conforms closely to the conservation of ancient public rights in the land, and it has adopted native customary titles to the needs of a civilization in close touch with modern ideas. Much the same can be said, too, about Malaya, another territory under British rule. Further reference to the former country will be made immediately. Unfortunately space forbids further reference to the interesting state of affairs in the Malay Peninsula.

An impartial observer, an American, Mr. R. L. Buell, of the Harvard University Department of Government, spent from 1925 to 1928 in investigating conditions in Africa. He published two volumes containing two thousand pages which constitute a complete survey of the subject. He gives as his well-considered conclusion definite support to the policy followed in the West African regime under British rule. He considers it is better to develop native institutions and agriculture, to the exclusion if necessary of European planters, and that this plan is more conducive both to native welfare and to a permanent increase of wealth than the contrasted East African policy of encouraging white settlement and the employment by whites of the native population. He believes the world at large in any way interested in these problems is watching British policy, which it will tend to judge not where it is strongest and most just but where it is weakest and is likely to follow British lead. So that the way these problems are settled in the near future may make a vast difference to future history, for, undoubtedly, one of the most important problems of the day is that of the economic relations of white and coloured people. Of course, differences of climate and culture must be heeded. The climate of Nigeria, for example, is undoubtedly unsuitable, when all is said and done, for Europeans to spend long periods of residence therein; whereas it is otherwise in many parts of the high tableland at the other side of Africa.

The twentieth century has seen tremendous advances in many directions, but in none more than in the realm of psychology. This science, as applied to individuals and to groups of people, tribal or national, may be said virtually not to have been born before the beginning of the present century. As knowledge of it spreads, a truer and deeper understanding of the relationships between white and coloured populations will render a fine co-operation between them easier and more lasting. In olden times a common rule was to put to the sword the men of a conquered race and generally to spare the women and children only to make slaves of them. By degrees other practices were adopted, but as often as not only for the material advantages of the conquerors, though a dim idea existed that it sometimes paid the conquerors to avoid upsetting the beliefs, the habits, and the customs of the conquered. But it is comparatively recently in the history of the world that it occurred to the victorious that it paid *both* sides to see to it, as far as possible, that the defeated got peace and plenty. In fact, even in this century—unfortunately—illustrations are not absent of a foolish spirit of vindictiveness gaining sway in making treaties after warfare. Throughout mankind the endeavour to be in the ascendant whether as an individual or as a race is now known to be about the commonest of all human traits; and this psychological proclivity must be reckoned with when the administration of such places as India and Nigeria is being considered.

On a previous page reference has been made to the instinct of getting as much as possible for as little exertion as possible. It has been this ruling passion above all others which has actuated those who have exploited native races, and this is perhaps especially true of Africa. Fortunately, another strong instinct, namely zeal for justice, has also moved many of those who have dealt with these problems. Because poverty is so rife, and wealth so badly distributed, fear of poverty produces greed. Greed for riches and power becomes a disease, well seen in the case of the exploiters of the resources of native territories and of the labour of primitive peoples. But intermingled with such failings is to be found, perhaps especially amongst British missionaries and civil servants, a strong desire to serve, and to see justice done to conquered races. The desirability of granting freedom to all is becoming increasingly recognized. The ambitions and aspirations of African people, from the dignified and able chiefs to the coolie boy and the black woman in her kraal, must be understood and respected. Africans generally exhibit a wonderful physical vitality, a cheerful and friendly disposition, and an unexpected adaptability. Though they lack initiative they are very teachable. Their moral values differ from ours. Amongst some tribes the idea of equality hardly comes within the scope of their imagination. Rapid and radical changes in their ideas ought not to be expected. They must not be expected to climb rapidly up the ascent from a kind of "feudalistic" to the "individualistic" outlook of persons of a more advanced civilization. Their development under the contrasting systems ruling in various parts of Africa under British administration (compare Northern Nigeria, for example, with Kenya) forms a useful study which may go far to decide the future development of civilization, as it will undoubtedly reveal the ways in which population should grow and be distributed. On the one hand (in Nigeria) there exists a system of administration which utilizes machinery created by the natives themselves; through their chiefs European influences allow the natives to absorb those elements of a more advanced civilization which prove most useful for their own progress. On the other hand, native customs and institutions have been, often ruthlessly, over-ridden; land has been taken away, and taxes have been placed upon the African. Truly all cannot be treated alike. Africa contains tribes differing as widely as our prehistoric druidical ancestors differed from ourselves in the Middle Ages. Each race must be studied separately and dealt with appropriately. The mistakes of the past have consisted in going to one extreme or the other, either assuming all to be ignorant savages, or attempting to push them too fast up the steep slope of civilization.

Nigeria, which contains a great diversity of climatic conditions, and ethnographical, sociological, and sectarian divisions, is governed by a Governor-General, assisted by an Executive and a Legislative Council. Its administration is through the native chiefs. Its land cannot be alienated from the native tribes. Northern Nigerian ordinances laid down this rule which came into force in 1910. In 1916 a further ordinance, of which the following is an extract, consolidated the principle:

"The whole of the lands of Northern Provinces, whether occupied or unoccupied . . . are hereby declared to be native lands. . . . All native lands, and all rights over the same, are hereby declared to be under the control and subject to the disposition of the Governor, and shall be held and administered for the use and common benefit of the natives; and no title to the occupation and use of any such lands shall be valid without the consent of the Governor. . . . It shall be lawful for the Governor: (a) to grant rights of occupancy to natives and to non-natives; (b) to demand a rental for the use of any native lands granted to any native or non-native; and (c) to revise the said rental in the case of (agricultural) land at intervals of not more than seven years. . . ."[1]

The tranquillity and commercial prosperity of Northern Nigeria's many millions under these ordinances have been amazing. The system of revenue from land rents is spoilt to a certain extent in the other parts of Nigeria by land tenures of the English pattern, especially in Lagos and in other places along the coast, and by the introduction of other forms of taxation. In 1925 Sir Hugh Clifford, ex-Governor of Nigeria, emphasized the root cause of contentment and progress in this colony by saying: "The day we forget that the land is for the African and not for the European, that day we lay the axe at the root of all that is best and all that makes for the solidity of our rule in the West African Colonies." How different from the expressions given vent to by the Governor of Kenya Colony! The culture of the natives in Northern Nigeria is rising steadily from chattel slavery and wage serfdom. They possess a big city with a population of about 100,000, the city of Kano. Including suburban areas there may be round about 1,000,000 inhabitants. Kano has a great trade and many factories, but no slum area to compare in misery with any large town in Europe, or places such as Bombay or Singapore. The Northern Provinces have agricultural resources, and plentiful crops of maize, yams, sugar-cane, sweet potatoes, etc., are grown for home consumption. The chief exports from Nigeria are palm kernels, palm oil, cocoa, and tin. They average over £17,000,000 in worth, and imports about £12,000,000. In 1928 tin exports, 13,000 tons, were valued at £2,209,000. The revenue and expenditure (Colony and Protectorate) in 1929–30 (and in 1931–32) were

[1] John Orr's *A Short History of British Agriculture*, p. 50.

each slightly over £6,000,000 and had increased since 1912 by £3,750,000. Unfortunately for the Southern Provinces the system, introduced from Lagos and the Gold Coast and other coastal towns, of raising revenue on the English plan, namely by taxation on houses and persons, is leading to dire results very different from the prosperity and increase in population and in the production of commodities in Northern Nigeria. In the latter parts there have been no serious disturbances in recent years, but in the former the lawyers are busy with land litigations and military patrols have to be multiplied. In the Gold Coast many tribal groups are literally bankrupt, and the peasantry gravely discontented by levies to pay for litigation on land. The local treasuries in the north are financed by the land rents, and carry out nearly all government duties without resort to taxation on trade or accumulation. In the Southern Provinces the treasury, local and general, is not easily filled; and there occurs profitless waste of public money in gross overcharges for land needed for public purposes, as at Port Harcourt and Aba. The public shortage of funds in consequence of the surrender of nearly all the southern land rents to monopolizing and speculating private interests has led to the imposition of vicious import and export duties. Warnings against many of these evils were given by Mr. W. G. A. Ormsby-Gore, formerly Conservative Under-Secretary for the Colonies in his report on his visit to West Africa in the year 1926 [Cmd. 2744].

The most stupid of all the restrictions on trade, on freedom of production and exchange which is hampering the people of Nigeria more and more are export and import taxes. The hindrances taxation imposes on free exchange of commodities between England (Lancashire cotton goods for example) and West Africa, together (it must be admitted) with the competition of whale oil—in the hands of Norwegians for the most part—is bad for the people of Nigeria. And it is because obtuse politicians in England and elsewhere, and officials blinded by the traditions and education they have received before entering into the civil services of the colonies, cannot understand and apply the system of just land revenues to finance all public services that hurtful taxes are imposed. They introduce disruptive friction into society. Abolition of all such stupid methods of raising public revenue and concentration on the system which is founded upon the age-long customs of African natives would fill the treasuries easily without hurt or harm to anyone. The rulers of Nigeria, of all grades, would be falling over one another to find new means of spending the funds for the common good, and at the same time the native peoples of Nigeria would be earning an abundance to spend on imported manufactured goods. True it is that much has been accomplished for the commonweal under British rule, even from funds raised to a large extent by foolish means. There is the splendid Achimota College, for example, on the Gold Coast. But much remains to be done, especially expenditure on better means of communication and on combating sleeping-sickness and the invasion of the tsetse fly. Mr. Ormsby-Gore, after his visit to West Africa a few years ago, came to the conclusion that what was wanted there more than anything else was more roads capable of motor traffic so that a cheap substitute might be found for human porters. In Sierra Leone, he says, porters carry an average of 80 lb. an average distance of 15 miles a day on either their heads or their backs. These porters have short lives and are everywhere the great carriers of disease to others. They have to sleep and eat in the open, and as they naturally choose a camp beside streams, all the streams along the trade routes are constantly getting fouled. A Commissioner of the Northern Province reported a few years ago that the men in his province, he estimated, carried loads for eight days, did unpaid work for some tribal service, such as road repairs, for ten days, and did four days' unpaid work for the Government in one year. But in other parts of Africa the natives would reckon such a year as the year of Jubilee. A network of motor roads paid for out of an equitably filled common pool would send up the earnings of the African natives, thereby benefiting all who traded with them.

The late Lord Leverhulme was interested in the palm kernel and oil industries of West Africa. His upbringing made him aghast when he knocked up against the fact that he could not buy any land in Northern Nigeria. The reply from the Colonial Office when he pushed forward his request explained to him very explicitly and lucidly that there was no one entitled to sell land in that great province. He had no knowledge about the principles inherent in a just system of land tenure and taxation. His mind was unable to grasp the possible lines of development under such a system. He conceived the plan of obtaining ownership of the ground on which to build crushing mills or what not, and could not visualize the possibility of Africans proving capable of finding the capital to erect and the ability to run such enterprises. He could not believe that anybody would put up substantial buildings "without the security of obtaining a freehold." Although leaseholds for monetary payments are in reality a violation of African customary law, he could not understand how a leasehold system under the Governor, as representative of the people, had been growing up in parts of Nigeria in a way which was compatible with a continuance of the tribal and family rights over land. So many Europeans are so accustomed to the heightened rents which an increase in the numbers and skill of communities gives to the ground, flowing into the pockets of private individuals, that they are blind to its injustice. They fail to realize what benefits accrue if such enhanced ground values inure to the public to be used as the fund which the community itself should decide how to spend. Northern Nigeria has been blessed by a succession of clear-visioned British administrators. Ground dues have flowed into the public treasuries. They have been used almost solely in proper ways so that popular control has been expanded and bureaucratic control lessened; and so that substantial and progressive increase of production from the land has been secured without in any way robbing the producer or reducing him to the rank of wage-earner. The continuance of such a policy, but not departure from it, is likely in due time to bring still better results. Areas, such as that situated in the neighbourhood of Kano where land is closely cultivated, will be extended; and cotton of good American type can be grown in abundance. Already this is being produced in the three provinces of Kano, Sokoto, and Zaria; and the Nigerian Department of Agriculture has succeeded in producing a new type, the "improved Ishan," which may raise cotton to the position of being the chief and most valuable economic crop of the whole country, that is if the world comes to its senses before long and abandons the foolish restrictive tariff measures which so severely hamper trade to-day, so that Lancashire is as hard hit as Africa in her endeavours to produce and sell freely. So long as Great Britain continues to set an example along such paths as in Northern Nigeria the example is one worthy for the world to follow. Then, as heretofore, it will be possible to say about our colonial policy in this part of Africa that our position has been used only to consolidate, to abolish inter-tribal strife, to assimilate common interests, to end the great injustice of the slave trade, to clear and protect a field in which native rulers may still exercise all useful authority and with dignity rule their people.

The population of Nigeria and the other three colonies on the west coast make up nearly one-fifth of the total population of Africa. Many parts of these colonies are comparatively thickly populated. The combined area of the Gold Coast, Ashanti, and the attached Northern Territories is 78,650 square miles, that of the Gold Coast Colony alone being 23,490 square miles. The colony in 1930 had 495 miles of railway and 4,687 miles of roads, besides 2,600 miles of telegraphs and 2,600 telephones. Several of the towns are lighted by electricity and have pipe-borne water supplies. The African population of the colony, according to the census of 1931, was 1,545,140 (compared with 1,173,439, including 1,500 Europeans, in 1921); of Ashanti, 582,866; of the Northern Territories, 717,283; and of the British sphere of Togoland, 275,925. The non-African population, mainly British, was about 2,400. The estimated population of the combined areas (not including Togoland) in 1908 was 2,700,000 (compared with 2,845,289 in 1931). The railways in the combined areas are State owned. The Government had sunk £8,000,000 in them by 1925. The first railway was begun in 1898. By the year 1928 there were also over 5,000 miles of main roads. In 1895 the chief exports were: rubber, £332,000 worth; gold dust, £91,000; palm oil and palm kernels, £308,000; and kola nuts, £30,000. In 1899 there were exported 714,000 lb. of cocoa valued at £16,000. But by 1924 from the Gold Coast over 200,000 tons, valued at over £7,000,000, were exported; and in 1930 it was stated that half the world's cocoa supply came from these colonies. The towns of Accra and Kumasi in 1931 had populations of 59,895 and 36,200 respectively. The revenue of these Gold Coast colonies, which was £122,000 in 1887, averaged, from 1894 to 1898, £244,559, and was £1,331,000 in 1914, is now about £5,000,000. Since 1902 the chief source of revenue has been the Customs; for example, in 1926–27, out of a revenue of £4,365,000 no less than £2,244,000 was from Customs. In that year the expenditure was £4,812,000. The colonies' public debt in 1907 was £2,206,964.

The colony of the Gold Coast is in area half the size of Kenya; its population is less by 300,000. Yet the value of its imports in 1925 was nearly £4,000,000 greater than those of Kenya, and of its exports nearly £5,000,000 greater. The Gold Coast imported in 1923 nearly £1,750,000 worth of cotton piece goods, mainly from Manchester.

If Nigeria had more roads the building of more ginneries for baling cotton would be possible. Compared with Uganda, which has over 160, the cotton-producing districts have only about a dozen in an area as big as Uganda and more populous. But ginneries cannot multiply in Nigeria until there are roads to convey 400-lb. bales of cotton from them to the railway. Sierra Leone alone in West Africa has a railway system comparable to its present needs, and with the possible exception of the Gold Coast the development of the road system of the whole area lags behind requirements of West Africa, although in the Gold Coast 3,434 miles of roads possible for motor traffic have been constructed since the Great War. In March 1926 no less than 2,401 motor-lorries were in use in the Gold Coast, and now many more.

Contrast the shrinking, non-progressing African population of Kenya with the prosperous and increasing peoples of the West African colonies, and the causes of the difference become obvious on learning the divergent systems of administration which are followed on the two sides of Africa. And what of the future? How will populations increase and develop? The Europeans in Kenya, the comparative handful of white settlers (about 14,000 in all), have been intriguing from time to time for some years to import labour from outside the colony, even indentured labour. By taking away three-quarters of the land from the native African of these parts, by imposing heavy poll and hut taxes on him, and by other means, the settlers have largely succeeded in converting the "landless proletarian" into a "wage-slave." The settlers find possession of land without cheap native labour is not worth much. A continuous pressure of one sort or another is exerted on the young male native to keep him busy working for the settler as a wage-earner. Surpluses in the public revenues in Kenya are not found as they quite frequently have been found on the west side of Africa. Budgets are with difficulty balanced partly by selling land to more settlers. Public loans proposals are pushed through the Legislature without the public knowing about them beforehand, and the money is spent on grandiose schemes to enhance the prestige of bureaucrats, or to build railways and harbours, often thereby enriching European land-lords and contractors. All these schemes do not do much to enrich the native Africans and remind one of Australia. Australia, even more than Kenya, is a country crying out for more popu-lation, in spite of healthy birth- and death-rates; but not accessions of inhabitants to the towns, which already (five of them) contain about 70 per cent of the total population of Australia. Roads and railways built through expenditure of moneys raised by means of the public's true revenue, the economic rent of land, and not by penalizing taxation, have a fructifying influence upon pro-gress. They increase prosperity and effect a sound and satisfactory distribution of the population. Sometimes roads and railways have been built by speculators, or by private or public tax-imposing, bureaucratic, place-and-power-seekers, in advance of the increase in the numbers and needs of population. Then their effect is anti-social, is against the true interests of the com-munity. Australia can show instances of this, for there railways have been constructed whose chief effect has been to stimulate a rise in land values, which rises have accrued to the speculating individual landlords, and not to swell the revenue for the com-munity's common pool. Enterprise is hampered and a niggardly production of commodities results. When taxes are collected, instead of filling the community's treasuries by collecting that revenue which is alone community-created, viz. ground rents, public debts and public loans are common. In this particular, comparisons between Nigeria, the Gold Coast, and Malaya on the one hand, and the Union of South Africa and Kenya on the other, are instructive.

A few years ago (in 1916) there was formed in England an

"Empire Resources Development Committee," which put forward specious arguments in favour of exploiting "selected resources" (beginning with oil palm trees, coco-nut palms, and other oil seeds) "under such conditions as will give to the State an adequate share of the proceeds." It was actually proposed to obstruct the expansion of local self-government, and to utilize the proceeds of this scheme for making good the deficiencies of the public treasuries of more "civilized" countries. It was suggested that the "savages" of Africa and the "natives" of Asia should be exploited to make good some of the financial difficulties resulting from wars. The devastating results on the population in the Belgian Congo and less horrible ones under the Chartered Company in Rhodesia were quite forgotten. Such schemes have only to be exposed to be condemned. Such ideas cannot be tolerated, especially in connection with British colonies, for they involve: (1) treating the Empire not as a trust but as an estate to be exploited for the benefit of the British tax-payer; (2) depriving the native of his rights in the land; (3) the establishment of monopolies in partnership with the State; (4) the conversion of the native from a free and independent producer into a forced labourer; and (5) the combining of government administration with commercial profit-seeking.

There is all the difference between working voluntarily for oneself and working under compulsion, between producing with ability to keep all the products of one's own labour, while knowing any of one's exertions which inure to the commonweal are going to be shared in by all, and on the other hand, working with the knowledge that much that results from one's labour goes to persons who have done nothing to earn it. Fortunately nature's impulsion, hunger, acts as a constant urge. But, unfortunately, in the present day this law of nature is often not allowed full sway. Conditions are artificial so that there are on the one hand those who neither sow nor spin yet reap a fat living, and on the other hand many exist who would work for a livelihood if they could find occupation, but are debarred through the errors into which society has fallen, though nature is ever bounteous. These are fed, by charity or through State regulations, from the products of those who are labouring. So long as mankind does not follow the lead of bygone races in respect to the bounties of nature, only to be procured by the application of human exertion and skill to the resources of the earth, and so long as mankind refuses to place the earth in a different category from all other forms of property, so long will human beings suffer under the disabilities associated with compulsory labour of one kind or another. Look again at Africa: in Northern Nigeria contented production proceeds steadily amongst an increasing population under a wise administration recognizing the elementary rights of man, whether white, black, red, or yellow. In Kenya, where the African has been deprived of many of his rights, the Government, so *The Times*[1] informs us, finds it necessary to "inform the native peoples that they are expected to work," and to impose a "stricter supervision" upon them. Anxiety is shown that the exertion of the old men, the women and children in the native reserves should produce more than before—a laudable enough desire, but apparently in order to release the able-bodied adult males to work for Europeans in the mines or in agriculture on the Europeans' plantations. The value of the agricultural exports from native sources rose from £260,000 in 1922–23 to £546,000 in 1924–25. Yet about that time the number of European occupiers of agricultural land was 1,700, holding 4,500,000 acres, of which only 400,000 had so far been cultivated. Many of these cared little about agricultural production from native sources. They were more concerned about getting cheap labour to develop their own holdings. Such people see no wrong in taking away their land from the natives, in imposing taxes and stricter supervision, etc. They were used to such things in Europe where a landless proletariat has existed for generations. Little blame can be attached to them, therefore, for their outlook and actions, though to get cheap labour they occasionally forget their humanity and descend to dreadful deeds. For example, here is an extract from a letter from a settler in Kenya, who with another Englishman had taken up 2,000 acres of land for maize and coffee growing:

"When I arrived up here I found K. had been having a good old time with squatters. He and L. bought out the original owners about six months back. Up till it changed hands the squatters had the time of their lives. No work, or very little, and this land

[1] February 23, 1926.

here is very good grazing, with salt licks all over the place, besides two unoccupied farms, one on each side, also with salt licks. When K. turned up and started a little gentle work they weren't so happy. Every squatter makes an agreement with the owner before he starts squatting, like this: The agreement to be for a certain time, twelve months, eighteen months, and so on. The squatter can build his hut, have so many cattle and goats which he can graze where the owner permits him, also can grow maize, *wembe* in the native *shambus*. In return for these things he must work for so many days a year, about 270, and must turn out to work when ordered to do so, the owner taking into consideration the harvesting of their maize, etc. Wages range from 6s. to 12s. here, cooks and house boys more, of course, also head boy. You have to watch them all the time. K. is full of go-ahead ideas and they are buying a caterpillar tractor which will save a lot of labour, and also oxen. The last named are so slow and always breaking their harness or something.

"The only rotten thing about the country is the extremely high prices. Everything is dear. Petrol 4s. a gallon, butter in towns about 2s. 3d. a lb., bacon is for millionaires, whisky 18s. a bottle. The Customs are very down on gramophones and records, the duty on which is about 30 per cent, *ad valorem*. The revenue of the country is about £2,500,000 and expenditure always exceeds that. The Colonial Office is going to make us spend £80,000 in Government buildings, which are unnecessary, or at any rate that amount is not needed. Then these bloated Commissions and reports run up. There is a Commission on Local Self-Government which will cost £12,000. They got badly hit at M. last Friday as their proposals were flatly turned down. Experts make terrific fees out of the country. But I forgot to tell you about their shavies. One morning K. turned out and found that very few had turned up to work, so he sent his head boy to fetch them. They wouldn't come, so he warned them that if they were not out in a certain time he was going to burn their huts and shoot their cattle. They didn't come, so he and L. went and burnt five or six huts and shot ten head of cattle. This had a very satisfactory effect but it cost K. and L. £25. This happened three months back and was finally settled by the District Commissioner on Saturday. On Friday we were busy running people in to the D.C. for not working and various offences. K. went out one night and found the night *chunga* (headman) asleep in his hut about 10 p.m. when he was supposed to be chungering the cattle. K. called him to the door of the hut and told him to bring him 100/c. fine next morning. The fellow didn't wait but dashed past him into the night. K. chased him with a revolver and then got L. and some natives to look for him. They caught him, but when he was about to give him a hundred with the Kiboks he gave a start and fled naked into the night, leaving his blanket in their hands. However, for that and for various other offences, such as letting the cattle into the wheat, he got three months' jug in O. and 190/c. fine. You ought to have seen K. afterwards, he was so bucked. The case cost him several sleepless nights and he simply leaped for joy, there was no holding him. We also got four others jugged at the same time. They are absolute devils for not working. Yesterday they were cutting weeds from the swamp about half a mile away and they had the impudence to only bring four loads the whole day, from 7 a.m. that is. To-day I got six up before 3 a.m."

The occurrences which are described in the foregoing letter happened only a few years ago in a country where a direct tax, difficult for the native to meet unless he goes out and works for wages, is imposed only on the poorest; where a system of compulsory registration of natives is in vogue, enacted by law, and enforced; where already forced unpaid labour is regularly exacted, in native reserves only, for twenty-four days per annum by law. It is also in the country whose administrators have taken away three-quarters of the land from the natives and allowed Europeans, some only—others have suffered (the subsequent history of the above correspondent is interesting in this particular)— to get rich quickly. As W. McGregor Ross retails,[1] a prominent and influential white man received a grant of 100,000 acres in Kenya for a merely nominal payment and, as shown in a Government White paper, had sold 82,000-odd acres up to 1926 for more than £150,000 profit. This author repudiates the "hoary and indecent libel" that the natives are lazy in their own villages. If they are working for themselves even when engaged on public

[1] *Kenya from Within: A Short Political History* (Allen & Unwin, 1927. 18s. net).

works, that is on improvements which will come back to them incidently but definitely and substantially as part of the community, they will work well. But let them feel, however dimly, that these public works will best go to swell the profits which landlords get in enhanced values for the land they claim to own, and their exertions will be poor ones.

Archdeacon Owen thus describes such proceedings: "In 1925 I watched with great interest the experiment of the Uganda Government in bringing on to the labour market thousands of men from Ankole, Kigezi, marching them down 200 to 300 miles to work on the roads over which Uganda's cotton crop is transported to the lake steamers. A more dispirited lot of men than those whom I saw working in gangs on the roads I have not seen in twenty-two years in Uganda and Kenya."[1]

But to return to the subsequent history of the settler from whose letter a long quotation is given above, after which some more will be said about Uganda. Mr. K. was originally in partnership with Mr. L. whose father had acquired on very easy terms indeed the farm of 2,000 acres which they were working, as well as a vast quantity of other good acres in Kenya. Incidentally, the family knew a good deal about landowning, having similarly acquired generations ago plentiful rich acres in England. Before very long Mr. K. bought his partner out, borrowing from a bank to do so. Within a year or two trade depression and the ravages of locusts made him bankrupt, the bank having foreclosed. Now he is working as a salaried servant, managing part of a big estate belonging to another great English landlord holding wide acres both at home and in Kenya. Though crops have been eaten by locusts, though fortunes have been lost, the land both at home and in Africa is still there! And the landlords! It is indeed a poignant irony that the class from which Mr. K. comes is the bulwark which by its voice, newspapers, and vote supports not only landlordism but systems of taxation which hinder Mr. K., and others like him in far parts of the Empire, from alleviating their solitude by wireless and gramophone apparatus.

The population in Uganda, which has an area of 94,204 square miles including 13,616 square miles of water, according to the 1931 census is as follows: Africans 3,515,910, Asiatics

[1] *Manchester Guardian*, October 23, 1926.

15,077, and Europeans 2,023. The most important and valuable crop grown in Uganda, almost entirely on land which has not been alienated from the natives, is cotton. The quantity of this crop grown in this colony increased steadily so that its value rose in fifteen years (to 1923) from about £20,000 to over £2,000,000; and in 1929 the value of the cotton lint and seed exported from Uganda reached £3,600,000. Yet a few years prior to 1929 the settlers in Kenya were saying that there was great wastefulness of labour in Uganda in producing these crops, because it took over a third of the population to produce them, and that resort to the plantation system, growing it on land owned by white with black lowly paid labour, would be more economical. In arguing thus they forgot one or two things, namely, amongst others: (1) That the native in Uganda cultivates his plots by families, each unit doing that part for which he or she is best fitted. With a great many families it is doubtful whether even one member of, say, five would be available for labour on white-owned plantations situated many miles from the home. This is a point of great importance, referred to previously (see p. 112), in regard to the proper distribution of population. (2) The native of Uganda is growing cotton just as the natives of the Gold Coast and Nigeria grow cocoa and palm kernels, because they own their land and can make it produce both domestic needs and economic material for export in exchange for coveted manu-factured articles from Sheffield, Birmingham, Manchester, and London.

The secret of good production is the presence of willing workers, not as was once suggested—by Mr. Stanley Baldwin—a subsidy of £10,000,000, though encouragement from such a body as the British Cotton-Growing Association, and the expen-diture of some money for education and research (preferably out of the native's own "common pool"), is of undoubted help. By such methods peoples not only flourish but increase in numbers. When opposite policies are followed they neither flourish nor increase. At the present time the population on the reserves in Kenya is equally as dense as in Uganda. Not that everything regarding the growth, development, and distribution of popu-lation in Uganda is all plain sailing. It has taken time and pains for doctors and veterinary surgeons to combat the diseases so prevalent in some parts of the colony, and these efforts have had distinctly disturbing effects at times upon the distribution of population. There stands to the credit of veterinary science the fact that the numbers in the herds of native cattle were doubled in five years a few years ago. The population is increasing rapidly in the Buganda province, the difference between births and deaths being probably greater amongst the people of that district than that amongst any other African tribe, despite the fact that there are very few doctors. But certain areas are still very unhealthy even for natives, on account of bad malaria and sleeping-sickness. There are, moreover, two game reserves north and south of the same district as the sleeping-sickness area, with the result that elephants and buffalo wander at will from one to the other, gradually pushing the population into what will soon be a congested area. But above all other disturbing influences are those due to administrative and political causes emanating from outside, especially from across the Kenya border. In Toro, for example, there is a little Kenya germinating because Europeans, mostly from the latter colony, have leased for ninety-nine years an unreasonable proportion of the best and healthiest part. It is true that vast stretches of fertile land are to be found at lower elevations, but malaria, to which the Batoro seem as susceptible as Europeans, is widespread and particularly malignant below 5,000 feet. This tribe even more than the Buganda are suspicious of an increasing European population because they fear the Kenya system of compulsory registration, and that indirect pressure may be brought to bear upon them to work on European plantations, the area of which long ago exceeded that for which local labour is available. In addition to these causes of unrest the combine of the cotton ginners has rather beaten down the price paid for raw cotton in Buganda as compared with other parts. Disquiet has been produced, too, by the agreements for a large measure of home rule through their Kabuka (or King) being set aside in certain particulars, especially in regard to their rights in the land. This has struck a blow at the structure of tribal and community life, and shows disregard of former promises and policies upon which the loyalty of the Bantu community has been based.

The whole future of the great British Empire depends, more

than it does on anything else, on our so ordering our ways that discontent and disquiet are not caused by such mistakes, however difficult it may be to avoid their occasional occurrence. The excellent book by the late C. L. Temple,[1] formerly Lieutenant-Governor of Northern Nigeria, ably puts forward cogent arguments for the system of indirect rule. He points out that we cannot check the development of the native population, we can only guide—hindering or assisting it. To the following hypothetical question he put to himself, "What, then, do you forecast as to the future of the natives if 'Ruled Indirectly'?" he replies: "By means of Indirect Rule you can so allow natural conditions to exert their influence in a manner modified to meet the requirements of the native group that in due course of time it will become robust enough to stand by itself."[2]

[1] *Native Races and Their Rulers*, p. 78 (Argus Printing and Publishing Co., Capetown, 1918). [2] Ibid., p. 255.

CHAPTER VII

THE FIRST DUTY OF GOVERNMENT

MR. C. L. TEMPLE maintains there are good grounds for believing that the populations in Nigeria under the sway of the greater emirs and chiefs were prosperous, well fed, and, according to their ideas, happy enough before the arrival of the Europeans. He considers that the method of indirect rule, unlike direct rule, does not tend to overmuch centralization; nor does it make difficult the introduction of measures beneficial to the natives but strange to European ideas. This question of home rule versus central authority tending to bureaucracy and autocracy is as old as the hills yet as new as fresh paint. Everywhere and in every age it springs up, for in no country has the art of government reached such a stage of perfection as to merit the name of an exact science. Some of the difficulties preventing the establishment of an exact science of government are definitely connected with the growth and development of populations. If the life of tribes and races were static, if peoples never migrated, never deserted rural habitats and occupations for towns and commerce, the art of government would be much simpler. But when all is said and done, and despite ever-present complications which the growth and varying densities of populations bring, the fundamental law of good government should always be this, viz. *It is the first duty of Government to collect the rent of land.* We have seen in previous chapters dealing with India, China, and Africa that rulers of old were renowned largely because they grasped quite clearly the connection between government and this law. But to-day quite a number of people have lost sight of the fact that the collection of the rent of land is the first duty of Governments, and still more fail to appreciate what land rent is. They confuse it with the rent of buildings and do not realize that the economists, defining it generally as economic rent, refer only to that value attaching to the ground which is not created by anything an individual does but which is created solely by the community's actions, needs, and growth. It may also be stated that the economic rent of land is the rate by which individuals measure the desirability of living within the jurisdiction of any community or nation. In districts remote from society, where there is no social service or government, solitary individuals live rent free. The difference between the social value of living in solitude and the value of living in society manifests itself in site value, which is the measure of government.

In the countries hitherto studied I have so far abstained from dealing with those places where people have become aggregated into cities. It simplifies matters somewhat to confine attention to begin with largely to primitive races, ancient civilizations, and to those following agricultural pursuits. But whensoever or wheresoever study is made of these things it is well to realize that the calm of even the best systems of government is occasionally ruffled by the friction caused by sectional economic selfishness. A conflict arises sometimes between the cultivator and the "authority" which comes to collect for rent some of the products. It was not always easy in days of old to arrive at a just assessment. Akbar the Great took one-third of the produce as land revenue. To-day, in the Native States of India, about a quarter is so taken. But the assessments to-day are on a better basis than of old in one respect (net produce not gross), and are in a much worse state than of old in another, for landlordism has crept in to an extent which was impossible in olden times and takes often a very high proportion of that which ought to be the public's revenue. The murder of Julius Caesar was not unconnected with these matters; for Brutus and the Roman nobility were much mixed up with the tax-farming syndicates, and Caesar shortly before his death had passed an order for the commutation into a fixed money payment of the tithe and other dues paid upon lands in various parts of the Empire in an effort to get rid of some of the worst scandals connected with the farming of the taxes. He attempted to establish fairer treatment for cultivators. The unsettled times which followed his death held up the reforms he introduced and so it fell upon Caesar Augustus to try and finish his work. According to one interpretation of Luke ii. 1, the fact that the birth of Jesus occurred at Galilee was due to the taxing reforms of Caesar Augustus; though others maintain that the enrolment of people which brought Joseph and Mary there was purely for census purposes. Dealing with recent times in Italy,

Professor O. Marinelli[1] has shown the connection between systems of rent collection in agricultural communities and the way in which persons live, whether concentrated or scattered. It has already been emphasized that a departure from the practice of assessing land for public revenue (or for landlord's rent, too, as a fact) on the crop-share tenure system is a good thing, because under that system when an occupier learnt to increase the output from his holding the revenue went up. This acts as a discouragement to the cultivator, and is apt to depress output. The introduction of a monetary payment is virtually essential as society develops, and if well-ordered schemes of assessment of the rent due, and a proper way of spending it when paid, are adopted, such payments conduce to the general welfare.

The second great class of conflicting interests which produce difficulties in both primitive and advanced nations depends upon the decision as to how to apportion the revenue collected between local and central administrative bodies. Amongst the somewhat primitive races of Africa which we have just been studying a varying amount of the public revenue collected is left in local hands. To-day, in Nigeria the collection of the State revenue is in the hands of the district and village heads. It is exacted in the name of the Emir, one-half being paid into the Government Treasury (the common fund of the Protectorate) and one-half into what is generally termed in the Northern Provinces the Beit el Mal or Native Treasury. The latter is used to meet the expenses of the native administration, such as the salaries of the emir, district and village heads, native justiciary, cost of labour and material for public works, etc. These arrangements refer to one of the more advanced groups of people in these regions. The amount of the revenue which central and local bodies, especially the former, want is rather dependent upon the amount they require for military purposes, and for the debts they have contracted. Now in both instances the requirements would progressively diminish and would eventually disappear if the individuals and the community's interests coincided. This blessed state can be consummated by a full understanding and a full

[1] Professor O. Marinelli, Union Géographique Internationale, *Report*, No. 1, 1928, p. 4.

use of the rule already laid down, viz. that it is the first duty of
Government to collect the land rent and use it for the public
weal. One illustration of this can be seen in Nigeria, without
plunging yet into the more complicated societies of Europe and
America. From official reports it can be discovered that in that
country where the inhabitants are the most contented there the
expenditure on military and police forces and on legal actions
and prisons is least, and that this tranquillity coincides with the
greatest enjoyment of home rule and respect for native customs
of land tenure and taxation. For example, the prison expenses
in the Southern Provinces and Colony of Nigeria where direct
taxation has been introduced since 1925 are more than ten times
as much as in Northern Nigeria, where native rights in land are
much more definitely respected, though there are far more people
in the Northern Provinces with its area of 281,939 square miles
than in the Southern Provinces and Colony with an area of
91,139 square miles.

A just apportionment of the revenue collected for public use
between central and local authorities has not become quite
easy with the progress through the ages in the art of government.
Sectional economic selfishness is discernible in civilized countries
despite all kinds of devices for "equalization" of local burdens
between one district and another and "grants-in-aid." As has
been well shown by Chuan Shih Li in his *Central and Local Finance
in China*[1] some progress was being made there, before Japan's
interference upset things, as a result of agitation for provincial
and local self-government. But he makes clear how difficult
this was without separation of the sources of revenue between
the central and provincial governments on the one hand and
between the provincial and the local governments on the other.
China at that time had not made any separation between the
local and the national taxes. Every tax in the provinces constituted a source of revenue for the national Government. Under
the rule of the emperor monarchs the land was supposed to be
the property of the emperor and the land tax, therefore, should
be his chief income. But owing to the fact that the land tax
supported the district magistracy and the prefecture administration, nourished the circuit governor, and fed the provincial

[1] Columbia University, New York, 1922.

authorities, only a fraction of this tax was returned to His Majesty. The land tax had been the mainstay of those different governing authorities from time immemorial. But in recent years these authorities were also supported out of the salt gabelle, the maritime Customs, and the inland Customs duties. And there were some provinces richer than others because their collected revenues exceeded their expenditures, and these were required to transfer their surplus via Peking to the provinces in less fortunate circumstances. These transferred revenues are unlike the English grants-in-aid inasmuch as they are without any condition for efficiency, and often have been utilized for wasteful and fruitless military expenses. Another drawback of these arrangements is that it encourages the concealment of revenues on the part of the richer provinces.

Questions connected with road and railways frequently give rise to sectional squabbles in both civilized and primitive communities. These are not easily settled even by the most wonderful formulae to ordain how "grants-in-aid" shall be dispensed. Such questions as the following are not easy to settle: Who needs the roads most, merchants or primary producers, home-workers or distant commercial concerns? Who wear out the roads most, which kind of user, and where from? Are railways, perhaps State subsidized or owned, receiving unfair aid as against road makers and users? And all such problems have much to do with the distribution of population. Matters are made less clear by modern taxing authorities so frequently being wedded to the bad principle of "ability to pay" in place of the good one of "benefits received." The latter principle at once turns attention to the using of obviously community-created funds for public services.

To return for a moment to the making of roads and railways in Africa—in Nigeria, for example: Some say that a native staff put at the disposal of an Emir is not capable of constructing such improvements unless educated in Europe and thus "detribalized," a deplorable thing to bring about for no other reason than that it seriously undermines the code of family, of paternal discipline, which is the bed-rock of all African well-being. But there is really no inherent objection to Native Administrations being lent European officers for the execution of public works; and the national spirit, once it has grown robust under the fostering care of a paternal Government, would be strong enough to permit of natives receiving European technical education without destroying the influence of their own homes. This national spirit has brought the tribe through a fierce struggle for its existence during past centuries. It will stand firm so long as Africans feel convinced that in helping to make better means of transport they are using common action for the commonweal. The native has not got reasoning powers like ours, but in this respect his instincts are keener. He can scent more easily than the members of a more sophisticated race what kind of action is for the commonweal. So also the native realizes better than does the European the fact that the number, health, and prosperity of the community are intimately connected with a proper use of the soil and its products, mineral and vegetable. To him this truth is patent. But to most Europeans it is lost sight of owing to the existence of vast agglomerations of persons living in cities who, to outward appearances, have little connection with the soil. With Africans the occupation of land is strictly conditional to its proper use and to the performance of those duties called for by the needs of the community. Failure in either of these duties is recognized as bringing disaster. Not so with us. In Northern Nigeria in no case had the land, prior to our advent, acquired a transfer value as between individuals. With them a chief might demand a payment before permitting an individual to occupy, but this was regarded as a legitimate form of raising revenue and did not constitute the chief an owner of the land or the tenant either. It did but help to confirm the individual security of tenure, already well established by such customs. Granted that an occupier met his obligations, it was regarded as an act of unpardonable oppression if the chief should deprive him of his holding, and in fact such cases were unknown among the pagans. It was found, when Europeans arrived and wisely continued the system, that a farm had been in the hands of the same family for generations. The very idea of a "landlord" class, i.e. private individuals who collect rent in exchange merely for permitting others to occupy land, appeared to be inconceivable to the natives. The same is true amongst the Red Indian natives of America; and it is fortunate that at length the opinions of

John Collier regarding the way of allotting lands to Indians in the United States are being put into practice. He proposes to return to tribal organization. Perhaps too late for the Indians, since at least two-thirds of their lands have already been lost to them, at least 90,000 of them are paupers, and since the small measure of restoration now proposed is based upon land purchase.

CHAPTER VIII

THE SIZE OF AGRICULTURAL HOLDINGS

THIS chapter deals with the size of holdings in areas of agricultural production. The size of the piece of land that any particular occupier holds depends upon the nature of the cultivation he practices. This depends to a considerable extent upon climate, soil, and accessibility to other mouths and hands, to sparse or crowded markets. At the present time at least two-thirds of the earth's land surface, counting in the uninhabited lands too, is in the occupancy of the peoples who belong to the lowest classes of producers. These lowest types of human development are: the hunting and fishing type, based solely on wild animals; the pastoral nomadic type, based on domesticated animals; and the type based on the "hoe and tree culture," which is the class of producer found in extensive regions in the tropics. The last-named type rely almost wholly upon the fruits of trees, as the coco-nut and the banana; or upon roots, as the yam, which can be cultivated with a minimum of labour among the trees and bushes. The size of holdings held for agriculture is affected also by the numbers of persons in the community under consideration, the rapidity of their increase during the period under review, and the state of their development sociologically as opposed to their stage of development in the science of agriculture. To illustrate the effect of these agencies reference may be made to the influence of the Black Death on the size of holdings during the fourteenth century. Before the plague came to England and Wales, on the occasion of its first devastating visit in 1348, certain economic and social changes were already beginning to be felt in the structure of society. By the late thirteenth century the mode of life and thought were beginning to change. Life was less hedged in by custom, less homogeneous in character, less "parochial." It revolved around the system of serfage and manorial government much less than before. The serfs, who had hitherto carried out their services in detail on the lord's demesne in each manor, were beginning to make small payments in lieu of performing the services. The practice of storing in summer food necessary for winter was leading to a fuller life, to more business-like methods and the accumulation of wealth. Individual initiative was becoming commoner, and the pursuit of trade. The manor was being worked for profit in the fourteenth century. Instead of being a grouped unit, a single organism, it was let out in numerous individual holdings, each worked by a "farmer" for his own profit, the lord thus becoming a rent-receiving land-lord. In Wales the tendencies towards a break-up of the manor system were more noticeable, partly as a result of the rebellion which arose there. The rights in land there were slowly passing to individuals. Then came the Black Death, and this assisted in these developments through diminishing the population heavily. It is believed that a quarter of the inhabitants of Europe, calculated to amount at that time to about 100,000,000, died in the few years in the middle of the fourteenth century, most of them in 1348 and 1349. The systems of land tenure in England and in Wales became gradually approximated, and this assisted in the union of the two countries. Alteration in the system of land tenure and the beginning of taxation helped to bring in money payments in lieu of services. Then the landlords themselves cast off their burdens due to the king, while culture in strips diminished and bigger holdings in the hands of "farmers" became commoner. All these changes paved the way for a central State as seen in the sixteenth century when the new groups—landlords, tenant-farmers, and workmen—became subject of the national State, and trade assumed national proportions

C. E. Woodruff, in his *Expansion of Races*,[1] points out that "the more dense the population the smaller are the land holdings," and gives a table indicating this, part of which is as follows. In doing this he adds that the States which are "Out of line have manufacturing interests."

	Acres per Farm	Population per Square Mile
Michigan	86	42·2
Ohio	93	102·0
Indiana	103	70·0
Wisconsin	115	38·0
Nebraska	190	14·0
South Dakota	227	5·2
North Dakota	277	4·5

[1] P. 27 (Rebenan Ltd., New York, 1909).

Woodruff says that the best paying farms, in the Eastern States anyway, are not more than 80 acres in extent, but the average in 1900 was 146 acres, and in 1850 it was 202 acres. It is said that for every 80 acres of cultivated farm land the country supported 15 persons in 1900. In the same year less than half of the land of the United States of America was occupied by farms, and only about 50 per cent of this land was properly "improved," that is cleared, reclaimed, irrigated, etc. In the last thirty years the percentage of improved land has, however, gone up considerably. But since then has come the fall in prices and financial crises, the outcome of the Great War. Farming, like other callings, has suffered despite more science and improved marketing facilities. The *Sunday Times*[1] states that over a million farmers—one-sixth of the total—have been sold up in the United States for debt during the past eight years. The main cause of these collapses was the preceding increase in the price of land. Until 1890 land was plentiful and man-power was scarce. By 1928 the reverse was roughly true. Between 1900 and 1920 the average value of all the farm land in the United States of America trebled, and in some regions, such as the State of Iowa, it increased five times. During the boom years corn land was sold in Iowa at $300 to $400 per acre, while not a great many years previously its selling value was only about $75 per acre. Possibly 100,000 Iowa farmers sold out. By 1932 the "greedy fools who bought were trying to pass on to the Government the burden of their mortgages." The power of the banks, and the bankruptcy of the banks in bad times, are founded upon their possession of land through mortgages. I have shown elsewhere[2] that roughly one-third of the assets of banking concerns is represented by land values, and there are times when the proportion is much higher than this. In England in 1923 the complaint was being made that the joint-stock banks were not supporting the farming industry to the same extent as the private banks used to do. This charge was rebutted that year in the annual address of the chairman of one of the biggest, Lloyds, by his telling his audience this fact, "We are lending to 12,800 farmers sums aggregating £14,000,000," and by his bringing forward figures to show "that the facilities by way of overdrafts given by the joint-stock

[1] May 7, 1933.　　[2] *The Commonweal*, Vol. VI, No. 49 (London, 1925).

banks were much greater than were formerly granted by the private banks." I guess some of the banking concerns in the United States of America are wishing to-day that they had not been equally generous to farmers about that time! It is not without its irony to notice that banks and farmers are always ready to welcome Government interference when they think they can wheedle it in their own favour, but are generally the first to complain when such interference seems to be telling against them, as witness the grumblings about the United States of America Federal Farm Board and the Cotton Stabilization Corporation, and the glee shown in many quarters when it was suggested the activities of these bodies should come to an end. On the other hand satisfaction was exhibited when President Roosevelt approved the legislation under which $200,000,000 were to be placed at the disposal of the Department of Agriculture for leasing land from farmers.

France seems bent on following the example of the United States of America in setting up a Farm Board with a capital of approximately £2,200,000, although, after Germany, she is already the most highly protected wheat-growing country in the world, and although French wheat production costs are two or three times those of Argentina and Canada. France has grown more wheat than she consumed only twice in one hundred years. If such a year occurred again the Board would balance the market in a year of surplus by strict regulation and try to recoup itself during years when there was a deficit.

It was reported in the House of Commons on July 21, 1913, that the number of agricultural holdings in England and Wales exceeding 1 acre and not exceeding 50 acres in extent, according to the latest available returns, was 292,720. In 1926 Great Britain had 436,000 holdings with 94,236 occupying owners, and 1,500,000 employed on them. The area under cultivation about that time was 29,000,000 acres. In 1923 Sir Henry Rew[1] stated that of the 26,000,000 acres of agricultural land in England and Wales, 13,500,000 are allocated in holdings of more than 150 acres, and 6,000,000 acres in holdings of over 300 acres. In 1931 there were about 325,000 holdings in England and Wales of over 5 acres, and of these 185,000, or 57 per cent, were under 50 acres.

[1] Sir Henry Rew on "Village Communities"—*The Times*, January 10, 1923.

There were only 12,000 farmers who farmed more than 300 acres.

According to figures published in Rome for the year 1930 by the International Institute of Agriculture, the number of holdings of all sizes in Ireland, namely 571,172, is very different from those in Scotland, 75,812, though the size of the two countries is approximately the same, Ireland 20,360,601 acres and Scotland 19,169,500 acres, excluding water in both cases. Scotland has more mountainous and unproductive land and a worse climate. But the difference in the number of holdings is by no means accounted for by such causes. It is connected with political agitation. Yet though politics have brought most Irish occupiers near to ruin, Ireland seems to be no nearer settling the land question than she was in the days of Gladstone and Parnell. The latter preached "the eternal truth that the land of a country belongs to no man. It was not made by any man, and belongs to all." Yet not long afterwards by switching the attention from the rights of the people in the land to age-old religious bigotries the landed oligarchy of Ireland were able to unload much of their property upon taxpayers. To this day bickerings continue over the interest on the land annuities, in spite of the multiplication of peasant proprietors and a better use of Irish land. Barren political changes are ever a sham safety valve for agrarian injustice. Scottish land holding, too, has had troublous times not unconnected with politics. But in Scotland the depopulation of many wide areas was deliberate a generation or two ago largely to allow sportsmen to go deer stalking.

The pressure of population is too readily blamed for splitting up land holdings into smaller and smaller pieces. Take China for example. Although droughts, floods, and wars have killed millions, population has increased by degrees. Though means of communication, education, and modes of cultivation have been stationary it is not this which has hindered progress in production so much as the unsatisfactory character of land tenure and of taxation. The same causes prevent population from spreading out naturally. Inherent conservatism, ancestor worship, and laws of inheritance all tend to tie the Chinaman to the place of his fathers. Good government rather than industrialism would prove a salvation for the peoples of these realms.

In Japan the size of holdings is on the average surprisingly small, though the intensive use to which the land is put and the succession of crops which the climate in many regions enables the cultivators to grow tend to a high yield. Japan is a mountainous country, and only about 16 per cent of the whole land (about 15,000,000 acres) is arable, and this is farmed as to about 80 per cent of the farmers in holdings of from 1¾ to 3¾ acres. Java is another country where a dense population in a tropical clime and with fertile land lives almost entirely by agriculture. Java, with Madura, has an area of 50,777 square miles and a population in 1930 of 41,500,000, of whom less than 194,000 were Europeans. Yet about 1905 the population was 28,500,000 and is said to have been only 5,000,000 in 1825. The present density in the plains and valleys is 568 persons for every square mile of surface, which is greater than in any province of China except Shantung. The Javanese are still able to raise all their food and to export (in 1930) £48,000,000 worth of the products of their plantations and forests. If the United States of America had the same density as the plains and valleys and terraced mountain sides of Java, its inhabitants would number over 1,200,000,000. Katherine Mayo pays this tribute to the rule of the Dutch in Java, though inferring condemnation of one feature of it, the use of force. She writes: "The population of Java has increased from 2,000,000 to 30,000,000 during their rule, and the yield of the rice and sugar fields has increased proportionately. The change was brought about not by capital expenditure but by an intelligent Government."[1]

By comparison with Ceylon, Java is a great contrast, in respect at least to the growth of population, for it is said that Ceylon had a bigger population in 500 B.C. than she has to-day.

To return to Europe: In France there are 5,505,000 holdings of which 2,200,000 are occupied by owners, and on them 8,777,000 of the population are employed. These figures relate to the end of 1925. At the same period for Germany the figures are 5,736,000 holdings, 5,000,250 occupying owners, and 15,000,000 employees. Denmark, the only country in Europe where a majority of land *owners* are opposed to private property in land, had (in 1925) one-third of its entire population engaged in production of food, and 88 per cent were owner occupiers. Holland had 27 per cent

[1] Katherine Mayo's *Mother India*, p. 208 (Jonathan Cape, 1927).

engaged on the land, and 50 per cent were occupying owners. The proportion of the occupied population engaged in agriculture in 1930 in France was 41 per cent, in Germany 31 per cent, and in England only 7 per cent; and these proportions remain about the same to-day.

A great number of interesting books have been written about the decline of the Roman Empire. All concur in ascribing the fall of this mighty civilization as being, at least in part, due to a decline in farming, especially associated with an increase in the size of individual holdings. These increases were one of the "glories" of war. The great ones of the Empire won marvellous victories. They conquered foreign races many of whose subjects were added to the number of the slaves who were used for working the land. The agrarian society planted on fertile lands was destroyed by successful war. War profiteering, confiscation of land because the owners had taken the wrong side, large indemnities, the making of life easy for a few who drew unearned wealth from all parts of the world, these were some of the results of the "knock-out" victories. They are interesting to contemplate and are well described by several writers on this subject: for example, W. E. Heitland.[1]

Professor E. Huntingdon has attempted to discover what were the climatic conditions in Greece and Italy in the centuries just before the Christian era, and he has brought together in a very able manner much evidence to demonstrate that these were cooler, stormier, and wetter than the average climate there to-day. Much of this interesting study is to be found in his *The Pulse of Progress*.[2] He has put forward the opinion that the decline of the Greeks and the Romans was partly due to this change of climate from the stimulating one, resembling more closely that of England to-day, to a warmer and more enervating climate. Even the wealthy Romans during the epoch of abundant storminess which culminated about four centuries before Christ, possessed, he believes, the pioneer quality and were not above handling the pick and the plough. The basis of the sturdy life of the early Romans was intensive agriculture. In those days about 4½ acres (7 jugera we are told) sufficed to support an average

---

[1] *Agricola* (Cambridge University Press, 1921. 47s. 6d.).

[2] Scribners, 1926. 21s.

family. But by about 220 or 210 B.C. there had come about a great decline in rainfall and storminess, and the conditions for agricultural operations were not so favourable. Professor Huntingdon surmises that some land hunger and poverty had arisen before the Second Punic War began in 218 B.C. This largely explains the ease with which people were hookwinked into "joining the colours" as aggressors in a war which brought seventeen years of bitter fighting. About this same time Italy needed to import food from abroad, and a society which had hitherto been military and agricultural began to be commercial. The year 196 saw the first public distribution of grain in Rome. Yet in spite of this demand for food it seems certain that farming became less profitable about this time. The peasants fell into debt; their lands were bought by capitalists or large proprietors. Country folk flocked to the cities. There huge wooden tenements were erected and bakeshops were established to furnish bread to the many unmarried tradesmen and labourers who could not get it at home. Several cities lodged complaints with the Senate between 187-177 B.C. against the influx of country people. At the same time, as the historian Ferrero puts it in his *History of the Rise and Greatness of the Roman Empire*, "there grew up a generation of arrogant and ambitious politicians." Even in the better years of the second century, Rome was never entirely immune from partial famines. Little by little the troubles of the farmers became the greatest political problem. It was in 133 B.C. that Tiberius Gracchus tried to remedy them by a series of laws for the redistribution of the land. Twenty-two years later these are supposed to have been improved upon by Spurius Thorius, and he is given credit for some improvement in agriculture. There is evidence, however, that meanwhile an amelioration in the climatic conditions with greater rainfall occurred. It may be that more rain and not doubtful improvements in the system of land tenure and taxation, etc., was responsible for the improvement which came about in agriculture. This improvement continued for many years. So did the bigger rainfall, according to Professor Huntingdon. Not many great geographers have emphasized so well as he has the importance of the way land is held, the size of the holdings, and its distribution and accessibility. The more these things are probed into, both in the past and in the present, the better. It is desirable also to collate them with questions of taxation. When further study still has been given to these influences on the development of human society it will become clearer how important they are, and how their influence on the growth and distribution of population increases as civilization advances. They may outgrow the factor which must be ascribed to climate.

E. Huntingdon has laid down the axiom that "the better the land, the larger the holdings of the rich and the smaller the holdings of the poor"; and he has raised it to an "important geographical principle."[1] I think that is going too far. In any case a thorough understanding of such a tendency regarding the size of holdings is worth attempting, though the matter is rather complicated. Under the regime of society which fails to discover and act upon the principle that community values should be collected for the public services, and values created by the individual belong quite strictly to the individual, the occupancy of areas of land which would become automatically smaller as numbers and knowledge increased is hindered. The means which would simplify and make smooth the natural changes in quantity of ground as well as in its usage go unrecognized, and therefore unused. A regime of society which has not discovered such means is clearly enough bound to produce conflicts and wars. It is also likely to lead and has surely been shown to lead to just those kinds of tendencies which brought the downfall of Rome. The agrarian laws of the Gracchi came too late and were not acted upon sufficiently to save the great Empire, and they were followed, too, by the disastrous though victorious later Punic Wars. Tiberius Gracchus enacted that no person should have more than 500 jugera of land as his absolute property; that if he had more it should revert to the State and be portioned out in small lots at moderate rents to the poorer citizens. The Gracchi, though on right lines, had not discovered the magic instrument which allows the changes to smaller areas of occupancy to occur automatically and smoothly and distributes population according to a natural geographical law.

The same mistakes are being made to-day in many particulars. State functionaries attempt to parcel out land to "small-holders" and to workers on "allotments." But they do not know how to do

---

[1] E. Huntingdon's *The Human Habitat*, p. 250.

it, and so their efforts, though well intentioned, are not really successful. And the same lack of success meets the costly State "land settlement" schemes. The last statement is well illustrated by reference to the one started in England in 1919. This settlement was to be on a profit-sharing basis. But the Committee[1] which reported in 1925 had to admit that "so far no profits have been available for distribution," and it recommended that "no new farming operations should be carried out by the Ministry." The total loss on the working of the Land Settlement Act of 1919 to the end of March 1926 was estimated, at the date of the publication of the White paper, to be approximately £9,500,000, which was at the rate of about £38 per acre and over £550 per tenant. The efforts of the State on behalf of allotment-holders, the users of small plots within reach of their homes, for workers to grow potatoes and other vegetables in their spare time have not been quite so costly and unfruitful. But difficulty of access to land, unless extortionate purchase prices are paid or high rents, prevents much being done, though loans to the extent of £1,285,091 were raised between 1908 and 1930. However, in all the following towns with over 100,000 inhabitants, the proportion of allotment holdings per thousand of the population is over 25, and in the first-named as high as 62 : Leicester, Coventry, Derby, Rhondda (urban district), Walsall, Nottingham, Bristol, Sheffield, Norwich, and Cardiff. The fate of the Labour Party's 1931 Agricultural Land Utilization Act, which aimed amongst other things at getting a lot of the unemployed "back on to the land," and which provided for the payment of £9,000,000 to landlords out of taxation, has met with little success. It would have been cheaper in many instances to import food and give it to those unemployed whom such Acts attempted to succour.

When the results of the efforts of the State to provide land for "small-holding" farmers come to be examined they are, on the whole, most disappointing. Under the Small-holdings Act 1908 only 13,000 small-holdings were provided by 1926. In 1930, when Mr. C. S. Orwin of the Agricultural Economics Institute reported that in the difficult times for agriculture the small-holders were the most prosperous, the difficulty of acquiring

---

[1] Select Committee on Estimates (Ministry of Agriculture—White paper published on August 14, 1925).

land under State schemes was such that 30 county councils had not attempted it in the year previous to his report. There existed at that time over 8,000 unsatisfied applicants for small-holdings, and nearly 14,000 applicants had withdrawn in disgust at the delays. When the 1926 Act came into force there were 5,565 unsatisfied applicants; and how many tens of thousands more would there have been had it been possible for them to get together a little capital for equipment, and had it been known that access to land on equitable and sure terms was readily to be got! It came out at a County Council inquiry at Brisley in Norfolk a few years ago that several of the county's tenants with from 2 or 3 to 10 acres were asking for more land up to 25 acres. I know full well from my own experience and observations how difficult it is to get access to land almost on any terms, not only for poultry farms, but often for such other ordinary uses as to build a cottage; and that is so even when one has capital behind one. To take a few figures for one county alone, Norfolk: In the 1930 estimates for the small-holdings accounts the expenditure under loan charges stood at over £70,000, and under the head of rates, taxes, tithes, etc., nearly £11,000. The estimated income from the Ministry of Agriculture from his contribution under the Land Settlement Act, 1925, was £55,630, which was equal to a subsidy from the taxpayers of £2 per acre per annum. An interesting brief account of the history of Small-holding Acts, starting with that of Queen Elizabeth's reign (an Act of 1597—not repealed till 1775—which forbade the erection of a habitation for an agricultural worker without providing at least 4 attached acres) was given a year or two ago in the *Manchester Guardian*.[1]

Now, besides being a physician I am a poultry farmer with over twenty years' experience of poultry farming on a small-holding, formerly 6 acres, now 14. I have lectured and written on poultry farming and continue to exercise supervision over a mixed poultry farm which goes in for pedigree layers, egg and table bird production. In a pamphlet I published in 1923 on *The Industry of Agriculture*, I point out how greatly the value of the food produced and the labour employed increases when good arable land is turned from ordinary farming to more intensive use. At the time of writing that pamphlet the poultry farm was

[1] September 4, 1930.

smaller than now, though profits in those days were propor-
tionately higher. With about 350 laying birds the profits then
were averaging £13 per month on receipts of £100 per month.
To-day receipts are a good deal higher, and still good profits are
made. For ordinary farming operations in England just a fraction
over four men per hundred acres, including the working farmer,
is usually put down as the labour required. With market gardening,
poultry farming, and similar intensive culture up to ten times as
much labour can be employed. The 14 acres I have as a poultry
farm give employment to two full-time men and one boy. Formerly, under arable farming it employed one man as a half-
timer. The value of foodstuffs produced is at least ten times as
much as formerly. It may be said, as it has been said to me, that
"if every farmer produced pigs and poultry extensively there
would soon be over-production," and that much land might have
to lie idle. We do not want every farmer to proceed to intensive
poultry, fruit, pig, or "truck crop" production, only greater
freedom to produce such products for those that do. Moreover,
ordinary farming, arable with animal husbandry, might be
more progressive in England. Take dairy farming, not hitherto referred to; production might be increased enormously by
improving the level of the breeds, by giving rationed foods, by
more up-to-date milking methods, and by raising the purity and
quality of the milk. If at the same time the ability to purchase by
the masses were enhanced, the consumption of milk would bound
up, especially if the public became less scared of the dangers of
milk drinking. To-day, though the idea of milk being a disease-
distributing beverage is grossly exaggerated, there is plenty of
room for improvement. Again, sugar beet cultivation, if it proved
worth while without State subsidization, might take up wide
areas, and large "factory farms" employing a maximum of
labour-saving machinery could produce cereals, with or without
stock raising. All these things could be accomplished without
burdening townsmen or rural workers with heightened prices
through systems of "protection," and without the other great
evil that import restraints impose, namely raised land rents and
monopolist's profits.

The paucity of ideas that farmers exhibit in hard times is
deplorable. They usually fly at once to cutting down wages,

asking for a reduction of rent (if tenants), for bigger overdrafts from the banks, while at the same time they "let the land down," that is, do not cultivate it so well. It may be rather difficult always to change the type of crop to suit the times, but more foresight, adaptability, and skill should be shown than is usually the case. Then the loud and persistent cries for import taxes, for subsidies, or for "quota" schemes would be unnecessary. If the evils of the present systems of land tenure and taxation could be abolished the natural tendency for more people to be producing food in a country where numbers and skill were increasing would be unhampered, together with the utilization of progressively smaller areas of occupancy. As things are, however, the tendency is for hard times to arise and relatively less food to be grown and fewer persons to be producing it. Take, for example, the case of certain estates in England close to the border of Hertfordshire and Buckinghamshire which are not far removed from the sphere of influence of expanding Greater London. The population of these regions engaged in husbandry is dwindling, but not because profitable agricultural crops could not be raised there. Oh, no. But the excellent soil there has been let down, under-cultivated for a generation. The farm labourers left the farm attracted by higher wages in London. The farmers had little capital and perhaps some of them less initiative. Advertisements of building sites in particularly favourable situations were put up so that actually as much as (at the rate of) £5,000 per acre was asked for land in small plots. The land speculators were apparently content to sell frontage and let the rest of the farm go to pieces. One of these farms (near Dagnal) had been in the occupancy of the same family for two hundred years, but it descended a year or two ago into being under-cultivated, giving diminished employment and more meagre crops. The inventiveness of man (for example, the advent of the motor-car and its cheap multiplication), the increase of population, and public expenditure on roads, etc., have sent up the value of the land. Those purely community values should be taken by the community for the public benefit. Because they are not that which is produced by the labour of individuals is taken from him in taxes. This omission and this commission of sin hurt society. They hurt society in many ways, amongst others they obstruct the path along which such transitions in the most profitable use of land can be traversed. Though the law that human progress entails access to areas of natural opportunity progressively smaller is working all the time, human blindness and folly, especially in the economical and political spheres, will not allow it to work smoothly. Consequently in place of cheerful and willing co-operation friction occurs and a proper distribution of population is hindered. The economists whose writings are most widely read pay no attention to the fundamental laws underlying all human actions. Many of them appear not to recognize that man seeks to satisfy his desires with the least effort. Few, indeed, mention that human beings are land animals and that therefore the land question comes into all economic problems. They are busy dealing with hare-brain schemes for issuing international paper money, or something of that sort. I wrote this passage on the day King George V opened a World Economic Conference in London. Just previously a prominent economist of the day was saying that "for the Conference to occupy itself with pious resolutions concerning the abatement of tariffs, quotas, and exchange restrictions would be a waste of time." But what did he propose instead? He urged that a concrete proposal should be brought forward for the creation of an international note issue which all central banks would undertake to regard as the equivalent of gold as a basis of currency and credit. Yet there would be little likelihood of any reliance being placed on such "gold notes," when it is well known that the Governments guaranteeing them have treated solemn contracts as null and void quite recently, contracts made in clauses referring to gold payments themselves. The craze of the day is for Governments to interfere and do this and do that when all the time they do not know what is their first duty. All present-day schemes envisage CONTROL. When will freedom and home rule come again as a battle-cry to aid society out of the slough?

CHAPTER IX

WHAT GOVERNMENTS DO

"IT is evident that the number, prosperity, and power of every community must depend in all and every circumstance to a very great degree on the use which the members of the community make of the natural resources of that portion of the earth's surface which they occupy. In the case of a primitive community surrounded by other hostile communities the importance of this axiom is liable to be brought home to its members in so drastic a manner, by the enslavement or extinction of a whole tribe, for instance, that the fundamental importance of a proper use of the soil to the needs of the community is never lost sight of. In such circumstances the monopolization by individuals of areas necessary to the very existence of the tribe is a thing not to be thought of. But in the complex conditions of life which the improvement of means of transport, the spread of commerce between nations, the invention of labour-saving machinery, the creation of immense reserves of wealth have brought about among civilized nations, the fundamental connection between the prosperity of the entire community and the proper use of the soil has been very often and to a great degree lost sight of. People living in one part of the globe may depend for the real necessities of life on the work of others living in another distant part, giving in exchange for these necessities perhaps objects of luxury only. And yet both nations may be to all appearances equally prosperous. The means of acquiring wealth, principally owing to ease of transport, are so varied for both nations and individuals that the importance of a proper use of land has in point of fact become a matter of less, or at all events less urgent and immediate, importance to a civilized community. So we find most civilized communities to-day tolerating laws which permit of individuals, if they choose to do so, occupying lands in a manner unhelpful to the community. Nevertheless, it is a fact that the immense stores of reserved wealth, the immense increase of the power of man over the forces of nature due to inventions which chain those forces to his service, and the general improvement in relations between races scattered all over the globe, enabling the produce of the world to be rapidly and easily conveyed to those who can make best use of it, have not resulted in so great an improvement in the material and economic situation of the people generally as might have been expected. The poor have remained as poor, if they have not become poorer; it is only the rich who have become richer. This has led to the institution of freehold in land being questioned."[1]

The institution of freehold, of private property in land, has arisen in different ways in different countries and at different times. In England, in law and in legal terminology, all holders of land are still holders under the Crown, as witness the following authorities: "The first thing the student has to do is to get rid of the idea of absolute ownership. Such an idea is quite unknown in English law. No man is an absolute owner of his lands. He only owns an estate in them."—Williams, *Real Property*.

"All lands or tenements in England in the hands of subjects are holden, mediately or immediately, of the King. For in the law of England we have not any subject's land which is not so holden."—Coke, *Institutes*.

"It being a received and now undeniable principle in law that all lands in England are holden mediately or immediately of the King." "It is against all natural and moral law to suppose that a set of words on parchment can convey dominion of land."—Blackstone, *Commentaries*.

"I recollect it, as a law student, as one of the first lessons in the law of real property—there is no absolute property in land."—David Lloyd George.

"All laws of property must stand upon the footing of the general advantage; a country belongs to the inhabitants."—Lord Chief Justice Coleridge, *Laws of Property*.

"No absolute ownership of land is recognized by our law books except in the Crown."—Sir Frederick Pollock, *English Land Laws*.

But these views, like some other things which the lawyers handle, are in the practice of everyday affairs largely figures of

[1] C. L. Temple's *Native Races and Their Rulers*, p. 136 (Argus Publishing Co., Cape Town, 1919).

speech and a mere fiction. The institution of freehold in England may be said to have arisen by degrees from feudal times. Very briefly stated, the outline of the changes which occurred to bring this about may be set forth thus: In the days of William the Conqueror the whole of the lands of England were vested in the office of the King. He partitioned these lands among the feudal barons, and they, in turn, subinfeudated to the lords of the manors. The peasantry were some freeholders and some serfs of the manor. The occupiers, from the feudal baron in his castle right down to the peasant in his hovel, retained their holdings only so long as the various obligations, under which they were granted, towards their liege lord (ultimately the State, as represented by the office of the King) were duly filled. The principal of these obligations on the part of the freeholder was that he should be ready to follow his chief to war, and, on the part of the serf, that he should labour on the lands of his chief. Gradually compulsory labour was abolished, the serf of the manor commuting his obligation towards the lord of the manor for a monetary payment, and, as the freeholder of the manor became no longer liable for military service, these two classes became landowners in the modern sense of the term, the first acquiring the title of copy-holder and the second that of a holder in fee-simple. The feudal barons and lords of the manors, losing their grip on the areas occupied by their dependents, carved for themselves estates from the common lands.

The excuses which give colour to the institution of freehold in land, to the private appropriation of pieces of land and subsequently of its rental value, are plausible. They are all primarily dependent upon a confusion between actual possession and ownership, and between that value which comes to be attached to a piece of the earth which has been produced by a man's labour, a so-called "improvement" of some sort or other, and the value which is purely a community-created one. Because such confusions arise the security of tenure which a title under a proper system of common ownership bestows is lost sight of, especially so in the complicated society of civilized countries to-day. Land holders, instead of being content with usufruct, assert a claim to dominion. Such, in brief, are the causes of the misunderstandings and perturbations which to-day appear to put insuperable obstacles in the way of the reforms necessary to set afoot a better distribution of population.

When society developed through the stages of nomadic pastoral, pastoral-agricultural, "hoe and tree" culture, to grain culture, to orchard and dairying, to spade culture and small-holdings, and still more when shops and factories came, the necessity for marking boundaries, for developing clearer systems of property regime, for written records, and for more complicated schemes for carrying out public works became more and more obvious. Compulsory labour for community concerns was superseded by payments in kind, later by money payments. In some countries to-day such recompenses swallow up a large proportion of the products of labour. Governmental interference, entailing more and more public work, gives rise to a huge army of bureaucrats. This is one of the causes of undue concentration in cities. The great capitals have to house and build the offices for an ever-increasing number of State or municipal servants.[1] But to this subject further reference will be made in the next chapter.

At the end of the last chapter an illustration, of a fairly simple kind, was given from the "home counties," near London. If the State had been performing its first duty, i.e. collecting for the public services annually those values which are purely community created, farming operations in that neighbourhood, though of an altered kind, would have continued without upsetting anyone's purse or temper. The land would have been put to still more profitable use. House building, good motor-road making, and, if desirable, shop and public hall provision could all have proceeded smoothly side by side with modern husbandry. But instead of attending to their primary duty, what do Governments do? They multiply bureaucrats who concern themselves with industry, distribution, and with schemes of social reform. Some groups of progressive thinkers consider that the State should not interfere even with education in an advanced and civilized country. The League of Justice in Denmark (which under Proportional Representation returns three or four members to Parliament) holds the view that if the State did what it ought to do

[1] A. F. Weber's *The Growth of Cities*, p. 215 (Macmillan, New York, 1899); Dr. M. R. Maltbie's *English Local Government of To-day* (Columbia University Studies).

and did not do that which it so often undertakes nowadays, poverty would disappear and everyone would wish to see to the education of their own children according to their own ideas. Behind most of the actions of our "servants" and "ministers" are arrayed a whole host of vested interests. Their manœuvres and manipulations generally play into the hands of privileged classes, who batten on the masses through monopolies. These, such as the banking, chemical, brewing, tobacco, and other combines and cartels, are all at bottom reared on land monopoly and taxation. Their leaders and employees and their followers nearly all hoodwink themselves into believing they act in the best public interests. Just as the outlook on moral questions varies from age to age, so too views about corruption alter. The behaviour of persons in high public positions in the days of Queen Elizabeth, "lining their own nests" by pieces of gross flattery and bribery, and thereby acquiring "grants" of land and other "privileges," is to-day looked askance at. But who shall say what comments may not be passed upon the actions of some of the present-day "big wigs" of commerce and politics when our great-great-grandchildren are living! May not they, too, become classed as clever thieves? Even the League of Nations has been called bad names by one writer,[1] who says:

"The basis of Peace is Justice, and no nation that has not annexed its own country, thus becoming a Sovereign People, may hope to find peace. So soon as a nation respects its own rights it begins to respect the rights of others. . . . First there must be a reign of Justice, which will bring about a profusion of Goods. Then will follow a reign of Benevolence.

"Landless nations, oppressed with an increasing burden of Ills, are filled with envy, hatred, and malice. Each is jealous of the other and possesses a consuming desire to dominate neighbours. Leagues of such nations inevitably become leagues of pickpockets, liars, bandits, and cut-throats."

By their actions to-day Governments upset natural movements of people; they interfere with the growth and distribution of population. Supermen herd themselves into offices to govern the

[1] John E. Grant's *The Problem of War and Its Solution*, p. 381 (Allen & Unwin, 1922).

masses, and to battle with the social ills arising from poverty. Interferences meant to help trade tend to foster it along artificial channels. Both actions give a wrong impetus, directly or indirectly, to the way population becomes distributed. New methods of food production on intensive or extensive lines cannot develop naturally and be utilized side by side with other uses of land. To revert to grain production again: the importation of this is often hampered just where it is most essential to let it come in freely.

Wheat production and grain exporting and importing have been, and are being, upset through the interferences of Governments almost more than the production and movements of most other commodities. This is well illustrated by contrasting the difference in prices of wheat for the years 1927–32 between those ruling in the countries of the exporters and those ruling in the protected markets on the Continent of Europe, and by brief reference to the actions of the Canadian wheat pools and the United States Farm Relief Board. This cannot be better done than by quoting a letter from Mr. F. W. G. Urquhart (of Liverpool) to the *Manchester Guardian*.[1] It runs as follows:

"Sir, I am indebted to the International Institute of Agriculture at Rome for the following table of average prices of wheat and other cereals. Prices are expressed in gold francs per quintal, and are for the January of each year:

Year	Exporting Countries	London and Liverpool	Protected Continental Markets	Variation between the Exporting and Protected Markets
		WHEAT		Per Cent
1927	26·96	31·09	36·05	33
1932	10·27	11·14	30·21	194
1933	9·22	9·74	24·84	169
		OATS		
1927	16·75	18·46	22·13	32
1932	7·91	8·7	18·92	139
1933	6·07	7·27	15·15	149
		MAIZE		
1927	13·19	17·28	20·52	52
1932	6·12	6·89	16·69	172
1933	5·33	7·53	15·36	188

[1] June 23, 1933.

"There is no doubt that the immediate causes of the world surplus of wheat are, first, the obstructions which have been put in the way of international trade, chiefly by Continental countries, with their high tariff barriers, quotas, and even prohibitions of imports; and secondly, the mistaken policy of those who administer the Canadian wheat pools and the United States Farm Relief Board.

"The pools in Canada, after the bumper crop in 1928, would sell only at their own prices, advised, most unfortunately, by economists and politicians. Their debts became, first, a burden on the Canadian banks: then on the provincial governments; and lastly on the Government of Canada, who carry that embarrassment to this day. The Farm Relief Board was a political conception which, far from relieving the United States farmers, depressed the international price of wheat and led directly to the farm crisis in the United States.

"If the wheat problem is to be solved, potential buyers of wheat grown in the United States, Canada, Australia, and Argentina must see that the tariff barriers are removed, and exporting countries must be prepared to take freely, in exchange for their produce, the goods and services offered by the importing countries. No manipulation of markets by politicians or economists can solve the problem in any permanent way."

Agricultural development in thickly populated countries, as things have been up to the present, requires as a prerequisite for success cheap foreign grain stuffs. The history of agriculture in Denmark demonstrates this most clearly. Before she developed her more intensive forms of food production she was a "protected" country actually exporting grain. But she soon became an importing nation of grain stuffs and opened her ports freely to them. On this subject Jacob Lange's little book is worth studying;[1] and H. Westergaard's;[2] also an article by Harold Faber.[3] Mr. Faber's article gives interesting comparisons between Danish, British, and German agricultural production. In 1870 Denmark exported 38,000,000 kilograms of grain; in 1882

[1] Jacob Lange's *A Danish View of British Farming* (John Lane, 1928, 1s.).
[2] *Economic Developments in Denmark* (Humphrey Milford, 1922).
[3] "Agricultural Production in Denmark," *Journal of Royal Statistical Society*, Vol. LXXXVII, No. 1, January 1924.

none. In 1902 she imported 50,000,000 kilograms. In 1868 her exports of butter were 5,000,000 kilograms; in 1902 they amounted to 70,000,000. In 1871 the area Denmark had under fodder plants was 5,000 to 6,000 hectares (a hectare equals about 2½ acres); in 1881 it was thrice this. In 1901 it was 142,000 hectares; and since then it has more than doubled. Similar figures indicate the remarkable progress in hog production in Denmark. Some farmers in England seem to think the progress of Danish farming has been largely due to Government help, but this is not correct. The Danish farmers organized creameries, bacon factories, and the egg trade themselves long before the Government gave them any aid; and in every case they made their own regulations for standards and quality, which in due course were adopted by the State. Furthermore, State aid is confined to technical matters; subsidies are unknown in Denmark. The Danes have shown a capacity for voluntary organization, self-help, and co-operation mainly due to good education, which includes their admirable system of adult education obtained in their Folk High Schools. These give them a wide range of interests and broad outlook. Hence, among other things, not only their co-operative organizations and good farming, but also their saner views on land tenure and taxation systems.

The Paris correspondent of the *Manchester Guardian* relates in its issue of August 8, 1933, how badly recent legislation regarding wheat was working in France. He referred to the absurd arrangement under which 150,000 quintals of French-grown wheat had just been sold for export at the world price of 45 francs per quintal. The exporters of wheat were entitled to a Government premium of 80 francs per quintal—an amount which in the last resort will be paid by the French taxpayer. The foreign consumer was consequently able to buy French wheat at about one-third the price payable by the home consumer. The minimum legal price was fixed in July 1933 at 115 francs per quintal, yet as soon as the good harvest was gathered, not many weeks later, farmers were found quite prepared to sell at a lower price, while wholesalers considered 115 francs too high. Bad laws generally lead to their being disregarded or evaded; so it happened that "adjustments" were made by traders, and the law could not be enforced. Some wholesalers bought the wheat at the official price, but obtained compensation by buying some of the other produce of the farmer at an exceptionally low price. Similar dodgings were not unheard of in England during 1933 to adjust and ease trading in grain stuffs. Some of the consequences of the wheat quota payments and the other kinds of interferences with freedom of production were even more undesirable and unsatisfactory for employment and the welfare of the masses in spite of the increased area under wheat which came about in the United Kingdom for 1933—1,744,000 acres as against 1,343,000 acres in 1932, an increase of 30 per cent. Except for 7 per cent of this increase it was balanced by a decrease of the acreage under barley.

Before leaving the subject of wheat production again it will be of interest to give the following table, which emanates from the Minister of Agriculture, in the House of Commons, in reply to a question early in 1931:

	Million Bushels	
	1913	1930
United Kingdom	57	40
Canada	232	396
Australia	103	215
Argentina	105	280
France	319	231
Germany	171	131*

* Reduced area.

It seems advisable, too, to add a few words about Russian wheat production. Present-day facts regarding it are hard to come by. Much of Russia's land is very suitable for wheat culture. A good deal of it was cultivated by somewhat primitive methods before the revolution. Noble efforts are being made to improve these by the Soviet Government, but without much aid from outside nations, who might help materially. So far these efforts have not been highly successful, as far as can be judged. In fact, it is questionable whether the Russians are to-day producing enough grain to feed themselves, much less to export a large quantity as heretofore. And there seems no doubt that this failure is due to the fact that the Government has not discovered how to restore the land and freedom to the people, though it came in on the cries of "abolish private property in land" and of "Peace, Land, and Bread." Also the Communists have been in too great a hurry. They have tried to hasten the conversion of an almost purely agricultural nation into one which is to become a big industrial one, but at such a pace as to make friction along the paths of natural development, instead of taking things a little more sedately. In this they have all too frequently been egged on by the foolish action of foreign politicians in a disregard of the spirit of co-operation between peoples of different nations. These persons have not curbed Russian enthusiasm to industrialize themselves by showing how satisfactory it often is to exchange the manufactured goods made by those having a generation or two's experience of such industries for the raw materials and foodstuffs easily produced in Russia. Instead, they have placed tariff impediments or prohibiting embargoes in the way of such natural trade.

The distribution of population cannot proceed along natural channels when freedom to produce and exchange commodities is hampered by artificial procedures. This can be illustrated by reference to the shipping industry. In 1933 less than half the available shipping of the world was being employed. The world's carrying capacity on the sea is 75 per cent greater than it was in 1913. Or, according to Lord Essendon's address in London at the end of July 1933, before the shareholders of Furness, Withy & Co., the world's steam and motor tonnage had increased from 43,000,000 to 66,000,000 tons during the period 1913 to 1933. That is slightly more than 50 per cent; or, if swifter ships and better handling facilities be taken into account, the effective increase might be counted as 70 per cent. During the same twenty years he estimated that world trade was only half what it was in 1913. At a preliminary sitting held by the Preparatory Committee of Experts before a recent World Economic Conference, it was declared to be "impossible to return to sound conditions in the shipping industry so long as the uneconomic policy of Government subsidies continue. This policy of excessive intervention requires to be checked by agreement between governments." The United States Treasury spent on ship construction and operations £745,000,000 from 1916 to the middle of 1931. France, Germany, Italy, and Japan have all spent lavishly, and even Holland and Great Britain have given some slight measures of artificial assistance. How far were the taxpayers of the United States of America consulted in these governmental expenditures? Are they fully alive to what they have done? Do they consider they have got their money's worth? How many of them benefited? These are interesting questions. At all events, they paid up meekly.

At the beginning of this century the United Kingdom owned half the shipping of the world, which stood at 24,000,000 tons and is to-day 66,500,000 tons. To-day the percentage is only 28. The following table comes from the Register Book, issued by the Committee of Lloyd's Register of Shipping:

PERCENTAGE OF STEAM AND MOTOR TONNAGE OWNED IN THE WORLD

	1901	1914	1934
Great Britain and Ireland	50·2	41·6	27·4
United States (Sea)	4·2	4·5	15·2
Japan	2·2	3·8	6·3
Norway	3·4	4·3	6·2
Germany	10·1	11·3	5·7
France	4·4	4·2	5·1
Italy	2·7	3·1	4·5
Holland	2·1	3·2	4·1

The 1934 figures are virtually the same as those for 1933.

The foolish systems of tariffs, subsidies, and taxation in connection with shipping have upset the natural distribution of shipbuilding workers, and of others connected with the shipping industry. These things go far to explain the descent of Britain's pre-eminent position due, no doubt, to her superior capabilities in production in this industry.

Other actions of Governments which upset things are the outcome of so-called Peace Treaties. For example, in 1919 Lloyd George gave his consent, which meant also the consent of the English Government of that day, for certain of the French to receive an annual amount of many millions of tons of coal from territory previously ruled over by Germans, which quantity was more than they wanted for their own and their fellow-countrymen's use. The miners extracting the coal were to work long hours and nearly all the week. But they got fairly well paid and did not mind much. Britain's export trade of coal to France began to dwindle, however; and it was not only to France. The French sold some of the coal to Belgians, Dutchmen, Italians, etc., previously good customers of the British, who carried it in their own ships. To interfere further with commerce and shipping it was arranged to sell German merchant ships to English and Continental shipowners at knock-out prices. That struck a further blow at British shipping and its subsidiary industries. In a vain attempt to right matters the Government again interferes in connection with coal by subsidizing the making of petrol out of coal. Though the process achieves many admirable objects, the result seems likely, once more, to advantage the few to the detriment of the many. That is the common result of these actions, whether or not founded upon the idea of "war reparations." It is at length dawning upon people, even upon the politicians, that "war debts necessitate unnatural transfers which provoke widespread economic evil," to quote from the British Note to Washington of December 1, 1932. Some of the economists of the eighteenth and nineteenth centuries were able to demonstrate the same thing a generation or two ago. When will it dawn upon people that nearly all these governmental actions provoke widespread economic evil?

But how can freedom be established? As heretofore, by the spread of knowledge and by vigilance. Those desiring freedom are not kept in thrall by Governments or dictators. It is lack of enlightenment, it is ignorance, too often due to harassing poverty and lack of opportunity for getting to know, which is responsible for slavery in any form. Until the captives learn that the door opens inwards and is unlocked they will continue to use force to push it outwards. At present Governments too often represent the reaction which results from the employment of wrongful means to obtain liberty. But might and power endure for a brief season. Nature ordains that the inherent desire for freedom increases at a greater rate than the building up of any restraint invented by man. People will awake; are, in fact, awakening. Perpetual financial crises, ever-recurring conferences of "economists" and "statesmen," while poverty in this world of progress persists, are making people think. Perennial unemployment, with a plenitude of natural resources staring everyone in the face, is leading the minds of the multitude back to the land question, which is of more moment to city than rural dwellers. True economic freedom brings about beneficial alterations in the way in which populations grow and are distributed.

The tendency of the present age is to look to Governments too much. Politicians try to do too much, and incidentally usually get swelled heads! Their doings actually affect the distribution of population far more than most people imagine. There is a spontaneous and unconscious co-operation which is always going on amongst neighbours and amongst the peoples of different nations; and there is a conscious and directed co-operation. As a matter of fact, the former is far wider, far finer, far more strongly and delicately organized than the latter—as anyone can assure himself by a little thought. Generally the best thing that actual Governments can do is to leave conscious direction out. They can so easily hinder when they are trying to help co-operative growth and combination in the action of individuals. When Governments perform their true functions, when they look after their own domain, when they collect their own revenues—then a healthy combination between actions of individuals striving after their own desires will coincide with the interests of the community: then society will not be based on theft, that theft which, on the one hand, confiscates for the State much that is a man's own, the products of his own labour, and, on the other hand, appropriates for the individual purely community ground values.

One of the ways in which Governments can and do help to-day is in the means of communication and transport. The collection of dues and fares for traffic upon the public highways (road and rail), especially in regions where population is dense, is sometimes a very easy way of collecting the public's revenue. Due consideration must be given to those who help in the traffic by providing the vehicles, the rails, and by driving the vehicles, directing the traffic, or collecting the fares. Exactly how to apportion the charges and the dues earned is apt to be a perpetual difficulty, and indeed the problems connected with it are often very thorny. In recent times, perhaps, private interests have been inclined to get too much and the public's purse too little. Eternal vigilance should be kept on the somewhat subtle ways of diverting the public's revenue into private pockets. Indirect methods of achieving this private appropriation of public revenue are over-indulgence in the financial support that Governments give to transport. This may be done by "trade facilities Acts" and "development Acts." Public convenience is often met in these transport concerns by creation of a monopoly. Unfettered competition between different warring organizations in transport concerns is generally senseless and costly. As that greatest of all authorities in such matters, Lord Ashfield, said at a recent meeting in the House of Lords when the London Passenger Transport Bill (now an Act) was under consideration: "It was only by complete fusion of all the interests concerned in the London area, by the establishment of common management which would have a common policy directed towards proper orderly development of this great system of transport, that it would be found possible to provide the facilities which the public wanted. . . . The Bill had his complete approval." This London Passenger Transport Act has brought about a unification of the London passenger traffic: main railway lines, tubes, trams, omnibuses, and coaches. The unification required negotiation with the numerous interests concerned, and the steerage of the Bill through the Houses of Commons and Lords, including a strenuous thirty-five days' sitting of the Joint Select Committee of Lords and Commons. Its passage was a triumph for the Minister in charge, Mr. Herbert Morrison. Its importance here is the connection it has with the distribution of population and with the knotty traffic problems connected therewith. The method of unification has been the formation of a complete monopoly of traffic under a public corporation. It is along much the same lines as those of the British Broadcasting Corporation and the Central Electricity Board, though the former involves much less capital and the formation of the latter enabled a more extensive preliminary "lining of nests" of private individuals than is the case with the London Transport monopoly. Since it may be taken as a precedent and as an example for the future of what Governments may do, and since it is so definitely concerned with the distribution of population, no excuse is needed for devoting a little study to it here. It must not be taken as a universal panacea for the ills of industry. The capital of this great corporation is to be held by private individuals; but the return on it is to be limited to a maximum but not guaranteed percentage. The whole organization is to be controlled by an independent board of the most competent persons available, whose aim must be to give the best service at the lowest fares consistent with earning the agreed return on the capital. One qualification for a directorship is that he shall hold no shares whatever. Herbert Morrison, who piloted the Bill through Parliament, met with considerable opposition from Conservatives because they considered it was Socialism, and from his own political friends, the Labour Party, because they condemned it as *not* Socialism! The points to emphasize, the alternatives possible, are summed up by saying that this corporation is not public ownership in the old sense; it is not under the direct administration of Parliament; and it is not Syndicalism. A stiff fight, in fact, with some of the Labour Party occurred over the last point, for Mr. Morrison would not give way to them when they demanded *ex officio*, so to speak, representation on the board, for the trade unions concerned with transport. He has written a book on this subject[1] in which he ably sets forth his reasons for adopting the plan of a "corporate board of ability" rather than a board of all the interests concerned, or of full-time technical experts.

This illustration of what Governments are doing is of particular importance because its chief author, Herbert Morrison, about the time when he was steering the Bill through Parliament, wrote a pamphlet in which he said: "The important essentials of Socialism are that all the great industries and the land should be publicly or collectively owned and that they should be conducted (in conformity with a national economic plan) for the common good instead of for private profit." Note the three words in this sentence, "and the land," showing that its author does not realize that land is in an entirely different category from the rest of the things he is dealing with—a sad state of mind, and one which is, unfortunately, not uncommon. Note also its author's designs on "all the great industries." This great precedent is almost more important than that of the Marxians in Russia. They have been trying to mould a nation of 160,000,000 into the mould of preconceived theories, but have found themselves beset with difficulties. On the other hand, this great piece of constructive planning is so far wonderfully successful because it is

[1] Herbert Morrison's *Socialization and Transport* (Constable & Co., London, 1933. 7s. 6d.).

along lines which follow those things appertaining to the real duty of Governments. It is perhaps more in accord with Nature's ordinances. These rule in the sphere of government, as in other spheres, and when that is better apprehended Governments will be found attending to their natural duties and leaving alone those unnatural ones which tend to interfere with the growth and development of populations.

Before leaving the subject of London Passenger Transport it is worth making two further observations, viz.: (i) The number of persons, with their dependents, who dwell in London for the purpose of moving people about London is more than equal to the number who inhabit Norwich, which has a population of 120,000, and the former is growing faster than the latter. (ii) Lord Ashfield, than whom no one knows better, has repeatedly emphasized how frequently and to what a great extent the landowners, especially of suburban land, newly opened up by fresh railway facilities, reap where they have not sown.

The shares that the varied interests should take in city transport concerns are generally very difficult to compose. They are apt to be greater than in other public undertakings just because it is rather more difficult to disentangle the ground value rent element in their earnings. The community's rents for sites do come in in some of the other undertakings, of course. But with many of these it is best to let the takings simply pay the expenses of management. It is generally a good principle for those who use these services to pay for them directly and not through rates and taxes.

One of the places where squabbles between various interests have been going on for many years is that great city, Buenos Aires. This has grown more rapidly than any other city has ever grown in the whole history of the world. It now possesses a population of 2,300,000, whereas only as recently as 1891 its population was only 1,000,00. The struggle to compose the conflicting interests in Buenos Aires has been a long and keen one. Even to-day all sides are not satisfied.

Almost no use of the at present much beloved word "planning" is made in the preceding paragraph or elsewhere in this book. It is well for industry to be so planned as to avoid wasteful competition. But the craze for advocating planning, for "technocracy," for "rationalization," is too often an endeavour to make it possible for combines and cartels to act smoothly, and these all too frequently are against the public interests, being chiefly concerned in profit making through monopolistic heightening of prices. What a lot of false virtue there is in the invention of a new word! By the time this book is a year or two old a fresh crop of jargon will probably have come into vogue.

Governments not only interfere directly with production and exchange through all kinds of taxes, restrictions, quotas, and regulations, but they also—it is a natural consequence—become increasingly bloated by having departments which actually plan and manage trading concerns, organizations which, unlike transport, have little or nothing to do with land values and therefore with the true function of government. Such actions have grown in most countries during this century, and they have increased regardless of the particular party in office. Even parties carrying the label Liberal vie with reactionaries and Socialists in restricting liberty and multiplying officials. The modern tendency towards dictatorships is thus fostered. People become more and more used to interference and regulations. They are taught to look more and more to governmental actions to save them from the results of too much government. They become dispirited and disappointed because the paternalism which is so common does so little to alleviate their state. Radical remedies are not allowed by Press and politicians, with all the vested interests behind them, to receive a hearing. Their support consequently is apt to lose ground.

In England the milk trade—to take an illustration—is in the hands of a Government Milk Marketing Board. Many dairy farmers are pressing the Board to go into the distributing trade. This is largely because the producers feel they are not receiving their deserts because the Board is too much under the thumb of the big distributing combines. A show is made of attention to hygiene by all concerned. But the march of progress to the universal production of liquid milk which is not only safe to the health of the drinkers but of essentially high quality is not really quickened materially by the combination of circumstances arising from the existence of the Board. The commercial interests, especially of the big companies capable of wielding a great deal of power, are usually quietly pulling the strings. All the time the interests of the consumer come off second best, and hardly anyone envisages the possibility of the heightening of remuneration to producers through a bigger consumption by the masses, who should be lifted out of poverty into prosperity. That happy state of affairs can only be brought about by attacking the root causes of poverty, namely taxes and private property in land. When Governments attend to their first duty and collect the public's own revenue, then, and only then, will all this Socialism be found to be unnecessary. But the change will be resisted by none so strenuously as by the present batch of politicians and their many friends in various official posts. These instinctively adhere to preaching more and more government, and hotly oppose Radical reform, though sometimes giving it lip service to placate those who are asking for it.

CHAPTER X

THE GROWTH OF CITIES

POPULATION originally began to agglomerate where sites were suitable for co-operation and when numbers and knowledge led to specialization in the work of human individuals. The meeting of clans occurred for the interchange of commodities and of ideas, and for religious ceremonies and governmental actions. Suitable sites were at the nodal points of all-weather tracts between nuclei, or at landing places beside fordable stretches of a river. Avebury was undoubtedly one of the former points in the Neolithic and the Bronze Ages. London arose because its site was one of the places lowest down on the River Thames where a crossing could be most readily made. Such sites owe their value to natural advantages found useful to the advancing needs of an increasing population. Their value is not due to anything some particular individual does. The commonest feature of these favourable situations is greater ease of communication or, in a word, accessibility. Where areas of good accessibility are, there cities arose. It is well to remember in this connection that neither steam nor machinery was used by the ancient Egyptians, Medes, Phoenicians, Greeks, or Romans, who nevertheless built great cities. Three good illustrations of the effect of accessibility on the growth and distribution of the population are: (1) The town of Calcutta, which arose in comparatively recent times chiefly through the advantage of its position. It was originally a collection of villages of comparatively modern foundation. These villages were situated on the fertile alluvial deltas of great rivers and were originally associated largely with the agricultural processes which were conducted in the neighbourhood. But as soon as difficulties of the shifting sands, etc., were circumvented and population, human skill, and knowledge advanced, the position of these villages was found to be more advantageous for commerce in connection with the network of great waterways of the Hoogli and the systems of canals leading to the Ganges and the Brahmaputra. (2) The French Riviera. There was a sudden change in the distribution of the population and a rapid increase in number shortly after the roads and railways were opened along the coast in 1890. Fishing villages grew into large coast towns and new industries flourished. Old towns waxed as they had not done for centuries. (3) Glasgow grew rapidly, especially last century, through the natural advantages of her position for commerce; firstly, as a port; secondly, as a manufacturing centre because it has a climate peculiarly favourable to the textile industry, like Manchester; and thirdly, because it is situated in the midst of a great coal and iron district like Birmingham. The town of Glasgow, with the adjoining thickly populated county of Lanarkshire, containing coal and iron, contains one-third of the population of Scotland.

The world has two cities with over 5,000,000 inhabitants, London and New York; three with over 3,000,000, Berlin, Moscow, and Chicago (not counting the 4,000,000 in close proximity to Chicago). There are five cities with 2,000,000 to 3,000,000 inhabitants: namely, Paris, Shanghai, Canton, Buenos Aires, Osaka, in order of magnitude Paris the largest. There are seven cities with a population of between 1,500,000 to 2,000,000. Between 700,000 and 1,000,000, twenty-one cities exist.

It is somewhat difficult to arrive at perfectly accurate estimates of the number of inhabitants in the ancient cities of bygone ages. But these matters have been carefully investigated and the following approximations, largely based on information obtained from the pages of A. F. Weber's book,[1] are probably fairly near the truth:

	Persons
Athens, about 300 B.C., exceeded	100,000
Syracuse, about 300 B.C., exceeded	100,000
Carthage probably reached	500,000
Alexandria, early A.D., probably reached ..	500,000
possibly	700,000
Rome, about A.D. 200, probably reached	600,000–800,000

After Rome's decay, Constantinople was the only European city exceeding 100,000 inhabitants. But in the Middle Ages it was overshadowed by Bagdad and rivalled by Damascus and Cairo. The modern period was well begun (A.D. 1600) before Paris wrested the first place from Constantinople, only to be overtaken by London before the end of the seventeenth century. Until the

[1] *The Growth of Cities* (Macmillan, New York, 1899).

end of the seventeenth century, when Paris and London grew to the half-million size, in all probability in the whole history of the world only twice before was the 500,000 figure reached, and that was by Rome and Alexandria. And let it be noted that Rome, when big and in her glory, did not exchange products of her own make for the food she required; she simply stole her foodstuffs for the most part. At the beginning of the sixteenth century Europe had six or seven cities with over 100,000 inhabitants, and at its end thirteen or fourteen. This century was the period of commercial expansion and New World conquests. The increase of city dwellers in Europe in the second half of the nineteenth century is calculated to have been as follows:

Year	Number of Cities of 100,000 or more	Aggregate Population	Ratio to Total Population
1850	42	9,000,000	3·80
1870	70	20,000,000	6·66
1895	120	37,000,000	10·00

A. F. Weber gives an interesting table showing the percentage of population dwelling in cities of 10,000[1] inhabitants and upwards in various countries in 1800, in 1850, and in 1890, or the nearest census year. Bringing this up to date, it is as follows:

	1800	1850	1890	1926–31
England and Wales ..	22·2	39	62	73
Scotland	17	33	49	59
Belgium	14	21	35	42*
Netherlands	29	28	39	64
U.S.A.	4	12	27·5	48
France	4·5	14·5	26	38
Denmark	11	9	24	37
Ireland	8	10	18	{ 22† { 43‡
Norway	3·5	6	17	23
Switzerland	4	7	17	30
Russia	4	6	9	—

* 1920. † Irish Free State. ‡ Northern Ireland.

The next table gives the actual numbers of persons living in cities of 10,000 inhabitants and upwards in the above countries:

[1] *The Growth of Cities*, p. 151.

PERCENTAGE OF POPULATION DWELLING IN CITIES OF 10,000 INHABITANTS AND UPWARDS

Country	Census Population			Year
	Total	Number in Cities of 10,000 and up	Percentage	
England and Wales	39,947,931	29,225,870	73	1931
Belgium	7,402,276	3,133,243	42	1920
Netherlands	7,935,565	5,044,060	64	1930
U.S.A.	122,775,046	58,340,077	48	1930
France	41,834,923	16,133,590	38	1931
Denmark	3,550,656	1,309,260	37	1930
Irish Free State	2,973,000	649,000	22	1926
Northern Ireland	1,256,322	544,555	43	1926
Norway	2,814,194	653,422	23	1930
Switzerland	4,066,400	1,237,776	30	1930

A. F. Weber also gives a table (Table XVII) for England and Wales showing how the population in towns, small or otherwise, were distributed according to the size of the town in three years, 1801, 1851, and 1891 respectively. In 1891 there were in England and Wales 817 "urban sanitary districts" with populations of over 3,000 and 194 with under 3,000 inhabitants. Only 1·3 per cent of the population dwelt in the latter. The aggregate population of the two together constituted 71·7 per cent of the entire population of England and Wales. Weber's Table XVII[1] is as follows:

ENGLAND AND WALES

Classes of Cities	1801		1851		1891	
	No.	Population	No.	Population	No.	Population
Over 20,000	15	1,506,176	63	6,265,011	185	15,563,834
10,000–20,000	31	389,624	60	800,000	175	2,362,376
5,000–10,000	60	418,715	140	963,000	262	1,837,054
Total 5,000 and over	106	2,314,515	263	8,028,011	622	19,763,264
Total under 5,000	—	6,578,021	—	9,899,598	—	9,239,261
Grand Total	—	8,892,536	—	17,927,609	—	29,002,525

[1] *The Growth of Cities*, pp. 42 and 43.

SCOTLAND

TYNE MOUTH
NEWCASTLE
GATESHEAD   SOUTH SHIELDS
              SUNDERLAND
CARLISLE   WEST HARTLEPOOL
STOCKTON   MIDDLESBOROUGH
        DARLINGTON

ISLE OF MAN

BARROW

IRISH SEA

YORK
BLACKPOOL   PRESTON BURNLEY   BRADFORD
                              LEEDS   HULL
SOUTHPORT   BLACKBURN HALIFAX WAKEFIELD
            BURY   DEWSBURY
            BOLTON ROCHDALE HUDDERSFIELD   GRIMSBY
BOOTLE   BARNSLEY
WALLASEY   SALFORD MANCHESTER DONCASTER
BIRKENHEAD WARRINGTON   ROTHERHAM
ANGLESEY   LIVERPOOL   SHEFFIELD   LINCOLN
                    CHESTERFIELD
            STOKE   NOTTINGHAM
                      DERBY

                                        NORWICH
                                        YARMOUTH
                    WALSALL   LEICESTER
WOLVERHAMPTON   WEST BROMWICH
      DUDLEY   BIRMINGHAM
      SMETHWICK   COVENTRY
                              CAMBRIDGE
              NORTHAMPTON   IPSWICH

                              LUTON
        GLOUCESTER

METHYR   OXFORD
SWANSEA   LONDON   SOUTHEND
NEWPORT   BRISTOL   SWINDON
CARDIFF   BATH READING   CROYDON   GILLINGHAM
BRISTOL
CHANNEL

                    SOUTHAMPTON
                    PORTSMOUTH   BRIGHTON   HASTINGS
EXETER   BOURNEMOUTH   EASTBOURNE

PLYMOUTH

FRANCE

POPULATION MAP OF ENGLAND AND WALES

The crossed line area starting from Yarmouth to Bristol indicates the area of greatest population in pre-industrial England. Dotted areas = principal industrial regions. Large black dots = towns of over 50,000 population.

In connection with the accompanying population map of England and Wales let it be noted that the population within a radius of 100 miles of Manchester is:

A. Nearly half the population of the British Isles.
B. Over three times the population of Australia.
C. More than the combined populations of Canada and the Union of South Africa.
D. Over fifteen times the population of New Zealand.
E. Equal to the total white population of the British Empire outside the British Isles.
F. Nearly one-fifth of the population of the United States of America.

In the ninety years between 1801 and 1891 over 20,000,000 people were added to the population of England and Wales; but while the rural inhabitants (those dwelling in places of less than 5,000) increased from 6,600,000 to 9,200,000, the town dwellers increased from 2,300,000 to 19,800,000. That is, of the total increase of 20,000,000, about 17,400,000, or 80 per cent, fell to the towns and cities. It is, moreover, noticeable that the increase of the rural population took place entirely in the first half of the century, and later turned into an actual decrease. Some 800,000 more people are classed as belonging to the *rural population* in 1851 than in 1891.

The figures for cities in England and Wales to-day are as follows:

ENGLAND AND WALES

(Census, 1931)

Classes of Cities	No.	Population
Over 20,000　　..　　..　　..	296	25,898,470
10,000 and under 20,000　　..	233	3,327,400
5,000 and under 10,000　　..	232	1,658,065
Total 5,000 and over ..　　..	761	30,883,935
Total under 5,000　　..　　..	—	9,063,996
Grand Total　　..　　..		39,947,931

England and Wales, taken as one nation, in 1801 possessed forty-five towns of 10,000 or more inhabitants. In 1377 she contained about one-fourth of the population of 1801 and in that year possessed only two cities with over 10,000 inhabitants: London, with almost 35,000 inhabitants, and York, with about 11,000. Defining urban populations as those dwelling in towns of 10,000 or upwards, in 1881 England and Wales had 50 per cent of her population in urban districts (that is, about the same as the United States of America to-day), and 72 per cent in 1891.

A. F. Weber, on page 468 of *The Growth of Cities*, gives the areas, total population, and the density of various cities in Europe and America about 1899, and shows how much greater the density is in Europe than in America. The "Population" Volume (I) of the fifteenth census of the United States, 1930, gives the area and population of the various counties and cities. Thus on page 128, Los Angeles (county) is given as having an area of 4,115 square miles with a population of 2,208,492, or 536·7 per square mile; and (on page 131) San Francisco (city) an area of 42 square miles and a population of 634,394, which equals 15,104·6 per square mile. On page 14 of the "Summary" Volume of this Census it is noted that the percentage of the total population dwelling in cities of over a quarter of a million increased from 11 to 23·5 per cent between 1890 and 1930. From the same census returns such facts as the following can be discovered: the population in Chicago City has a density of 16,723 persons per square mile, yet the percentage of increase of population from 1920 to 1930 was only 25 per cent there compared with 73 per cent in the districts just outside the city (the density of which in 1930 was 1,077 persons per square mile).

The tendency for the centre of great cities to lose inhabitants who actually dwell there is a phenomenon of modern times. Central areas are found to be more profitably used for shops, offices, warehouses, etc. For example, the Strand attained its maximum population last century as early as 1821, and after that lost inhabitants regularly, except during 1831–41, and London City, the business centre with its banks, Stock Exchange, etc., reached its maximum population in 1851, though the inhabitants of that year scarcely exceeded in number those of 1801. In 1801 it was, after Westminster with a density of 213·42 to the acre, the densest district in the Metropolis, with a density of 192·86 to the acre. By the beginning of the last quarter of the nineteenth century the densely populated areas of London had moved further east. The growth of suburbs all around most modern towns has not brought the happy solution of density and housing problems at one time expected. It has certainly not brought about that ideal of population distribution which Charles Kingsley put forward in the middle of last century, namely, "a complete interpenetration of city and country, a complete fusion of their different modes of life."[1] The ever-increasing impetus to move outwards from the centre has received some check in the last few decades through the habit of building large blocks of flats and tenements. The strain of "rush hours" is having a deleterious effect on the mental and on the physical condition of huge numbers of the population of to-day. It is beginning to alarm people, who wonder how to get over its drawbacks. But these will never be overcome until the fundamental principles which underlie the distribution of population are thoroughly studied and understood.

It is fortunate for London that the ground on which she is built is not so solid as to give builders the same confidence in soaring skywards as that possessed by the builders of New York. Besides which, the latitude of London is 700 miles further north than New York, so that buildings cast longer shadows. In New York there are many buildings of 300–500 feet high, and some considerably higher, yet the width of the streets on which they border rarely exceeds 100 feet, while most of them are narrower. Although the average building height may be only about ten stories, he who visits the southernmost section of Manhattan in the most congested district on a bright summer day will observe that many offices facing the narrowest streets—not to speak of the shaft-like courts—are artificially lighted all through the day. There is one block containing a business building which contains a resident population of 12,000 persons during working hours, and it is estimated that the total number of people passing in and out of this building during a working day is 50,000. Besides business buildings there were in 1919 in Manhattan 23,000 factories, employing over 500,000 workers, many, in fact, most of them, situated in the main business centre. For example, New

[1] Charles Kingsley's *Miscellanies* (essay on "Great Cities"), Vol. II, p. 339 (Parker & Son, London, 1859).

York produces more than half the yearly output of the garment industry in the entire United States. It has been estimated that by 1965, as things are going at present, there will be in the whole area a population of about 20,000,000, and nearly half these persons will want to enter Manhattan daily.

The tendency in London in the last few years has been to gain floor space on valuable central sites by burrowing down, so that two or even three stories below the street level are becoming comparatively common. It is in such quarters that artificial light has often to be used all day and that the amenities for and the health of workers go by the board. It has even been seriously suggested in recent times that "underground shopping" should be encouraged. Underground railroads have become so usual, electric lighting so much improved, and systems of ventilation too, that such an idea seems to present no shocks to some people. But even if the practice of burrowing under ground and building higher and higher be not persisted in, clean fresh air and sunlight will be at a premium unless smoke be abated. The New York Municipal Art Society issued a striking report in 1929 on the position in that city, which is generally believed to be less severely affected by soot and smoke than are many English towns. In this report it is stated that during 1928 approximately 45 per cent of the available daylight and 100 per cent of the ultra-violet rays were excluded from the city by reason of the smoke hanging over it; and that 20 to 80 per cent of light capable of entering is constantly lost by dirty windows, even though they were washed twice a month.

The devices enabling more people to work in the busy centres of civilization send site values up and up. Supposing conditions became so impossible at the centres that there had to be an abandonment of many central sites, then these values would slump. The bare possibility of such a thing happening conjures up awful alarms in the minds of the private holders of ground rents. But if such a thing happened and ground rents were flowing into the public coffers it probably would not matter much. Some people who have given a good deal of thought to the undesirable congestion of cities have put forward excellent suggestions of one sort or another. But most of these do not go to the root of the matter. For example, the London County

Council has built a town containing about 150,000 inhabitants at Becontree "to house the working classes," 10 miles from London. Incidentally, be it noted, the London County Council paid £295,544 for this housing site, previously assessed at a "net annual value" of £3,590. Those who dwell therein are undoubtedly better housed than formerly. But this has cost money which has to be raised partly out of the rates levied in London. The ratepayers there are being burdened, and especially the inhabitants of the poorest districts. That is not a result which goes to help slum clearances. It was reported by the Unhealthy Areas Committee a few years ago that if all the districts in Greater London with a density of more than 200 persons per acre were cleared and houses built to accommodate 100 persons per 20 houses on each acre, approximately 1,000,000 persons would have to move elsewhere. A lot of people find it distinctly inconvenient to move 10 miles away from where they have been working, and a number of workers cannot under any circumstances do so; for example, dock labourers, market porters, nightworkers, and certain professional men and women. Again, many hoped to find cheaper accommodation. But it does not take long to find out that rents of buildings vary directly with rents of land and not with the cost of similar buildings elsewhere. So it came about that those who had been paying such-and-such a rent for a cottage or a tenement in a slum, who thought they would get better terms further out, actually did do so; but when they and their family came to add to the rent payment the weekly cost of fares, they found they were not really in a better position. For Becontree is not a self-contained town but very much of a dormitory for London, and though a four-roomed house (nonparlour) can be got there for about 16s. 6d. per week inclusive of rates (local taxes) and water charges, the cost of getting to London is 6d. to 1s. per journey. This is important, because many go daily to London from such places as Brighton, and even Bedford, 50 and 60 miles away respectively. Then the towns of Becontree, Brighton (population 190,000), and Bedford (42,000)—not comparable at all in most respects—develop some of the drawbacks of the larger cities; and traffic troubles are made worse.

The congestion in certain districts round London is producing many problems. This can be appreciated if the growth and distribution of population in Middlesex is studied. The population of this county has increased at a really remarkable rate in the last ten years. The county is, in fact, the most rapidly growing area of its size in the kingdom. Between 1921 and 1931 the population increased by 30·8 per cent, and this increase was greatest during the last few years of the decade. Numbers went up in the ten years by 385,726 to 1,638,728. It may be noted in passing that at the first census, taken in 1801, the population of the extra-metropolitan portion of the county was 71,411 persons. Urbanization is proceeding in Middlesex at a pace probably unequalled in any other county in Great Britain, although there is, fortunately, still an appreciable amount of milk production and market gardening being carried on. The predominantly urban character of the county is shown by the fact that there are thirty boroughs and urban districts with an aggregate population of 1,589,397 and only two rural districts with 49,331 population. The former comprise 97 per cent of the population and 90 per cent of the area of the county. The urban areas with the largest populations are Willesden, Tottenham, Ealing, and Hendon, containing 184,434, 157,772, 117,707, and 115,682 persons respectively. Hendon grew fastest, slightly more than doubling the number of its inhabitants in the ten years. 68·1 per cent (that is 11 out of every 16) of the total population of the county are persons over twenty-one years of age and all but 34,200 of these are on the electoral register. A very large number of the people who live in these residential areas travel daily to London to earn their living. The average size of the family in the county has declined from 4·05 in 1921 to 3·66 in 1931.

The growth of industries in the South of England, more especially in or not far from London, has been remarkable since the war. Amongst the causes of this growth, diminishing relatively the proportions employed in industries in other parts of Britain, may be mentioned the proximity of a great market and the facilities for exporting provided by the Port of London. Between Acton and Slough it is estimated that there were in 1929 150,000 factory workers (involving a new population of about 500,000 persons) compared with only 60,000 five years previously, and the number has increased considerably in the last four years.

LONDON: THE GROWTH OF A CENTURY

The black portion represents London one hundred years ago, and the shaded the growth since that date.

By kind permission of Mr. W. R. Davidge and the Town Planning Institute.

The contraction of the old staple trades of the North of England, cotton, wool, iron, etc., and of mining, partly accounts for relatively more growth of industry in the South; but unfortunately the workers of the North, especially women workers, are tragically immobile. Decay in the North may lead the drift of the newer industries to the South to become more accentuated, though such changes would seem to be socially bad and of doubtful economic value. It may gradually bring about a migration of young and able-bodied, leaving behind the less mobile sections of the population to be kept alive amid a society tending to decay. As usual, those who become alarmed by such possibilities at present can think of nothing but State interference, regulations, and attempts at control. But some other way, along more natural lines, should be found to adjust or prevent such possible changes in the distribution of the population. Neither talking vaguely about schemes of national planning, reconstruction, or rationalization; nor schemes for "derating" depressed areas; nor State provision of capital at low-interest rates will really help materially or get to the roots of the difficulties.

Regarding the contraction of some of the oldest staple industries of the North of England, take the woollen industry of Yorkshire for example. What are the influences which have been at work tending to the relative decline of this? It is true to say that peoples in other countries are learning to manufacture cloth; it is true that England and Scotland cannot be expected to manufacture cloth for the whole world; and that the use of cotton, silk, and artificial silk, especially the latter, has increased very much in recent years. But who shall say that the Yorkshireman can be excelled in his ability for producing the best and most durable stuffs in woollen materials, or that woollen cloths are being superseded for clothing to any great extent? No, it is not correct to answer either of these questions in the affirmative. It is what Governments have done (and so far as their first duty is concerned, omitted to do) that has interfered with the natural development of industries here and there, and hindered the natural way in which population would have become distributed. Where can the wool of sheep be most efficiently and cheaply produced? On the South Downs of England and the plains about the South Coast of Kent and Sussex, and in Australia. But instead of encouraging the free production and exchange of wool from Australians, Governments have put tariff barriers up and have passed legislation to encourage the congregation of people in cities engaged in the so-called "back-yard" industries. The scandals connected with these are notorious, though the newspapers —naturally enough—are not overflowing with accounts of them. Instead of collecting the dues from site holders of the public domain, levies to equalize people's opportunities, levies collecting the public's true and only revenue, Governments have imposed taxes on the products of an individual's labour which have burdened production and hampered commerce. Instead of spending the true income of the Commonwealth for enhancing the commonweal by developing helpful irrigation schemes and encouraging a useful influx of population where it could best be performing useful functions in some of the primary industries, they have spent public funds in building railways in advance of population and thereby lining the pockets of a few fortunate individuals who have been able to lay claim to land in the vicinity of the railroads.

Again, the Commonwealth Government has spent, some would say wasted, large sums on a big-scale Socialistic experiment in shipping. This has not contributed to freedom in the overseas carrying trade and has probably interfered with commerce and the distribution of population to a greater extent than at first meets the eye. It is not easy to tell when the extra cost of production which must be added to commodities carried long distances outbalances the cost of production nearer home unless true freedom reigns. When will this happen? Who can tell! In connection with this matter of State shipping, undoubtedly some heavy losses were incurred by the Federal Government of Australia. But it is a principle that when financial losses of this sort occur it is common for some people to gain financial advantage. A craze for gambling which is so rife to-day is primarily due to the poverty of many. The obverse of the coin which has the fear of poverty on one side of it is the greed of the rich. When a few people get something for nothing (or next to nothing), many people lose something for which they get no return (other than a pathological excitement). It would be interesting to find out, if it were possible, who were the few who —almost for certain—made some handsome profits out of the deal when the Australian Government entered and abandoned the shipping trade. Given the right actions of Governments and not constant wrong actions, that is given freedom, Australia might gain the population she wants for her development. Furthermore, the complaint that this population is congregated too much in the towns (about 73 per cent of it is in the seven capital cities of Australia) would probably not arise. It has been estimated that the population of Australia instead of being about 10,000,000 could easily be at least five times this number. Yet some say the world is over-populated!

In the past, industries have appeared to develop in a rather haphazard way. To ordain how they shall develop in the future, to zone their location, is not a sure guarantee of improvement. To know why and how they have sprung up and how to influence the causes affecting their disposition are necessary to better planning. It is not sufficient, for example, to assert: things will be less centralized if greater use is made of electricity. A thorough knowledge of things as they are is a prerequisite to progress. In that direction much good work has been done by such bodies as the Committee for the Regional Planning of New York. Numbers 5 and 6 Monographs of this Committee deal with an Economic Industrial Survey of the Tobacco Products and the Printing Industries. They are excellent illustrations of useful surveys. The maps in these monographs divide the region into three zones, namely: (1) Manhattan, south of 59th Street, the most congested and over-centralized portion; (2) the 25-mile industrial area; and (3) the outlying region. The printing industry is concentrated in the first zone. The tobacco industry is in both the first and the second zones, a larger and a gradually increasing portion of it in the latter. If New York people are wise they will effect in time a grand redistribution of some of these centralized industries. But with the best will in the world, and with an abundance of knowledge and wisdom, these redistributions are generally by no means easy. Take, for example, a friend of the present writer at the head of a large pipe manufacturing industry. When asked why he did not transplant his factories from London to a garden city, such as Welwyn, where air was cleaner, more space available, and lower local taxes had to be paid, he said his body of workers, experienced and skilled, descendants of other similar workers, were tied to London. Their relatives and dependents had jobs in other parts of London as typists, shop assistants, and whatnot; and these persons could not easily be uprooted. Supposing the factory were transplanted 12 miles out and a new housing estate were built close to it. Even if transport facilities for those who still found it necessary to travel to London were wonderfully augmented, matters would not really be vastly improved. Witness the crawling of London out over Middlesex just described. That kind of extension is going on in the case of scores of large towns in various parts of the globe. These questions are but parts of larger problems. An immense amount of energy and money has been put into town and regional planning in the last thirty years. Less than two years ago a book was published on "a new principle in town planning,"[1] the building of satellite towns—so the advertisement runs. This book examines the present tendency of industry to move to the outskirts of big cities and analyses the resultant economic wastage. But Letchworth, the first garden city, was founded as long ago as 1901, and it is rather pathetic to find that the writer of the Introduction to this book, Dr. Raymond Unwin, in an address he gave at the Council Meeting at Welwyn Garden City about January 1932, said: "As a movement it behoves us to consider how it is that we have worked for thirty years and have only succeeded in that period in accommodating about 24,000 persons in the two garden cities of Letchworth and Welwyn; whereas during the last ten years that number of available persons have settled in the Greater London area every twelve weeks."

He goes on to say in the same address: "When the new Town-Planning Bill is passed it would appear that practically all the requirements of the generally accepted *definition of a garden city* could be satisfied through the medium of regional planning, except perhaps that which *requires the land to be held in trust* for the garden citizens." (The italics are the present writer's.)

Sir T. Chambers, Chairman of Welwyn Garden City, was getting close to the same point when he said (on May 31, 1929): "The real economic unit to be considered was not that of the individually owned plot but nothing smaller than the whole town." He stated that: "London was far from being an over-

---

[1] *Decentralization of Population and Industry*, by several authors, with Introduction by Dr. Raymond Unwin.

crowded city. . . . There were vast areas in London which are really very sparsely inhabited. These areas are often thickly strewn with wretched little obsolete, disreputable-looking cottages, which ought long ago to have been demolished. . . . The commonsense treatment of such areas lay in the direction of wholesale pooling of ownership, wholesale demolition of buildings, complete clearance of the sites, often breaking up and obliterating the old roads and then with broad vision replanning the whole . . . but without greed."

Calculations easily made prove that, if it was desirable, 36,000,000 people could be housed within a radius of 30 miles of Charing Cross and yet occupy only one-third of the land. That would leave one-third for roads and public open spaces and one-third for factories, offices, and shops. Yet the 36,000,000 could live 5 to a house and 12 houses to the acre, each house having a frontage of 30 feet and a depth of 120 feet. Supposing Sir T. Chambers' views just mentioned were carried out, what would happen to the fortunes of those who pooled their ownerships? Would it not come about that their fortunes would simply be more evenly spread, and that they would all tend to reap a good deal more than they had sowed through pocketing values made by the community's expenditure, needs, and natural growth? Dimly town-planning reformers see these things. They also see clearly the paramount importance of accomplishing improvements "without greed," and of getting the private advantage of individuals to coincide with the community's interests and welfare. The first essential for abolishing any conflict between the interests of the individual and the commonweal is to respect the rights of property, the community's no less than the individual's. To establish this reign of justice it is necessary to recognize that each man has an exclusive right to the use and enjoyment of what is produced by his own labour; but to make quite certain of his securing this the elements of nature and the value which attaches to land must be treated as common property by taking for the community what belongs to the community. Otherwise, in order to finance public services, something other than what belongs to the community has to be collected.

A proper and natural distribution of population depends directly upon an instrument being found to make easy the displacements involved in the less for the more remunerative use of land. That instrument has been discovered but is not extensively used. Cities grow, but they grow badly, with many attendant evils, because the passage from one use of sites to another is not a smooth one; the navigation is stormy; and the passage is an especially difficult one because the compass and the charts have not been brought aboard. Human progress, in numbers and ingenuity, leads to smaller areas of natural opportunity, of ground, being all that men find necessary and advisable. The smaller areas now capable of being put to better use are more valuable, but these values measure the community's rather than the individual's gain. The individual gains through them only if they are pooled. As individuals take up new areas they gain by the advantages in accessibility, etc., of their new position and also, and to a great extent through, what they get from the communal services financed from the common pool. Those individuals who are displaced also receive benefit, if the true instrument is used, by having relatively less to pay into the common pool than formerly for the services financed therefrom, which services, however, in their new positions they need less. They receive benefit too, indirectly, through cheapening of commodities by specialization in production, and by having bigger numbers better grouped to whom to sell their own productions. There is only one instrument to make smooth the proper and natural growth of populations. Whether these be distributed sparsely or in dense agglomerations, community values must be collected for the community and the rights of individuals to their own property must also be left intact.

CHAPTER XI

WATER SUPPLIES: SANITATION: FEEDING THE EARTH

NOTHING is more important and interesting in connection
with the growth of cities than their water supplies. This is
the first civilization in the history of the world which has known
the cast-iron pipe. The Romans built beautiful aqueducts to
convey an ample supply of water to their cities over long distances. But these did not carry water under pressure. New York
and many other cities of this era could never have come into
existence but for the discovery of pipes capable of carrying
water under pressure. Buildings of many stories housing busy
humans heaped up one above another are comparatively hygienic
because pure water can be conveyed to them and watery effluents
from them. One hundred and fifty years ago London had wooden
water mains made from elm 7 inches in diameter. To this day
the laying of a main water-pipe is usually referred to amongst
water engineers as "driving a main" because in the old days the
habit in constructing a main pipe was to drive the upper thinner
end of the hollowed elm trunk into the lower thicker end. In 1809
when London's population was about 1,000,000 water was
obtainable over a great part of the town only in the basements
of the houses and for less than three days a week. The mains
were largely kept empty because they were leaky. Hence, if a
house caught on fire a very dangerous situation arose because
it often took an hour or more for the water to reach the plug
holes. St. James's Palace got damaged by fire about this time
in spite of the action of watchmen, one of whom was always
stationed in the Green Park, to open the valve and bring out
horses to pump. Iron pipes first made their appearance in 1746.
But it was not till 1810–20 that they came to be extensively used.
In 1817 an Act was passed requiring all new mains to be made of
iron after ten years.

Some idea of the quantities of water used nowadays can be
gathered from the following miscellaneous facts: Birmingham gets 75,000,000 gallons per day from the Elan Valley in

mid-Wales 73 miles away. The inhabitants of London use 36 gallons a day per head. The inhabitants of Norwich use about 23 gallons a day. Many American cities have to supply 100 to 200 gallons per head per day, largely because their citizens are extravagant and wasteful in the use of water. New Yorkers use rather over 100 gallons a day per head. It is calculated that British water users (not counting those in London) supplied by undertakings connected with the British Waterworks Association waste at least 100,000,000 gallons of water a day, and that this represents an expenditure of not less than £2,000,000 per annum. Chicago stockyards require, for cleansing purposes chiefly, as much water as is equivalent to that required for over 1,250,000 people. That city requires 10,000 cubic feet per second of water to flow to and through it in order to deal with the disposal of its sewage, and this water, since the year 1920, has been made to flow along the deepened and widened bed of the Chicago River, which used to flow into Lake Michigan but now flows in the reverse direction into the Mississippi Basin. A perceptible fall in the level of the water in the Great Lakes has actually occurred in the last twenty years, and most authorities consider part of this is due to Chicago's geographical Acts.

Los Angeles obtains its water supply from 223 miles away. The capacity of its aqueduct equals 280,000,000 gallons per day. San Francisco brings 400,000,000 gallons a day from 155 miles away and nearly half of the pipe line consists of pressure pipes. The revenue of the public water supply undertaking of New York is $20,000,000 a year, and its expenses about $7,000,000. Its capital value is $415,000,000 and its liabilities $196,000,000. The revenues of the public service waterworks in 247 of the largest municipalities in the United States amount to $158,000,000 per annum and their expenses ("cost payments") to $76,000,000. The similar expenses of these cities for sewers and sewage disposal come to $20,000,000 per annum. £5,500,000 in loans were sanctioned by the Ministry of Health for schemes of water supply in Great Britain in the two years 1930–31 and in 1931–32, besides other loans for the same purpose amounting to nearly £2,000,000 in the first of these years under the Public Works Facilities Act and in local Acts. The average loans sanctioned by the Ministry of Health each year for the ten years 1921–30 for water schemes is just over £2,250,000. In the year 1930–31 loans sanctioned for expenditure on sewerage and sewage disposal works amounted to nearly £8,900,000, though this was considerably above the average. Ninety per cent of the urban population in the United States is served with water by public plants. It is said that in Manchester the change from hard to soft water effected a saving in soap and soda of between £80,000 and £100,000 a year. The inhabitants of Manchester use 36½ gallons per head per day, and rather over a third of this is used for manufacturing and trade purposes.

In England as late as 1845 a Royal Commission reported that only six out of fifty large provincial towns had a good water supply. But in 1911 the 36,000,000 people inhabiting England and Wales used over 434,000,000,000 gallons of water annually. Sixty or seventy years ago the waste of water in towns was chiefly due to faulty fittings and carelessness. In 1869 Manchester obtained powers against such waste. This reduced the consumption from 35 gallons to 14 gallons per head per day. To-day it is in America where water is used most extravagantly. This is in some places largely due to dilution being used as a cheap means of sewage purification.

In the provision of public utility services vested interests arise and are difficult to dislodge. Unduly high profits are apt to be extracted when pipes and plant for water supply and sewerage are constructed, and unduly high prices when the public acquire the undertakings from private companies. Owners of the private undertakings get so used to making swollen incomes out of the needs of the community, ever increasing as numbers rise, that one is reminded of the story of an old lady who lived close to a railway coal siding. She was so used to lifting a few pieces of coal for her modest requirements from the ample store opposite that she complained bitterly on losing her "privilege" after a watch had been set up and she was thereafter obliged to buy coal.

The people of London made repeated efforts over a space of more than two hundred and fifty years to get possession of their own water supply. This was obtained from the Thames at old London Bridge from 1580 to 1822, and originally a Dutchman, Peter Morise (in whose family the privilege continued till he sold it to Richard Soams for £38,000 in 1703) got a lease of one arch for five hundred years for 10s. a year. Soams floated a company with a capital of £150,000. It was not till 1902 that London secured its own water supply, and in the end it had to pay £40,000,000 for it. The history and an outline of London's water is most interestingly told in William Garnett's *A Little Book on Water Supply*.[1] The story of the municipalization of Glasgow's water supply has been graphically told in a pamphlet by John S. Clarke, and he gives his booklet the sub-title of, "a revelation of business graft and landlord trickery."[2]

In sewerage plant and service vested interests are common, though towns usually keep these schemes in their own hands from the outset. Many private interests, however, are not very obvious amongst the crowd of contractors for pipes, cement, tanks, pumps, etc. In a little English market town surrounded by rich arable land where water carriage is very difficult because of the undulating contours of the ground and the low elevation above the sea not very far away, some dilapidated cottages exist. The local authorities insisted on these being connected up to the sewers. This cost the owner more than £60, though the cottages only let for less than 5s. a week; and when joined up along came the rate assessor and put up the local taxes. Thus is the provision of good cottages hindered. The waste of nitrogen and phosphorus that occurs through methods of sewerage and burial contributes, too, to the power of the combines who claim the ownership of those parts of the earth where these substances are most readily exploited. But such ramifications of the evils of private land ownership, of the sins against the rights of property, are really generally too complicated for people to grasp. Other indirect effects of such evils leading to the growth of bureaucracy would require a book to themselves. But it is well to remember in passing that many of the worst crimes against society are belauded as smart, and others are noiselessly sunk in the silent bogs of Blue books, or carefully shrouded by the censorship of some official. Yet they are crimes which have a big effect on the growth and distribution of population.

It is not only amongst contractors that in all openness and honesty costs creep up unduly in these ways. Political influences,

[1] Cambridge University Press, 1922.
[2] *An Epic of Municipalization* (Forward Publishing Co., Glasgow, 1928. 6d.).

too, often lead to unexpected multiplication of persons drawing remuneration for some public service or other. Present-day systems seem to breed "tax-eating" bureaucrats. One authority,[1] W. J. Roberts, Professor of Economics at Cardiff, indeed, goes so far as to define the adjective "political" as that which is due "to habits and institutions whose origin and purpose is mastery and privilege and monopoly." At all events it is too often the case that political action involves work and income for officials which produces no commensurate return in public benefit. One wonders sometimes whether the practical benefits received for the energies of Government staffs in Great Britain are worth while. Their total number in 1921 was 341,279; and their wages and salaries, £69,000,000, in 1921, were three times as much as they were in 1914. Towards the end of 1932, when a National Planning scheme was set up in England, a plan for the control of the pig industry was proposed with the following new Boards, Commissions, and Committees to secure an improved standard of technique and organization in the production and marketing of bacon: a permanent Reorganization Commission; a Quota Advisory Committee; a Bacon Imports Advisory Committee; a Pig Industry Development Board; a Pigs Marketing Board for Great Britain, and another for North Ireland; and two Bacon Marketing Boards. Not only do Governments by direct action set up such Boards and Committees, all of which tend to bring people into big cities, but indirectly their actions have the same effect. When in the spring of 1933 vast plans sprang up for the reorganization of American economic life, Washington had not seen such a bustle to find or build new offices since 1917. Hundreds of experts from all parts of the country hurried to the national capital to aid in administering the new laws—and look after their own interests. But has Industrial Recovery been established? Is it indeed possible if the plan of smaller markets, higher wages, and shorter hours be the means for bringing about better business!

A distinguished English water engineer, Dr. A. Parker, has stated recently[2] that the public demand for water is increasing,

---

[1] See *British Medical Journal*, 1923, II, p. 482, on "The Falling Birth-rate."

[2] Article in Vol. XVI (1931) of *Applied Chemistry Reports* on "Sanitation and Water Purification," p. 585.

and the available sources of unpolluted water, both surface and underground, are gradually being depleted. Rivers which are to some extent polluted are in many instances being utilized as sources of supply for both domestic and industrial purposes. As long ago as 1911 Sir A. Houston said: "About 80 per cent of the London water supply is derived from sewage-polluted rivers."[1] Waters from sewage-polluted sources can, of course, be made safe nowadays by chlorination. Most of London's water and the great majority of water supplies in Canada and the United States are now treated in this way. But it is unpleasant to read about the Great Lakes (Michigan, etc.) that: "There are practically no points at which water can be secured free from pollution. In a general way the pollution hugs the shore in the neighbourhood of the cities, and there is danger of the pollution of waterworks' intakes due to wind-driven currents."[2]

The water supply to 7,000,000 Londoners, one-seventh of the population of England, is almost all from polluted sources. Yet London is one of the healthiest cities in the world, and the freest from water-borne disease. This is an immense triumph to the late Sir A. Houston and the water engineers who defend the citizens of London by means of storage, chlorination, and filtration. It is an illustration of the greater safety of water supplies as a general rule nowadays, compared with some years ago, despite increase of pollution.

Pollution means waste. Dilution of sewage means expense and immense diversion of water. There is destruction of fish. Trade and sewage effluents defile estuaries particularly, and no longer do once famous salmon rivers contain these fish. An enormous waste of soap and grease down the sewers is a problem which few have even begun to think about. Reference to Chicago has already been made, but a few further particulars are of interest. In 1840 there were only 4,480 inhabitants in this city. At the end of last century the serious amount of typhoid there led to the reversal of the Chicago River and the construction of a canal which, via the Illinois River, flowed into the Mississippi. Canadians complain about the fall in the water in the Great Lakes and New Orleans. Navigation improvements, too, make waterway trade more possible now between the Great Lakes and New

[1] *Aquarius*, Vol. VI, p. 156.   [2] *Surveyor*, 1926, pp. 69 and 389.

Orleans. These changes may have important geographical consequences one of which will very possibly effect the distribution of population, for more than half the United States population and three-quarters of her industry are situated in the basin of the Mississippi.

Water supplies in pipes capable of bearing considerable pressure enable population more readily than ever before to be densely herded together. Sewage disposal by water carriage is a method only extensively used in the last one hundred years or so. It is true that water-closets were used at Knossos in the Island of Crete in the Golden Age of the Minoans—that is, about 1580–1200 B.C. But the palace itself was probably one of the few buildings to use this system, and it was not of more than three or four stories high. Besides which it seems probable that only collected rain water was used to flush the water-closets, and the pipes and conduits were made of earthenware, stone, or concrete. The occasional water-closets found in England from Tudor times also can hardly be classed with modern sanitary arrangements. It was the witty and famous godson of Queen Elizabeth, Sir John Harrington, who introduced them into England and described his innovation in a broad and humorous pamphlet, *The Metamorphosis of Ajax*.

Another important geographical effect of modern systems of city water supplies and sanitation is an interference with the natural increase of soil fertility which generally went with denser populations in previous ages. Conservant methods of disposal of all kinds of animal waste were formerly practised. Nowadays the soil is robbed of its natural food, animal waste and excreta, not to mention animal corpses. Most of the former are to-day swept down the drains out to sea; and dead bodies are buried deep in dead sub-soils. The result is that communities which would have been more agrarian and less industrial—more mixed, in fact—would have been more dispersed, and the modern tendency for excessive numbers to participate in the secondary occupations would have been counteracted. A study of the interdependence of plants and animals, and of conditions of habitat upon numbers, is revealing the ways in which nature regulates the aggregation of populations. Man is able to modify his habitat wilfully to such an extent that evils may occur unless he is careful to learn and to obey natural laws. One of these is that, where animal excreta and dead bodies increase, there plants will be likely to proliferate the more.

There are certain thickly inhabited parts of the globe where the method of burial is of some moment in connection with soil fertility. Professor E. Huntingdon makes reference to a province of China, south of Yangtze, where, in spite of the ancestor worship of the Chinese, the living agricultural producer is in the habit of constantly encroaching on the land allotted to the dead. The plots for burial are in the midst of cultivated fields. Whereas these at first are spaces 3 feet by 7 feet, they dwindle to "2 feet by 5 feet and then 1 foot by 3 feet. Finally, in some districts the grave is represented by a little pottery cylinder 6 inches in diameter and so small that it merely occupies a space that must anyhow be left between most kinds of plants in order that they may get light and air. . . . If all graves were allowed to remain the full size, most of China would now be a graveyard."[1]

In the days when most people lived in villages everyone knew that a rotting cabbage leaf was not waste. The grocer had his potato plot; and even the village blacksmith, if he did not cultivate his own cabbage patch, had a son or daughter who did, and they knew that vegetable matter left in a heap at the bottom of the garden was in no way an offence, and that presently there would be a heap of useful material to add to the soil. At the annual pig slaughtering the superfluous blood and offals, if not made into "black puddings" and "chittlings" for the household and all the neighbours, would be added to the heap. There was neither waste nor want. To-day, when 60 to 80 per cent of the population live crowded together in cities, there is both. To-day much additional knowledge is in the possession of the agriculturist about humus and about animal manures, and their inestimable value in keeping up soil fertility. Consequently, as population increases, agricultural production can increase also. Yet there is less and less humus produced from decaying vegetables in civilized communities, just where it is most wanted, and a great proportional diminution of animal manure. At the same time city dwellers are ever and again crying out about the difficulties and evils of refuse disposal. Animal manure is scarcer, not only because

---

[1] E. Huntingdon's *The Human Habitat*, p. 179.

of the introduction and wide use of the water carriage system of sewage disposal, but also because of the supercession of animal traction by mechanical transport. Artificial manures are being supplied and used more and more. But without decomposing organic matter the soil fertility cannot be easily preserved. The "humus" so produced aids the soil to make use of "artificials" given to feed it. Humus enables soils to absorb water, ammonia, potash, and other plant foods, is necessary for the welfare of beneficial bacteria, and by means of the carbonic acid gas produced in the course of decay corrodes mineral matter and reduces to a soluble form the phosphate and potash which would otherwise be useless to the plants. If a ton of beanstalks be reduced to ash it is found they produce 29 pounds of potash, 16 pounds of nitrogen, and 9 pounds of phosphoric acid. It stands to reason that there will be waste if agriculturists have to go to the expense of purchasing much material of a manurial nature, often from afar, which is actually the same as that which every household has at its disposal nearly every day in the year. But the agglomeration into towns, mostly paved and divorced altogether, at all events in their most congested districts, from every kind of agricultural production, not only robs the earth of her food, but also leads to great difficulties and evils in the disposal of "refuse." The chief of the difficulties are financial and chief of the evils are sanitary.

Ancient cities are always found buried deep. This is largely due to the dirt and débris which city dwellers accumulate. The exploration of ancient cities in various parts of the world has shown that they deposit on the average a foot of débris per century. Since the day when town paving became more extensive and since the discovery and wide use of coal in many cities, the rate of accumulation, of growth in height of the ground has probably slowed down, largely because the débris is nowadays mostly carted out of the cities. The composition of town refuse in recent decades has shown that generally not less than 30 per cent consists of cinders, much of it useful fuel, and a good proportion of the 45 per cent of fine dust comes from the ashes of coal. But gradually everyone is using less coal, consequent upon a greater use of oil fuel and of electricity. Man acts as a geological agent in a variety of ways. R. L. Sherlock[1] points out that a total

[1] *Man as a Geological Agent* (Witherby, London, 1922).

of 50,000,000 cubic yards of earth had been excavated in the City and County of London up to 1922 for sewers, wells, railways, docks, etc. This is equal to 3¾ inches over the whole surface of 117 square miles.

New York produces 15,000,000 cubic yards of garbage, ashes, and rubbish annually, and over 9,000 persons are employed for the collection and disposal of all this "waste." The Boroughs of Richmond and of Queens incinerate their refuse, while the other boroughs of New York, nearly all, dump the stuff 30 miles out to sea. The expense of the garbage disposal of 247 of the largest municipalities in the United States mounts up to $40,000,000 per annum. The London borough councils expend rather over £2,000,000 per annum on their public service enterprises of this kind. To two dump heaps alone very nearly 1,000 tons a day are taken. The collection of the house refuse is not done in the most up-to-date ways. Continental towns such as Zürich and Cologne, and some English cities such as Bradford, Liverpool, and Birmingham, employ much better methods of collection and disposal than does London. The present writer stood a fortnight ago at the window of a house in Westminster within view of the towers of Westminster Abbey and the House of Lords at 10 o'clock one morning watching the open high dust cart making its round. Various kinds of bins were lifted up, scattering dust, just as the milk man and the baker were delivering their goods, the latter at the same door from which the garbage bin was being removed; and the loaves were heaped uncovered in the baker's cart to be handled by baker's man and housemaid, etc. A doctor in Harley Street rather further north in London, the centre of the doctor specialists district, wrote a month or two ago to complain that there, too, an open lorry, eventually over-filled and defiling the street on a windy day, collects the garbage from small, miscellaneous sized, often overflowing buckets between 8 a.m. and 10.30 a.m.

A town's solid refuse consists of: fine dust as to about 45 per cent; cinders about 35 per cent; glass, stone, brick, and heavy debris about 10 per cent; vegetable matter 5–10 per cent; paper and light debris about 4 per cent (though this is increasing); and metals 1–2 per cent. There are six ways of dealing with it, two of which ought to be utterly condemned, viz. depositing out at sea, and dumping, for they have two or more of the following defects: they waste what is worth salving, they are insanitary, they are cumbersome, and often costly methods of disposal. The best schemes are so organized as to be capable of being completed in one operation. The remaining four methods are: controlled dumping, separation, incineration, and pulverization.

The chief evils of uncontrolled dumping are: flies, rats, crickets, and odour. London, chiefly the boroughs of Westminster and the City of London, produce two of the worst dumps in the Kingdom; these are the notorious twins at South Hornchurch, near Dagenham, and Becontree, which receive about 350,000 tons of house and trade refuse every year. One of these "reeking masses" has been growing for more than thirty years and at one point reaches 90 feet in height. In 1932 the Parliamentary Under-Secretary to the Ministry of Health pointed out that they will "probably go on growing." Since then, however, at last the step of getting as far as a joint committee has been taken to see whether a unified controlling board can be set up for the whole of London to tackle the difficulties. But Liverpool and Bradford have controlled dumps which work well. Suitable land can often be reclaimed decently if the advice published by the Ministry of Health is followed. The way Bradford deals with 200 tons daily is held up sometimes as a model. Birmingham deals cleverly with the animal and vegetable parts of its refuse. The Corporation Salvage Department deals with 4,000 tons of this a year, and, in the midst of a densely populated area, turns out 100 tons of feeding meals and fertilizers and nearly 100 tons of fat without smell or nuisance. Slaughter-house and animal trade refuse is incorporated in the materials sold. Manchester within recent years has brought itself up to date in many of its schemes for refuse disposal. It uses slaughter-house offals to mix with its dust, thereby making a "town's manure" much valued by celery and lettuce growers and market gardeners on Chat Moss. It also makes a more valuable manure (over 500 tons in a year fetching £5 a ton) out of bone meal, wood ash, and the ash of banana stalks; and sells its oyster shells, ground up, to poultry farmers. Sir John Russell has written on the subject of the utilization of town refuse as manure.[1]

[1] *Journal of Ministry of Agriculture*, Vol. XXIX, November 1922, p. 685.

An unsatisfactory feature of improving the means for living more healthily in crowded towns is this: the more bearable crowding is made, and the greater the facilities for comfort in overcrowded centres, the greater seems to be the increase of over-concentration in urban areas. Economic causes are always at work drawing persons from rural surroundings and occupations to the cities. But sometimes causes of concentration in cities seem to be inadequate. Dallas in Texas, e.g., with a population of 262,000 inhabitants, has skyscrapers. Yet it is surrounded by prairie land. The concentration is doubtless largely the result of matters connected with real estate, but also, apparently, partly a result of following the fashion set by New York, Chicago, etc. It is, of course, labour saving to speed upwards in an elevator instead of moving along horizontally to the next appointment. A certain amount of concentration is convenient. It is said a man can make sixteen business calls in New York in the time it takes to make three in London. The house where the doctors have their offices in Dallas is sixteen stories high. It is convenient to physicians and patients alike to find the medical wisdom of the town all under one roof. But the example set by those American cities where ground values are prodigiously high, an example followed by Dallas, is not by any means followed widely in the United States, for, compared with most European towns, American cities have extensive areas relative to their population.

There are still towns in England where in the case of a large number of the houses the human excrement is disposed of by the conservancy methods. The dried and granulated "night soil" from the pail system of sewage disposal contains some $5\frac{1}{2}$ per cent of nitrogen, $5\frac{1}{2}$ per cent of phosphates, and $2\frac{1}{2}$ per cent of potash. The price that Rochdale and Warrington obtained for night soil in dry form, unmixed with ashes, twelve years ago was about £7 a ton. The comment that Sir John Russell[1] makes on this is as follows:

"If the methods used in these places were generally applicable to town and city conditions the problems arising out of the waste of sewage would be solved and the shortage of organic manures on the farm would be greatly relieved."

Other towns in England with a high proportion of con-

[1] *Journal of Ministry of Agriculture*, Vol. **XXIX**, November 1922.

servancy closets are, amongst others, Hull, Middlesbrough, Darlington, Bolton, Huddersfield, and Rochdale. Conservancy methods are sometimes condemned chiefly for four reasons, namely: (a) the method is not properly worked. Abominations known as privy middens are only emptied once a week or even at such long intervals as once a month. Sometimes the front door is the port of entry and exit for emptying the earth-closet, especially in wornout, city slum districts. But even on modern estates poor arrangements are frequent. The writer was visiting the property of a county council run under its Public Health Department not long ago, situated quite in the country. One big building had water carriage closets, but these flowed into a cesspool in a garden not 100 yards away. It was full, the land around it was water-logged and smelly, especially in hot weather, and the cesspool had not received any rest for over nine years. New cottages had earth-closets in them, but these were ill-supplied with earth, were in the house, next the larder, used carelessly also for some house refuse, and were emptied only once a week. True it is that the water carriage system can be equally badly worked. In several countries, in some French towns for example, stroll along some of the chief residential streets in the midday dinner hour when no one is about and the tank pumping cart can be found outside a house emptying—a rare event—the cesspool through a big tube which is running across the threshold of the front door! The accompanying odours are a pleasant appetiser for anyone who happens to be late for his dinner! Even Paris is in a bad way in many of these particulars. Many of the older houses are built over cesspools. Some authorities maintain that nearly a quarter of the houses in Paris are unfit for human habitation and are reeking with germs. The high death-rate in France is not unconnected with these things and accounts for the stationary population. Conservancy methods of sewage disposal are often condemned, too: (b) through the inability of finding suitable land nearby for working the system properly; (c) through prejudices, generally caused by (a) and (b), but also caused by ignorance and the fashion of the day; and (d) through vested interests. Yet if the manurial values of sewage were conserved throughout the United Kingdom they would be worth about £22,000,000 per annum. In 1919 it was stated[1] "the total

[1] *Journal of Ministry of Agriculture*, Vol. XXVI, August 1919, p. 502.

excrements of the inhabitants of the United Kingdom would be worth £18,000,000 per annum as fertilizers if they could be applied to the land. Only a fraction is so used at present."

There are essential antagonisms between the water carriage and conservancy or dry methods of the disposal of excreta which might well be freshly considered now that so many housing estates are being developed in open or semi-rural neighbourhoods. They are both dependent upon biological purification; but in the one case *putrefaction* is the basis of the process, and in the other *nitrification*. Putrefaction is encouraged by (1) water, (2) darkness, (3) absence of air—all the circumstances of drains and septic tanks. The end product is "a satisfactory effluent"—that is, the dissolved relics of squandered manurial wealth (1 part per 100,000), always useless, often laden with bacteria. Nitrification is encouraged by: (1) a moderate amount of moisture in the soil (33 per cent is the optimum); (2) exposure to the air—hence the need for surface burial, and for the cultivation of the soil so that air shall gain access; (3) sunlight; its warmth in fine growing weather awakens to activity the nitrifying bacteria in the soil. The end product of this system of sanitation is garden produce. In cold weather manure consigned to the soil lies dormant and harmless. What some villages and housing estates in semi-rural neighbourhoods want is a few enlightened Chinamen or fastidious Japs to show the inhabitants how to work the dry method decently, how to encourage an enviable agricultural wealth, and how, too, to keep down the costs of land development for housing. Dr. Lionel Picton, writing in the *British Medical Journal*,[1] has described how the alignment of the dwelling-houses on the site can eliminate the slightest unsightliness and the most transient offence, and yet obtain for each house a maximum of sunshine with beauty of outlook, pleasant and productive gardens, and convenience of access without expensive roads. In the days of Hippocrates medicine depended upon the four elements earth, air, fire (in the form of sunshine), and water, from both the preventive and the curative aspects of the art. Are we not apt to reverse their order to-day, or in any case use water too much to the exclusion of the other elements?

London requires an added area of 2,000 acres every year to house the normal increase of its population. The cost of this

[1] 1924, I, p. 250.

land to users is always getting higher. Though in the case of small suburban property the cost of the site is but a small fraction of the cost of house building, the cost of the development of land for building by the construction of sewers, roads, etc., is very high. When prices were ruling rather high this cost was from 20s. to 25s. per foot frontage; and when the roads are taken over by the public authorities there is another heavy charge to be met. This, in some suburban districts where the need for houses was great, amounted to £2 per foot. The total cost of development was at the rate of £1,200 per acre in such districts. Taking this cost at half this amount on the average to-day it means that £1,200,000 is required every year for these purposes alone to meet London's annual increment of population. It is interesting to examine who pays these charges and who gains most out of them. Scrutiny into the facts reveals that for the most part the consumer pays and the landlords gain. Even where and when some portion of the charges for such developments are met out of local taxes, these are paid by the householders and hardly at all by the landlords; besides which the landlords (by which is, of course, meant the lords of the *land*) are often able to pocket, sometimes in advance, the increased values which public expenditure gives to the ground needed by an increasing population more densely aggregated. Bye-laws, generally drawn up by the same vested interests who dispense the land in small parcels and the pipes, curbs, etc., which come from the land, seem made, almost expressly sometimes, to keep up the cost of development. Sewerage and road making especially contribute to these costs. Unduly wide roads and badly grouped houses are common. There are miles and miles of small houses built with 12- or 14-foot frontages on 40-foot roads and their construction is such, an almost unavoidable result of the bye-laws, that the staircase can never get adequate light and ventilation, the back room (generally the dining-room) is ill-lit because of the scullery, etc., extension towards the rear. This extension looks on a similar one belonging to the next house.

In ancient times houses were crammed closely together, sanitary laws were ill-understood and badly carried out; the health of the inhabitants of towns was poor and their lives short. But without water under pressure close density of population was unusual. The areas of ancient cities are difficult to estimate accurately. Nineveh, according to G. Rawlinson,[1] was 3 by 1½ miles and contained about 1,800 English acres. Babylon was a great deal bigger, though the description and particulars of dimensions given by Herodotus are obviously far from correct. He made out that it measured 14 miles each way in 450 B.C. Priene is believed to have contained 400 individual houses and a population of 4,000 in an area of 750 yards in length by 500 yards wide in the early Macedonian age. Pompeii covered 160 acres. Turin, in 28 B.C., enclosed about 127 acres in its walls enclosing an area of 745 by 695 metres. Tmigad, founded by Trajan in Algeria in the Province of Constantine, covered about 30 acres within the walls at the middle of the second century.

In 1348 the Papal City of Avignon was roughly 124 acres and it contained a population of about 80,000 inhabitants. That was at the beginning of the year which saw a death-rate from the plague which rose from 100 to 1,000 a day—in fact the English chronicles record a maximum of 4,000 deaths on one day there in that year. Housing difficulties in Avignon in the twelfth and thirteenth centuries were acute. The overcrowding must have been terrible. In 1348 the density was about 645 persons to the acre. To-day there are but 40,000 inhabitants in the larger Avignon and its suburbs. Paris at this time (and before it was affected by the plague) had about 275,000 people in it, and its area was about 800 acres. The Hague grew in area and population as follows; the first column gives the date, the second the number of inhabitants, and the third the surface areas taken up by building sites (1 hectare = 2½ acres):

Date			Population	Building Sites Area, Hectares
1820	..	..	50,000	120
1870	..	..	100,000	250
1900	..	..	200,000	560
1920	..	..	350,000	900

At the present time the largest city (in area) in the United States is Los Angeles. This covers an area of 281,509 acres and has a population of 1,238,048 persons, very nearly double the population of San Francisco.

[1] G. Rawlinson's *Five Great Monarchies*.

CHAPTER XII

HEALTH IN TOWN AND COUNTRY

IN times past rural workers were stronger and healthier than town dwellers. Even in the days of the Roman Empire there is evidence to show that this was so.[1] The towns were constantly being replenished from the country districts. Infant mortality was higher in the towns and the physique of city inhabitants was notably inferior. Soldiers from rural districts were decidedly taller and stronger than those who came from towns, especially large towns. Not a great many decades ago it was difficult to find a Londoner who was a pure-bred Londoner unto the third generation,[2] and the same was probably true of many other similar cities in other parts of the globe. Doubtless this was partly owing to the fact that the populations in such cities increased far more rapidly by attracting people from outside than from natural increase from within. But it was also due to lower birth-rates and higher death-rates in the towns than ruled in the country. These differences were more due to the insanitary state of the towns up to even fifty years ago than to the better conditions of diet, fresh air, and sunshine which prevailed in rural districts. But nowadays things are changing, especially during the last thirty years. The healthiness of town life, as well as health generally, has improved a great deal. Birth-rates, though falling everywhere outside Asia and Africa, are becoming equally as high, or even somewhat higher, in towns as in the country, and death-rates in town are nowadays quite often lower than in the country districts; while the physique of town dwellers is occasionally quite equal to that of rural dwellers. These changes are in some degree just a measure of the greater equalization of the standard of living. Knowledge of what is sound and good in the way of food is often greater amongst the inhabitants of towns than it is amongst rural workers; and the facilities for getting good food supplies in cities have increased tremendously in the last forty or fifty years. Furthermore, unfortunately, many

---

[1] See Professor Frank's *An Economic History of Rome* (Baltimore, 1920).

[2] See Sir A. Keith and Dr. T. B. Layton, *Lancet* (letter, November 8, 1930).

agricultural labourers have to put up with a very low wage and get fewer perquisites than once upon a time. In the middle of last century, and even later, the agricultural labourer got a good deal beyond his money wage of 9s. to 15s. a week. There was the cottage garden, some milk, a rabbit often, a little corn occasionally, besides having the inestimable advantage of eating wholemeal bread. Free litter for his pig was generally his, and even a right to some feed for his geese or donkey on some common or heath. To-day the lowliest paid of agricultural workers, like his confrères in the towns, gets little milk, eggs, or bacon, and much emasculated bread and margarine, and he drinks too much tea. In former days the pace and strain of life was not great in cities as it is to-day; and, on the other hand, equanimity and contentment were fostered in village life much more than they are now, for there was more of the community spirit about, even though many squires were terrible tyrants. This showed itself in village music, games, and sports. To-day, in place of the social life with many amenities and perquisites, the labourer has won the right to combine and the right to vote—advances indeed, but reforms which do not seem to inure into bread and cheese. The influence of individual mental peace and contentment within the community has probably got much more to do with health, vigour, and longevity than is usually realized.

The expectation of life in cities has varied very much through the ages. Before towns became unmanageable in size their hygiene was not very different from that of the country districts except that they were much more affected by epidemics. When they grew bigger and before modern sanitation and preventive medicine worked so beneficially to improve their health, the people in them were less healthy and shorter lived than those who dwelt in rural surroundings. This was due chiefly to the terrible infant mortality and the greater prevalence of illness in late adult life.

The general death-rate in London and other large towns was 50 per 1,000 in the middle of the eighteenth century, whereas it is estimated that for the whole of England and Wales at this time it was 35 per 1,000. In 1815 the death-rate for England and Wales was reduced to about 20 and for London to about

30 per 1,000. A comparison of statures and weights of boys employed by the Post Office in London twenty years ago with similar boys in 1932 shows, according to Dr. H. H. Bashford's research,[1] that the present generation are over an inch taller and more than a stone heavier than their predecessors. He also compared these modern messenger boys with public-school boys and found they were equal to the latter between 14 and 16, but between 16 and 18 the public-school boys averaged 1 inch taller and 6½ pounds heavier. Dr. F. C. Shrubsall, too, in his address before the anthropological section of the British Association in 1924, rebutted the view that the British people were degenerating.

That close aggregation and high industrialization does shorten life can be seen by examination of short-life tables. For example, compare the expectation of life at 20 years of age of males in the County of London, the Boroughs of Liverpool, Birmingham, and Sheffield with those of the following non-industrial areas: East Suffolk, Lincolnshire (Holland division), Wiltshire, and Oxfordshire. It appears from these figures that life in an industrial centre rather than in the country is shortened by 5 to 9 years, for the years of expectation of the former are from 38 to 42½, whereas in the latter four districts they are all between 47 and 48 years. A. B. Hill[2] has shown that in the first five years of life the rate of mortality in our urban counties is more than 50 per cent higher than in the mainly rural counties, and that in the age group 55–65 men die in urban counties at a rate more than 40 per cent in excess of the country rate and women show an excess of nearly 40 per cent. But in adolescence and in young manhood things are different, for between 15 and 25 the rural dwellers have a higher death-rate than the townees. The explanation of this is, with but little doubt, to be found by a consideration of the type of individual, both physical and mental, who leaves the country for the town. In France, though up to the age of 19 the death-rate is considerably higher in the urban than in the rural groups, the general death-rate

---

[1] *Manchester Guardian*, June 22, 1932 (London letter).
[2] Report No. 95 of the Medical Research Council, *Internal Migration and Its Effects upon the Death-rates: An Inquiry in Rural Essex* (H.M. Stationery Office, London, 1925).

(15·3 per 1,000) in urban districts is lower than that (17·8 per 1,000) in rural districts, and than the death-rate for France as a whole (16·5 per 1,000).[1] In Ireland the highest death-rates in 1930 were in the county boroughs and the lowest in the almost purely rural areas.[2] The preliminary return of the census for England and Wales in 1931 gives a table on page 10 which compares the death-rates for certain diseases in rural and urban districts, and the results as a whole are strikingly in favour of the rural districts.

In spite of advances in the sanitary state of modern cities human life is healthier in the country than in the town. The stature of human beings has slowly increased through the centuries with the gradual improvement in the standard of living; but there was a check to this increase when people became huddled into big cities. Dr. A. K. Chalmers[3] has connected the greater lack of fresh air and sunshine associated with the greater prevalence of tenement dwellings in cities in Scotland as compared to England with the higher death-rates in Scotland. Professor Noel Paton and Dr. L. Findlay[4] show that town children, at all events from poor quarters, are, on the average, lighter and less tall at every age than the children of rural miners and agricultural labourers, the last class being largest at each age. They believe that a smaller town race is being evolved as being really better adapted to environment now that there is a relative decrease in the emigration from country to town. They state that efficient mothers are to be found in relatively greater numbers in rural rather than in town districts and that this influences nutrition and growth quite a lot. Figures show that women are more prolific in the country than in the urban districts; and Dr. Kathleen Vaughan,[5] and others demonstrate that maternal mortality (3,500 mothers a year in England) is least when the mothers have enjoyed an abundance of fresh air and sunshine from childhood onwards. Since about 80 per cent of people in Great Britain now live in towns, and the towns are

---

[1] *Lancet,* 1931, II, p. 647.

[2] Ibid., 1932 (January 23rd), under "Ireland."

[3] *Transactions of the Royal Society of Medicine,* November 27, 1925.

[4] Medical Research Council Special Report, No. 101, *Poverty, Nutrition, and Growth: Studies in Cities and Rural Districts of Scotland* (H.M. Stationery Office, 1926).   [5] *Sunlight,* Vol. II, No. 7, 1932.

breeding more and more their own population, these points are of increasing importance.

A comparison of some of the most recent figures (1931) of the crude death-rates in urban and rural districts[1] shows that these are now lower in towns than in rural districts in Germany, Switzerland, Holland, Belgium, Sweden, Finland, and Bulgaria. In Italy the mortality in rural districts is now exactly the same as in towns, and the rural mortality is only a little lower than the urban in England and Wales, Denmark, and Norway. At the present time only France, Spain, Hungary, Scotland, and the Irish Free State show a fairly marked urban excess. Although formerly infantile mortality was much higher in towns than in the country, it is now almost everywhere in Central Europe lower in towns than in rural districts. In Southern Europe, on the contrary, there seems to be little difference between urban and rural infant mortality, and in England and Wales both the birth-rate and infantile mortality are higher in towns than in rural districts. After the age of forty the urban death-rates are everywhere higher than the rural death-rates, but in youth, especially in the case of the female sex, the position of the rural population in this respect is in most countries unfavourable. The researches of Dr. Percy Stocks[2] into mortality and population density largely corroborate the above views.

[1] *British Medical Journal*, October 3, 1931, "Mortality Conditions in Rural Europe."

[2] Royal Society of Medicine (May 1934). Summary given in the *British Medical Journal*, 1934, I, p. 1000.

CHAPTER XIII

RURAL DEPOPULATION

NOW that cities are healthier places in which to live apprehensions about rural depopulation are less than they were. The vast improvements in transport, too, have enabled thickly populated areas to obtain adequate food supplies easily, and except in war time fewer alarms arise about food shortage. In most countries peopled by those coming from European stock the decline from rural residence and pursuits has been progressive and rather rapid. In England and Wales, for example, the percentage of population dwelling in rural districts has gone down as follows:

ENGLAND AND WALES

Year				Percentage in Rural Districts
1851	..	..	..	49·8
1881	..	..	..	33·3
1891	..	..	..	28·0
1911	..	..	..	21·9
1921	..	..	..	20·7
1931	..	..	..	20·0

This is not due, except to an infinitesimal extent, to the shrinkage of the area of rural districts owing to the operations of building, but almost entirely to the attraction and the increase of the towns. Similarly in the United States the percentage of the total population residing in other districts than in towns of 8,000 or more inhabitants has gone down as follows:

UNITED STATES OF AMERICA

Year				Percentage in Rural Areas
1790	..	..	..	96·6
1810	..	..	..	95·1
1840	..	..	..	91·5
1860	..	..	..	83·9
1880	..	..	..	77·3
1900	..	..	..	66·1
1910	..	..	..	61·3
1920	..	..	..	56·2
1930	..	..	..	48·0

Or counting as rural those other districts than towns of 2,500 or more inhabitants the percentage in recent years is:

UNITED STATES OF AMERICA

Year				Percentage in Rural Areas
1880	..	..	..	71·4
1900	..	..	..	60·6
1910	..	..	..	54·2
1920	..	..	..	48·6
1930	..	..	..	43·8

In Australia half a century ago 44 per cent of Australian bread-winners were working on the land; by 1921 this figure had fallen to 25·8 per cent. To-day only just over 30 per cent of Australia's population live in the country districts and 50 per cent in five cities. In 1891 the total population of Australia was 3,810,000 and one-third of these lived in cities of 10,000 or more inhabitants. In 1921, 62 per cent of Australians were city dwellers, and 46 per cent lived in the six capital cities. Greater Melbourne is stretching out at such a rate that it must within measurable time cover an area equal to that of Greater London. This emphasizes the fact that there is a spaciousness about the cities of Australia. A majority of the country acres which the cities have brought into their own and their suburban boundaries have more garden space than is to be found in English towns, so that the clerk and the retailer retire with spade and watering can to satisfy the primitive half-forgotten instincts of their villain and yeoman ancestry. The drift to the towns has occurred somewhat similarly in New Zealand for in 1901 the rural population was 61 per cent, twenty years later it was only 51 per cent, and in 1926 it was 48 per cent.

In Germany though the population of the towns more than trebled in the twenty years from 1891 to 1910 the urban population is not more than about 55 per cent of the entire population. In France from 1851 to 1925 the town population rose from 25·5 per cent to 49·1 per cent, the country areas having lost nearly 6,000,000 inhabitants while the towns gained 10,000,000. In Italy the urban population in 1921 represented no more than 42·5 per cent of the total population. The figures are even lower for Sweden in 1929 (32·9 per cent), and Switzerland in 1930

(29·5 per cent). The total population of the world is estimated to be about 1,800,000,000 persons. The total population of those countries which distinguish between urban and rural areas is 782,320,000 and 31·8 per cent of these (that is 248,426,000) are inhabitants of rural areas.

Rural depopulation is undoubtedly associated with the rise of industrialism and commerce. Where agglomerations of population into urban centres are greatest, namely in England and Wales, the proportion of workers engaged in manual labour is lowest.

PERCENTAGE OF POPULATION* IN CERTAIN OCCUPATIONAL GROUPS ACCORDING TO VARIOUS CENSUSES

Occupational Group	Country						
	England and Wales	U.S.A.	India	France	Germany	Denmark	Czecho-Slav.
Agriculture, fishing, etc.	6·8	26·3	72·3	41·5	30·5	34·8	33·7
Mining, quarries ..	7·5	2·6	0·3	1·5	3·2	—	2·8
Industry	39·7	30·8	11·2	28·4	38·1	27·0	37·7
Commerce	13·9	10·4	5·9	10·4	11·7	10·8	6·4
Army and Navy ..	6·5	0·5	0·3	2·0	0·4	0·7	2·6
Public administration ..	6·5	1·2	1·1	2·6	2·0	0·8	2·0
Census year	1921	1920	1921	1921	1925	1921	1921

NOTES.—As the classification of occupational groups varies from country to country the above table does not furnish a precise comparison.

* The figures relate in most cases only to those gainfully occupied.

Extracted from the *Statistical Year-Book of the League of Nations*, 1933–34.

In England and Wales, too, agriculture employs fewer persons per 1,000 acres than other countries. People are drawn away from agricultural pursuits into manufacture, commerce, and the professions. These occupations are carried on increasingly in big cities. But exactly what forces there are at work producing these changes it is rather difficult to determine. Agricultural production is not progressing as fast as knowledge about it has been and is being increased, especially in some parts of the world. In India, for example, up-to-date methods might be widely taught and used, but they are not.

Fewer people and smaller areas are required to produce food than formerly because facilities have increased. Yet suitable new methods adapted to differing climates, soils, etc., are not as widely adopted as they might be. The United Kingdom produces approximately only half of the food its inhabitants eat. The proportion is usually put rather lower than this because the returns from gardens and allotments are not reckoned in, nor the home consumption of farmers and their families, and because too much attention is paid to certain commodities (such

CHANGES IN INDUSTRIAL DISTRIBUTION IN THE UNITED KINGDOM, 1923–33

CHANGES IN THE DISTRIBUTION OF THE INSURED POPULATION IN CERTAIN OCCUPATIONS

	July 1923*	July 1933†	Change
Distributive trades	1,253,980	1,992,000	+738,020
Hotel and catering trades	258,960	398,780	+139,820
Trams, bus, and road transport	257,140	393,830	+136,690
Motors, cycles, aircraft	191,830	261,720	+ 70,890
Electrical trades	84,020	153,180	+ 69,160
Coal-mining	1,243,580	1,023,910	−219,670
General engineering	666,950	528,190	−138,760
Shipbuilding and repairing	269,970	169,310	−100,660
Cotton	567,650	499,930	− 67,720
Iron and steel	210,960	164,670	− 46,290

* Aged over 16.   † Aged 16–64 inclusive.

Extracted from *Ministry of Labour Gazette*, November and December 1933.

as wheat, butter, and cheese), where the proportion is much lower than 50 per cent. But with better capitalization and organization of agriculture, with readier access to land, with removal of tax burdens and Government interference much more could be produced, and more persons would be employed in this, the most important of the primary industries.

The proportion of total population which is engaged in agriculture to-day varies widely even in Western Europe. In Great Britain it is 3·4 per cent; in France 22·5 per cent; and in Germany 22 per cent. The same is true about the percentage of the working population engaged in agriculture, which is 7·2 per cent in Great Britain, 40·7 per cent in France, and 36·7 per cent in Germany. C. B. Fawcett[1] states regarding the United Kingdom that, "the one-thirtieth of our population which is engaged in agricultural work produces nearly half of our supply of the principal foodstuffs. Thus under the conditions now existing in Great Britain the food produced by the labours of some 1,500,000 agricultural workers is sufficient to feed a population of 20,000,000. . . . Under the conditions now ruling in Great Britain, on the average the work of one agriculturist can produce a food supply sufficient for 15 persons." Further, he maintains that, "the minimum rural population for a self-supporting country is about 25 per cent of the total."

Agriculture includes not only the food-producing industry, but also the production of a large group of important raw materials for other industries, such as the animal and vegetable fibres used by textile industries. Scientific discoveries enable such production to be more prolific and intensive. A greater concentration of population is a result, a fortunate one since human beings increase in numbers. It is a natural law that *as numbers and knowledge increase the area of land required by humans for their maintenance and comfort can be decreased.* From it another law follows, namely that the value of sites rises steadily, site values which are the property of the community. These can be used for the common good. Primitive peoples recognized, and still recognize, this second law; but the complications of advancing civilization have hidden it from a majority in most nations to-day. Had not the second law been hidden every fresh advance, every new complication in society would have been smoothly traversed without any conflict arising between an individual's self-interest and that of the community. Population would have been very differently distributed than it is to-day. Examine the introduction of factories. In olden times the work of weaving, for example, was done in the home, or in small workshops. Division of labour and specialization came. Factories came to be put up just when the tribal custom of holding land as the property of all was departed from. The products of a man's own labour were no longer regarded as sacredly his own because arbitrary taxes of one sort or another were imposed and infringed his rights of

[1] *Geography*, June 1929, pp. 104, 105.

property. The tribal revenue fund was not collected as labour for the community or as money payment for ground rent for exclusive possession of sites. Consequently, some individuals got advantages over their fellows and a maldistribution of wealth set in. Those, for example, in possession of more favourable sites than their neighbours did not square their position with their neighbours by paying for their privilege into the common pool to be used by all. Those in the least favourable locations were apt to become poor because they did not get their share of the common heritage, viz. the revenues from the ground; and very possibly they were hit too by taxes (just as to-day those striving against adverse natural circumstances on the frontiers of civilization are gravely hurt by import duties and poll taxes). Those most capable of utilizing the best sites often could not get access to them. Instead of facilitating production through the encouragement of leaving to the producer all the products of his labour, and collecting for the public services all those rents of the ground which naturally arose from the growth of population and knowledge, production was hampered. Some were compelled to work for others at a wage which was less than the measure of the enhanced values given to materials by their labour. When private property in land was allowed, when, in other words, some of the public's rent went into the pockets of private individuals, the corollary evil, the evil of taxation, arose. Maldistribution of wealth increased. Some gained unfair advantage over rivals. (Fair competition and friendly rivalry are good.) Certain manufacturers found it possible to enlarge their factories more easily than their competitors. They attained a greater division of labour and more rapidity of production. They could afford to pay somewhat higher wages than others. They attracted labourers from those that were poor. A vicious circle was inaugurated. Governmental and guild (trade union) action began to exert itself and to interfere with production. A Weavers Act and other similar measures were passed. The number of journeymen a master might employ was limited by legislative action; and numerous guild restrictions sprang up. Yet these actions did not undo the evils wrought through the lack of realization of what was truly public and what truly private property. Factories which might have been unmitigated blessings had drawbacks and introduced difficulties and hardships. The mediaeval clothier concentrated his workers in a factory for economic reasons, but the economics on which they were based were to some extent wrong, and not altogether conducive to the best kind of combination and co-operation, and not altogether conducive consequently to the best way of arranging a thicker population. The immense advantages of specialization, of the division of labour yet of combination to produce, were bound to accrue from the use of concentration of special bands of workers, but instead of benefiting all, the economy of factory co-operation benefited only a few. To-day in spite of the advantages of "mass production" factories stimulate anti-social feelings at every point; and it is all through society having taken the wrong turning some time back by permitting private property in land. Despite the altruism which burns in the breast of most folk even in modern society, factories too often bring strife into the community. The competition of workers with one another, the antagonism between employers and employed, between factory and factory, and between sellers and buyers, all contribute to these conflicts.

The factory system affects the distribution of population in several ways. It destroys family industry prosecuted in farm houses; it diminishes the number of agriculturists; it destroys industries in the handicraft stage (village shoemaking, milling, etc.); it removes population from villages. But it probably has less influence on rural depopulation than commerce has. And whether the factory becomes located in the small or the big town—the latest tendency is towards the latter—depends on a nice balancing of the factors involved. Amongst these factors those of most importance are transportation facilities, both those of getting the raw materials and those of distribution of the finished article, and ease of getting adequate skill and numbers to labour in the factory. Density of population has little to do with depopulating the country-side and producing the massing of people into cities. This can be appreciated by comparing Bengal with England, two areas with a very close approximation to one another as to population density, but where those living in cities are less than 5 per cent of the population in the former case, but over 65 per cent in the latter; also by reference to the following table giving the density of population to the square mile on the one hand, and the percentage of population in towns of 100,000 or more inhabitants on the other:

	Population Density	Percentage of Population Urbanized
		per cent
Egypt (valley and delta of the Nile)	1,047	12·2
England and Wales	668	39·1
Japan	403	14·6
Germany	350	26·6
India	177	3·6
U.S.A.	38*	26·5

* In 1926.

Urbanization goes with industrialization rather than with density, and still more with commerce. A. F. Weber confirms this last view by comparing Holland and Belgium. "Belgium is a great manufacturing country, consuming more coal and iron *per capita* than any other European country except Great Britain. Holland has few manufactures, but carries on an extensive commerce. It is also less densely populated than Belgium (138·7 persons to the square mile, against 206). Those who maintain that cities are the product of manufactures would expect to find a much larger urban population in Belgium than in the Netherlands. Yet the actual percentages are as follows:

	Holland	Belgium
Township of 2,000 and over ..	(about) 85	(about) 75
Township of 10,000 and over ..	43	34·8
Township of 20,000 and over ..	31·3	26·1[1]

So much has been written by various authorities on the decisive steps towards the abolition of community rights in land which were taken when the great enclosures took place in England and Wales, that it seems unnecessary to enlarge in these pages upon that great cause of rural depopulation. It is the less obvious ways of depriving the community of its property which especially need emphasis to-day. That the way to get cheap labour is first of all to create a landless proletariat has already been shown in

[1] Adna F. Weber's *The Growth of Cities*, pp. 181, 182 (Macmillan, New York, 1899).

an earlier chapter of this book in connection with Africa. But a few remarks are called for about the English enclosure Acts, and a few references must be given. First of all, here is a quotation from F. E. Green's book on the agricultural labourer:

"The rural labourer, deprived of the opportunity to exercise peasant thrift through the Enclosures Acts, which from 1760 to 1867 put a fence round 7,000,000 acres over which the peasant's cow, his donkey, his geese, fowls, or swine used to graze, and from which he derived fuel for his household, fodder for his beasts, and even corn for his daily bread, had now little else to sell but his labour, and the labour of his family. It is difficult to see what course was open to him as a voteless, voiceless man, if the farmers refused to meet him, but to strike.

"In spite of the fact that Land Commissioners had instructions to reserve sufficient Common Land for the needs of the rural poor, even in as late a period as from 1845 to 1867, out of the 614,800 acres enclosed, the Enclosure Commissioners had only assigned 2,223 to the poor."[1]

A great authority on rural depopulation, Christopher Turnor,[2] places amongst the causes of rural depopulation peculiar to Great Britain the following:

"For the fifth cause of the depletion of the British country population, one must look into past history. The Enclosure Acts necessitated by the need for higher production to feed the growing towns, were operated in such a way as to reduce the number of those directly interested in the land, and to turn the agricultural labourers into a landless proletariat entirely dependent upon wages. These evils were avoided in Germany, for instance, by taking effective measures to enable 'ex-commoners' to become small occupying owners." He also makes the following statement: "The rural population of Great Britain is not only inadequate, but dangerously so."

There were two great periods of enclosures in Great Britain. The first in the sixteenth century when the chief object was to provide more pasturage, especially for sheep which became very profitable about then, and the second mainly at the

---

[1] F. E. Green's *A History of the English Agricultural Labourer*, 1870–1920 (King & Son, Ltd., Westminster, S.W., 1920).   [2] *Ency. Brit.*, Vol. XIX, p. 670.

beginning of the nineteenth century. Since an object of the enclosures on the second occasion was to increase tillage, the effect, immediate at all events, on rural depopulation was not so marked as on the former occasion. Arthur Young found in 1801 that of 37 enclosed parishes in Norfolk, one-third of which county's total area was taken from the common possession by enclosure, the population had increased in 24, diminished in 8, and remained stationary in 5.[1] These enclosures have been but one method of creating a landless proletariat and they, and the other methods employed, have undoubtedly had a lasting and depressing effect on agricultural production, and depopulating the rural districts. Ever since the end of the period of the enclosure Acts Parliament has been swayed too much by the territorial interests. A multitude of Land Acts (for example the Purchase Acts for Ireland), Small-holdings, Land Settlement and Land Utilization Acts, of Derating Acts, Sugar Beet, Wheat Quota Acts, etc., have streamed from the legislature, ostensibly to aid the farmers, and better food production. But they have not been particularly successful in these directions, while they have generally helped the landlords very materially. They have, on the whole, certainly not conduced to a better distribution of the population; and not a single one of such Acts has done anything towards the Government's first duty which is to collect for the community what belongs to the community.

For decade after decade the population of most Norfolk villages of the type based on farming has been stationary or slowly declining. These villages can be taken as typical of the same kind of agglomerations of persons chiefly dependent on agriculture throughout the rural parts of England and Wales. This decline of population has happened when the total population has been increasing rather rapidly. Yet with increased facilities of transport, more scientific agriculture, more specialization in food production oftener than not involving smaller areas of land utilization, and with bigger markets, there is no inherent reason for the stagnant villages. The decline, the stagnation are due to the regime of property which exists everywhere in England nowadays, the regime based on the private ownership of land, and the accompanying taxation systems,

[1] Prothero's *The Pioneers and Progress of English Farming*, p. 72.

local and national. Some would say, "Not at all; they are due to the inherent conservatism of the farming classes." But this conservatism, too, is based on the same foundation. What leads so many farmers all over England to adhere so closely to the good old-fashioned four course "Norfolk" rotation of crops long ago shown to be entirely unsuitable to present-day conditions? With this rotation something like 70–80 per cent of the crops must be sown in a brief period in spring-time, and harvested in an equally brief period in autumn. The result is that the rotations do not provide an even distribution of labour throughout the year. Also great harvesting risks have to be faced, and it often happens that through bad weather at harvest time the corn is much lowered in value. Again, too large a proportion of the land is left idle during the late autumn, winter, and early spring months, and much grain is produced which has to compete with foreign grain produced more cheaply. Yet adherence to the Norfolk crop rotation, but slightly modified, is widespread. The farmers certainly are a conservative lot. They suffer, too, from insufficient capital and they are poor at organization and co-operation. Their very lack of capability to imbibe fresh ideas, to acquire capital, to learn to organize and co-operate is all wrapt up with the continuance of things as they are in the matter of land tenure and taxation. Suppose they, their marketing plans, and all their clients were entirely freed from the burdens of taxes and from Government interference, suppose they had security of tenure as tenants of the public domain, would they not be more progressive, or give place to those who were? And could not the most capable of the highly skilled men working under them, as they cannot now, get access to land to put it to more intensive use? Food production would increase by leaps and bounds and there would be a thicker population in rural districts utilizing smaller areas.

An excellent intensive study of a typical English village, Crawley in Hampshire, throughout the ages and up to the present day, has been made by N. S. B. Gras and E. C. Gras. In some of the earlier pages of this big volume written by them in 1929 the departure from the common ownership of the land is traced. The following passage is worth quoting:

"The manorialization of Crawley had taken place, at least

in structure, by the time of Domesday Book. By that date the lord was deriving from the village not only lordship rents but an income from unfree predial service on his home farm." A regime of small-holders followed. "So far as we know, this was a regime of small-holders and small tenements. The ups and downs of these small people cannot now be discovered for the earliest times. While they seem to have been held pretty much in check in the period 1208–30, they appear to have been restless in the period 1231–1314. From 1315 to 1383 the restlessness continued and apparently led to a diminution in the size of the home farm and a rise in the wages of special workers. In the period 1384–1448 the small people succeeded in getting free from the most objectionable services, the landlord meeting his difficulties by leasing the home farm. Just what happened during the 100 years following 1448 is not clear, but the small tenantry appear to have maintained their position as a class. The rise of the middle class of yeoman farmers occurred in the sixteenth century. This class was the dynamic factor on the manor until about 1880. It made an increasingly good income until the nineteenth century, but tended to become less and less numerous. Finally it proved unable to withstand oversea competition."[1]

An old, ill-rhymed doggerel verse on a tombstone in Crawley churchyard is worth quoting as indicating that the inhabitants in those days perhaps understood the history and causes of rural depopulation better than the average inhabitant of England to-day.

> Rights are for those who fight even as they lose,
> Under such circumstances Crawley men refuse;
> England made her choice long years ago
> Wealth, great cities, industries—all villages know.[2]

Crawley in Hampshire had an Enclosure Act applied in the year 1794. Its results in the long run were far-reaching. "After enclosure there was to be nothing really common in Crawley."[3] Several census returns for the village are given in the Grases' book, namely:

[1] N. S. B. and E. C. Gras's *The Economic and Social History of an English Village* (Crawley, Hampshire, A.D. 909–1928) (Harvard University Press, 1930), p. 162.
[2] Ibid., p. 163.   [3] Ibid., p. 597.

Date			Population of Crawley Village
1841	..	..	.. 372
1851	..	..	.. 402
1901	..	..	.. 502*
1921	..	..	.. 563*

* In these years from 139 to 152 persons in two schools or colleges which had sprung up, outside the village but in the parish, are included.

In 1927 the population in the village of Crawley had declined considerably.

It has been said by Lord Ernle in an interesting book published in 1908[1] in which he compares agriculture and land tenure systems in England with those in France, that "the uniformity of English agriculture, land tenures, and civilization imprint monotony on much of her rural economy. But throughout France diversities of climate, land ownership, and land tenure have left their mark." He then goes on to say, "Each different system of land tenure affects the grouping of the rural population," and illustrates this statement by reference to various provinces. Lord Ernle looks upon the defects and deficiencies of French farming as having as their ultimate cause the slow growth of the population in France. It does not occur to him that it may rather be the other way round and that both are due to and dependent upon the firm establishment of the twin evils of private ownership of land and the burdens of taxation. He describes and enlarges upon the poverty of the small owners whose increase the State promoted, and states[2] that in 1842, with a population of 33,000,000 or 7,000,000 families, 5,500,000 owned land. Nearly all had very low incomes.

Several geographers in recent years have brought out the connection between regimes of property and the distribution of people in village communities. But few carry this idea further. Professor M. Vahl has shown that the density of the farming population in Denmark is by no means everywhere proportional to the fertility of the soil. The population is thinner in rural districts in Denmark where the landowners hold big estates; and this is so even in those parts of the country where the soil is chiefly boulder clay and the fertility only varies within narrow

[1] R. E. Prothero's *The Pleasant Land of France* (John Murray, London, 1908).
[2] Ibid., p. 61.

limits. Denmark is the one country in Europe where the majority of land *owners* are opposed to the private ownership of land. It is in Denmark that a reversion to natural conditions regarding the regime of property is best seen to-day in Europe. The small-holder is re-colonizing his home land there with holdings of only moderate extent, while fighting steadily for lower taxes and the collection for the common use of the communal values (land rent). Two other papers show clearly the connection between regimes of property and village settlements; these are: Miss S. Harris on "The Village Community of Alderney" and Miss I. F. Grant on "The Highland Openfield System."[1] The last three references, as well as the next one, and a paper by the present writer on "Causes of Rural Depopulation," are all to be found in the 1928 publications of the International Geographical Congress. Professor O. Marinelli points out that the distribution of population in rural districts in Italy depends more upon the property system than upon the agrarian system; for he has shown that it varies according to whether the *podere* unit and the *mezzadria* regime or the *contadini* system based on the contract of rent be adopted.

In earlier chapters of this book indications have been given of how easy it would be to utilize English land so as to produce far more food stuffs of the finest quality if only easy access to the soil were possible and better use made of the scientific knowledge now possessed. Danish experience and that gained in recent years on the farm estate at Crawley (and elsewhere), described towards the end of the book to which reference has just been made, all go to show that growing more forage crops, adopting a system of intensive arable farming ("continuous cropping"), using land in small parcels for poultry, fruit, vegetables, pigs, etc., will produce more and will employ more persons despite more machinery being used. It will also give occupation to more persons in all kinds of subsidiary callings, such as the making of poultry houses and appliances, etc. But these changes in the settlement of people on the surface of the earth cannot come about so long as man is not a free agent to work at that occupa-tion towards which he feels most disposed, and at which he is

[1] *Report of the Commission on Types of Rural Settlement* (Union Géographique Internationale), No. 1, 1928.

most likely to prove capable, nor so long as he cannot get freely the raw materials for his work, all of which come from the land. Some say that access is there to-day; and that under a regime of collecting all land rent, according to the site value of the ground alone, into a common pool and abolishing all taxes, access will be no easier. But neither of these assertions is correct. Anyone who attempts to get a site on which to build a house, open a factory, run a poultry or fruit farm, though he be blessed with influence and capital, will soon find that he is up against great difficulties. The obstacles preventing him from obtaining secure possession of a site for his venture and a certainty of holding the improvements he himself makes, are often insurmountable. How quickly does he not knock up against the exactions of land-lordism! It matters not where he searches he will be extraordinarily lucky if he gets what he wants easily and on terms he considers fair. If successful he soon experiences the awkwardness, to say the least of it, of the system of taxes which is in vogue. What, too, of the poor "wage slave" which the present regime produces? What chance has he got of getting access so that he can produce freely howsoever capable he may be? Hardly any! I could multiply instances by the score out of my own experience, first-hand knowledge, and observations. But under a new regime, a return to ancient customs, at last recognized as just and applicable to modern conditions, the regime of no private property in land and no taxation, such difficulties would vanish. To-day the speculative value of land, being in the private hands of a few, leads holders to keep land unused or underused. They have not to pass the rent of such ground on (it may be very highly valued sites), to the exchequer to finance the public services. If they and hundreds of others like them were forced by public opinion, enlightenment, and legislation to do so it would have an immediate effect on production and wages, and upon the distribution of wealth and of population. They would quickly discover that neither they nor anyone else derived any advantage by withholding the ground so that it was not being put to a good use.

The industries of the human race may be conveniently grouped thus: (1) extractive, including agriculture, and mining; (2) distributive, including commerce, wholesale, and retail trade, transportation, communications, and all the media of exchange; (3) manufacturing; (4) services, including domestic servants, government officials, professional men and women, students, etc. All previous writers on rural depopulation and the growth of cities have emphasized the importance of an unnatural upset of the proportions occupied in these various classes. But adequate attention has not hitherto been called to the primary cause of such a disbalance. What Governments do to-day, and leave undone, generally interferes with producers and burdens them. Their actions, too, subserve the present regime. If agricultural workers, who now get such miserable wages, were not ever on the look out for the better living they hope and expect to find in the towns; if rural labourers could get small plots of land to work intensively for themselves, if only an eighth of them could do this would not the low wages of this primary industry rise? Of course they would, and with that, even apart from similar effects of a better regime in other industries, wages in other occupations would also rise. Still more would these results come about if a small proportion of such labourers could get some modicum of capital. But capital is simply wealth put aside to aid in the production of further wealth, and like all wealth it comes from the application of human labour to the resources resident in the earth. Again, therefore, it is a question of land tenure, and of property rights.

The English depend on industry and commerce more than any other nation, but less so than formerly, since other nations have learnt, or are learning industry and participating more than before in commerce. The English must take the step of producing far more foodstuffs, not because wars may otherwise lead to our starvation, nor because it will be a healthier life for people to live, but because our very existence depends upon the attainment of a better balance in productive activities. This cannot be done by any scheme for "putting people on the land," by any governmental "back to the land" plan. People don't want to be put. Natural and equal opportunities, freedom to produce, room to live, space to work for a living: these are the things people want. To some extent the day has gone by when, because workers cannot grow food intensively in thickly populated England, more people have to build ships to bring food across the seas, and more people have to busy themselves in the insurance, transport, and freightage of those foods. Such persons naturally congregate in cities, because in closely aggregated centres it is easier to carry on their business.

There is another aspect of under-use of agricultural land which has an effect on the distribution of population. The craftsmen were to be found of old making most things wanted by the rural worker and his dependents, in the villages or market town. To produce things in great numbers in factories has many advantages. But the craftsman of old took a pride in his work. He had not lost his soul and become a piece of machinery. There is still plenty of room for more hand-made goods. Examination of old buildings in most villages—the church, the manor house, the farm-houses, and the cottages—will generally reveal how skilled were the village tradesmen in the arts and crafts, and how superior in quality and lasting powers most of their work is to that of the present day. Here are some details of the calling of the heads of households in the Norfolk village of Southrepps in 1800–2, and this may be taken as typical of most English villages of that time: Among the 161 heads of households there were 8 carpenters, 5 bricklayers, 4 gardeners, 3 shoemakers, 2 bakers, 2 barbers, 2 carriers, 2 glovers, 2 shopkeepers, 2 tailors, 1 blacksmith, 1 butcher, 1 collar-maker, 1 mariner, 1 publican, 1 weaver, and 1 wheelwright. Seventy of the inhabitants were engaged in agriculture, 8 as farmers, and 62 as labourers. One hundred and thirty years ago the inhabitants of Southrepps must themselves have been capable of supplying practically all the needs of the community. The skill of the craftsman, largely unappreciated throughout the Victorian era has increased in favour in recent years. But much of it, which was often handed down from father to son, has now been lost. Consequently the efforts at revival which are now occasionally made are rather futile. Again, the prosperity of these secondary rural industries fostered a high standard of appreciation of beauty. Though numbers have gone up, and standards of living improved—yet not commensurately with the advance of knowledge and ability to produce—the general level of taste, and demand for beautiful things has gone down.

Concentration of population upon smaller areas as civilization

H

advances is naturally more obvious in commercial centres than in the regions where the extractive industries are pursued, or even in those where manufacturing is being carried on. But it occurs almost everywhere more or less regardless of what the main occupation of the people is. An exception is when the fertility of the soil, and the situation of the site is such as to lead to extensive agriculture with the use of a good deal of machinery. Such exceptions, however, are comparatively rare, and the particular one cited in the last sentence should be rarer than it is. In Russia, for example, mistakes in this direction have been made in recent years. Society there is based upon wrong theories. Moreover, when more haste is made along wrong lines less speed is indeed the result. Wrong-headed notions pursued auto-cratically bring privation and lack of freedom—to teach the next generation. To obviate such mistakes it is necessary to get back to the ideas of property which ruled in primitive times for centuries; and to learn how to apply such ideas to modern conditions. The primitives distinguished between the earth, the source of all wealth, and the commodities produced therefrom by human labour. Ownership of the former, bespeaking some form of rent collection (or its equivalent in services) for the common benefit, was vested in the tribe. But the private owner-ship of the latter was respected. To-day when every variety of production and enterprise is apt to be more complicated, specialized, "intensive," and occupying smaller areas, when consequently more public services are required and bigger values attach to sites with a corresponding higher rent roll, it is considered more difficult and by some less just to continue the old regime. As a consequence radical departures from the out-look on the rights of property of primitive peoples have taken root. But the necessity for collecting for the community the values which the community creates, and for preserving the property of the individual for the individual's own possession is greater than ever. Fortunately the ease whereby this could be accomplished is greater than ever. There is no value easier to assess than that accruing to the ground in a thickly populated area from the needs, increase in numbers, and the public expen-diture of the community. Land cannot be hidden; everyone is interested in its value; and even if its value is not public many people know it. Yet the rent-roll for the common benefit has become replaced by another idea, namely, the property-regime upon which all taxation is based. Tribal action instead of seeing to its rent nowadays takes products of labour as common property.

A distinction between possession of a site for use and ownership of the earth is not appreciated in the complicated society of the present day, and this is at the root of many of the difficulties. Because it became necessary to enclose land to protect crops, or to mark off sites to be held exclusively for other reasons than agriculture, people lost sight of the essential wrongness of private ownership of land; and it has not until comparatively recently become obvious how to make exclusive possession secure while continuing to honour public ownership, nor how unjust it is to all to abstain from making the necessary changes. Those are the changes which, above all others, must be made to stay the flight from the country districts. Minor causes of rural depopulation all essentially devolve from the primary one. But some consideration of these secondary causes is now desirable.

It is said to be dull to live in the country despite wireless and cinemas in most market towns. Truly dullness and monotony exist. Village life has not reaped its due proportion of the progress of the last thirty years. On the other hand townsfolk are becoming a somewhat jaded lot, often full of a peculiar kind of irritability, the only cure for which is a more natural life in sex and family matters and through a closer contact with mother earth. Townspeople's only idea of looking at scenery, poor things, is all too often the somewhat unprofitable occupation indulged in by holiday-makers in charabancs. To enjoy new sensations is doubtless refreshing; but the senses, unlit by understanding, are not enough. Mr. de Sélincourt[1] describes meeting a woman who declared she would rather cut holes in stockings and darn them than waste her time looking at scenery. Contentment signifies a proper fulfilment of function. But the right exercise of our powers is all too often but vicariously carried out in towns. Much irritability is due to poverty and woeful lack of opportunities, wheresoever people live. The cinema is a natural and cheap form of diversion, restful to the body of a tired worker. Moreover, it furnishes fine dreams of romance in love and riches,

[1] *Hibbert Journal*, Vol. XXVIII, No. 4, July 1930.

so that even a down-and-out unemployed will say, " the cinemas make you think for a little while that life is all right." The late W. H. R. Rivers[1] has shown that the love of adventure finds an outlet still in warfare, excessive speed, dangerous sports and similar pursuits, but that in a truly orderly and advanced state of civilization such outlets ought generally to be considered pathological. Yet to-day the daily Press and wireless glorify them more than ever. If closer contact with the earth and all that this means were commoner, more natural pursuits for such instincts would be found. Adventurousness is often a reaction to ennui; and irritability a reaction to discord. There would be less room for boredom, fear, and conflict suppressed or other-wise, and for unnatural excitement if the miseries, sorrows, and hardships which are now so often the lot of those who suffer from scanty sustenance and vile conditions of housing and work in overcrowded city quarters, were banished. Over-development of the gregarious instinct, allied to, or really part of the instinct of self-preservation is one of the traits of modern society arising from a maldistribution of population. People recognize the importance of maintaining cohesion in the group to which they belong. But the complexity of grouping which characterizes human society to-day cramps freedom. The magic instrument to smooth the path of change as populations grow has been lost. The individual's position in society is damaged. His social instincts are upset, just when his other two instincts, sex and that connected with sustenance, cannot be obeyed in well-balanced activities.

It is no good blaming education. Defective upbringing, deficient training are a result rather than a cause of the present state of affairs. Who shall say that 50 per cent of the boys of Norfolk should become agricultural labourers? Yet such is their fate. They lack opportunities of development even in practical agriculture. Compare the Danes. Elementary education in Great Britain has made great strides and has reached a much higher level during this century. But beyond the elementary schools education for a majority is the hard training obtained from life. The cultivation of good taste, even in things to eat, and of a fine civic spirit is difficult amongst overtired workers benumbed by poverty and beset by anxiety.

[1] *Instinct and the Unconscious* (2nd Edition, p. 120).

CHAPTER XIV

BIRTH, DEATH, AND MARRIAGE RATES:
A STUDY OF THE FALLING BIRTH-RATE

DWELLERS in rural areas are generally more prolific than city dwellers. Poor people breed more children than rich; primitive races more than civilized. The birth-rate is declining in most countries. The average birth-rate in Europe at the end of last century was about 40 per 1,000 living persons, that is, 40 children were born in a year for every 1,000 people alive in the middle of that year. To-day it is questionable whether

ENGLAND AND WALES

Period	Annual Birth-rate for 50 Years		Annual Death-rate for 50 Years	
	Average per 1,000 Population	Excess of Birth-rate over Death-rate per 1,000, Population per Annum	Average per 1,000 Population	Infant Mortality† (under 1 Year) per 1,000 of Live Births
1881–90	32·4	13·3	19·1	142
1891–1900	29·9	11·7	18·2	153
1901–10	27·2	11·8	15·4	127
1911–20	21·8	7·5	14·3*	100
1921–30	18·3	6·2	12·1	71
1926	17·8	6·2	11·6	70
1927	16·6	4·3	12·3	70
1928	16·7	5·0	11·7	65
1929	16·3	2·11	13·4	74
1930	16·3	4·9	11·4	60
1931	15·8	3·5	12·3	66
1933	14·4	2·1	12·3	64
1934	14·8	3·0	11·8	59

* Civilian mortality only.
† In 1900 the deaths of infants numbered 142,912 out of 890,248 live births. In 1930 the deaths of infants numbered 38,908 out of 648,811 live births.

it is above 30 per 1,000, despite a high birth-rate in Russia. The decline in the birth-rate began in France, in Normandy at the opening of the nineteenth century, spread to the Garonne Valley, then to various other parts of France and Central Europe. This movement, although checked for a few years immediately after the war, has now recommenced, and is spreading to such an extent that the birth-rate has fallen in several countries to less than 20. It did not affect England and Wales until about 1876; and according to Dr. Brownlee began in rural Wales and not, as is commonly supposed, in the better class districts of great cities. From 1875 to 1895 the birth-rate fell in Germany from 42 to 36, in England from 36 to 29, and in France from 26 to 25·2. Some of the lowest birth-rates recorded in 1925 are as follows: Sweden 17·5, England and Wales 18·3, Switzerland 18·4, France 19·1, Irish Free State 19·6, Belgium 19·7, Norway 20·0, Germany 20·6. Professor Carr-Saunders considers the theory that the fecundity of races tends automatically to decline with the growth of civilization is quite unfounded and believes that the deliberate use of contraceptive methods is the explanation of the decline in the birth-rate in modern times. The evidence, however, that can be deduced in favour of this latter view is by no means conclusive. But then he is one of those who considers that a necessity for the deliberate limitation of population growth has always existed and always will exist. Other authorities believe nations are passing through a period of natural ebb.

A decline in birth-rates is not a simple matter to explain. If it is to be ascribed to one cause only, that cause is late marriages, and that depends on a variety of causes, though most of them are economic and political. Late marriages are a sign of an effete, used-up nation. The matter is not by any means purely physical, but is undoubtedly partly psychological. If the Britisher emigrates to Australia or the French to Canada they will breed more prolifically than at home. The birth-rate in Australia is 24·6 per 1,000, and of French Canadians is 31, whereas that for the rest of Canada is 25. French Canadians were 28 per cent of the population of Canada in 1925 and the percentage of the population of Canada of British stock was 55. When Canada was conquered by the English in 1759 it contained a French population of 65,000. Without further immigration the number had increased in 1901, including 800,000 in the United States of America, to 2,400,000.

One of the most striking illustrations of the difference between the birth-rate (as represented by the crude birth-rate figures at all events) amongst well-to-do and poor people is to be found by reference to Kensington, a borough in the west side of London with a population of 178,700 people in 1924. Here there are two distinct districts, North Kensington, the inhabitants of which are poor people, and South Kensington, where poor folk constitute only a small portion of the population. The birth-rate in the former district was 21·7 in 1924 and of the latter 9·2. An illustration of the decline in the birth-rate in a more or less typical working-class neighbourhood in London is the case of Bermondsey. This, with a population of about 130,000 has an extensive river front lined with wharves, docks, and warehouses, and a hinterland of crowded streets with many factories and workshops. The birth-rate in Bermondsey in 1901 was 34·2 per 1,000 of population and 18·5 in 1927. During the same period the death-rate fell from 20·8 to 12·9.

In England and Wales the highest birth-rate was attained during the years 1865–80 when it exceeded 35 per 1,000 population; from that time it diminished by gradual stages to 23·8 in 1914, and since then to 18·8, and in 1932 to the lowest rate on record, viz. 15·8 per 1,000 population. The decline in the birth-rate in England and Wales has produced this result, namely, in 1925 double the number of people produce only the same number of children as in 1861. The general decline in births per marriage in England and Wales is striking in the last half-century, for in 1878–82 it was 4·63, and to-day is less than 2·20. It has been a steady and gradual drop. The average number per family in the United States was 5·8 in 1790 and 4·6 in 1900, according to C. E. Woodruff;[1] and is to-day less than 4. The average in Europe was given ten years ago as 4·2 by Mulhall in the *Dictionary of Statistics*.

All sorts of fantastic theories have been put forward to explain the decline in the birth-rate. As long ago as 1750 and 1830 publications on this subject appear. At the former date a Dr. Short thought town dwellers begat fewer children than the inhabitants of country districts, because they ate and drank more and were more idle; and in 1830 Mr. Saddler in his *The Law of Population* rather supported the same view. Ancient Greece and Rome noticed similar phenomena in birth-rates. The Emperor Augustus offered lavish prizes to the parents of large families.

[1] *Expansion of Races*, p. 225.

To-day some persons suggest such parents should be excused taxes—indeed a prize in many countries! Four generations or so ago Malthus crystallized the views of the educated classes, or so it rather seems to-day, and quieted the people's consciences when notice was taken of the condition of the masses at the beginning of the nineteenth century by ascribing their dire state to the hand of God. He thought population was increasing faster than the means of subsistence, and his views are exerting some influence even right down to the more enlightened times of the present day. He brought forward some excuses for counting wars, pestilences, famines, poverty, and vice almost as blessings or, at least, as having some purpose even in an otherwise well-ordered society; just as so-called Neo-Malthusian practices to-day are lauded as commendable because limiting population. Lots of people still imagine rather vaguely that poverty is the result of the "pressure of population," and so spare themselves the trouble of thinking. Consequently they never make the discovery that such things as government, tyranny, taxation, tariffs, land monopoly, etc., are the real causes of poverty. Not twenty years ago certain people held the theory that the world war was explained by Germany's over-population and her need for expansion; and to-day other wars are predicted by learned authorities as likely to arise from similar causes. It is a curious thing, but worth noting, that the impulse to expansion seems proportioned to the strength or weakness of standing armies, and the possession of the power to seize the lands of weaker peoples, rather than to the density of population (compare Belgium, Holland, Denmark, etc.). Last century Malthus, no doubt, gave some comfort to those devout people who believed in religion, in natural law, or an All-Wise Creator. During the second quarter of this century a certain scepticism even in respect of belief in natural laws, has become common.

Mathus' theories have been shown up time and again in the last one hundred years. His *Essay on Population* was followed by his *Political Economy*, which came near to discovering some of the real causes of poverty, yet the latter has always been more or less ignored and the former exerted an influence for a long time. Is it because it furnished an easy and to some extent comforting explanation of social misery? He wrote before modern advances in food production and before all the wonderful inventions of the last century and the great developments of commerce had been accomplished. His theories now seem more than ever discredited and absurd.

Now let the case of France be considered. The total population of this country to-day is roughly the same as before the war of 1870. During the same period the populations of two of her neighbours, Germany and Italy have increased, in the first instance from 39,000,000 to 65,000,000, and in the second from 25,000,000 to 42,000,000. Under Louis XIV (1638–1715) France had three times the population of Britain, twice that of Germany, and almost twice the population of Russia.[1] In the middle of the seventeenth century in France the size of the family averaged 5. By the end of the eighteenth century it had dropped to 4; by the end of the nineteenth to 3; and it is now about 2. In the last sixty years the birth-rate of France has decreased by more than 30 per cent, in spite of an abnormally high marriage rate (159 per 10,000 of total population) immediately after the Armistice. The average number of children for every marriage has fallen in France from 4·5 in 1831 to 2·5 in 1913, and 1·7 in 1921, and 1·8 in 1926 and 1932. Figures published in the census taken in 1926 give France a population of 40,475,000 which is almost exactly 1,000,000 less than the population of 1913 for the same territory, Alsace-Lorraine included. Figures published with this census disclosed the startling fact that there were 2,000,000 fewer children attending the schools (public and private) in France than in 1913. This is one of the eloquent proofs of what war means. France lost 1,500,000, killed during 1914–19. The slow rate of increase of the French population is not due, however, so much to a low birth-rate as to the appalling death-rate. This is higher than in any other country in Western and Central Europe except Spain.

The decline of the birth-rate in France is almost universally put down to voluntary birth-control, dependent partly upon economic causes which make it difficult to rear children. Wages are low, hours of work are long, and decent housing difficult to obtain. Therefore, man, the vertebrate with the most brain, the animal with the most cunning, whose inventions have given him

[1] Lothrop Stoddard's *Racial Realities in Europe*, p. 93.

H*

the most wonderful tools to facilitate the furnishing of his needs, is in innumerable instances prevented from rearing offspring easily. He commands the processes of nature by his skill. Yet the inventions accumulated through the centuries do not help him materially—so it seems—to perform one of nature's most primitive set of instincts, the production, protection, and upbringing of young. Do these primitive instincts really tend to become incompatible with those pleasures of the mind and body which are developed as the intellect becomes more cultured, and must they perforce take a back seat? But before attempting to answer that question another demands a place. It is: Is there ample evidence that the declining birth-rate in France is due to voluntary birth-control? Although there is a certain amount of indirect evidence, the answer is, No. Those given this answer who persist in believing in an affirmative reply fall back upon the obvious difficulties that exist in collecting the evidence, difficulties distinctly greater in former times than in the last decade or so. People are now less shy in discussing these delicate matters and franker in answering inquiries. But there is one glaring piece of evidence against the affirmation answer and that is the absence of so large an industry in contraceptive manufactures and distribution as the case would require. According to C. E. Pell there were in France in 1890 2,000,000 couples without children, 2,500,000 with only one child, and only about 1,000,000 with more than three children.

"So if we assume that the decline of the French birth-rate is due to the use of contraceptives, we must assume that they are used with regularity by the vast majority of married couples of child-bearing age from week to week, and this would be true of all the other leading countries of the world. This would necessitate a trade comparable in magnitude with that in some of the commoner necessaries of life, such as mustard and salt. No evidence has ever been produced as to the existence of a trade of such magnitude."[1]

It can be presumed that voluntary birth-control was not much practised in any class as long ago as 1870. Now at that time, and even before then, it is known that there was a con-

[1] C. E. Pell's *The Law of Births and Deaths* (T. Fisher Unwin, 1921).

siderable variation, which could not therefore be put down to the use of contraceptives, amongst couples in different classes. For example, the number of children born to couples who married in 1871–81 and who had lived thirty to forty years in wedlock was, to each 100 such families, in the upper and middle classes 497, but in miners 717, so that the average family varied between roughly 5 in upper and middle classes to just over 7 in miners. This variation in fertility has increased in the last fifteen years. Professor Hogben[1] brings further arguments against ascribing the decline in the birth-rate so largely to the factor of voluntary birth-control. He considers that many modern changes in social habits, such as bodily cleanliness associated with thorough washing with ordinary soap, have a big effect in lowering the birth-rate.

To return to the question of the causes for an apparent incompatibility between intellectual advance and enhanced knowledge and the breeding and rearing of children: inherently there are no reasons which suggest themselves as clear and sound to explain any such incompatibility. France is blessed with good natural resources and an excellent climate. Her people are blessed with many advantages and considerable ability and knowledge. Those who try to explain her declining birth-rate and stationary population hardly ever seek explanations in man-made causes dependent upon political and economic influences. Yet once these are called in question much light can be thrown on the matter. Some of these influences acting over many decades are well illustrated by reference to France. This country is pre-eminently one of peasant proprietors. The many in several wide areas in France are landowners rather than the few as in some other contiguous countries. The attraction of population city-wards has none the less been as great in France as in many other countries. Again agricultural production has gone up at a rapid rate in France. Have these facts been influenced by political actions, and have they any bearing on the absence of the growth of the population? Assuredly they have. For example, the laws of France, which have prevailed for a long time, lead to the breaking up of estates into smaller and smaller holdings through division at death and equal distribution amongst the children of the

[1] Professor Lancelot Hogben's *Genetic Principles in Medicine and Social Science* (Williams & Norgate, London, 1931).

deceased. Denis Gwynn[1] says that areas immune from a falling birth-rate, besides those in the north where an influx from other parts has occurred, are found in those districts, like Brittany and the foot of the Pyrenees, where the law bringing about the sub-division of agricultural holdings does not operate. He thinks the persistence of a strong religious tradition, too, tends in these same areas to check the use of contraceptive methods, and so aids in the maintenance of a higher birth-rate. But he reiterates that where the people have succeeded in maintaining the old custom of handing on their properties undivided to the eldest son, the birth-rate has invariably been higher than elsewhere in France. Although the Physiocrats, in France, were (about 1760) amongst the first economists in comparatively modern times to indicate some connection between systems of land tenure and taxation the French do not recognize the injustice of the private ownership of land. They regard the ground as if it were on a par with the forms of property resulting from man's own indi-vidual exertions. The private ownership of land is entrenched in France very firmly largely because of the extent of peasant proprietorships (there are 7,000,000 of them); and the cause of the attendant evils of taxes is not appreciated even though there is much outcry against and evasion of taxation. Lack of freedom to produce from nature's storehouse through man-made political and economic obstructions preventing access on fair and just terms to that storehouse, is the most important cause, not only driving people into the towns but also hindering the breeding and rearing of children under happy and easy circumstances.

Largely at the expense of the taxpayers some of the more thinly populated parts of France are slowly being repopulated. But this has not materially aided either agricultural production or rural wages, nor has it stayed the suck to the towns of France. The percentage of the population dwelling in cities of 10,000 and upwards in France in 1800, in 1850, and in 1890 was respectively 4½, 6½, and 26; and it has gone on increasing since 1890, for to-day it is about 45 per cent. It is low wages in agri-culture which is one of the chief causes of the attraction of the cities. A majority of the rural workers never get a foothold on the soil in their own right. The peasant proprietor sweats the

---

[1] *The Catholic Reaction in France*, pp. 167, 170.

members of his own family. More efficiency in agriculture, too, enables more people to engage in the industrial pursuits generally to be found in cities. There was a decline in the persons occupied in agriculture from 8,500,000 to 7,250,000 during the decade ending 1921, and there has been a slight further decline since then.

Some would-be leaders of economic thought seem to consider that industrial success and national prosperity can be founded upon low wages, political chicanery, and bankruptcy in public finances. French bureaucrats and politicians have become renowned for public borrowing, for inability to balance budgets, and for playing with the currency and the taxes. The French were taxed at the rate of over £8 per head per annum in 1925, and the rate now (in 1934), like that of the United Kingdom, is over £14. Wages in 1926 were said to be especially low in France. The comparative figures given by Mr. Sisley Huddleston[1] were: America 5·6, England 2·28, Germany 1·55, and France 1·35. There are many lowly paid workers in France to-day who hardly consider it an advantage to have poor wages, and too many of these, especially in the cities, work under conditions of hygiene which are reminiscent of the worst days of sweated industries in England. The height of prices, too, in France is such as to bear heavily on the poor. The density of the population in France is 193 per square mile, that is, five and a half times the density in the United States of America. But the population is very unevenly distributed, and both this and its stationary nature have economic rather than biological causes.

In considering birth-rates there is a difference between crude and standardized birth-rates. The former can sometimes be misleading. The latter take into account the proportion of married women of childbearing age in any country. But space forbids entering into these details. Suffice it to say, figures show that it is diminished fertility and not a decline in the proportion of married women in the whole population which explains the decrease of the crude birth-rate.

A factor affecting the natural fertility of marriage is the age of the parents. The age of the father is secondary in importance but has some influence. For the man fertility remains stationary

[1] *France and the French.*

between the ages of 20 and 35. For the woman fertility increases from the ages of 15 to 25, remains stationary till 30, declines from 30 to 40, and after 40 it declines very rapidly. The mean age at marriage of those not previously married did not alter greatly in a good many European countries during the period 1876 to 1915. But in most countries it is steadily but slowly going up. During the forty years just mentioned in England and Wales it went up for males from 25·9 to 27·4, and for females from 24·4 to 25·7; and since 1915 it has risen further. In England and Wales in 1871 out of 1,000 wives there were 607 under 35, whereas in 1921 only 538.

Stevenson has shown that the proportion of males born has some definite relationship with the prices of commodities. It goes up with a rise in wholesale prices. Dr. C. C. Morrell of Christchurch has demonstrated the connection between prosperity and marriage rates. It can therefore be assumed that relative luxury and relative want have an effect on total births. The desire for sex gratification in either partner may be depressed by a variety of causes, for example, by ill-health and mental anxiety, and if intercourse takes place in spite of a lack of such desire on either side fertility is depressed as well as satisfaction being less for both.

Knowledge about a great many more facts is necessary before anything like a full explanation of the causes of a decline in the birth-rate is forthcoming. It is only within the last few years that any scientific investigation has been made into the effects of stress and strain of work, of mental anxiety, and of childhood phobias, repressions, or indulgencies. A comparison of these effects on peoples of the civilized communities with the condition of more primitive races is bringing out interesting points.

The distinguished statistician, Professor Raymond Pearl in his book *The Biology of Population Growth*, has set forth certain conclusions about the growth of populations which have received a good deal of attention. He has studied such growths in a variety of populations. He bases his studies particularly on the two first-order variables (birth-rates and death-rates), and on the second-order variables (density of population). He states that growth of populations of the most diverse organisms follows a regular and characteristic course, as follows: The population at first grows slowly, but gains impetus as it grows, passing gradually into a stage of rapid growth, which finally reaches a maximum of rapidity. After this stage of most rapid growth the population increases ever more and more slowly, until finally there is no more perceptible growth at all. He makes certain assumptions partly based upon an enormously laborious piece of investigation into the life of flies in bottles! He is proud to find that the little fruit-fly *Drosophila* under controlled conditions behaves in accordance with the theoretical assumptions he postulates. He thinks he has been able "to get deeply into the biology of the business of the mode of growth of populations,"[1] even though admitting that a human population is not as simple in its biological relationships as a population of flies in a bottle. Here is one of his conclusions: "It is the form of the birth- and death-rate curves which determines the form of a logistic curve for a population, and not vice versa." Another is: (1) That populations grow in size according to the same mathematical law as individual animals and plants follow in the growth of their bodies in size. Now when the biology of population growth has been reduced to mathematical formulae and laws, that ought to mean full knowledge of the causes which underly the growth and development of populations; and when the causes are known precision in forecasting and guiding the future should be possible. But that is not the stage to which knowledge in these matters has arrived as far as human society is concerned. Mr. Pearl's years of labour are sterile. Flies in bottles are really very unlike assemblages of human beings! To understand human society properly necessitates a discovery of the fundamental influences which underly human behaviour. Unfortunately most statisticians and economists have not yet discovered the basic principles which govern society. This explains how it is that Professor Pearl can perpetrate such a statement as the following: "Perhaps the most impressive thing which has come out of the statistical study of human population growth is the evidence that the steady onward march of this growth is not sensibly influenced by the host of economic

[1] Raymond Pearl, "Population Growth," *Time and Tide*, May 18. 1928, p. 483.

and social events which are supposed of logical necessity to affect it."[1] Such writers in the twentieth century as Raymond Pearl, unfortunately, are well-nigh as ignorant as most of their predecessors of the nineteenth, and they cling to the exploded doctrines of a generation or two ago. They fear an increase of population beyond the limits of the food supply and show no knowledge whatsoever of the root cause of poverty. But the resources of nature are indestructible and inexhaustible, and the enhanced knowledge Man has acquired in the last one hundred years alone has multiplied the productiveness of decent agricultural land and the means of transporting the products about the face of the globe at least five or six times, leaving out the enormous strides that have been made in other directions, all of which should contribute to his ease, comfort, and welfare. Authorities who ignore such essentials cannot help in the elucidation of the complicated problems underlying the growth and distribution of populations. Truly, as in the days of Malthus, the "haves" can sit in their studies more complacently if they can convince themselves that the difficulties which are apt to arise by the growth or decline of populations are due to Providence. But it does not help the "have-nots" to be told that the growth of a given population is a "biologically self-regulating process."

Declining birth-rate and size of families have occurred in America as in Europe. The average American family in 1790 was 5·8, whereas in 1900 it was 4·6, and to-day it is only 2·6. The birth-rate has fallen steadily in the United States from about 35 in 1880 (estimated), and as follows: 1924, 22·4; 1925, 21·5; 1926, 20·7; 1927, 20·6; 1928, 19·8; 1929 and 1930, 18·9 per thousand. One cause of this is undoubtedly an increase in celibacy. The census of 1900 in the United States showed nearly 11,000,000 celibates over 20 years of age, 6,726,000 men and 4,000,000 women. The average age of marriage in the United States in 1928 was 27 years for men and 24 for women. According to C. T. Brumer[2] three years' delay in marriage means one child less per family. And it is generally agreed that at least three births per marriage, on the average, are required to maintain

---

[1] Report of the World Population Conference at Geneva, September 1927, *Lancet*, 1927, I, p. 726.

[2] Article on the Marriage Rate, *Economic Journal*, March 1925.

a stationary population. C. E. Woodruff says,[1] "the increasing number of celibates is another universal phenomenon of civilization which reduces the birth-rate. . . . In time it will be as natural to marry at 30 as it is now at 25 and once was at 20, and as it now is at 15 in the tropics. Hand in hand with this change will be delay of puberty by natural selection of the most fit." This same author refers also to the increase in the number of sterile marriages and quotes Dr. G. J. Engelman of Boston as stating in 1901 that whereas a century ago only 2 per cent of American marriages were sterile, now 20 per cent are so; and that the average family has dropped from 6 to 2.

E. Huntingdon said in 1924,[2] "Amongst people of the same race and social position the birth-rate is lower in cities than in the country"; and "The early farmers of the United States, quite unlike the peasants of Europe, were the backbone of the country and produced a large share of leaders. This condition continued more or less vigorously so long as there was new land to be taken up in the West, so that there was an incentive to men of ability and initiative to remain on the farms."[3] Further, he states that, "The census does not show how many children are born[4] per family in the cities *versus* the country." But by comparing occupations he arrives at certain conclusions. Thus:

	Average Number of Living Children
Farming, fishing, and lumbering ..	3·3
Mining and quarrying	3·5
Manufacturing and industry	2·4
Trade	2·2

There are more fecund immigrants in the last two classes. "Therefore if racial and social composition were similar in the two groups, and if both contain the same proportion of immigrants, the constrast between rural and city birth-rates would be greater. . . . In other words, the mere fact of city life, with its mercantile and industrial conditions, seems to reduce the size of families," despite the fact that those who have vigour and possess initiative are attracted to the cities. Of some significance

[1] *Expansion of Races*, pp. 197 and 200 (Rebman, New York, 1909).
[2] *The Character of Races*, p. 346 (Scribners, New York, 1924).
[3] Ibid., p. 352.   [4] Ibid., p. 353.

is the connection between ability, vigour, initiative, and enter-prise and access to land, referred to by Professor Huntingdon in the above-quoted passage. It is necessary, however, to add three things, viz: (1) It is, generally speaking, many generations since European peasants had free access to the earth, for landlordism in some shape or form has been established in most parts of Europe for a long time. (2) New land cannot be taken up in the United States nowadays without paying the landlord's price, either out West or further East, either in rural or in town districts. (3) In quite recent years farming, of all industries in the United States, has suffered from a slump more than most others. For various reasons, therefore, fewer enterprising persons are to be found following the occupation of farming.

The connection between national prosperity and the birth-rate has been investigated carefully by Professor G. Udny Yule, who in a paper before the Royal Statistical Society in London in 1905 showed "that the birth-rate is intensely sensitive to changes in national prosperity." Undoubtedly, when trade is prosperous young couples can find the means to set up house and have children more readily than in hard times and they will marry the earlier. Of all the obstructions to early marriage, a high birth-rate, and large families the economic is pre-eminent. One of the commonest effects of poverty in civilized com-munities is the lack of houses for the newly married. Living temporarily with a mother-in-law is an expedient which seldom conduces to thorough happiness. Yet how frequently is such an expedient followed! How frequently, too, does not the mother-in-law soon become the grandmother of one or two (often one or two only) grandchildren! And generally this is not conducive to the mental welfare of any of the three generations.

The rate of increase of population depends, of course, upon the rate at which people are dying as well as upon the rate at which they are being added to the world. Thus the growth of populations involves a study of death-rates and the rates of natural increase (i.e. the excess of births over deaths) as well as a study of marriage rates, birth-rates, and the proportion of persons living at the various ages. The rate of natural increase of a population also sometimes has to take account of immigration and emigration. Even when the latter movements can be disregarded, two nations whose rate of natural increase is the same may be very differently situated. For example, compare the United States of America with Chile. The rate of natural increase of the former in 1924 was 10·8 and of the latter 10·7. But in the United States this rate of increase resulted from the difference between a moderate birth-rate (22·6) and a low death-rate (11·8), whereas in Chile it resulted from the difference between a birth-rate of 40·5 and the very high death-rate of 29·8. It is obvious that these figures reveal a much more satisfactory state of affairs in the first case than in the second.

Death-rates are usually high amongst primitive races, especially if grouped together in thickly populated areas, and in tropical climates. They get lower as civilization advances and in spite, in recent times at all events, of greater density. The progress of the sanitary and medical sciences leads to definite improvement so that lives on the average are prolonged. Children under ten, and especially at the youngest ages, and, of course, old people tend to die more than others. The improvement in death-rates has been especially marked, in recent decades particularly amongst infants. The general death-rate is expressed by a number which represents the total deaths in a country during the year per 1,000 of persons living at the middle of the year. And infantile mortality is reckoned as the number of infants under one year per 1,000 births.

The birth-rate and the death-rate are tending by degrees to approximate to one another everywhere. The death-rates in the United States have fallen steadily as follows: In 1880 the death-rate was 19·8 per 1,000 living; in 1900, 17·6; in 1910, 15·0; in 1924, 11·8. That is, they fell 8·0 in forty-four years, or 40·4 per cent. Some death-rates in tropical or sub-tropical climates are: in Japan 21·2 (in 1924); in Jamaica 21·5 (in 1925); in Chile 30·6 (in 1916–20). In the town of Rio de Janeiro the death-rate was 48·9 in 1872–76, but fell to 22·2 in 1917–21.

The expectation of life in England and Wales has increased by twelve years in the last fifty years and by about fifteen years in the last eighty-five. Since 1881 there has been a gradual ageing of the population, partly produced by the continual fall in the birth-rate and the improved vitality of the middle-aged. In 1881 the average age was 26·2 and in 1921

COMPARATIVE TABLE OF VITAL STATISTICS

Country	Birth-rates per 1,000 Population						Death-rates per 1,000 Population					
	1880	1890	1900	1910	1920	1930	1880	1890	1900	1910	1920	1930
England and Wales	34·2	30·2	28·7	25·1	25·5	16·3	20·5	19·5	18·2	13·5	12·4	11·4
Scotland	33·6	30·4	29·6	26·2	28·1	19·6	19·6	19·2	18·0	14·8	14·0	13·3
Ireland	23·9	22·8	23·3	23·3	22·2	{ 20·8* / 19·8†	—	17·9	18·1	17·1	14·8	{ 13·8* / 14·2†
Australia	36·0	35·2	27·7	26·7	25·5	19·9	—	14·8	12·7	10·4	11·0	8·6
New Zealand	38·0	31·2	25·7	26·2	25·1	18·8	—	9·9	9·6	9·7	10·0	8·6
Canada	—	—	—	—	26·6	23·9	—	—	—	—	10·9	10·7
Union of South Africa (Registration Area)	—	—	—	—	29·0	26·6‡	—	—	—	—	11·0	9·7‡
United States	—	—	—	—	23·7	18·9	—	—	17·6	15·0	12·7	11·3
Germany	37·7	36·5	36·0	29·8	25·9	17·5	26·1	24·4	21·2	16·2	14·8	11·1
France	25·2	23·1	21·4	19·7	21·4	18·0	22·6	22·0	21·9	17·9	17·4	15·6
Italy	33·6	37·5	33·0	32·9	31·8	26·7	30·5	27·2	23·8	19·6	17·0	14·0
Denmark	31·8	31·4	30·0	27·5	25·4	18·7	20·4	18·7	16·4	12·9	11·8	10·8
Sweden	29·4	28·8	26·9	24·8	23·6	15·4	18·1	16·4	16·1	14·0	12·8	11·7
Austria	37·3	37·8	37·6	32·5	22·7	16·8	29·6	28·9	25·2	21·2	17·9	13·5
Hungary	42·9	43·7	39·4	35·7	31·4	25·4	38·6	32·1	26·9	23·6	20·9	15·5
U.S.S.R. (European)	49·1	48·2	49·3	44·0	—	—	—	35·7	31·1	28·9	—	—
Belgium	31·1	29·1	29·0	23·7	22·1	18·7	22·3	20·8	19·3	15·2	13·8	13·3

* Northern Ireland.   † Irish Free State.   ‡ Whites.

it was 30·6. The fall in the death-rate in the twelve years to 1923 applied to both sexes and all age-groups up to seventy-five years.

The longer lives attained to-day compared to the time of our grandfathers is partly due to improved environment, especially the gradual improvement in cities, but probably more than that it is due to a higher standard of education and material comfort, and to a better knowledge about man's body and the influences which hurt it. These advances are well illustrated by the life table published by Sir William Hamer in 1923 :[1]

LONDON LIFE TABLE, 1841–1922

Period	Expectation of Life (years)		Period	Expectation of Life (years)	
	Males	Females		Males	Females
1841–50	34·6	38·3	1891–1900	41·2	45·4
1851–60	36·4	40·4	1901–10	47·2	51·9
1861–70	35·7	39·9	1911–12	49·5	54·5
1871–80	38·0	42·4	1920–22	53·8	59·1
1881–90	40·1	44·5			

Because there are to-day in several civilized communities disproportionately few very young and old people, who supply comparatively more deaths, the death-rates in such communities are somewhat misleading. With that reservation a survey of a few death-rates is worthy of study. The death-rate for England and Wales in 1871–80 was 21 and in 1924 it was 12; in the same period the infant mortality rate was brought down from 149 per 1,000 born to 75. The average infant mortality was still 146 in 1900–2. In the middle of the eighteenth century the death-rate was about 35 per 1,000 for England and Wales and considerably higher in London and other large towns. But in the year 1815 it had been reduced to about 28 for the former and 34 for the latter. These now stand at 12 and 14 respectively.

In recording the following facts from the 1931 census returns for England and Wales this estimate may be mentioned, namely

[1] *Annual Report of London County Council*, 1923, chaps. xxiii and xxiv (*Report of the County M.O.H.*, p. 13).

BIRTHS, MARRIAGES, AND DEATHS (GREAT BRITAIN AND NORTHERN IRELAND)

Year	Births	Rate per 1,000	Marriages	Rate per 1,000	Deaths	Rate per 1,000
1926	825,174	18·2	318,332	14·1	536,411	11·9
1927	777,520	17·1	348,138	15·3	568,655	12·5
1928	783,052	17·2	343,449	15·1	543,664	11·9
1929	761,963	16·7	353,709	15·5	623,231	13·6
1930	769,239	16·8	355,999	15·5	536,860	11·7

that to maintain the population a birth-rate of about 19·5 per 1,000 is required. The birth-rate and death-rate per 1,000 population were as follows in 1931:

	Births	Deaths
England and Wales	15·8	12·3
107 county boroughs and great towns, including London	16·1	12·3
159 smaller towns (population 20,000 to 50,000	15·6	11·3
London	15·0	12·6

Deaths under one year per 1,000 live births were:

England and Wales	66
County boroughs	70
Smaller towns	62
London	67

Some of the lowest death-rates to-day are in the following countries: New Zealand, Australia, Netherlands, Canada, Denmark, Norway, Sweden, United States, Germany, England and Wales, Switzerland, the highest in this series being the last two at about 12 per 1,000 and the lowest the first mentioned at about 8. Some of the highest death-rates to-day are in the following countries: Chile, India, Japan, Bulgaria, Roumania, Spain, France. These range from 29 to 17 per 1,000 living.

About the middle of last century Farr put forward the theory, and brought forward a good deal of evidence to prove its correctness, that death-rates varied with the density of the population. He said he found that though the general health improved, the power of the density remained unchanged for forty years. J. Brownlee[1] has made investigations into the applicability of this so-called law. In this century it has been demonstrated that though density and high death-rate usually coincide, the correlation between them does not amount to so close a formula as was once believed. To-day hygienists are concerning themselves to analyse the complex causes of insalubrity, especially that which may occur in cities, into its constituent elements. Density is without question one of these, but recent work indicates it is more density as represented by the number of persons living in each occupied room than density represented by the number of persons to the acre. This subject will be referred to again under housing. Atmospheric pollution, more noise and vibration, and greater amount of indoor occupations, it must be borne in mind, are factors influencing health which generally go with density of population, besides many other factors.

Most writers on population questions profess a good deal of alarm about what they call the differential birth-rates. By this they refer to the fact that the poor and indigent masses show a higher effective fertility than the rich and favoured, even sometimes to the extent of the poorer producing more children the poorer they are.[2] Dr. F. C. Shrubsall referred to this subject in his presidential address before the British Association at its meeting at Toronto in 1924, and pointed out that the last census returns published a table showing the influence of differences in effective fertility in changing the distribution of the population among different social classes. A majority of those who are so concerned over the differential fertility seem to me to worry themselves because they place an undue reliance upon hereditary as against environmental influences and training, and because they have little idea of the unbounded possibilities of improvement of human stock if once real equality of opportunity were opened up for all classes. Most of them belong to the upper and middle classes themselves, and are too apt to cling to the feelings

---

[1] "Density and Death-rate," *Journal of Royal Statistical Society*, March 1920, p. 280, and article on "Farr's Law" in the *Lancet*, February 2, 1922.

[2] The subject has been extensively investigated by Dr. J. H. C. Stevenson. See his article in *The Journal of the Royal Statistical Society*, Vol. 83, Part 3, on "The Fertility of Various Social Classes in England and Wales from 1850–1911"; and his contribution on "The Decline in the Birth-rate," in the Registrar-General's report on fertility (census, 1911).

of superiority which swell the bosoms of those who have been born amongst the "haves" and whose opportunities of education are above the average. Try as they will there is a tendency to look down with disdain upon their less fortunate fellow-countrymen. Research and experience go to show that the basis of these class distinctions is but a flimsy one. Reference can be made to innumerable recent books on education which tend to prove that the superior person is not bred specially from the privileged classes. Two only may be referred to: G. M. Bennett's *The First Five Years of a Child's Life*, a little book published in 1920 by George Harrap & Co.; and H. A. Bruce's *Psychology and Parenthood* (W. Heinemann, 1915). Sir A. Newsholme[1] says "neither mental nor physical superiorities are a class characteristic." And[2] "The time spent bemoaning the disproportionate contribution of the population of the very poor were better spent in promoting the more efficacious prevention of destitution."

The experience of those who have to deal with some of the primitive races of mankind shows that these peoples can be trained along new paths wonderfully well if the pace is not unduly hastened, and especially if their prejudices and the traditions and customs of their tribe are not—as too often used to be the case last century—ruthlessly overridden. It is unnecessary, therefore, to spend anxious moments over fears engendered by a study of the differential birth-rates. So long, however, as the writers, politicians, and economists do not get down to the fundamental causes of poverty, unemployment, and the maldistribution of population such alarms will be rife. So, too, it is with all that mass of thought and the many writings which are given to the "menace of the coloured." Books, many of them most interesting and some of them excellent in their way, have been produced for half a century or more dealing with this and cognate subjects. To mention but a few of them: *The Yellow Peril* (Karl Pearson), *The Clash of Colour* (Basil Matthews), *The Rising Tide of Colour* (Lothrop Stoddard), *Mankind at the Crossroads* (Professor E. M. East), *The Shadow of the World's Future* (Sir George H. Knibbs), *Expansion of Races* (C. E. Woodruff).

[1] *The Elements of Vital Statistics*, p. 110 (Allen & Unwin, 1923).
[2] A. Newsholme's *The Declining Birth-rate: Its Nature and International Significance* (Cassell & Co., 1911—Race and Sex Booklets, 6d.).

Some of these writers are dominated by the fear of over-population and by qualms about the ability of humans to go on producing enough food. Some of them look upon war as a purifier and as "a natural phenomenon whose benefits have outweighed its disadvantages." Some consider it is the prerogative of the white man for ever "to control the tropics." Too often such ideas are associated with the exploitation of tropical mankind for the benefit of a few whites, as has been so ably demonstrated in that wonderful little book by E. D. Morel, *The Black Man's Burden*. There is a book by Professor Lancelot Hogben[1] which shows clearly the inadequacy of the alleged scientific evidence for the genetic superiority of white and inferiority of coloured races. Professor J. B. S. Haldane in a recent address, too, said, "Tests suggested that there were not many innate differences in intelligence between races so far apart as negros and white people."[2] The menace of "no prospects" has a terribly stunting influence on development. This psychological factor accounts for much.

The study of human heredity is a very difficult one. It strains the intelligence partly because it is so hard for man to be unbiased about himself, and because he is so apt to consider he already knows so much. Whereas, as a fact, present knowledge of human heredity is fragmentary and cannot easily be extended until social conditions are much more uniform than they are now. Environments vary so enormously. It has always been difficult to detect which part of human behaviour is due to heredity and which to environment; and sure it is that until recent decades the tendency has been to ascribe too much to heredity. Probably further research will show that these things are particularly true of racial behaviour. Furthermore, the rapidity of the changes in environment in modern times is sometimes so great that the chances for changes to become stereotyped are scanty. "Social change—industrial, economic, and the like—is everywhere modifying the conditions of life . . . too rapidly for the exercise of the *natural* powers of adaptation of the human race."[3]

[1] *Genetic Principles in Medicine and Social Science* (Williams & Norgate, 1931. 15s.).

[2] *Manchester Guardian*, August 7, 1933, p. 11.

[3] F. S. Marvin's *Science and Civilization*, p. 248 (Humphrey Milford, 1923) (in chap. x, by Dr. F. G. Crookshank, on "Science and Health"); see also *Trans. of International Congress of Anthropol. Sciences* (London, August 1934).

CHAPTER XV

LOVE: PROCREATION: CONTRACEPTION

THANK goodness we are emancipated from the nineteenth-century outlook on matters of sex! In Victorian days these things were treated as if they were a dirty little secret. Increased knowledge and frank discussion produce progress. But some reticence is inevitable and right when sexual matters are discussed; and liberty does not mean libertinism. The greatest, the most important thing in life, love, is not purely a private affair. Friendship, the companionship of two beings, while largely and primarily their own concern, is also linked closely to the family and the tribe. Moreover, every form of liberty presupposes an equal freedom to others, and that imposes some measure of limitation. Many somewhat superficial thinkers imagine that the new freedom of this century has made the path clear and the outlook satisfactory. But is this so? The tense emotions aroused by sex are nowadays frequently treated with an irrational and irrelevant flippancy or with a cold, scientific, and assertive assurance which are both equally inappropriate. The latest information and views on birth-control are accepted as if these settled everything. Contraceptive practices settle neither the personal and private concerns of individual pairs nor the future developments of society.

Most of the advocates of the use of contraceptives to control and limit pregnancies are extravagant in their advocacy. This extravagance casts a doubt upon the worthiness of their enthusiasm. That is a pity, considering how sensible and sound many of their arguments appear. The following are a few of the strong sayings which come from the lips or pens of this group:

(*a*) On the last pages of J. Swinburne's *Population and the Social Problem*, he writes: "A new hope has arisen, . . . due to enlightened self-interest. . . . The limitation of families will gradually extend until it changes the whole of the relations of society. The limitation of offspring, and the means, form the greatest discovery man has ever made."

(*b*) Dr. C. W. Saleeby wrote in 1925: "Poverty would be

abolished if only mankind would recognize the glorious gospel of the empty cradle as the solution of all our problems."

(*c*) "It was a crime against humanity to bring children into the world at the present time," said Mrs. Spivey at a Women's Labour Party Conference in May 1925.

(*d*) Francis Place, renowned for being amongst the first to advocate birth-control, in his handbill distributed to working people in 1823, wrote: "By limiting the number of children, the wages both of children and of grown-up persons will rise; the hours of working will be no more than they ought to be; you will have some time for recreation, some means of enjoying yourselves rationally; some means as well as some time for your own and your children's moral and religious instruction." . . . By such means you will remove "the causes of the wretchedness which afflicts you."

(*e*) Professor H. T. Laski, at a conference in London on November 23, 1931, said: "To give the working woman a conscious control of parenthood was one of the most considerable pieces of liberation that had ever come to the human race. . . . The control of the population problem would place in the hands of society a weapon whose significance is comparable with the discovery of fire. It may give us a power over nature whose consequences no one can see."

(*f*) Havelock Ellis writes (*Views and Reviews*, Second Series, 1932, p. 31): "We are about to witness, not merely in Europe, but in Asia, a fateful race between the brute instinct of unchecked procreation and the reasoned and deliberate impulse of birth control, and on the issue of that race the existence of our civilization will depend."

(*g*) E. Huntingdon (in *The Character of Races*, 1924, p. 370), in advocating the use of contraceptives, writes that society, as a whole, must decide "what kind of people shall increase in number and what kind shall diminish."

Most supporters of birth-control start on the assumptions that a natural increase of population endangers the food supply, and that control and limitation of births is the only alternative to famine and war. Bertrand Russell, for example, takes this view, and supports his commendation of a world parliament amongst other reasons so that "it may see to making subject races less prolific."

Man's most sacred trust is so to live as to use his gifts to the best advantage of mankind. There are very few individuals who are fulfilling their most sacred trust if they do not exercise their sexual faculties to procreate children. Yet as civilization advances the procreation of children becomes less and less common. This is an indictment against our present civilization. One of the sayings of Confucius is: "The art of life is to live untiringly and undismayed." Love is an art. Sex love is likewise an art not by any means always easily learnt. To-day there is much more effort made to instruct the young in the biological and psychological essentials on which the activities of sex are based. Nevertheless, how often is love spoilt and sex debased because men and women cannot live untiringly and undismayed in the society of to-day, and because the art of loving has not been acquired. It is not only the rearing of children which is hindered by fatigue and dismay, but the begetting of them. Keyserling says, "The whole of life is a state of tension." . . . "One can only play on tightened strings." Havelock Ellis quotes from his "The Correct Statement of the Marriage Problem" in his own essay on "The Philosophic Problem of Sex,"[1] and explains how contradictions in marriage, if taken in concert, act contrapuntally. The added force harmonizes with the original theme. As there is a state of tension yet harmony in the case of a well-mated pair, so in a healthy sexual life there must be some natural and largely unforced balance between sex indulgence and sex abstinence. Such well-adjusted balances contribute to a full vigour and to vitality in the physical, mental, and so-called spiritual plane. Havelock Ellis says: "We cannot well have a rich human nature without some sexuality; we cannot have a fortified and self-controlled nature without some asceticism; the whole art and discipline of the emotional life lies in preserving that harmonious conflict."

The old-fashioned idea was that romantic love had no physical lessons to learn. On the other hand, the modern old gentleman, Bernard Shaw, has recently said he would like to place D. H. Lawrence's *Lady Chatterley's Lover* in the hands of every young virgin shortly before marriage that she might be properly acquainted with the physics of mating and not unduly bashful.

[1] Havelock Ellis, *Views and Reviews*, Second Series, 1920-32, pp. 206-7 (D. Harmsworth, 1932).

How sensible such advice is compared with the view that the procreation of children is the real purpose of all sexual pleasure. The desire for a child is really only occasionally a cause of conception. Childbirth is not caused by a desire for parenthood, but is an end result of a physical craving. This century understands these things better than last. The fiction of a masculine superiority, somewhat obtuse views on female chastity, and the maintenance of ignorance amongst youths and maidens, are not much practised nowadays. The following quotation from *The Joyful Wisdom*, published about fifty years ago, is appropriate:

"There is something quite astonishing and extraordinary in the education of women of the higher class; indeed, there is perhaps nothing more paradoxical. All the world is agreed to educate them with as much ignorance as possible *in eroticis*, and to inspire their soul with a profound shame of such things, and the extremest impatience and horror at the suggestion of them. . . . But here they are, intended to remain ignorant to the very backbone: they are intended to have neither eyes, ears, words, nor thoughts for this, their 'wickedness'; indeed knowledge here is already evil. And then! To be hurled as with an awful thunderbolt into reality and knowledge with marriage—and indeed by him whom they most love and esteem: to have to encounter love and shame in contradiction, yes, to have to feel rapture, abandonment, duty, sympathy, and fright at the unexpected proximity of God and animal, and whatever else besides! All at once!— There, in fact, a psychic entanglement has been effected which is quite unequalled! Even the sympathetic curiosity of the wisest discerner of men does not suffice to divine how this or that woman gets along with the solution of this enigma and the enigma of this solution; what dreadful, far-reaching suspicions must awaken thereby in the poor unhinged soul; and forsooth, how the ultimate philosophy and scepticism of the woman casts anchor at this point!—Afterwards the same profound silence as before; and often even a silence to herself. . . . Wives easily feel their husbands as a question mark to their honour, and their children as an apology or atonement. . . . In short, one cannot be gentle enough towards women."[1]

[1] Nietzsche's *The Joyful Wisdom*, p. 104 (English Edition, Allen & Unwin).

Two other brief passages from Nietzsche's writings, from *Ecce Homo* this time, may here be quoted. He denounces (p. 140) those whose aim seems to be "to teach the contempt of all the principal instincts of life; to posit falsely the existence of a 'soul,' of a 'spirit' in order to be able to defy the body; to spread the feeling that there is something impure in the very first prerequisite of life—in sex."

And on page 34 of the same book, "All depreciation of the sexual life, all the sullying of it by means of the concept 'impure,' is the essential crime against life." Also from his *Will to Power* (p. 196) there is this further passage which has a good deal to do with the difficulties so frequently still met with in bringing about normal and proper gratification of the sexual craving: "Every power which forbids and which knows how to excite fear in the person forbidden creates a guilty conscience. (That is to say, a person has a certain desire but is conscious of the danger of gratifying it, and is consequently forced to be secretive, underhand, and cautious.) Thus any prohibition deteriorates the character of those who do not willingly submit themselves to it, but are constrained thereto." There are more than prohibitions to-day which hurt character and lead to the exercise of the sexual functions being secretive, underhand, and beset with difficulty, and more than shyness, modesty, and natural reticence. What are these obstacles; and how do they affect the growth of population?

Behaviour depends upon mental traits which are much more dependent upon environment than upon heredity. The advances in the science of psychology which this century has brought— and this science from a practical point of view can be said hardly to have existed before the Great War—have brought out that childhood is the most important time for moulding character and influencing mental traits. Sexual aberrations, the homosexual tendency, for example, which is quite common in many individuals at some stage or other of their development, when pronounced is always found to be associated with inordinate ambition and pronounced caution and fear of life; and these traits can generally be traced to the environment of childhood, very often to the mental influences of one or both parents. Aberrations of this sort always indicate a failure in personal and social integration which can generally be attributed to incorrect handling and training in childhood, or bad environment. The abnormal behaviour strives after regaining a satisfying personal and social life, and is contributed to by the frequent difficulties in matters of sex which are to be found in present-day society. Children too often grow up in an atmosphere of ridicule and discouragement if not of actual hostility. Amongst the proletariat over-pronounced docility and even sometimes a bearing as of being crushed can be traced back to the fact that the man or woman has grown up in an atmosphere of fear and punishment. Parents and teachers do not realize at all fully how great a part of the education of a child is not that to which they are constantly giving their attention, but emanates from the surroundings of the child. All the events and conditions of life impress themselves upon children even more than the conscious training and education which are imparted to them. That is why harmony between husband and wife is so important. But the harassing economic circumstances, the fatigues and worries which are so common, are apt to make harmony more difficult to maintain. It is surprising at what a youthful age a child may be affected by the hard struggles to make ends meet which so frequently assail his parents, or by the domineering character of his father, or the nagging disposition of his mother. Children too seldom can face life gladly and courageously. The present industrial system is apt to lead one man to be the enemy of another and this produces an ineradicable demoralization. The shadow of this demoralization, a by-product of the struggle for existence, falls early across the soul of the child, destroys its poise, increases its craving for power and importance, and tends to render it craven and incapable of co-operation. When the child reaches puberty and matures, shortcomings which may have become more or less ingrained will hinder normal and happy sex relationships, especially if he or she has not been wisely handled in gaining knowledge of sex. As Alfred Adler has put it,[1] "An individual who has been well prepared for social life in childhood will not have great difficulties in the sexual life. Courage, an optimistic attitude, common sense, and the feeling of being at home on the crust of the earth, will enable him to face advantages and disadvantages with equal firmness.

[1] *Problems of Neurosis*, p. 47 (Kegan Paul, 1929).

His goal of superiority will be identified with ideas of serving the human race and of overcoming its difficulties by his creative power. Deviations from the norm of sexual expression will be instinctively excluded as unattractive."

In early training no point is more important than to illuminate and dispel that still all too prevalent opinion that the male is a superior being to the female. The permeation into mean minds of the idea of male superiority has perhaps a more poisonous effect on society, and upon sexual life and happiness, than any other. It forms an obstacle to satisfactory mating, normal procreation, and the happy rearing of a family. This leads men into vain expectations of rulership and makes women rebel against their feminine function. If either of the partners is looking for a weaker mate in order to rule, disappointment is certain. It appears to be an inescapable law of love and marriage that it can only succeed where the attitude is one of giving. There is, of course, an element of selfishness in love. Donations may subserve ulterior ends. But many marriages are wrecked because there is not an equal and mutual amount of give and take. People do not sufficiently realize that entire mutual satisfaction in the sexual act contributes not only to its pleasure but also to that mutual co-operation and companionship in life after which ideal all married couples strive at the outset of their partnership. Nor do people adequately appreciate how paramount a human trait is the desire for superiority. Somehow satisfaction for both in the physical act of sex helps to smooth over the immense difficulties which often arise in bringing compatibility between these desires for ascendancy on the part of each. It is perhaps on this rock, the hard rock of mutual adjustment of the will to power of both, that more marriages are wrecked than on any other; and that rock is often hidden and surrounded by rough seas. The behaviour of an individual is modified by the amount of communal feeling that is included in his individual striving for prestige, and this is settled by childhood influences more than by any others. Hence the immense importance of the mother and the happenings of nursery years. Many an adult's powers of adjustment to meet the difficulties of sex, and the trials of marriage if that be undertaken, are ruined before the individual has left the nursery. An interesting short study bringing out the duties and powers for good or evil of parents, as well as the influence of the place of a person in the family constellation (that is, his position in the family, whether first-born, or youngest, etc.), is that written by Dr. T. E. Lawson.[1]

One of the best antidotes to the mistakes and shortcomings of parents which nature so kindly provides—there are fortunately many—is the influence of other children in the family and, to a less extent, in the school. The only child is very apt to come off badly. The members of a large family score. Because the size of families is growing smaller, maladjustments are more common in the civilization of to-day in spite of an increased understanding of individual and group psychology. Two short quotations are much to the point in these connections. They come from the pen of H. E. Stearns,[2] who has not much belief in the view that American nerves come from the hectic haste of business and industrial life. He says: "The groundwork for fatal ruptures in the adult personality is laid in childhood and in the home which produced the victim." And again: "Obviously the tired business man cannot properly substitute for a roistering, shouting brother who never came into the world at all; nor can all the concentrated care of the most devoted mother take the place of the companionship and discipline which children get from other children." Nursery schools, or still less the State as super-parent, are a poor substitute for the rough and tumble of children in a large family. One authority (Dr. H. P. Newsholme) goes so far as to hold that children of large poor families, born at close intervals, gain, from contact with other children of their own age, more than they lose from the physical privations to which they are exposed by the extra financial responsibilities of their parents.

The greatest obstacles to the natural and happy procreation and rearing of children are grouped under the heading "economic." Even when other impediments exist, the economic one usually looms large. I know a girl of nineteen and a half who is desperately in love with a man of twenty-one. She is the eldest of six. Though the parents are not of the poor, as usually labelled, they cannot be said to be at all well off. For example, no servant

---

[1] *The Robinsons: Do You Understand Your Child?* (C. W. Daniel & Co., London, 1932. 1s.).

[2] *Civilization in the United States*, pp. 335–36 (Harcourt, Brace & Co., 1922).

is kept. One motive for marriage is to get away from some of the turmoil of the house and from some of the duties of a domestic nature which fall upon her night and morning. She is in a good post earning nearly twice as much as her young man, but will have to give it up if she becomes married, according to the regulations of the body employing her. She pays a contribution from her salary towards the household expenses of her parents. She is devoted to her father and gets on well with her brothers and sisters and with her stepmother and her two (part of the six) step-brothers and -sisters. What should she do? What does she do? She takes a holiday with her young man and they buy a wedding-ring and pose as a married couple, afterwards meeting and indulging in congress whenever possible. Of course they feel compelled to use contraceptive measures to avoid pregnancy. Yet they would like children. They feel their lives unsatisfactory and stilted without them and without a home. The girl's parents are shocked when they accidentally discover the state of affairs. What should they do? They are apt to consider the young man a scamp and they know he reads "oh, most nasty and advanced literature for he actually lends her some of it!" But they realize their own partial dependence upon their eldest and her ability and devotion, and they conclude discretion is the better part of valour, and that sometimes silence is best. If the girl's parents could do without her help through having the larger income, of which they are worthy, and if the opportunities of the pair for lucrative employment were not cramped by the presence of masses of unemployment, even then other obstacles of an economic kind to marriage would still crop up.

Women should not be debarred because of marriage from following occupations which they find congenial and good outlets for their abilities. They help society by their work. Even when children come they should be able to follow their bent and they would be able to do so if it were not for economic difficulties. Again, if the couple mentioned in the last paragraph could marry they would at once find it almost impossible—unless having very ample means—to discover a house to live in. The housing difficulty, whether in town or country, is in no respect more direful in its effects than it is in this direction. How many homes are wrecked, how many young children are spoilt early in life, how many children never get born simply because of the presence of a mother-in-law! Are parents-in-law welcomed as residents in the new home? How often does the natural inclination of a mother, and sometimes of a father, to decline to realize their children are grown up, find itself coupled with the excuse of a housing shortage? Even the contributions of two grandparents on the ten shillings a week State old-age pension are often requisitioned to eke out the low and precarious earning of a poor young couple, and in return, and because of house shortage, a common roof is shared.

The exercise of the sexual function, congress between man and woman, takes place in the society of to-day too often solely through the emotional tension aroused by the physical craving involved. The act coming after a period of courtship which is, compared with that of most other animals, unusually long should have an abandon about it. But this abandon should join together the physical, mental, intellectual, and spiritual affinity of two beings. How otherwise is it correct to say that two become one? And there should be nothing underhand, nothing involving dismay or fear about the act. But is this so as a general rule in the civilization we have built? To begin with, choice of mate is not as free as it should be. Secondly, the courtship is frequently a hampered affair. Then barriers to a fine communion of souls are often present, subconsciously if not consciously, through all sorts of difficulties created by the taboos of society. Maladjustments of character arise owing to hurtful conditions of environment and to economic difficulties. Two independent persons striving through their mutual relationship, and later it ought to be through the presence of children, to attain a sound self-development helpful to all those with whom they come in contact must necessarily encounter some discomfort or even pain as well as much joy. But preventable maladjustments, economic hardships which in a world better founded would not be present to harass them, stupid prohibitions, and old-fashioned views are constantly multiplying the discomforts and increasing the pain. It is true to say that obstacles occur for us to show courage and skill in getting over them, that no advance is ever made without the consciousness of a hindrance. But it is only a born opportunist and a man well blessed with the material gifts of this world who can say,

"Nothing that happens in life is disaster, but opportunity." (Lloyd George.) Amongst the ill-paid masses disasters are frequent and often simply crushing. Again taboos and prohibitions, teaching that there is opposition between the body and the spirit, and that the things of the body are "sinful," produce either a woeful obsession with sex, as seen amongst the young of to-day (especially according to some authorities in America), or a wrong feeling of shame about acts which under freer conditions should produce nothing but elation and satisfaction. There should be no cleavage between the joy of the body and the joy of the soul. Baffled desires produce another crop of abnormalities which can be met with at every turn in the society of to-day. Cravings are balked, desires cannot be fulfilled generally through the necessity of economic circumstances, in other words through shortage of material goods.

In the classes who have plenty, revolt against strict upbringing often produces licence, even licentiousness, or maladjustments leading to reticence and fear of mating; or other kinds of disharmonies may arise due to causes already outlined. All tend to result in postponement or the shirking of marriage and to the propagation of fewer children.

Take the case of Sheila Y., for example, aged twenty-two, who only has an elder brother, and whose parents for as long as she recollects have not got on particularly well together. Her mother, like herself an only daughter, but also an only child, was brought up in a typical Victorian atmosphere, and was decidedly spoilt, also very conceited, romantic, and high and mighty in her ideas. She, the mother of Sheila, married rather above her station. She was brought up in a small village, in rather a narrow circle. Her husband is a rather bluff, practical, and astute man a few years older than herself. They both wanted to rule, especially their two children, and by the time Sheila was a year or two old their frictions had sometimes become rather glaring. Of course, Sheila was rather spoilt. After one or two rather minor flirtations she fell in love with a man a year or two older than herself who was not well off, and was therefore not much esteemed by her people. But he was very handsome and had other good qualities. She did not feel too sure about her feelings—until it was all off through the following circumstances. She refused him twice, then accepted him, then proceeded to have fearful tiffs from time to time, once ending in a breaking off of the engagement. In her heart, though herself decidedly frightened of marriage and unwilling to give up her freedom, "to be tied always to a man," she felt quite sure of the warmth of his attachment and fidelity to her, so sure that she was appalled and heartbroken when the rupture proved final, and when she discovered before many months had passed that he was paying attentions to another girl, large and handsome, somewhat resembling herself, and one who had lots of money. Her sense of self-importance—she was clever and attractive, well shaped, and a good athlete—received a fearful shock, and she only then, too late, knew how deeply she loved him. Now, years later, Sheila is still single, still somewhat disconsolate. She is a successful and ardent missionary in a foreign land and seems well set for being childless.

Or take the case of Gertrude B., aged twenty-four, the third child of four. Her father was very pious and her mother very strict. They were elderly by the time she was born. The eldest child, her sister, was austere and domineering. She had a very isolated and repressed early childhood. The facts of sex were completely unknown to Gertrude till she was twenty-one. Each bit of half-knowledge gleaned by chance came as a fresh shock. Never did she receive information with any explanation of how or why and the pieces were scrappy. Even in the nursery the sexes were very much kept apart; seldom were outside children introduced. Later, her brothers and their boy friends nearly always played separately from the girls. The idea of male superiority was early instilled. When quite young she met with a serious accident which produced a certain amount of permanent deformity of a leg and left her a trifle lame. Subconsciously she felt this very much, and suffered from a sense of inferiority which worked in two ways, making her very timid and also very self-assertive. When timid she was left alone and became more timid, when bumptious she was squashed and became more bumptious. When quite small she was teased as being a flirt because she preferred her father's elderly male friends to female ones and became very self-conscious about it. Later she was twitted about her lameness and told no one would ever want to marry her. The theory that "grown-ups know best" was practised to such an extent that she never had any opportunity of making a decision of any kind. She grew up with a pronounced decision-funk (always greatly worried till someone or some circumstance helped a decision to be arrived at), with an ultra-romantic idea of love and a scare of making a hash of marriage. For long she believed in the theory that there was only "one right man as mate for each woman." At twenty-four she broke off an engage-ment she had contracted with a man she really loved, and soon afterwards gave her services to a welfare society, where her abilities and work for human uplift and education were much appreciated. She found these decisions very hard and chose the least pleasant path because she felt it was most likely to be the right one, and because she felt Providence would intervene if not. At twenty-five another man rather younger than herself proposed to her. She took a little time to decide, but refused him, not having forgotten her former love. Shortly after this she heard her previous fiancé had become engaged and he soon got married. Then she began to wonder whether she did not love number two after all. But by this time he had developed considerable hesi-tancies about marriage; and in any case had never been an ardent seeker after her affections. Though she felt admiration for him and that love would grow, his diffidence and indecision, due to very similar causes to her own, were great. So nothing came of it and she is now, after a short period of ill-health of an indefinite kind, devoted again to her studies and to her welfare work, probably to die an old maid but always showing great fondness for children.

Amongst the poorer classes similar maladjustments occur, though probably not so frequently; but the economic causes postponing marriage and the propagation of children are, of course, commoner. Marriage is shirked and postponed, propor-tionately to numbers, less often in the working than in the pro-fessional and well-to-do classes because the former group are less proud and sensitive about keeping up a high standard of living. According to A. Newsholme,[1] 7 per cent of the husbands of the professional classes and 57 per cent amongst coal miners are married at under twenty-five. In both a proper mixture of motives

[1] A. Newsholme's *Vital Statistics*, p. 100.

for marriage is too often absent. The possessive instincts of the female over the male partner, and the domineering instincts of the male over the female, are exaggerated by the condition of present-day civilization; and such exaggerations militate seriously against happy marriages and against the procreation of a decent-sized family. The wife tends to claim exclusive possession of her husband, and natural tendencies to jealousy are fostered, because subconsciously she has behind her mind the feeling of insecurity which the common shortage of this world's goods engenders. The husband, too, treats his wife too much like a material possession and tries always to domineer over her because he wants her too much as a mere housekeeper and because he has been taught the superiority of the male as a correct attitude. Either one or the other may sometimes take to matrimony chiefly in an effort to escape from drudgery in employment, or home surroundings, or both. The romance and pleasure of independence in a little home of their own with their own possessions in it, and their own friends visiting it, appeal to them. All too often, however, before long a life of greater drudgery and less independence becomes their lot. This is especially apt to occur for the wife. The husband, more frequently, particularly if he is selfish, gets off to the nearest "pub" or finds some other form of relaxation. Both are relieved from monotony by the distractions and joys of a bevy of youngsters. Then, however, both, the wife especially, suffer from inability to get out of the home and away from the labours and duties there. I know an old lady, now over eighty, the eldest child of a large family. She married very young a man in her own village. Having been blessed with a goodly number of children she was over sixty before she had had time to visit anywhere so far away from her home village as two miles!

Or take the case of Lilly B. She lost her father, a village blacksmith, and found herself at fifteen the second of the five daughters of her widowed mother. All save the eldest, who had gone into service, had to be brought up on about 28s. a week. She found a temporary post and then went as a milliner's assistant in a neighbouring small town. She was well brought up, though somewhat innocent. She was very good looking and received a number of proposals before she was eighteen. Eventually, she fell more than half in love with one of her admirers who was slightly her senior, though she was in reality more attached to much older men, having still a subconscious romantic feeling towards those who in a way represented the protective and guiding influence of the father she had lost, for whom she had had a strong affection. She tired of her job. Meanwhile her eldest sister had married happily and settled near by. She had wonderful notions of a home of her own, with fresh work, and more personal devotion to someone who loved her upon whom she could lavish her care and kindliness. So she left her job. Her young man was out of work at the same time, and they were able to enjoy much of one another's society. A month or two later she was in the family way. Her lover prevented her seeking the advice of her mother and her greatest female friend. She was advised to marry the man and, being in love with him now and thinking it best, this she did, only to find within a few months that he was a lazy, pleasure-seeking, unfaithful Don Juan. He took no pains to find a cottage. She had to live with her parents-in-law, who treated her as a wicked and disreputable woman. Her mother-in-law hated her for many a day for stealing her eldest son's affections, and even the birth of a grandson and the sweet disposition of her daughter-in-law took a year or two to change that attitude materially. To-day the young wife has still only the one child and she is completely tied to a small house where she is little better than the slave of the four others. The two males are often out of work and seldom do a thing to help in household duties. The younger one is philandering after pleasures which he never shares with his wife, and the mother-in-law is frequently "enjoying ill-health," so that she escapes her share of the labours of the house. What will be the end of this fair maid, whose budding years were so full of promise? Is it astonishing that more children do not appear "to bless the house"? How can that desirable harmony be attained between the emotional, the intellectual, and the spiritual aspects of the mind of two beings who are thus mated? How can noble self-development of either of the partners be reached? How even can frequent repetition for years of the joys of sexual intercourse be expected? Under such circumstances is it surprising that the birth-rate goes down? Yet this is not an exceptional case. It only differs from hundreds and thousands of similar ones in the exact admixture of the circumstances.

In 1901, according to Dr. G. I. Engelmann, of Boston, quoted by Woodruff,[1] 20 per cent of marriages were sterile in America then, whereas only 2 per cent were sterile one hundred years previously; and the average family had dropped from six to two.

Take another feature of our present civilization which is at times bad, one which works adversely against freedom of choice of mate and ease of following an open, healthy, and congenial courtship: I refer to gross inequality of means, coupled with class distinctions and snobbishness. Compare, for example, the traditional outlook inculcated into the minds of the youths and maidens of the so-called public schools of England, or even similar young people in the New England States, with the happier freedom and less stilted ways of those who live and are brought up in the Western or Middle West States of the United States. It is not a flat equality which is to be aimed at, for that is undesirable and impossible, but less class consciousness, less snobbishness, greater equality of opportunity. These things at bottom depend on economic conditions. Why is society so acquisitive? Why are wives so possessive? Essentially because of the fear of poverty, which coin has as its obverse the greed after riches.

The dreariness and emptiness of modern Bohemian life, its flashy excitements and short-lived exhilarations, lead to an ennui or to excesses neither of which conduce to orderly, decent, and continued procreation of children. Nor do the many hardships which the proletariat encounters conduce to a satisfactory multiplication of children. Even the growth of popular education, and the greater facilities, through the cinema, etc., for getting knowledge, have not improved matters much, for they have led to a greater consciousness of poverty and insecurity. Again, to the ambitious, children are a handicap. Ambition is too often an exaggeration of the will to power reflex or an inordinate striving after riches, both of which over-emphases are more rife to-day than formerly.

I know a newly married couple whose standard of living and comfort is such that they expend a little money and trouble over

---

[1] *Expansion of Races*, p. 205.

contraceptive measures rather than give up a motor-car, and they intend to continue in these practices for several years at least. Another married couple from France who settled in England years ago behaved similarly after they were married for a good many years though their income, starting at about £400, went up quickly and is now over £1,500 per annum. With what result? Now twelve years later they have but one child and they are never likely to have another. They look back with deep regret to their former practices and realize, too late, what a mistaken policy they followed. They can no longer obtain any satisfaction from sexual intercourse together. The health of both is at times far from good. The temper of both is bad. They find it difficult to continue to live together. And the child's outlook for future happiness, health, and equanimity is already probably ruined.

Another couple, a Welsh pair, now middle-aged, have no children and will never have any because in early married life they did not learn to adjust themselves together either in physical or in mental congress. The woman has the will-to-power instinct and jealousy excessively developed. The man falls in love with his fellow-creatures readily, and especially with attractive females. His wife wilfully encourages his "extra-mural" amours in order to enjoy a kind of vicarious sexual excitement, and the pleasurable miseries of jealousy combined with those joys she gets by the crackings and lashings of the whip to bring her erring spouse to heel again. Constant quarrels have hampered their life and work, as have also the burdens and costs of the woman's ill-health. These phenomena of sickness have varied considerably and have seldom been absent during a period of more than fifteen years. She has consulted many doctors and has received all kinds of treatment, including surgical operations, elaborate regimes, and expensive courses of physical and medicinal "cures"; but all to no lasting purpose. Yet not once has any one of her medical advisers recommended attention to the psychological side of her make-up; and now she is too old to be likely to derive any benefit if skill were spent in that direction.

Women are less likely to attain full sexual satisfaction when indulging in sexual intercourse than men, and they are somewhat more liable to be hurt thereby. Either sex, however, may suffer, and the harm may be of various kinds. It is often much more far reaching than is generally imagined. That is why more attention should be given to this matter than has been the case until quite recently. It is too often assumed that all the so-called "finer" sides of love—as if the physical were shameful—would make up for any deficiencies in the physical. So they do to a considerable extent. But the point is the other fine qualities associated with love and mating would thrive much more if this side is satisfying. Furthermore many marriages now wrecked before any children are produced, or when only one (or two) have been born, would continue happily and result in larger families. Better mating and bigger families would produce augmented family happiness and mentally healthier children to carry on the next generation. The old-fashioned views on romantic love and the hush-hush policy about sex did not really conduce to the ideal mating, even though they were coupled with the accepted masculine dominance and the very straitlaced morals of the nineteenth century, and were capable of producing larger families and fewer divorces. They will not do, however, in the twentieth century. It has been said, "where love rules the marriage is unbreakable." But love must be complete in every way to make a happy and lasting marriage, and even people of the present day have still much to learn about it. Let it never be forgotten, however, that the mishaps and mistakes in mating that are made to-day, though they may appear to be frequent, and perhaps more frequent than formerly, are only a small proportion of the marriages which take place. Further, that the persons connected with the mishaps are more vocal than the others. A great body of humble, inarticulate people do not manage badly in spite of the difficulties and hardships of this world.

Another social evil often partly caused by repressed or maladjusted sex produces much devastating slandermongering. Backbiting, interferences with other people's business seem to be the chief diversion in some places. Both slanders and jealousies are engendered by frustration of natural instincts and desires. It has been truly said the "only begetters of jealousies are discouragements and disparagements." But the world is full of discouragements and disparagements and so is full of jealousies.

Some believe that the enhanced and wider opportunities for

recreation and pleasures in all grades of society which are now open are a detriment to childbearing and the rearing of children. But in a more prosperous and better organized society there would be plenty of room for gratifying all legitimate pleasure seeking and for a satisfying use of leisure. To spend an undue amount of energy, money, and time upon "the circus" is rather a symptom of the ill-health of society than a cause of its maladies. Furthermore, by comparison with previous ages the increase in pleasure seeking is but commensurate with the increase in the standard of living, and many of the comparisons do but bring out alterations in tastes and in the means of recreation rather than in its amount. Again, in a society enjoying ampler freedom and plenty, childbearing and upbringing need not cramp the activities of women desiring to pursue vocations of one kind or another. The rearing of the children can be delegated to others who enjoy such work.

A study of the use of contraceptives and their relationship to love and the growth of the population is called for in the next pages. Two of the most ardent and persuasive advocates of birth-control are Judge Lindsey and Dr. Marie Stopes. A striking feature of all the advocates of birth-control is their belief in the theory of over-population. Fear of a continuance of unemployment and poverty enthrals them—somewhat naturally. This book tries to indicate that poverty is curable; that voluntary unemployment is unnecessary; and that there are no substantial reasons for fearing food shortage and over-population. The advocates of birth-control start with incorrect major premises. These should be abandoned. Nevertheless let their very specious arguments recommending the use of contraceptives in certain circumstances be examined. On the face of it a plan which permits earlier marriage and allows the postponement of the production of children until the parents can better afford to rear them seems to have much to be said in its favour. Then, too, the state of affairs which sends plenty of children to the poorest and least well educated and a very few to those blessed with the opposite advantages is very sad, and if birth-control will mend that we ought to be thankful for it. If again the use of contraceptives will lessen the number of unhappy marriages, separations, and divorces, well and good. Couples can mate before they set up a home if birth-control is the vogue. They can continue to do their jobs, earn their salaries, accumulate some capital, learn to know one another better, and find out whether they are compatible for life partnership. If they cannot afford to acquire the means and knowledge for preventing pregnancies as surely and safely as possible out of their own resources, then the municipality or State authorities, it is proposed, should provide these things; and they cost a little! Presumably the poverty-stricken teeming millions of India and China will get them this way!

That very human and humane man, Judge Lindsey, of Denver, has undoubtedly helped many and many a couple to avoid tragedy. His writings, especially *The Companionate Marriage*,[1] make out a strong case for the use of contraceptives. He defines companionate marriage as "legal marriage with legalized birth-control, and with the right to divorce by mutual consent for childless couples, usually without payment of alimony." He maintains that companionate marriage is already an established social fact in the United States; and that it is conventionally respectable. He points out how it differs from trial marriage, and is far removed from "free love," for "what makes a marriage is the spirit and intent of it." He and his co-author set out an account of a number of cases in a picturesque form and with the attractiveness of a well-written novel. His exposure of the revolt against existing laws, conventions, and customs is fine. He treats the unrest and rebellion against these in a broad Christian spirit. He believes that poverty breeds divorce, and that the fear of poverty makes happy married life impossible. Lack of goods—"not enough to eat, rent overdue, etc., wreck lives, poison happiness, make sex a source of misery, and sow the seeds of divorce" (p. 115). He goes further and writes (p. 113): "The lack of contraceptive information does not act as a restraint on the unmarried; it merely results in a kind of trouble which helps nobody and does no good. Illegitimacy, social disgrace, abortion, and even suicide, are among the fruits of such ignorance." He states (p. 64) that he "has not a doubt that on an extremely

[1] Judge Ben B. Lindsey and Wainwright Evans, *The Companionate Marriage* (4th Edition, 1927. Boni & Liveright, New York, and Brentanos Ltd., London).

conservative estimate there are a thousand abortions a year performed in Denver," a city containing about 300,000 inhabitants. He considers that the emotional tension of sex is too often mistaken for congeniality of taste and temperament and that it plays for safety and future happiness if this tension is relieved through sexual intercourse for a time before any possibility of pregnancy can arise. He thinks under his plan, openly recognized, the interest of the community in marriage and the concern of society would be an excellent protection of the children when they arrived, and would maintain a high standard of morals. In this connection reference may be made to a book by B. Malinowski[1] in which he points out how the code of morals differs very much from place to place and from age to age, and how in Melanesia freedom of sexual relation is universal from the earliest years. Yet it is not immorality there. It has a place in the system of morals and leads by stages to a permanent matrimonial union. Judge Lindsey holds that the companionate marriage as suggested by him would conduce to permanence far more than would the unmarried union, because the eyes of society and the weight of the compulsions of custom would rest upon it. The law should give married couples, he says, no legal hold on one another as long as they are childless. Couples would go on working until ready to have children. "Thus the number of marriages would increase; and the number of divorces and broken homes would decrease" (p. 138). He emphasizes the immense mass of corruption which is associated with the vested interests, bringing about, through covert legal practices, collusive divorces. He caused questions to be put to a thousand women, and 70 per cent of those who answered (754) were college graduates, as to the proportion of them using contraceptives and found that 75 per cent admitted their use (p. 223).

It is an extremely difficult thing to estimate at all accurately the prevalence of the use of contraceptives. There are persons who ascribe nearly all the fall in birth-rates in various countries in the world to the increase in their use. On the other hand, a good many arguments, some of which have already been set forth in this book, show that that view is quite untenable. Considering the frequency of the sexual act it is quite clear that,

[1] *The Sexual Life of Savages in N.W. Melanesia* (Routledge, 1929. 42s.).

even in those countries where the drop in birth-rates is most striking, a comparatively cursory count of all the factories and workshops where these things are manufactured reveals the impossibility of ascribing the decrease in births to any great extent to voluntary birth-control. There are certainly not enough factories to be found to supply the need if the practice was as widespread as it is supposed in some quarters to be, unless the practice of onanism is very much commoner than there are good grounds for believing. The widespread practice of birth-control as the chief cause of the drop in the birth-rate can hardly explain, without other corroborative evidence than has hitherto been supplied, why it took the English thirty years for the birth-rate to fall from thirty to eighteen whereas it took the French a hundred years to bring about the same drop. Some authorities consider that increase of abortions has more to do with the falling birth-rate than at first sight seems likely. Dr. W. Pust said at the Seventh International Birth-Control Congress at Zürich in September 1930 that "between 1900 and 1930 Germany lost five times as many lives through the practice of abortion as she lost in the late war." It is stated on good authority[1] that in Leningrad, where abortions are now tabulated like births, and where the birth-rate for a population of 1,700,000 is still as high as 23 per 1,000, there were 53,512 abortions (legally procured there) in 1929 against 39,058 births. Similarly, in Moscow, with a population of about 2,500,000, 60,000 births and 70,000 abortions per annum are registered.[2] If any woman is uncertain who is the father of her child, when one is born in the Soviet Union, it is the duty of a statutory court to make up her mind for her, according to the same authority. But here again, in spite of these startling statements which must be taken as rather exceptional, the practice of abortions cannot be counted as one of the chief causes of the fall in the birth-rate. No, the chief causes are more subtle and, I believe, must be looked for as arising out of those influences which are dealt with in the first half of this chapter. Undoubtedly *the* most important cause of all is later marriages.

Reticence about sex is a natural and commendable phenomenon. No amount of biological and psychological training and

---

[1] See *Lancet*, December 27, 1930.
[2] *Manchester Guardian*, October 14, 1931.

instruction can dispel it, however desirable more education and knowledge in such matters may be. Largely for this reason an assessment is very difficult of such things as the prevalence of promiscuous sexual intercourse in any community, of the use of contraceptives amongst youths and young women both before and after marriage. Undoubtedly all these practices are much more frequent than they were a generation ago. They vary in different classes of society. There is evidence, which seems good evidence to the present writer, that these things are practised more frequently by those in the highest ranks of society than by the middle classes and the poor, and by the last class least. Amongst certain more or less limited communities new customs sometimes become infectious. Judge Lindsey, in his *Companionate Marriage* (p. 315), relates the goings on of a group of senior high-school boys and girls. "Nine of the girls had gone the limit with an average of five boys each. These nine of them had had such relations, collectively, more than 200 times . . . yet not a single pregnancy resulted." Probably as with prostitutes and animals, promiscuity and over-indulgence militate against pregnancy. Dr. G. V. Hamilton[1] made an investigation which leads to the following observation: "In view of the common opinion concerning the prevalence of sexual licence to-day, it is instructive to observe that 41 per cent of the husbands and 53 per cent of the wives had never had any sexual relationship before marriage; and 46 per cent of the men and 61 per cent of the women never except with the future partner in marriage. Dr. Hamilton's analysis, moreover, enables him to separate the younger from the elder of his subjects. He is thus able to ascertain that men of the younger are more 'conventional' as regards pre-marital sexual intercourse—that is, are more chaste—than men of the older generation. But not so the women. Our men are becoming more virtuous and our women less so." A large collection of data of this and a cognate kind are to be found in one of the latest publications from the Bureau of Social Hygiene. The secretary of the Bureau, Dr. Katherine B. Davis,[2] records the frequency of

[1] *A Research in Marriage*, 1929 (reviewed by Havelock Ellis in his *Views and Reviews*, Second Series, p. 179).

[2] *Factors in the Sex Life of Twenty-two Hundred Women* (Harper & Bros., London and New York, 1930. 12s. 6d.).

the use of contraceptives, of conjugal relations, as well as information about pre-matrimonial sex instruction, sexual desire, orgasm, masturbation, and homosexuality.

Advocates of birth-control for overcoming the many difficulties of life, especially those related to marriage and the growth, nature, and distribution of populations, all admit that economic factors are the chief cause of those difficulties. But they do not see that economic ills cannot be cured by other than economic methods. The earth is full of riches. The ingenuity and skill of man is great. The lack of an abundance of *goods* is due to the mistakes man slips into through not bringing human skill into full play to produce plenty of commodities from ever-bounteous mother Earth. Poverty cannot be cured by any method which strikes at the very root of our procreating capacity. Besides which the evidence is that birth-control methods, as devised up to the present, are neither sure nor harmless. In the last few months I happened to acquire the following first-hand confirmation of the fact that the best methods are not sure: A medical friend who was an expert in contraceptive measures had a delicate wife whose doctors had warned her at the peril of her life not to become pregnant. In spite of precautions being taken this event happened and an abortion had to be induced. Another friend, the father of ten, when he married his second wife, said he could not afford to have more children than the six he already possessed by his first wife. His new spouse agreed and went to the most up-to-date clinic for help. Within a year she gave birth to twins, and since then, despite precautions, she has had two more children—all doing well!

Indications have already been given in the first half of this chapter that birth-control measures are not harmless on the psychic condition of society. A great many doctors maintain that they give rise to ill-health. Just to give one illustration. One of the ablest of doctors who happens also to be an advocate of birth-control, Lord Horder, has said about one of the most favoured means of preventing pregnancy "that a satisfactory solution of the practical problems of contraception could hardly be in the production of prolonged irritation of the uterine cavity."[1] But it is not so much bodily illness as various major and minor mental

[1] *British Medical Journal*, 1933, II, p. 120.

illnesses which can often be ascribed to the practice of birth-control; and mental upsets are at length coming to be recognized as amongst the commonest causes of ill-health. Even more than illness, unhappiness can be traced to the use of contraceptive devices. It is not so easy as people seem to think, with all the skill in the world, to arrange the use of these things so that both partners attain the same amount of satisfaction as they would reach if they were not used, assuming that the pair have naturally become well mated or have learnt the way to maintain as much repetition of sexual gratification as they require. Apart from these ways of harm to marital congress and to a happy and lasting partnership there is the fact that children help to educate and bring a closer communion between the parents. Nature meant it to be so and it is no answer to say "the action of nature is blind and needs to be guided and corrected by the deliberate action of man." As Bacon said, "Natura enim non nisi parendo vincitur" ("Nature can be commanded only by obeying her"). The joy in children which the mother usually gets ought to be shared in more than is sometimes the case by the father. People talk a lot about the education of their children; but little is said usually about the education of parents by the presence and doings of their children. These joys and this training are all too often cramped and spoilt by an insufficiency of sustenance and comfort. But economic battles cannot be fought by other than economic weapons.

A scientific study of contraceptive methods has come to be looked upon as an appropriate one for doctors. It has been pertinently asked: Are medical students, then, to be taught how to prevent life and how much new life is to be produced? One of the latest announcements from the National Birth-Control Association is to the effect that a method of controlling and limiting fertility which may one day be welcomed is that which will be invented through researches now going on in the isolation and administration of extracts from glands of an African clawed toad![1] But whatever methods are found best they always have this objection, that they are least effective for the poorest classes; and they often have a further drawback, they generally leave out the family adviser, the general practitioner. Again, birth-

[1] *British Medical Journal*, 1933, II, p. 120.

control has been likened to night hoeing. The wheat is cut down with the tares. Who can say what the world loses by preventing children being born? There is much evidence showing that the reason why the poor do not produce quite so high a percentage of clever persons amongst their descendants is due to the handicaps of environment from which their children suffer. The proper way, therefore, to improve the quality of a population is to attack the causes of bad environment. Birth-control is no way to overcome the differential birth-rates.

Population could grow naturally and without any grievous results when the means for the multiplication and more even distribution of goods is discovered; that is, when poverty and unemployment are cured by allowing willing workers to get ready access to the earth and all that therein is, and when the producers are allowed to have and to hold all the products of their work without deductions by tax-gatherers and landlords. (What they paid in rent to the common pool would be no more a subtraction from their earnings than any other exchange they made of their goods or services.) With that discovery nothing further need be heard of "the differential birth-rate." With it, too, sex, including the preliminary flirtation and courting periods, would gain a freedom which is difficult in the society of to-day. For with the new liberty would come a new education, and fresh knowledge which would quickly banish present inhibitions, obstacles, and fears. The full advantages of a big family—no longer a burden to anyone—would come to be realized. A more humane code of morals, free from jealousies, would arise. Reasons for separations and divorces would grow fewer, and when they became necessary wiser and easier legal proceedings would come into existence.

The science of eugenics is very apt to direct its endeavours along wrong channels. Dr. Saleeby has written, "The concern of eugenics is not the right to live but the right to become a parent"; and there are many who follow this idea. For example, Lothrop Stoddard[1] talks about the enforcement of fundamental biological truths, which are apparently to include supermen, defining who are the élite, so that the multiplication of the least

[1] *The Revolt against Civilization : the Menace of the Under-Man* (Chapman & Hall, 1922).

fit at the expense of the élite shall be forbidden. But as Dr. C. C. Hurst says,[1] "Neither the outward appearance of the individual, nor a knowledge of its ancestry, is a safe guide to its breeding potentialities"; and he goes on to point out that until much more is known about genetics it is most unsafe and improper to venture far in eugenics. Foundations must first be made sure. At present these are not sure. Eugenics, he protests, is simply applied genetics, and sound eugenics can only be founded on sound genetics. Again, the professor of sociology in the University of Minnesota, Mr. L. L. Barnard,[2] comes to the conclusion that it is environment which is of paramount importance in the determination of human behaviour and in the formation of character; furthermore, that the future control of the human race lies, not through selective breeding of the higher social qualities, but through their transmission by social contact and control. With these opinions I entirely agree.

The increase of promiscuous sexual intercourse as a result of a further spread of knowledge about contraceptives and the harmfulness of such increase cannot be lightly set aside. As J. Lionel Tayler[3] demonstrates, the moral atmosphere of regions where contraceptives are widely used and of places where they are manufactured and sold is generally low. The same can be said about the classes and groups in society which use contraceptives. Over-indulgence and promiscuity are undoubtedly dangers of such use and lead to various evils the greatest of which are unhappiness and the absence of children and an orderly family life. Sir John Robertson, Medical Officer of Health for Birmingham, in his annual report for 1925, refers to the mischievous results which had come to light in Birmingham owing to methods of birth-control becoming widely known among young people.[4] Many examples could be given from literature, but let one suffice. In Richard Aldington's *Death of a Hero*, the hero and heroine, George and Elizabeth, freely discuss and practise birth-control. They extol it "because England has three times as many persons as the land can feed." They think themselves wonder-

[1] *Experiments in Genetics* (Cambridge University Press, 1925. 50s.).
[2] *Instinct : A Study in Social Psychology* (Allen & Unwin, London, 1925. 15s.).
[3] *The Population Problem*, 1924.
[4] See also Sir J. Robertson's article in *Medical Views on Birth-control* (M. Hopkinson & Co., 1926. 6s.).

fully modern, sensible, tolerant, and free. But, as so often happens, freedom must be only for one side, not for both. Presently George has his Fanny and Elizabeth her Reggie, and there is much unhappiness. These things breed unhappiness, neurosis, and ill-health—and lack of the divine gift of children.

Finally, it must be admitted that despite research and recent advances in knowledge much profound ignorance prevails on these questions. It is only necessary to peruse the small book entitled *Medical Views on Birth-Control*[1] to show how little of relevance scientific inquiry has yet discovered and what irreconcilable differences exist not only of ethical opinion but also with regard to method. Exact scientific knowledge should enable approximately accurate predictions to be made. Yet who can precisely tell what answers to give to the following questions, for example: What are the environmental conditions of the fluctuations of parental desire, of sex attractiveness in the married, and of pleasure or distaste in intercourse? Do any of these conditions directly bear on fertility? What are the most important *natural* influences producing checks to human over-growths of population? What are the factors which govern the natural intervals between confinements? Does marrying early cause an earlier cessation of childbearing? Until such questions can be answered more precisely and until the fundamental causes of present difficulties are exposed and properly tackled, it certainly is unwise, to say the least of it, to interfere with the eugenic and hereditary problems of love and mating. Again, class and national rivalries must follow fluctuations in the distribution of the quality and quantity of human birth-rates. It would be folly to stir up such rivalries unless it is possible to control them satisfactorily. That can only be done by knowing what are the scientific principles to follow.

[1] By Eight Writers (Martin Hopkinson & Co., 1926. 6s.).

CHAPTER XVI

THE GARDEN CITY IDEA

A GARDEN CITY is defined as "a Town designed for healthy living and industry; of a size that makes possible a full measure of social life, but not larger; surrounded by a rural belt; the whole of the land being in public ownership, or held in trust for the community." It must not be confused with a Garden Suburb or a Satellite Town, nor with such places as Bournville and Port Sunlight, towns founded by and more or less each belonging to one firm of manufacturers. Bournville, near Birmingham, was founded in 1879 by the firm of Cadbury, the cocoa and chocolate manufacturers; and Port Sunlight, near Birkenhead and Liverpool, in 1887 by Messrs. Lever Brothers, the soap boilers. Garden suburbs and some satellite towns are not necessarily self-contained or do not conform in one or other particular to the above definition. Bournville is the home of one industry. A garden city is the home of many. A garden city must organize its own public services and the essential amenities associated with town life. Bournville is dependent upon a neighbouring town, Birmingham, to a considerable extent for its public services and social recreation. Nevertheless, a garden village such as Bournville serves as a fine example of good site planning, and has a world-wide influence as a model single industry town.

Most of the efforts to establish satellite towns have broken down through the difficulties associated with moving industries to new sites. Occasions have arisen when far-seeing men have managed to do this. A travelling salesman gave a tip to Thomas A. Edison about some unfinished buildings in Schenectady at a time when he was desiring to move his factory to rural districts, with a romantic result. For now the works there founded—of the General Electric Company—normally employ some 20,000 people, and the town of Schenectady only falls short of 100,000 inhabitants by a few thousands. But usually the difficulties of transporting even a small concern are so great that factories remain where originally planted, even though success usually means paying landlordism handsomely when expansion becomes neces-

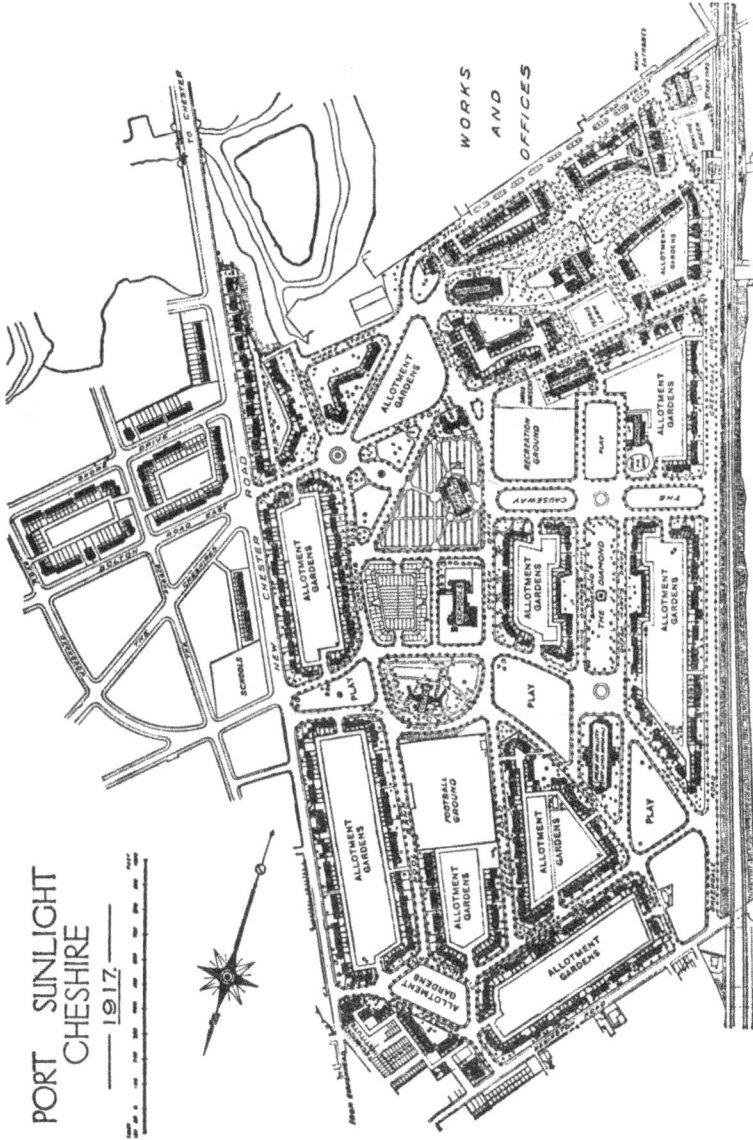

PLAN OF PORT SUNLIGHT, CHESHIRE
By kind permission of Lord Leverhulme

sary. The lack of mobility of labour is one of the greatest obstacles. If fathers are skilled in some industry they often cannot move because their daughters living at home have got jobs in shops and offices in the old town. Moreover, transport facilities for bringing raw materials and taking finished products to a good market where population is thick are not built in a day.

In 1925 some 4,000 families of Bermondsey signified their willingness to move out to a satellite town. This was a move in reply to the proposals for building ten-story flats to provide accommodation for persons displaced from slums. Conferences were held. An ideal of halving the population of Bermondsey was suggested. A Conservative Member of Parliament proposed that the Government should aid manufacturers to move out of London by lending them money. But the project never came to anything, and to-day the population of Bermondsey is greater than ever. It is not surprising that the inhabitants of Bermondsey and other densely populated districts in the centres of towns object to high tenements. For unless they are of only moderate height, and arranged as nicely as are those in Vienna, where bath and washhouses, restaurants, kitchens, and laundry houses, crêches, real kindergartens, etc., are provided in admirable fashion, the drawbacks of high tenements are acutely felt. Particularly are they detrimental to children.

In 1849 James Silk Buckingham proposed the formation of a company to build an entirely new town very much on the lines of a true garden city. He suggested 10,000 inhabitants as an appropriate size, and these were to combine industrial with agricultural pursuits. There was to be "zoning," as it is now called, that is, buildings for various uses were to be grouped together on different sites, thus one area was to be for factories, another for dwelling-houses, etc. Sanitation and health were to be constantly studied. For example, fuels were to be so used as to avoid smoke; and abattoirs, smelly factories, and places for carrying on other disagreeable operations were to be situated outside the town, and sufficiently far away as not to cause any nuisance nor yet to be inconveniently placed. The convenience, comfort, and well-being of the citizens was to be met by suitable communal baths, kitchens, laundries, restaurants, schools, libraries, playing fields, gymnasiums, etc.

In 1857 Charles Kingsley, in an address, afterwards published, on "Great Cities and their Influence for Good and Evil,"[1] advised building better things than cities, and advocated "a complete interpenetration of city and of country, a complete fusion of their different modes of life, and a combination of the advantages of both." Before his time, in fact as early as 1775 Thomas Spence had conceived the idea of local authorities as ground landlords whose revenue should maintain all public services.

Many of these suggestions were crystallized into more concrete plans by Ebenezer Howard in his book *To-morrow*—afterwards rechristened *Garden Cities of To-morrow*—published in 1898. In 1903 was formed the First Garden City Company. By skilful manœuvring it acquired some land belonging (though the owner knew it not until after the sale) to the late Marquis of Salisbury. Very soon other land was added thereto, bought from a dozen other owners, without any one of the dozen learning about the whole plan which was afoot. By skilful management of this sort, 3,800 acres were got at an average cost of £40 15s. an acre. On the central part of 1,400 acres Letchworth has been built. In the first eight years the virgin population of 400 had expanded to 6,500. To-day there is a population of 15,000. 116 factories and workshops and 3,800 houses have been erected. Although persons come into Letchworth to the extent of about 2,000 from neighbouring villages to work during the day, the city contains about 1,000 season-ticket holders to London. The neighbouring Garden City of Welwyn was started in 1920 and aims at a population of 40,000 inhabitants on the central area of 1,600 of the total 2,400 acres. The land was bought at an average cost of £50 per acre, much of it at a public auction, from Lord Desborough, and a quarter of it from Lord Salisbury. The former was annoyed when he heard about the sale as he did not wish his land sold for building. It was fortunate, therefore, that when Ebenezer Howard called on his Lordship at the House of Lords to try and negotiate the purchase of the land Lord Desborough was busy, and unable to see him. The purchase of the land and the starting of Welwyn Garden City was due

[1] Charles Kingsley's *Miscellanies*, Vol. II, p. 339 (J. W. Parker & Son, London, 1859).

to the energy and determination of one man, Ebenezer Howard. His keenness and initiative, and the actions he took to found Welwyn, are described in D. MacFadyen's biography[1] of this pioneer. Welwyn now contains a population of 10,000 and about 40 factories and workshops.

Sir Raymond Unwin, in his presidential address before the Society of Architects at Cambridge in July 1933, said that although he and his friends had advocated garden cities for more than thirty years, they had only succeeded in accommodating 24,000 persons in Letchworth and Welwyn, whereas during the past ten years the same number have settled in the Greater London area every twelve weeks. Despite the great strides in town and regional planning, dealing with industrial decentralization, housing, transport, etc., very few garden cities have been built anywhere. What prevents better progress? The answer is twofold: garden cities do not spring up because insufficient weight is given to the facts of geography and to the economics of the situation.

Geography treats of man's home and of man's work. The physical environment in which man finds himself has a profound influence upon his home and his workshop. Hence climate, weather, position, accessibility, contour of land surface, altitude, etc., all influence housing and industry and, secondarily, civic co-operation. The advocates of better planning and of smaller and healthier cities are valiantly striving to improve the relations between man and nature without seeing how close the connection is even in the civilization of to-day. What attracts the multitudes to life and work in London, in New York, in Chicago? There are many drawbacks to residence in such "great wens." Are not the chief attractions still precisely the same as those which originally led people to live in these places, viz. the advantages of position? Set the ball rolling and it continues to move. People attract people. Accessibility, and climate are still most important factors. New York City contains more than half of the population of the whole State of New York, though the latter has seven cities with over 100,000 and sixty-nine with over 10,000 inhabitants in it. New York has a population of 7,000,000 because it is so well situated at the mouth of the Hudson River,

[1] *Sir Ebenezer Howard* (Manchester University Press, 1933. 10s. 6d.).

THE
GROWTH OF LONDON

THE WALLED CITY — WHITE
ELIZABETHAN — DOTTED
QUEEN ANNE — HATCHED
GEORGE III — BLACK
18ᵗʰ Cᴱⁿᵀ ROADS ▪▪▪ 19ᵗʰ Cᴱⁿᵀ IMPROVEMENTS

VICTORIA PARK 1841

THAMES

DOCKS

CITY

THAMES

WESTMINSTER

REGENTS PARK 1820

BATTERSEA PARK

By kind permission of the Town Planning Institute

on the coast, at a latitude which enables the great ships which come to its docks to ply there all the year round. For similar reasons the older City of London continues to attract inhabitants. All the secondary ones are added thereto, such as: the proximity of the thickly populated England and many of the most closely populated parts of the Continent of Europe; its choice as the centre of government; and of financial brokerage and insurance business, etc. Similar primary geographical advantages are at the bottom of the attractiveness of Chicago as a centre. There the population has grown from 500,000 persons about fifty-five years ago to over 3,250,000 to-day. It had a population density in 1917 of 12,360 per square mile on its 199 square miles. Within a short distance from its centre there are at the present day actually as many as 7,000,000 people. It is now the fifth largest city in the world. More than one-half of the land values of Chicago are within the square mile containing the business section; and in 1917 the Marshall Field Estate owned approximately 43,000,000 dollars worth of land in this section. The total land value of Chicago in 1915 stood in the assessors books at 1,196,000,000 dollars. Its growth is due to its position in the very heart of the continent, to the fact that it is served by twenty-seven railway systems supplemented by its fine situation for water-borne traffic, and that it is near to the rich-soiled prairie lands of the central west. No wonder, therefore, that it should become the most important grain market in the United States. Because it is able to get cheap power from low-grade coal and has an abundant supply of high-class labour it has become a great manufacturing centre, especially of agricultural implements and machinery, and iron and steel products. It is the largest live-stock market, and has the biggest meat-packing business in the world.

Though the primary geographical influences still affect the distribution of population enormously, their sway does not take as prominent a place as it did once. Economic factors have grown in importance. Both influences, for example, account for the following facts about New York, but the economic probably counts highest. In 1929 three-fourths of the nation's apparel for women and nearly half of the clothes for men were made in New York. Nearly one-fifth of all the life insurance in force in

America, both ordinary and industrial, is held in New York. New York pays in income taxes and internal revenues nearly two and a half times as much as she would if the reckoning were on a *per capita* basis. The total population of Long Island in 1930, 4,103,000, is approximately three times that of New Zealand, and a shade more than that of Cuba. The Island of Manhattan was bought by Peter Minuit in 1626 from the Red Indians for $25 worth of beads and ribbons. Americans to this day are to be found who exhibit a wampum, a string of beads made out of rough torquoise, which, they say, was the exchange value of Manhattan Island in Minuit's time, and tell the tale of how the Red Indians came back to the purchaser periodically demanding further objects to pay to the new members of their clan who had arrived in the world. When the Dutch settlers tried to explain to them that was not the way land was sold according to their custom, they could not understand it. They said, "But how under such customs could the new generation get along without their inheritance, the land, from which all lived?" In 1750 Manhattan had a population of but 10,000 to 11,000 souls. To-day it has a population of nearly 2,000,000 and one which is much larger still in the daytime, so that its population density during working hours is above 20,000 per square mile. One business building alone contains 12,000 people in business hours, not to mention the approximately 50,000 visitors streaming in and out daily. The ground value of Manhattan in 1915 was $3,184,441,505, and that of New York City in 1930 was assessed at over £1,500,000,000, or at $5 to the £, $7,500,000,000. Two years later it was up to $9,000,000,000. A farm worth $50 an acre half a mile wide and girding the earth ten times would not quite equal in value the assessed value of the bare land of New York City. Mr. John D. Rockefeller, Jnr., is credited with having paid in 1928 more than £25,000,000 for a block of real estate in New York City, extending between 48th and 51st Streets and from Fifth to Sixth Avenue. It is stated that early last century this block was sold by New York City authorities for less than £900. This brings to the mind some of the real estate deals of the astute John Jacob Astor, the flutist and fur-dealer. For example, he bought the farm of Medeef Eden for $25,000, a piece of land bounded by what are now 42nd and

46th Streets and Broadway and the Hudson.[1] The rent-payers occupying this land to-day contribute, through the channels of the Astor family's taxes paid to the Chancellor of the Exchequer of England, several millions of pounds, some of which is spent in building battleships which might just possibly (though heaven forbid) be used to bombard their own city. Even if never so used, they aid in extorting extra taxes from Americans to build and maintain a navy in readiness to meet a foreign one. Far better would it be if Americans woke up and started to collect the rent of their land and to abolish all taxation. Even as I write the British Government announces that England must build bigger cruisers because the United States and Japan are building heavier cruisers.

Manufacturers are able to combine to form trusts and cartels under the all-pervading shadows of taxation and land monopoly. Cheap labour is procurable from similar causes. Workers drift to the cities of many inhabitants because more factories and jobs are to be found there, because ready access to land is nowhere to be had on reasonable terms. Wages are depressed. Some forces impel the manufacturer outwards from the congested areas. High rents, high taxes, limited opportunities for expansion, insecurity of tenure, congestion of traffic all tend to press him to more rural surroundings. But he hesitates to go far from the sources of labour supply, and from the mechanized public services which are worth so much to him—drainage, water, gas, electric light and power, the telephones, the various means of transport, etc. These arterial and intestinal systems of the big cities, forming a most complicated system of pipes, wires, rails, conduits, tunnels, along or under the public highways for the most part, have cost immense sums. If similar services have to be built up elsewhere these again will be costly undertakings. Hence, if the manufacturer does venture to move to new ground in more rural surroundings the respite he gets from the economic pressure of high rents and local taxes will be but short lived. The civic task of providing the elements of a civilized common life is distressingly heavy under the present regime of legalized theft. There is a perversion of the rights of property. What

[1] See Arthur D. Howden Smith's *John Jacob Astor* (Lippincott, New York, 1929. $3.50).

belongs to the individual, the products of his labour, is persistently taken from him in part by taxation. On the other hand, what belongs to the community, the values attaching to land due to the community's presence, growth, activities, and expenditure, is allowed to be the possession of a few privileged persons, the landlords, instead of becoming the revenue for public use. This double theft which society tolerates is the chief and primary cause of producing the agglomeration of persons into overcrowded cities. It is the chief and primary cause why the garden city idea makes such poor headway. A body, such as a limited liability company, formed to provide a garden city, Letchworth for instance, is handicapped from the start because it has to found its city upon land purchase. That handicap is removed once definite action is taken after recognizing that the value of land, apart from "improvements," is truly due to nothing else than the community's presence, growth, needs, activities, and expenditure (and this is a conclusion to which all who have examined the matter closely and without bias have come). The collection of these values annually into a common pool to be used for the service of the public will take away all purchase values from land. Moreover, Letchworth would not have to meet the constant handicap, howsoever modified by its constitution, of living in a world wherein the present bad polity is in vogue. Examine a few of the facts which this particular company has to face. Almost at the beginning of its existence it had to grapple with a group of landlords. Though a big tract, the most important piece, was bought from Lord Salisbury, there were fourteen other owners from whom options had to be got. One of these, a clergyman to boot, was represented by a lawyer who said, "His word is as good as his bond," when a request for something in writing was refused. But later this owner broke his word and screwed several extra thousands of pounds out of the company. His was central land. Shortly afterwards he was "gathered to his forefathers." Again, at one stage Letchworth wanted about 5 acres at a high spot (actually 130 feet above its highest point) a mile or so away for a reservoir. To this plot at Western Hill water is pumped from the Baldock wells for the water supply. Though it was purely agricultural land, the cost, including the sum paid for a wayleave, worked out at nearly three figures an acre. On two other occasions more land was wanted for Letchworth sewerage. On both occasions the landlords were able to "reap where they had not sown." The inhabitants of Letchworth and the Garden City Company have also had to pay tribute to the lords of the land in other ways during the last thirty years, either directly through the rates and taxes or indirectly. An important new main road giving direct access from the Great North Road to London was completed in 1931 and in the cost of this a good deal was represented by land and materials obtained from privately owned land. Similar tribute was paid some years before this in building and extending the electricity supply station. The capital invested in this latter undertaking amounted to over £350,000. The gasworks has a capital invested in it of over £130,000. Both these concerns now show a credit balance on the profit and loss account. But how much more cheaply could these services have been supplied to Letchworth residents had it been possible to eliminate the tribute to landlordism? To calculate the answer to such questions is no easy task.

There need be no surprise, therefore, that the First Garden City Company had an uphill fight at its inception and during its early years, even though at the end of its first eight years buildings had been erected in its area to a value of £365,000 and though it was able to claim an annual ground rent of £4,159. This had been accomplished at a total expenditure of £282,500, most of it on land and land development (roads, etc.). For the year ending September 30, 1932, the net profit was £12,436 (roughly the same as eight years previously), and out of this the directors paid in dividends to the preference shareholders £2,359 (5 per cent); to the ordinary shareholders (also 5 per cent), £9,760; and a little on account in dividends accrued on the 5 per cent cumulative preference shares, namely £393, equivalent to two months' dividends. The position a year later was substantially the same. In the 1932 balance sheet it is stated that the ordinary share capital is entitled to a cumulative dividend of 5 per cent per annum; and that the arrears of dividends amounted at that time to £116,555, more than half the total amount of ordinary share capital issued. It further appears that there stand under the head of loan capital the following sums: £228,960 of 6 per cent first Mortgage Debenture Stock, £200,000 of 6 per cent Registered Debenture Stock, and loans and mortgages on freehold properties £207,731. Be it noted further that in the Estate Profit and Loss Account, the total income from ground rents amounts to a meagre £14,719. Ground values cannot always expand properly to-day because neighbouring big cities attract population in rivalry to small country towns, and because the incubus of taxation strangles enterprise and quick development. In the general Profit and Loss Account a profit of £20,696 from electricity and £9,104 from gasworks is shown. On celebrating its twenty-first birthday the Company was still unable to make the first payment on account of arrears of dividend on its debenture stock. It was not until about seven years later that it could manage this. When the company was formed the principle was set forth that after paying a dividend of 5 per cent on capital, all profit should be utilized for the benefit of the town and its residents. From the annual report of the First Garden City Company for the year 1932 it is found that the total assets on the balance sheet in freehold property was £628,522 and on the liabilities side there was a total loan capital of £681,100. Reference to the General Profit and Loss Account shows a net profit of £12,436 after payment of £38,935 in interest on mortgages, loans, and debentures.

The first garden city, Letchworth, was established to be an example to the world of the principles laid down by its founders. It has been in many respects a fine example too. But one of the principles is that "the whole of the land should be in public ownership or held in trust for the community." As one of the best-known supporters of the garden city idea, Mr. C. B. Purdom states, "bringing population to land gives it value: that is the practical economic basis of the garden city idea." Land values at Letchworth have gone up a great deal in the thirty years since its foundation. Their collection annually or biannually for the people of Letchworth should have enabled them to finance all the public services they require without resorting to any other source of revenue. But because the city was founded on land purchase, and because its inhabitants are not only living in the midst of a society which is based on the private ownership of land, but also because the law of England compels them to pay taxes levied in a very stupid way, they are not able to benefit and

K

prosper by the full and proper adoption of the principle, which the founders of the city set out to illustrate. Meanwhile, and despite this, a large section of the shareholders of the First Garden City Company have hardly ever got any interest on the capital they invested, and many unpleasant speculative dealings and transactions in the stocks and shares of the Company have occurred to the detriment of some people and without due compensatory gain to others. Before the ordinary shares began to pay a dividend, brokers and jobbers tried to buy up shares cheaply for speculating in. The Company tried to confine dealings to existing shareholders. At one time £1 shares were offered by dealers at about 8s. 6d. In the event of these so bought starting to pay dividend, a return of 12 per cent on the money invested would have been shown. There were, in addition, arrears of dividends to be some day paid. The Company actually thought at one time of issuing further shares in settlement of these arrears, but found it impossible. Ordinary shareholders who took a good deal of risk were displeased when further sums at a higher rate of interest were borrowed. They had made considerable sacrifices. Many of them do not live in Letchworth. Not many of them, it can be presumed, looked forward to twenty years without a dividend. It will be a tragedy if the inhabitants of the First Garden City wake up one day to find their city in the possession of the debenture holders of a limited liability company. Such a possibility is by no means remote, at least for Welwyn Garden City. This Company has, unfortunately, had more adverse circumstances even than Letchworth has had. Such are the trials and dangers, however, of trying to base high principles on wrong foundations. The world to-day in which the advocates of the garden city idea find themselves has to contend with private ownership of the public values attaching to the ground. That great wrong involves another, viz. taxation. Speculative dealings in shares and in land follow; and these foster the gambling instincts and do few people any good. Another consequence is disappointment amongst supporters of the garden city idea that their principles are not practised more extensively.

Welwyn Garden City has to meet very similar difficulties of finance. It was ordained to be a self-contained city but it is trying to attract inhabitants by advertising its nearness to London and the excellent travelling facilities that are available to take people to and from London. It is also quite openly granting 999 years' leases for some of its sites. Yet it was founded to demonstrate the principle of employing land values in the public benefit instead of in the enrichment of an individual.

The stalwart pioneers of the Garden City movement have been harassed by a perpetual dilemma. From the outset they have seen the desirability of the land being held in trust for the community. They have realized that it is essential to get community values used for the public services. They know that enhanced values of sites are not meet rewards for any private individuals, whether these be attached to a house or factory site, or whether the individuals be banded into a company or not. Yet they have been perplexed and beset by puzzling how to bring this about. Also they have lived in a world where their views have not been shared by the majority, especially by those who have to do with land holding and all the legal formalities connected with interests in land. Their efforts to get the best of both worlds have not been successful. Their difficulties have, unfortunately, not led them to see the solution in the abolition of all taxes and the financing of public services from the revenue of site-values. They have discovered that a company founded with the best intentions and with public-spirited restrictions is apt, like others, to get in its midst those who think chiefly of the dividends to be earned. They find it difficult to decide for how long a period a lease should run, and how often valuations for assessing rents should be made. They have discovered that to run subsidiary public utility undertakings (water, gas, and electricity, for example), so as to show profit, possibly used to help the parent land-holding company, is apt to give rise sometimes to adverse criticism on the part of the users of the water, gas, etc. Again, the issue has been obscured through an unfortunate term, the taxation of land values. The use of this term to denote the collection of ground rent, whether all of it or some of it sometimes, suggests the idea of a burden on producers, which all taxes are. It connotes ownership by the payer of the amounts due; that is, it denies their public ownership, their creation exclusively by the community. The demand for the payment of a ground due, asserts the rights of the community to such dues. Such duties are owing to the public for exclusive holding of a piece of the community's property. They are paid to finance public services and to allow the sweeping away of all tax burdens. The payers choose to pay them, recognizing they get value for the payments in the use they get of the public services. The principle of "benefits received" replaces the perverse one of "ability to pay." Once such a principle is adopted all perturbations disappear on the question: Who is the community? For once the public's own revenue were collected equitably from the various interests involved, and *in toto*, the apportionment between the various bodies, State and local, and the method of expenditure would present far fewer difficulties than do the collection and expenditure of taxes to-day.

The distribution of population along the lines of the garden city idea is not such a simple matter as some of the advocates of this excellent idea would have us believe. Geographical and economic influences are so strong. Yet the statement of a few bald facts of numbers and space will demonstrate how badly packed the inhabitants of most countries are, how ill the space is used, and such statements alone should stimulate the attack on the problem of better distribution. Whenever such endeavours flourish better regional planning and the garden city idea will receive ever closer attention and support. A few calculations will show that the whole of the population of England and Wales could comfortably be housed in the County of Somerset at ten houses to the acre. This county is 1,599 square miles in extent. The Greater London region contains 1,846 square miles. Supposing, therefore, that the County of London, containing 117 square miles, be given over to public buildings, shops, warehouses, offices, and industrial buildings, on the basis of ten houses to the acre, the whole of the population of England and Wales could be housed on the remaining land of the Greater London area and still leave 130 square miles for open spaces. A year or two ago L. J. Johnson, Professor of Civil Engineering at Harvard, wrote: "It can readily be shown that there is room in our little Massachusetts, a mere speck on the map of this country, to house the whole population of the United States in detached one-family houses, five to six persons in a house, with a quarter of an acre per ground per house. Even then the density of population of the State would be no greater than of Boston—and more than half of Boston land area is vacant—and only one-eighth as dense as that of Manhattan."

In attempting to solve the intricate problem of a better distribution of population it does not suffice to say, "we have scattered the dwellings of London over a belt 10 miles wide because we have not had any proper planning or control." Planning and control, more and more of both, are the fashionable panaceas for all the ills we suffer from to-day. Planning and control will not do much to get rid of those workers in factories which are still in crowded Manhattan. Fifteen years ago Manhattan had 22,981 factories in it, employing 519,647 workers, and most of these factories were situated in that part of the island which constitutes the main business centre covering only about 6,000 acres.

The problems are much the same in various parts of the globe as they are in England and America, and the solution of them is to be found along the same lines. In Czecho-Slovakia reforms in the distribution of population have been suggested which involve the remodelling of cities so that they form centres of business, industry, and public doings and actual residence is outside them in rural surroundings. Dr. Ruzicka has written a book[1] (which has been translated into French) which contrasts the life of a family in the country with that of a family in the town. He estimates that, on a basis of 2,000 square metres (approximately an acre), being the requirement for a country cottage for a family of five, 1 square kilometre would be sufficient for a garden city of 500 families; and as the area of Czecho-Slovakia is 141,000 square kilometres and the population about 3,000,000, only 6,000 square kilometres of the total area would be needed to house the whole of the population "in constant touch with nature." Cheap and rapid transport, he thinks, could easily be provided through an extensive use of electrical power which in his country can be produced fairly cheaply.

Rural surroundings influence mind and body. Reference to this is rightly being constantly made; it is so important. Not long ago Sir Raymond Unwin, in the course of the speech before the Royal Institute of British Architects (July 1933) said: "I have

[1] *L'Eubiotique Sociale* (Paris, A. Malonie et Fils, 1923. Fr. 8.50).

been fortunate in bringing up my small family in a house where the children could run in and out of the garden; I believe there is more value in what my children called "diggling" than in any other form of education that could have been given. There is education mental, moral, and physical in contact with the earth, the weather, and growing things—animals and flowers. When father becomes grumpy and tired with the noise they make, the children have but to slip out into the garden! The difference between tenement and a home is to me not one of degree, it is one of kind. It is the difference between a home in which a family is likely to grow healthily, and a mere house to contain them."

Now the question is: Cannot even bigger cities than those envisaged by the Garden City Association have all the amenities, and most of the advantages, of the country, and cannot rural beauties be combined with all the dignity of well-planned and finely built towns? This should be possible, but only after the causes working against such happy conditions are understood and eliminated.

When Charles Dickens (1812–70) was writing, in *Barnaby Rudge*, about the district of Clerkenwell in the year 1775, he says that although this part of London was parcelled out in streets and plentifully peopled, "there were gardens to many of the houses and trees by the pavement side, with an air of freshness breathing up and down which in these days would be sought in vain. Fields were nigh at hand. . . . Nature was not so far removed or hard to get at as in these days." Clerkenwell to-day is notoriously slummy, dirty, and over-crowded. Even those open spaces, like the many squares and private gardens, which for several generations have been the pride of the west and west-central districts of London are to-day disappearing or threatened, and in some of the parks, St. James's, for example, the public are not allowed to walk on the grass. How Lord Palmerston must turn in his grave! For when he was Prime Minister, on hearing that hurdles had been put up in the Green Park, he ordered their instant removal. Yet the pressure of population and the paucity of parks and open spaces in the great centres of population, especially in the poorest quarters where they are most needed, often makes such restrictions quite necessary nowadays. Sad to say, hunger for the sights and sounds of wild nature is tending to die out in the breasts of many thousands of town dwellers. There is a true affection implanted in the human heart for the influence of those things which nature produces without much or any aid from the hand of man. Yet the crowds of city dwellers have but poor opportunities for culture of that kind. Present conditions hurt their moral and spiritual condition too. They become apathetic and irritable, easily led by the often unreasoning and inane crazes of the crowd, and stampeded by the mob oratory of dictators. If individuals could but get away sometimes from their fellows and commune with nature they would learn to call nothing common and only cruelty and greed unclean. The birds are given a sanctuary in the heart of London, in Hyde Park, in memory of that great nature lover, W. H. Hudson. But what of man? In times of yore sanctuaries were not so much places of hiding as places of healing. There is no inherent reason if population were not too thickly agglomerated, and if Kingsley's idea of a fusion between the different modes of life and an interpenetration of city and country was followed, why sanctuaries for human souls should not be provided in cities. These need not necessarily be associated with the inside of a building. Quiet woodland glades are all too seldom to be found in the middle of a town. But why not? Every-one needs to give more play to the sentiment: live and let live. But in the hustle and constraint of modern crowded cities little room is found for the cultivation of that sentiment. The evils of urbanism could be banished by the multiplication of opportunities for freedom and for the greater enjoyment of natural beauty.

The frustration of better town planning sometimes emanates from some of the town planners themselves. They are over-zealous and the unconscious servants of those who regard town planning as having the purpose of restricting the user of someone else's land to maintain or improve the value of their adjacent property (on which they are often paying no rates or taxes). Such people, who do not see the fundamental causes of haphazard develop-ment, will never do much to make the common weal coincide with the profit and well-being of individuals. These are they who constantly look to control from the departments, and regula-tions from authority. But governmental authorities are sometimes the worst offenders against good taste. There are plenty of reasons for this. One is the unwieldy size of some local bodies. Reforms can be brought in to establish better representative systems of election to public bodies and to ensure better co-operation between individuals and governments, local and national. But even if clashing interests are eliminated, towns should be of such a size as to make it possible for elected representatives and permanent officials to be fully acquainted with the needs and aspirations of the town to be administered. Loss of time in travelling about and loss of interest in the welfare of the town are risks which are run if the town is too big. This is not to say that common action by adjoining towns and districts is undesirable in certain instances, as, for example, in water schemes. Again, the load of debt charges that big cities have to bear is another source of trouble and frequently, under present methods of assessment and taxation, leads to squabbles and expense over definition of boundaries—matters which would be of no moment under a good system of raising revenue for the public services.

The supporters of the garden city idea are frequently town-dwellers who follow sedentary occupations. They have a hankering after rural beauties and after working with their hands. But they do not emphasize enough the healthiness of combining some manual labour with some brain work. Hence people are apt to consider that cities are made up of persons who do not cultivate the soil and they leave out of their calculations the necessity in many instances for that combination of the different modes of life which Charles Kingsley advocated (in 1857) in the days when city agglomerations had not grown to such vast dimensions. I remember walking along the Euston Road, London, not many years ago at the time that an age-long open space in front of Endsleigh Gardens Terrace was being dug up to be utilized for the foundations of such buildings as the finely designed Friends' House, now completed several years ago. I was arrested by the sight of the most beautiful rich loamy soil which was being dug up. Upon inquiry from ancient Londoners still alive I learnt that in the days of our grandfathers that piece of ground was the site of nursery gardens and vegetable plots which grew plentiful and fine crops for Londoners. What a pity that that open space has gone, that smoke abatement is not further advanced so that clean and nice crops could grow in the midst of even so big a town as London, and that certain inhabitants of the Metropolis could not get the health-giving and satisfying joys of cultivating the soil there unto this day. Much fuss is being made over the development of the Wythenshawe Estate near Manchester, acquired by the Corporation of that city. But few are those who point out the richness of the soil there and its usefulness for producing big and successive truck crops for the inhabitants of those parts; and still fewer are those who see the possibility of using such land not only for housing but also for cultivating crops, not oats, wheat, and sugar-beet, but vegetables, salads, celery, cauliflower, fruit, flowers, etc. There are at times good reasons in favour of an agricultural belt surrounding a garden city. But this plan is generally not so good as arranging pieces of land for cultivation within the town itself. Then workers combining brain with hand work will often replace wholetime tillers of the soil. Such an arrangement, too, minimizes one of the greatest of the difficulties which huge cities encounter, namely the transportation of foodstuffs in and out and round about their centres and their suburbs. The immense advances made in intensive agriculture in the last half century make such suggestions far more feasible.

With the greater freedom of production which a better system of land tenure and taxation would inaugurate more independent workshops and small factories would arise, and we do not here forget the many advantages of combining to produce on a large scale. The year 1924 was the first one in England and Wales to record the outnumbering of workshops by factories. In the report of the Chief Inspector of Factories and Workshops for the year 1924,[1] this fact is recorded. The number of factories was 142,494 and of workshops 133,729. With more workshops, more small factories, more home-grown foodstuffs, more production and less commerce, more intensive use of tilled land and less transportation and marketing difficulties, there would be better chances for the building of garden cities.

Again, another cause of rural depopulation and of drifting of population into the largest of the cities, namely the ennui of village life and the love of the society to be got in towns, could be counteracted by the multiplication of true garden cities. In

[1] H.M. Stationery Office [Cmd. 2437], 1925 (pp. 145. 2s. 6d.).

these the advantages of country and town are interwoven. In them open spaces and garden land for tillage give healthy occupation and surroundings; civic pride is fostered, as well as good educational and recreational opportunities for both child and adult. When the dream of clean, spacious "garden" cities has become a reality man will have recognized, as very few town dwellers do to-day, that he is a land animal, and that the social ills of the present persist because man's connection with the earth is not properly appreciated.

An attack has been made on the garden city idea by Mr. Thomas Sharp in a book which is not without attractions.[1] But a good deal of the criticism, aimed particularly against Ebenezer Howard and his work, *Garden Cities of To-morrow*, is somewhat misdirected and unjust because the supporters of the garden city idea are incorrectly accused of having no regard for civic design, and no love for town beauties, and because no credit is given for, indeed little mention is made of the specific suggestions which are incorporated in the garden city idea. It has been said: "Plan and single-land-ownership are half a garden city; zoning of the several elements is another; industry, society, and amenity complete the thing." Yet Mr. Sharp who sets out to destroy garden cities—largely, it seems, because he is dead set on "close development" for town structure and seems to have a strong aversion to "open development"—never says in his book one single word about their *principles*. He picks out beautifully designed bits of cities for admiration and emulation, such as the new town of Edinburgh started by Craig in 1767, and eighteenth-century Bath. He considers these attainments were reached through the unity of outlook among the collective creators, and because the spirit of that age understood the possibilities of the town-medium as a separate work of art. But he forgets that these productions were exceptional and that for occupation to-day their drawbacks from a utilitarian point of view condemn them. Present-day requirements differ from those of even a hundred years ago. Old bridges and old terraces, however finely designed and well built, have to be pulled down sometimes. Let modern requirements meet good culture

---

[1] Thomas Sharp's *Town and Countryside: Some Aspects of Urban and Rural Development* (Oxford University Press, Humphrey Milford, London, 1932. 15s.).

and taste, then modern developments will be all right. He says, "there is very little likelihood of the multitudinous inhabitants of modern England ever reaching the unity of outlook, the common inspiration, that once gave us beauty and urbanity in our towns. The only way we are likely to attain any beautiful civic expression is by stringent but enlightened control from authority. And the only way we are likely to maintain and extend the rural beauty that we have inherited is also by enlightened control." In making one of his very few references to land ownership—in an aside— he adds a few pages on, "it is most unlikely that real control will ever be established over county developments except through the national ownership of the land. But of what use would such ownership be at present when central authority itself is so dismally unenlightened?" The possibility of enlightenment through ownership does not seem to occur to him; nor the possibility of the growth of a fine civic spirit and an educated and refined taste. Such a growth would flourish once the clash of interests, public and personal, and individual against individual was banished. These effects would follow amongst the other results of abolishing the private ownership of the ground and at the same time doing away with all taxes. Public authorities have had a fair amount of power and good opportunities during the last dozen years or so, for during that time nearly 1,000,000 houses have been built with State financial assistance and more than half of them by local authorities. During twelve years, 334,000 dwellings have been built in Greater London alone—enough to produce forty-five satellite towns of 30,000 population, or twenty-six towns of 50,000 population. Numerous housing and town planning Acts have been passed. Good will, good intentions, and control by public authorities are not enough. Yet Mr. Sharp, while deploring the lack of enlightenment shown by modern democracies (have we got a democracy anywhere yet?), says "fresh control is needed"!

The Garden City idea has done much in the last thirty years to direct attention to town planning. It has helped towards a wider civic sense. It has encouraged efforts towards a better distribution of population. It has increased people's desires for better, more, and more beautifully arranged open spaces in cities. And it has aided in a more sane treatment of various kinds of roads and other lines of communication. It has failed to make much headway because its supporters have not appreciated how sadly they have been thwarted through land monopoly and through taxes. The constant desire of people for access, in some degree, to natural surroundings has generally expressed itself in vast sprawling additions to suburbs instead of in garden cities. Taxation and the private collection of ground values almost more than geographical influences have led to these changes in population distribution; and greatly improved facilities of transport have aided these tendencies. People can now live twenty miles from their work places just as conveniently as they could, not so many years ago, two or three miles away. These things lead naturally to the subjects of town planning and traffic which will be dealt with in the next two chapters.

One corroboration of some of the views expressed in the last paragraph is to be found by a study and a comparison of one city with another. Dwellings in Greater London, for example, are more spread out than, say, in New York or Berlin. In the latter town the majority of people live in two or three rooms in five-story buildings. Yet the towns of "close development" have spread out into their environment as much as or more than those of the more "open development" type. This at all events shows that it is not the method of development but some other commonly acting causes which lead to such things as sprawling suburbs, "ribbon development," and disorderly arrangement of buildings. Persistent advocacy of the Garden City idea will gradually help to enlighten people and may enable them to discover what these other causes are more easily than they otherwise would. It is not control; it is not authority that is needed. It is enlightenment, better distribution of wealth, and freedom that will inaugurate the new era.

CHAPTER XVII

TOWN AND COUNTRY PLANNING

TOWN planning has been defined as the art and science of arranging beforehand for the extension of towns and the protection of the country. But this definition belongs to this century. In previous centuries no thought had to be given to the protection of the country, and towns were often planned *ab initio*. It is an old science, but in the last few decades it has excited a new interest. In England several Acts of Parliament have been passed to aid a study at least, and in part to guide a practice of town planning. Regional planning strives to arrange beforehand the development of the countryside in the neighbourhood of towns. It has become necessary because the aggregations of population have become so great, as, for example, in South Lancashire and in many regions neighbouring London and other big cities, such as New York and Chicago. The art of planning cities as harmonious wholes was to some extent practised in every age. The mark of civilization is co-operation, and one of the earliest methods of co-operating was to plan a town beforehand so that it was convenient and pleasant to those about to live in it. Co-operation of this kind is seen to be a condition alike of material efficiency and of intellectual and spiritual development. City building and opening up lines of communication were two of the first ways in which co-operation between human beings came into force. Mutual benefit, the commonweal, was the motive.

Even in the days of the building of the Pyramids, about 3,000 years B.C., orderliness was shown in the layout of a town though the town was probably used only by the slaves who built the Pyramids. The small town of Kahun is usually given as an example of this and as an example of the first town known to be planned. It is an interesting reflection that the slaves of those days, who were looked upon purely as tools with life in them, were probably housed in a more sanitary way than are some of our own people in neglected slums. This despite the fact that the people who inhabited such towns, or even places like Athens in the height of the best Greek period, lived much more out of doors than is possible in colder countries.

Nebuchadnezzar, as inscriptions found at Babylon record, paved the city with limestone flags for purposes of procession, and Herodotus speaks with enthusiasm of Babylon as a city of straight streets running at right angles planned in relation to the river and to the gates of the city wall.

All town planning necessarily takes into account the contour, elevation, etc., of the site. Town planning, especially in previous ages, has been much influenced by considerations of religion, defence, and centralized government. The beauty of a town may depend upon a combination of circumstances. Athens, for example, like mediaeval Durham, depended upon harmony in the ordered grouping of a unified scheme of buildings in relationship to the religion of the day and upon the skilful use made of a fine site. Because cities had to be surrounded by walls and placed in a position where they could be defended against enemies, many ancient cities are built on high ground and are cramped. For such reasons very few gardens are enclosed in such cities and sometimes there are many cross-streets with steps. But since wheeled vehicles were not very common these steps did not matter very much. The City of Priene, a little town on the Aegean coast, built in the Macedonian age, is thought to have contained about eighty blocks of private houses, numbering in all some four hundred dwellings and housing a population of about 4,000. Its size is thought to have been 750 yards long and 500 yards wide. One of the purposes of cities was to have centres where Governments met and issued their decrees. Hence governmental buildings are conspicuous and sometimes very fine in old as well as in modern cities. Another important function which is always conspicuous in town planning, ancient and modern, is the market place or places. In ancient towns this was usually in the middle of the town at crossroads transecting the town.

The Greeks adopted the plan of making owners responsible for the repair of their property and of the adjacent roadway. They appointed officials to see that this duty was not neglected, and it seems likely they had rules and bye-laws designed to secure order and convenience in streets and to safeguard the health of the citizen. The Romans added to such arrangements. Even in those times many-storied buildings went up because ground values increased rapidly and expansion of towns was difficult. Augustus sought to check the evils of overcrowding in cities by a decree that no house should exceed 70 feet in height and Trajan reduced this height to 60 feet. But no attempt was made to rebuild insanitary areas. How similar to present conditions! But in ancient times occasional extensive fires swept away whole districts and effected slum demolition. To-day other methods have to be sought. The most notable instances of great fires affording great opportunities for planning and reconstruction are perhaps the cases of London in 1666 and Chicago in 1871. About nine o'clock one October evening in 1871, as Mrs. O'Leary was milking her cow in a small Chicago barn, the cow kicked over the lantern. That was the start of the great fire. Within not much more than twenty-four hours the main business and residential sections had been burnt, and there had been property loss of $190,000,000. But it was a wooden city which burned, and this was replaced by one of brick and stone. Chicago's expansion since then has been unprecedented. It became a place of 1,000,000 people in 1890, and now it has nearly 7,000,000. Only New York has more in the New World, and only London has more in the Old World. The Great Fire of London in 1666, in the reign of Charles II, led to fine designs being made by Sir Christopher Wren. These still remain as an example of one of the saddest "might have beens" in history, for the scheme was frustrated by the "other commitments" of the King, mostly wars. It is interesting, however, to speculate how far Wren's plans (see next page) would have fitted in with modern methods of life. Without doubt they would have made subsequent town planning easier. But even the most skilled reformers cannot plan towns and countryside so cleverly as to assimilate the discoveries and progress which take place in the course of two hundred and fifty years.

Fortunately for London, successive Governments have recognized their responsibilities to her as the Metropolis of a great Empire and have helped, from time to time, to make many improvements. It is only the present generation which seems inclined to default in the carrying out of such duties. The great Charing Cross Bridge question is constantly hung up for two or three main reasons. Compensation to landlords represents not less than £11,000,000 out of a total contemplated cost of nearly £17,000,000 for this improvement. A new road bridge at Charing Cross will concentrate traffic on the south side of the Thames This will block the roads in the bend of the river at or close to the Elephant and Castle crossroads where six main roads meet. A scheme has been put forward to minimize the present

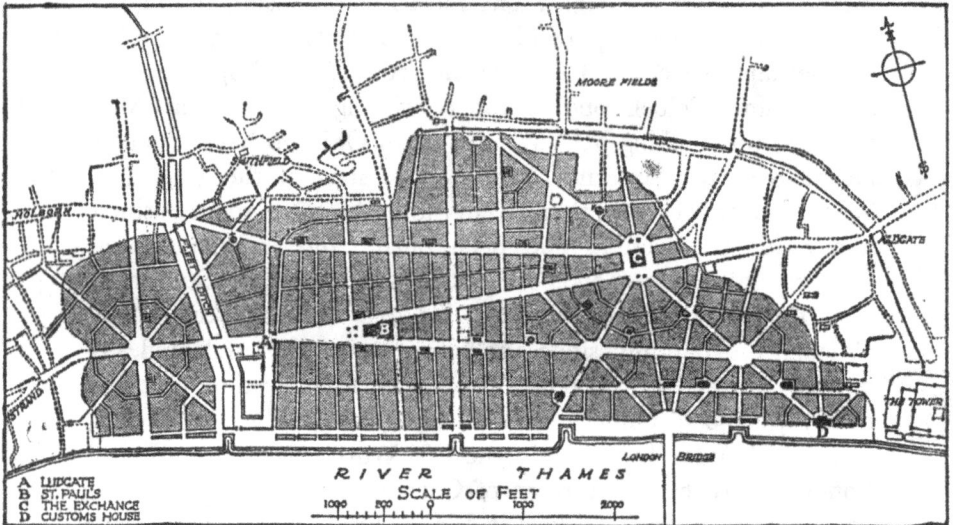

A LUDGATE
B ST. PAUL'S
C THE EXCHANGE
D CUSTOMS HOUSE

RIVER THAMES
SCALE OF FEET

WREN'S PLAN FOR REBUILDING LONDON, 1666
From "Towns and Town Planning," by T. H. Hughes and E. A. Lamborn. By kind permission of the Clarendon Press

traffic congestion there. But again, out of a total estimated cost of £1,970,000, just under £1,500,000 would go in acquiring the necessary land and easements from private owners. In neither case does the estimate take any account of the enhanced values which under our present system of land tenure and taxation would flow into private pockets as a direct result of spending public money on carrying out the improvements. Another cause of delay in putting through such schemes of town improvement as the Charing Cross Bridge scheme in London is a feeling that traffic problems are not by such means being dealt with in any really radical way. Nevertheless it is to be hoped that the appropriate authorities, viz. the National Government and the London

County Council, will follow the traditions of their predecessors. Past Governments have, amongst other improvements in London, assisted in financing the following: rebuilding old London Bridge, constructing Westminster Bridge, Regent Street, New Oxford Street, Victoria Street, Westminster and Thames Embankment improvements, the provision of Regent's, Battersea, and Victoria Parks; and, in conjunction with the London County Council or its predecessor, the Metropolitan Board of Works, the Rosebery Avenue, and the Kingsway and Aldwych improvements. This generation has so far done comparatively nothing compared with the generations which have preceded it.

One or two other big improvements in London in contradistinction to those just cited have been carried out without burdening the payers of taxes. Neither directly through taxes nor indirectly through debts have people been hurt by the building, for example, of Southwark Bridge. This stretches across the Thames in the heart of the City of London itself. It was paid for out of the natural fund accruing to the community through its own growth, needs, and expenditure on public services. It was built in 1815–19 after a design by Sir John Rennie and cost £800,000. The fund had accumulated in the coffers of the Bridge House Estate which held land, constantly rising in values, in the City. Similarly more recently Tower Bridge, costing £1,500,000, has been built without one penny falling upon London's ratepayers. "Between 1800 and 1894 the Bridge House Estates Committee expended over £2,500,000 in connection with its bridges."[1]

A further apposite quotation from the book just cited runs as follows:[2] "Away back in the early times, when London Bridge was the only bridge over the river between the town of Kingston-on-Thames and the sea, patriotic Londoners were wont to bequeath land and houses, scattered about the country, for the upkeep of London Bridge. The number of such bequests grew as time passed until, in 1818, a special committee of the City Corporation, the Bridge House Estates Committee, was established, charged with the duty of administering the trust; to-day the annual income from those lands has grown to more than £200,000.

---

[1] J. W. Graham Peace's *The Great Robbery*, p. 119 (Commonweal Press Ltd., London, 1934. 3s. 6d.).   [2] Ibid., p. 118.

"Other lands were left to the City from time to time, but as these were not specifically earmarked for the Bridge they were placed in charge of the City Lands Committee. The average revenue from these estates exceeds £300,000 a year, and forms what is now known as the City's Cash. Out of this fund is borne the expense of maintaining the structure of the Central Criminal Court, the Magistracy, the Mayor's Court, the Guildhall, and also one-quarter of the expense of the City Police Force. A great part, too, of the expenses of the mayoralty comes out of this convenient nest-egg.

"Blackfriars Bridge, built and subsequently widened, drew a contribution of £506,289 from the land rent of the Bridge House estates.

"King William Street, named after William IV, who opened the present London Bridge on August 1, 1831, is Bridge property. The old leases fell in in 1914; they were originally granted for a term of 99 years, but the war intervening, rebuilding was delayed until 1918. The new leases are for 80 years only, and it was a condition of them all that a building to plans approved by the City Surveyor, and to cost not less than a specified minimum, should be erected.

"The City Corporation adopts a perfectly simple method of 'fixing' the rent. A site is advertised to let, tenders are invited, and opened upon a day appointed. The highest bidder usually is accepted as tenant, and both parties are satisfied. There is no fuss over valuation, nor are there costly, interfering tax-eating officials to hamper proceedings. This simple and effective method could as easily be adopted for all the land."

The area now covered by the Greater London Regional Plan is 2,000 square miles. That of the County of London is 117 square miles and that of the City of London is but 1 square mile. Would that the public welfare were so well served throughout this whole area as it is upon occasions by the Bridge House Estate! It could be if the people woke up to the true rights of property.

Baltimore's parks furnish a further illustration of how the cost of town improvements can be met out of the community's own income without robbing any individual. The method by which the park system in Baltimore, Maryland, was acquired and is maintained is unusual. Many years ago a private company sought powers to run tramways in the city streets. The council granted the franchise only on an understanding given by the company to pay annually to the council for park purposes a sum equal to 9 per cent of the company's gross takings, this being calculated as a fair measure of the public's income from the franchise monopoly. Out of this income an unusually fine series of parks and parkways has been acquired and maintained. The maintenance of this source of public revenue has not been easy to arrange in recent years. Like other cities, complicated questions of competitive traffic for conveyance of the public along the streets have arisen and are difficult to settle. Another urgent problem in many cities in America and elsewhere is the finding of space for parking cars. Sites for temporarily leaving a car are all too scarce, especially close to business and shopping centres.

The original parent of all books on town planning is Sir Thomas More's *Utopia*. More's vision saw the importance of wide streets, and the dignity of close development if associated with large gardens and open spaces as a background for important buildings and for recreation. He emphasized the necessity for planning market places conveniently and for having control over land for expansion. But to give an illustration of the impossibility of even so great a man as More looking far into the future, he failed to foresee how river pollutions would grow, for he recommended that the filth of the city should be washed away by diverting streams. He knew well, however, what moderns have lost sight of, viz. that occupiers of land "count this the most just cause of war, namely when any people holdeth a piece of ground void and vacant to no good or profitable use, keeping other from the use and possession of it, which notwithstanding by the law of nature ought thereof to be nourished and relieved." This observation strikes at the root of all the problems which surround town and country planning. Recent years have brought out most of the admirable methods and aims to which planners must aspire. But always they are knocking up against the difficulties over the means for carrying out their plans, and most of these difficulties centre round the powers of ultimate control of landlordism. Landlordism is able to hold ground vacant or under-used which obviously ought to be put to different use, ground covered with slums, or with dwelling-houses where shops or public buildings ought to rise, or where trees, flowers, or grass should be growing. Private ownership can also thwart schemes of improvement by obstinacy or extortionate price of land. The planners ordain which region should be set aside or rebuilt for resident dwellings; which for offices, stores, public buildings, factories, etc.; which for open spaces and park, and where roads should run and what kind of roads; but every time the landlord has to be coaxed, cajoled, or compensated. Even the wheedling advantage of self-interest is generally not sufficient to coax him without use of the other two influences. For he is either out for immediate returns at whatever cost, and not far-seeing enough, or else he is in a position to consider it worth his while to wait for the rise in land values that inevitably occurs in an advancing country. His powers are only temporarily curtailed or apparently clipped by proposals for compulsory purchase. Plans for municipalities to expropriate and hold land in advance of development do not as a rule come off.

Great advances in the power of the public authorities to control town development were made in England by the Public Health Acts of 1872 and 1875, and in Germany in 1870. The Act of 1875 was rightly counted a great landmark. Amongst other things it gave powers to local authorities to make bye-laws regulating the construction and width of streets, the amount of air-space round buildings, the construction of the buildings themselves, and the closing of houses which were not fit for human habitation. But, like the outcome of similar regulations in Germany and elsewhere, one of its striking effects was to raise the value of the ground, and with these values going to a few private individuals who did nothing in return, housing and town difficulties were increased. Also many bye-laws raise the cost of buildings without increasing their efficiency. J. S. Nettlefold, in his *Practical Town Planning*,[1] has shown how grievously overcrowding has been encouraged by those regulations in Germany which, while aiming at better town planning, allowed too high a building density. Land values in working-class districts in many German towns consequently went up to £5,000 and even occasionally to £15,000 per acre. He goes on to say: "The landjobbers are well paid, but their tenants have been badly caught by these

[1] Pages 20–21 (St. Catherine Press, London, 1914).

successful philanthropists, on whose land they are huddled together with the ostensible object of providing houses at lower rents, and the best German town planners are now taking measures (largely successful since this was written [Author]) to reduce building density in residential areas. In the words of Professor Eberstadt, of Berlin, 'The power of town planning passed . . . into the hands of the professional speculators.' "

It matters little what kind of public authority it is which attempts to control and regulate town planning, the effects on ground values are always much the same. In Great Britain Acts of Parliament have been for the most part the authority for public control of town planning. In Germany powers are given to the municipalities. In America, on the other hand, the powers controlling planning and zoning are vested in town officers acting under ordinances based on what is termed the "Police Powers" to institute regulations for the health, morals, safety, and general welfare of the community. In all circumstances such powers are really secondary to those entrusted to the assessors and gatherers of taxes. Because these property and appraisal influences are not felt as directly as they ought to be and are not based on justice and equity, no driving force is behind to ensure better planning. Laws can be enacted by the score, regulations ordained by the hundred, yet still it is possible to say, "There is absolutely no statutory power that definitely provides for restricting the growth of towns or determining the direction of their growth." This is a sentence from a regional planning report that has just been published in England by the South-east Essex Joint Committee, and its truth will remain until property rights are respected, both those of the community in the revenue it creates and those of the individuals in the products of their own labour.

If a survey of English towns and villages be made a sense of bewilderment is produced. "There seems no trace in England of a definite type of plan such as the chess-board arrangement that marks so many cities of the ancient world. Yet a little further study, concentrated especially upon the central portions of our town plans, will lead to the discovery that English towns fall into two classes. The street plans of the first, the vast majority, resemble an irregular spider's web with the main lines radiating from the centre; those of the second are like a gridiron, formed by parallel lines. But in all the larger towns of the second class the central, gridiron, portion is surrounded by later accretions arranged like the spider's web.

"This difference in design reflects a difference in origin and history; the town with parallel streets began as a town and must at some period have been laid out as a whole; its roads are contemporary with its original buildings. But the town with

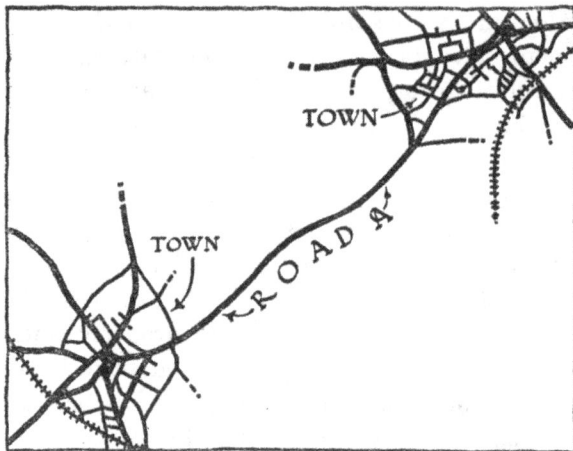

DIAGRAM ILLUSTRATING "STAR" AND "RIBBON" DEVELOPMENT

Towns develop along roads radiating from a centre and buildings tend to arise on these roads of accessibility to persons and public services

By kind permission of the Garden Cities and Town Planning Association

radiating streets began as a village and grew to its present form without an organized plan; its main streets are the roads and tracks which connected the original nucleus with neighbouring places, the fortuitous lines of which have largely determined the lay-out of the side streets that branch off from them."[1] Both types of town planning can be understood when the laws which govern human action are appreciated.

Two axiomatic propositions should ever be borne in mind when town and country planning are under consideration, namely: (1) easy accessibility to fellow human beings for co-operation with them must always underlie good planning; and

[1] *Towns and Town Planning Ancient and Modern*, by T. H. Hughes and E. A. G. Lamborn (Clarendon Press, Oxford, 1923).

(2) a man generally likes to live within comfortable reach of the place where he works. These two propositions are the direct outcome of the first law of economics, viz. man seeks to gratify his desires with an expenditure of the minimum amount of exertion. From the first law of economics, a law as inescapable as the law of gravity is in the physical world, follows the second law of economics, the law of rent. The rent of land is the price paid for the right to occupy and use the earth as well as for the advantages of superior soils and sites. Or it can be defined as economic rent representing the natural bonus which attaches to the more productive lands in consequence of the presence, industry, and demand of the people. It is impossible to escape from rent. Society always collects rent for itself or pays it out to individuals who have not earned it and do nothing in return for receiving it. Unless the economics of the situation, and the fundamental principles underlying the growth of cities and the distribution of population are recognized and understood, no real headway can be expected.

The cause of star development is largely due to a denial of the rights of property, especially the rights of the community to the values it creates by its growth and expenditure. Take the influence of the public services, say the provision of water and sewers, upon continuous building abutting on to public roads. These services, even as soon as projected, send up the value of adjacent land. If the paving and metalling of roads and the sewering are done by the owners of private roads they are generally done cheaply so that the owner can make as much profit as possible. When the roads become adopted by the corporation it is found sometimes that the owners have been successful in getting on the blind side of that body or of the magistrates and they have thus been enabled to shunt their responsibilities upon the ratepayers. Trouble and cost to the community then arise because the owners have used less durable materials and less good construction than they should have done. In any case a large city has to spend big sums annually on these services. Manchester, for example (population 766,000), in 1925 spent £287,393 on paving, sewering, and highways—which was equivalent to a rate of 11d. in the pound. Such expenditure was high that year because of new housing estate development. Yet the rate is not levied on the holders of site values, as is done to some extent in New York and some other places. Naturally these holders "make hay while the sun shines" by "realizing" the

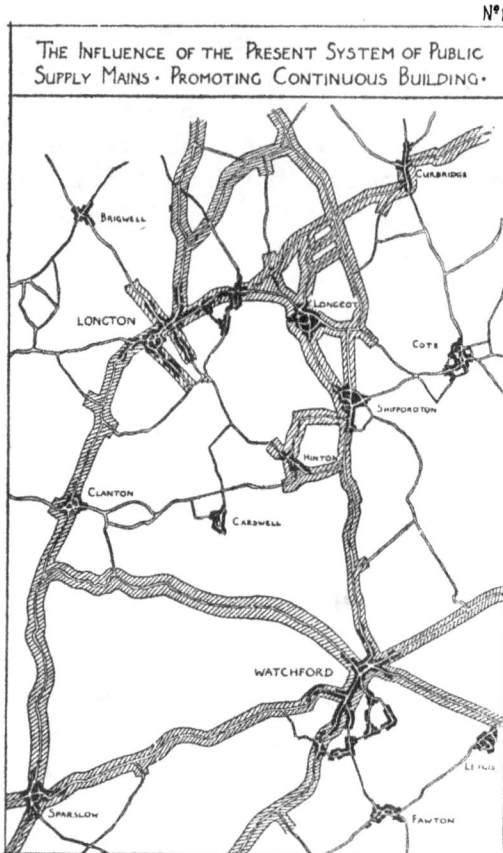

By kind permission of the Garden Cities and Town Planning Association

value of "their" property as quickly as they can. Few of them are far-seeing enough to realize that sometimes they can reap more by preserving a good hinterland behind their frontages. That great town planner, Jocelyn Abram, in an interesting article[1] has shown with illustrative diagrams how much better it would be, where possible, to use localized sources of water rather

---

[1] Miss Jocelyn F. Abram, A.M.T.P.I., "The Inter-Relation of Public Services and Town Planning," in *Garden Cities and Town Planning* (Garden Cities Association, London, December 1929).

than to depend, as is occurring increasingly, upon public supply mains. These ideas should be read in connection with the views expressed above (see pp. 194 and 202) on more natural methods of

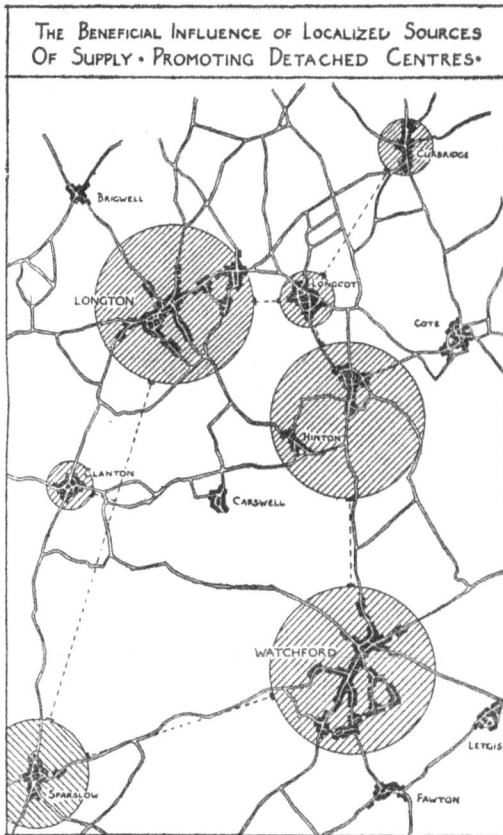

N° 2

THE BENEFICIAL INFLUENCE OF LOCALIZED SOURCES OF SUPPLY · PROMOTING DETACHED CENTRES·

By kind permission of the Garden Cities and Town Planning Association

sewage disposal.[1] Another article in the same journal and the same date is to be found on "Roads and the Public Services." It is by Rees Jeffreys. It deals with the methods whereby the public roadways can best be exploited by having subways along underneath them for service pipes and cables, etc. It also refers to difficulties arising when efforts are made to take such subways at the back of buildings or across land which is private thereby involving costly negotiations for wayleaves. Such difficulties

[1] See also pp. 317 and 318, under the heading of "ribbon" development.

would not be great if once private interests could be made to coincide with public benefit. The magnificent systems of sewers and pipe-subways of Paris, Brussels, and Nottingham are referred to.

Only one advantage of moment has been discovered about the prevalent star-shape development of cities, and that is it has enabled "by-pass" roads to be built more cheaply than would

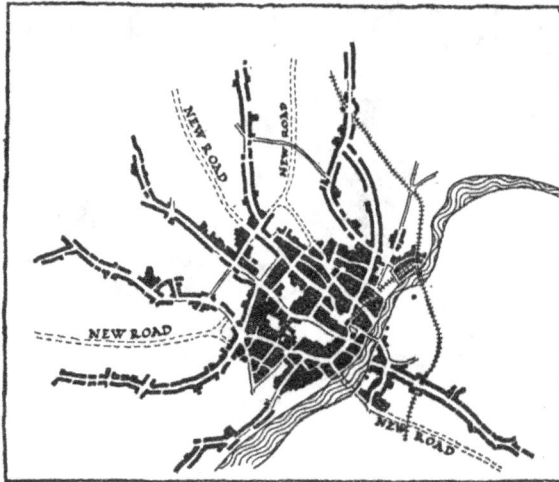

"STAR" AND "RIBBON" DEVELOPMENT. POSITION OF NEW
TRAFFIC RELIEF ROADS IN SUCH TOWNS
By kind permission of the Garden Cities and Town Planning Association

otherwise have been the case. Thus, because building takes place along main roads radiating from a centre, land is left undeveloped between these roads. The existence of these spaces between radial roads has made possible the construction of the by-pass roadways without having to meet the heavier cost of compensating landlords along the radial roads.

At a recent Public Health Congress (held in London at the Royal Agricultural Hall, November 1932), Mr. J. R. Oxenham, of Brigg, read an illuminating paper on "The Future Development of Large Towns, with special reference to their size and population."[1] He shows that towns grow slowly in England and Wales until the 15,000 mark is reached, but from this point to

[1] See the *Journal of the Institute of Municipal and County Engineers*, Vol. LIX, No. 12.

the 100,000 population mark the rate of increase is at its maximum. He says, "It would appear that the most effective aggregation for large towns is a population of 50,000 to 100,000. There are now in England and Wales sixty-two such towns, twelve having been added to the group during the last intercensal period." He favours garden cities and satellite towns and the limitation of the size of towns by a national decree. "As soon as it became patent that any town was about to reach the decreed limit of population, the regional authority would proceed to seek the most suitable site in the neighbourhood and establish there the nucleus of another large town, . . . at least 12 miles from the centre of the old town," . . . which would leave an "agricultural belt of a width of about eight miles between the two towns." All very well in theory, but again an example of powerlessness in practice through no grasp of the fundamental underlying economics of population growth and distribution. Without regard to these radical influences town and country planners cannot reach that happy goal on which Mr. Oxenham has set his heart "when all conflicting interests will be fused into concord for promotion of the common weal; . . . when all development will be co-ordinated and directed by wise foresight and control; when rashness and hastily conceived projects hurriedly executed will give way to weighed and considered judgment followed by deliberate action; when every forward step taken will be illuminated by recorded experience of the past; and when a blindly gregarious instinct will surrender to the definite ambition of forming perfect civic entities." No, Mr. Oxenham, that Utopia will only be reached when a bloodless revolution has occurred, and all these forms of Socialism which are based on the taking of public revenue by the few and its necessary concomitant, taxation, have been swept away. An appreciation of causes, and a return to justice, can alone lead to that Utopia. Meanwhile, the good offices of quite a number of worthy persons will have shown the way, though one cannot help feeling at times that a vested interest is growing up. The number of professional people (including the lawyers, of course) who are earning fees by discussing and drawing up reports on town and country planning is rising rapidly and out of proportion to the accomplished results. In this last connection it is worth while mentioning that a few years ago, but eleven years after the first town planning scheme had been produced in England (Birmingham in 1913), the chapter dealing with the acquisition of land took up nearly fifty pages of a book on *The Law and Practice of Town Planning*. This is by Sydney Davey (Thornton Butterworth, 1923, 25s.). In a review of that book it states: "Whether land is acquired by agreement, or, as the law provides, compulsorily, there are definite legal conditions, each of which must be fixed in as exactly as the pieces in a jigsaw puzzle." True it is that since that time new laws have been enacted. But have they simplified things, or given less work to the lawyers? The briefest of studies of one of the latest Acts will not lead to an affirmative answer to this question.

To return to the problems of accessibility to one's neighbours. It has taken a great many years for town planners to discover that roads for through traffic cannot well also perform the function of being "development roads." This term means roads with buildings having direct access to the road frontage. It is now considered of the utmost importance to put strips of parkland on each side of roads for through traffic, and not to permit access from buildings fronting on them. Otherwise high land values are created at the public expense and have generally been made a free gift to those who own the land through which the road passes. Also such roads have been made unattractive. A development road should not invite but should discourage through traffic. A famous English architect and town planner, Mr. Barry Parker, in a most interesting article on "Highways, Parkways, and Freeways,"[1] states that our realization of these points has created a new era in town planning. The labels just mentioned were invented by that great American town planner and zoner, Edward M. Bassett. His definitions are as follows: "A 'highway' is a strip of public land devoted to *movement* over which the abutting property owners have the right of light, air, and access. A 'parkway' is a strip of public land devoted to *recreation* over which the abutting property owners have *no* right of light, air, or access. And a 'freeway' is a strip of land devoted to *movement* over which the abutting property owners have *no* right of light, air, or access." Mr. Barry Parker points out that

[1] *Town and Country Planning* (a quarterly review), Vol. 1, No. 2, February 1933, p. 38 (Published by the Garden Cities Association, London).

open spaces for leisure and pleasure which are provided along main roads are more likely to be used and enjoyed than if placed elsewhere. So main roads should pass along places of natural beauty. He illustrates his article by diagrams showing the old-fashioned errors producing smell, noise, and dust from traffic near dwelling-houses, and awkward corners, stationary vehicles, and many cross roads interfering with moving through traffic.

It has been frequently argued that to attempt to prevent ribbon development is to attempt the impossible. By ribbon development is meant the erection of buildings with access to the roadway along roads originally constructed primarily as lines of communication. But to say that to prevent ribbon development is impossible shows that its causes are not understood. What, then, are these causes? The chief one is the natural temptation of landowners to capitalize the value that lies ready to hand in sites already furnished with good frontages and probably also with services, for example, drainage, water, etc. Now if the principle adopted amongst primitive people that land is the property of the tribe had been recognized, and if the values given to land had always been employed in public benefit, there would have been no clash of private and public interests and no individual would have felt aggrieved in being unable to reap where he had not sown. Further, it would have been impossible for a town planner to have said a new era was created by discovering the folly of partially blocking by stationary and local vehicles roads made for through traffic, for such folly would not have been perpetrated. But frontage development along new roads still goes on, though recognized as inappropriate for many years. Such development causes traffic troubles and precludes decent communal life and pleasant rural surroundings for those who live in new houses.

Other disadvantages of ribbon development, now well recognized, are: the spoiling of appearances of main roads, increased costs later of road-widening, increased costs in provision of such services as drainage, and water supply. Main traffic roads should have grass verges, paths for pedestrians along them, and trees, parkland, and pleasant streams in their close vicinity. Dwelling and shopping houses should be grouped nicely together, not spread out in too formal straight lines, and not so as to sprawl out and spoil the countryside. Another cause of ribbon development is the suck to the towns. So many people want to live in a position of easy accessibility to the big cities yet in surroundings bearing some semblance to "unspoilt nature" that they abhor any added obstacle, even an additional corner to go round or an extra quarter of a mile to walk to their work. In England population has become so concentrated into one or two regions[1] that the vision of town and country planners has now become directed almost entirely to turning England either into a series of suburbs or of satellite dormitory and week-end residence towns, or of seaside, moorland, lakeland, or mountain pleasure resorts for town-dwellers. Since in so many countries the proportion of people who live in towns has increased so much in recent years it is the town-dweller's point of view which is the one now constantly considered. As Mr. Gilbert H. Jenkins has aptly said:[2] "In town and regional planning . . . the city or town and all its needs is the focal point. Here should be placed the shopping centres, there the factories and workshops, this is the best site for the better residential quarters, that for those of the working classes. To make the town healthy so many acres of park or playgrounds are needed and to provide proper communications these great trunk roads and those by-passes must be provided, while in the outskirts so much land must be left for the vegetable and milk supplies of the urban population. There is nothing in this philosophy which considers the needs and amenities of the rural population. We, as architects, were the originators of town planning, and the great regional schemes are in our hands to make or mar. I would strongly urge that the time has come when a constructive policy for the preservation of rural England is as necessary as that for the orderly development of our industrial and commercial centres, and their dependencies, the residential districts. The gist of the problem seems to be in the means whereby the gradual absorption of the whole of rural England by its towns is to be prevented. One way to prevent this would be to ensure that our towns shall be more compactly planned, but the whole present-day tendency of town planning

[1] See map on p. 174.
[2] Discussion on Regional Planning in *Journal of Royal Institution of British Architects*, Vol. XXXVII, No. 6, January 25, 1930, p. 198.

is to spread the buildings out over a wider area." By all means let towns be compact so long as this is consistent with aesthetically beautiful planning.

The principles of aesthetic planning, according to the worthy conceptions of Dr. Vaughan Cornish, have been enumerated as follows (in his speech at Norwich in 1932 at the Fifth Annual Conference of the Preservation of the Countryside) :[1]

"The first foundation of aesthetic planning is the adoption of such tone and colour for rural architecture that all new buildings shall take their place quietly and unobtrusively in the natural landscape.

"The second foundation of aesthetic planning has to do with our cities. . . . Whereas we can neither foresee nor effectively control the forms which future methods of construction may impose upon civic architecture, we can establish this foundation of urban planning, namely, that every city should be a garden city; the rigid lines and hard surfaces of architecture relieved and offset by the tender foliage of trees, the weaving of their sinuous boughs, and the restful colour of soft, spreading lawns. In this way, moreover, we shall bring the fragrance of the country to the dweller in the town. . . . Thus our second foundation is gardening and afforestation in the city.

"In a well-ordered countryside, the isolated building takes its place quietly amidst vegetation; in a well-planned city, the houses with harmonious elevation and definitely grouped, are offset by trees and lawns; but the radial suburb and the country road which has been subjected to ribbon development lack pictorial grouping and are as unsociable as they are un-picturesque. Thus the third foundation of aesthetic planning is the formation of the satellite suburb as a small garden city.

"The fourth foundation of the new plan of England is an unimpaired outlook on the sea-front from watering places which are the chief holiday resort of our people. . . .

"These four foundations have to do with the *aspect* of the scenery of civilization; the fifth and last foundation has to do with its *prospect*, or outlook. . . . An axiom for the planning of

[1] Quoted from *Town and Country Planning*, Vol. 1, No. 4, p. 113 (London, Garden Cities Association).

England is that complete landscapes of wild nature must be preserved. Thus one other of the foundations is the reservation of areas of wild country as National Parks for free rambling; containing, however, in their remoter recesses Nature Sanctuaries for the protection of rare species of animals and plants, in order that the variety of wild life may not be diminished."

In front of the question of "zoning" comes that of the growth and distribution of industries. The Chief Inspector of Factories (for England and Wales), in his report for the year 1928, writes: "The growth of industry during recent years in the South of England has been remarkable, and probably in no part of the United Kingdom has there been a more striking increase in factory work than in the neighbourhood of London. The reasons for this increase are, doubtless, many, but among them may be mentioned the proximity of a great market, the facilities for export furnished by the Port of London, and excellent transport facilities for raw materials and for the finished products. Some indication of the industrial expansion in the Southern Counties is given by the progress of the Southern Division of the Factory Department. During the last eight years the number of registered factories has increased by over 3,000 and some of the new works are of great size. Between Acton and Slough it is estimated that there are now 150,000 factory workers compared with only 60,000 five years ago. The expansion has, in fact, been so rapid in some industries that difficulty was sometimes felt in obtaining suitable workers, and, owing to scarcity of workers, one firm has made arrangements not only to lodge for five days weekly those workers who live at a distance but also to pay week-end fares so that these workers may return home on Saturday."[1] But note this is the act of one firm only out of many hundreds. In most cases no such arrangements are made, and one of the causes of scarcity of workers, when thousands of persons are unemployed, is the difficulty firms find to pay wages high enough to compensate the workers for the travelling expenses they have to meet and, in many cases, the additional expenses of running two establishments. This is an illustration of the conglomeration of industries with but

[1] *Garden Cities and Town Planning*, November 1929, p. 260.

inadequate forethought as to "zoning." The attractions of good sites, at first obtained on somewhat favourable terms, and of ready means of transport, etc., explain this growth of industry and of population. But once they became established up went the speculative value of land in their vicinity and this, more than anything else, has prevented better town and regional planning.

A fault of the 1925 Town Planning Act was that it led owners to get their land scheduled for building. They, perhaps rightly, thought that it would thus be possible to be assured of high ground values in the future. The 1925 Act made it necessary to prescribe the future use of every yard of the area planned. This, somewhat falsely and prematurely, tended to send up the speculative value of land against the interests of the public and of land users. Even the new Act, which came into force in May 1933, tends in the same direction. Owners are seeking to enlarge the already considerable area on which development is being allowed. Through the adoption of the plans of some only of the Joint Regional Planning Committees, an absurd state of affairs has arisen. An area has actually been planned which can house nearly 200,000,000 *additional* population, more than four times the population of the whole country!

Another way in which Town Planning Acts spell gains to landlords and help to increase rather than decrease the speculative value of land is in connection with demarcation in advance of parks and open spaces. On November 24, 1933, for example, it was retailed at a meeting of the Norfolk (East Central) Joint Town Planning Committee[1] how about seventy acres of land should be reserved for recreation ground, parks, and open spaces at locations around Norwich, where future buildings, dwelling-houses chiefly, were likely to arise. Though efforts were made to fix the price of such plots in advance, such prices were not by any means the present value of the land, almost purely agricultural, but took into account the speculative values likely to accrue owing to the future growth, needs, and expenditure of the community.

Norwich is a particularly interesting city to the town planners. It is one of the oldest cities in England. Its plan shows vestiges of the mediaeval streets which circled round the protecting walls

[1] *Eastern Daily Press*, November 25, 1933.

of the ancient castle. This is built on a mound thought to be, to some extent at least, artificially made and surrounded by a foss or moat, still traceable, piled up in the prehistoric Neolithic or Bronze Age. It is a fine specimen of a Norman castle, now used as a municipal museum of archaeology, natural history, and art. In the seventeenth century Norwich was described as "a city in

MAP OF CENTRAL NORWICH
By kind permission of H.M. Stationery Office

an orchard or an orchard in a city." To this day it is sometimes spoken of as a city of gardens, though it contains plenty of foul slums despite the repeated and, to a great extent, successful efforts to improve the town and rehouse its inhabitants. Three or four good housing schemes undertaken by the Corporation referred to in the chapter on housing (see p. 369). Many historical points of great interest to town planners are to be found in a book by the Rev. Wm. Hudson.[1] From the pages of this work the conflict between the privileges of the few and the rights of the many can often be followed through the centuries, and the importance of geographical influences, particularly of accessibility and transport communications, can be traced. Norwich is fortunate in the possession of a good number of public open spaces. These are

[1] *How the City of Norwich Grew into Shape*, with five maps (Goose & Sons Norwich, 1896).

well dispersed in various quarters of the town and their aggregate amounts to over 10 per cent of the city's area, which is the proportion usually prescribed by town planners.

One of the gravest evil results of the system of taxation and land tenure which oppresses the people of most nations to-day is the increased frequency of governmental action. This, almost to a worse extent than an overbalanced amount of commerce in society compared with production, increases the tendency of persons to congregate into cities. Although people are becoming alive to the burdens and drawbacks of too much government, this secondary result is not sufficiently appreciated. In the United States of America the National Industrial Conference Board is calling the attention of taxpayers to the increasing cost of government and this is at last beginning to attract attention. With the Federal Government struggling to meet a large deficit, with many of the States casting about for new sources of revenue, and with numerous local governments in financial straits, the American people are more keenly conscious than ever before that the cost of government is not merely a problem for the legislator but one that concerns every taxpayer. The tendency to look to organized government in nation, state, and local community for the solution of every problem of society has led to the multiplication of offices, and bureaus, some of questionable value, all of which cost money that must be drawn from the income of the people. The latest volume published by this Board on the *Cost of Government in the United States* 1929–30, gives the three main expenditures in the United States in 1929 compared with 1890. The following are the figures in dollars for (1) Federal, (2) State, and (3) Local expenditures, and show an amazing increase:

	1890	1929	1929 per cap.
(1)	291,000,000	3,932,000,000	32·36
(2)	77,000,000	1,990,000,000	16·38
(3)	487,000,000	7,126,000,000	58·64
	885,000,000	13,048,000,000	107·37

Incidentally it is worth mentioning that the gross public debt of the United States Government has increased by $6,300,000,000 (£1,260,000,000 at par) during the past three fiscal years to a total of $22,500,000,000 (£4,500,000,000). This more than cancels the reduction, $6,100,000,000, effected during the previous seven years, according to the National Industrial Conference Board.

A vicious circle comes into force as people get sucked into the great city centres. For example, the persons with their dependents who live in Greater London who are employed in moving people about London number more than all the inhabitants of the City of Norwich put together, namely, about 120,000. Several factories erected close to London draw their workpeople from London itself. Hardly any successful efforts to provide dwelling accommodation close at hand have been made. To Greenford, in Middlesex, not 10 miles from the centre of London, where some big factories stand, several special trains run daily to take the employees from London to and from their work. Similar arrangements have to be made to bring factory hands to Slough, 20 miles from London. The prohibitive cost of providing dwelling accommodation adjacent to new factories is generally found to depend on the rise in land values which comes about as soon as the factories are even prospected, values which accrue to private individual land holders.

Much has been said about through traffic and by-pass roads, and about ribbon and frontage development. When, as is usual, such improvements are paid for out of the community's coffers, the public advantages are not generally up to expectations and much gain often accrues to landlords. A good example of all the worst evils coming from lack of foresight and adoption of wrong principles of planning and ownership is to be found by a study of developments along the Kingston by-pass road, constructed only six or seven years ago. Already this is often being abandoned by motorists who find it quicker to go through Kingston, with its narrow streets, and no end of public values have been raked off by landlordism. For example, a plot of land at the Merton Connection Corner, close to Raynes Park Station, an area of 14 acres of rough grazing land, was worth £300 per acre, though so used, in 1921. In June 1928 it was sold by auction for £11,780, or about £835 per acre. A little further along the road the Bodley Road Estate, formerly owned by Merton College, Oxford, was worth only about £60 per acre (as agricultural land) before the road was thought of. In 1928 it was fetching roughly

£600 per acre for back land and treble this for plots close to the main road. Further along still, rather nearer Long Ditton and Surbiton, land opposite Fox and Nicholl's Garage was "zoned" under town-planning powers for business premises and shops. In 1921 this land was worth at most £100 per acre. After being zoned and the by-pass road was in contemplation, it was bought in small lots at from £2,000 to £3,000 per acre. Some years previously some of this land was secured by H. C. Jones & Co. at about £350 per acre.

Legislators in various countries have tried to tackle the problems connected with the rise in land values resulting from the making of roads and other means of communications and transport. The twentieth century opened largely unprepared for the revolution in transport which the advent of motor vehicles brought. Road construction in recent years has more or less caught up. By comparison with the building of quick transit electric railways, however, new roads have done little to increase city congestion, to add to the huge "con-urbations," as Professor Patrick Geddes[1] calls them. Some most surprising results of the construction of these means of passenger transport have occurred, especially in the neighbourhood of London and New York; and one of the results has been the acquisition of vast fortunes to a few lucky individuals through phenomenal rise in ground values. This wealth has not usually gone to the railway builders and owners, but quite often to persons who were innocent of foresight and genuinely surprised at their luck. The extension of the Hampstead line—to illustrate what has been happening—from Golders Green to Edgware, 4¾ miles in length, was opened in 1923–24. It was taken largely through a rural area. In two years the annual users had become 9,000,000 and in 1933 they were 24,500,000.

The people of some nations, especially since town planning Acts came more to the fore, have become alive to the injustice of landlords appropriating values to which they have contributed nothing. They have concerned themselves about this even more than they have about the obstructing power of landlordism. When, for example, the Housing and Town Planning Acts of 1909, 1919, and 1925 were passed in England they were hailed because they enacted that ratepayers were entitled to half of

[1] *Cities in Evolution* (Williams & Norgate, London, 1915).

the betterment due to improvements such as road widenings, etc. But in practice these clauses have not been particularly effective; and it seems stupid more or less to encourage theft and then to excuse it by taking a share in the swag. One of the ways to discourage such robberies, though only a partial and half-hearted remedy, is to prevent frontage development along arterial thoroughfares and along many other main roads. These should have grass and park land along them. The aesthetic value of trees along roads and well grouped in cities is becoming increasingly appreciated. Along roads they should not be so placed as to make these dangerous, or awkward from the point of view of upkeep through the fall of leaves in the autumn or through too much shade from very large trees close to the road. The Continent oj Europe has longer experience or, at all events, generally follows a better practice in these ways than does England or America, though there are many notable exceptions to this statement. Besides the attention given to the aesthetic considerations and the provision in many places of shady walks for pedestrians in some parts of Austria and Germany, the local taxes are actually relieved by granting leave to local farmers (in return for a small rent) to plant fruit-trees on public land on condition that the public can pluck and eat fruit therefrom but never carry any away.

It seems desirable to say a little more in this chapter about zoning. This term is a comparatively new one. But even in Queen Elizabeth's day she tried to establish a green belt round London by commanding that everyone should refrain from building within three miles of any of the gates of the city. In the same edict (July 7, 1580) she attempted to prevent overcrowding by forbidding more than one family per house. Before her time many kings and potentates planned cities in advance, and even sometimes ordained "zoning" as cities grew, often with great success. A zone does not mean marking out a belt, but the reservation of different areas for different uses, this for dwellings, that for factories, and the other for a park. In America zoning ordinances also prescribe building lines, character, and height, width of streets, and density of houses to the acre. The proportion of public open spaces to the total area of a town is generally put down at a minimum of 10 per cent. But this should generally be considered too low, and in any case no hard-and-fast rule should be made. London requires an addition of 15,000 acres to its playing fields to bring it up to the standard of 10 per cent, that is, in the Metropolitan Police District area. As a rule, public open spaces are most scarce where most needed, namely, in the poorest districts. Efforts to preserve spots of natural beauty, even in the middle of big towns, and in as natural a state as possible, are being more frequently made now than formerly. The often lovely effects produced by grass, the fine old trees, and the curling lake of St. James's Park and the Government offices, etc., adjoining it in Westminster, can be cited as examples of this. Many towns have been beholden to private landlords for the gifts of parks and public open spaces. When commemorative statues are erected to such benefactors, however, never is any record made on the pedestals as to what the town has done to benefit the line of private owners, in England often noblemen. In some instances it can be seen how few years it takes for a landlord to recover from his gift more than all he gave. Increased land values giving him a greatly swollen rent roll result from the enhanced amenities of the neighbourhood where the park is situated. (Sefton Park, Liverpool; Eastbourne; Bournemouth; and Cardiff are places which occur to one as illustrating this). How much more frequently, however, is it not the custom, still tolerated in most civilized lands, for the landlord to hold the town more or less to ransom by asking the inhabitants of the day a very high price for the purchase of the open space! The price takes into account the speculative rise in value (as likely as not to inure into his own pocket) which accrues before long from an increase of population and a continued expenditure of public money on public services of some sort.

Lucky is the town that has acquired land far in advance of its growth and importance. The City of Vienna was lucky in having already got possession of certain sites at two important junctures in its development. After it was decided to extend the town beyond the boundaries of the walls and ramparts of the old city it was possible to arrange wide roads, esplanades, promenades, and gardens between the old city and the suburbs. More recently, since the world war, in fact, when the municipal authorities did so well in erecting fine blocks of flats for housing the people, they had their efforts facilitated by ready access to sites. The municipality owns or is trustee for practically all the sites of the 60,000 flats it has erected since the war. Most of its property was acquired at advantageous prices long before the war. It finds blocks of flats more economical to build than small houses. This is rather against the experience of builders in England. One of these blocks, the Sandleithen, accommodates 8,000 people;

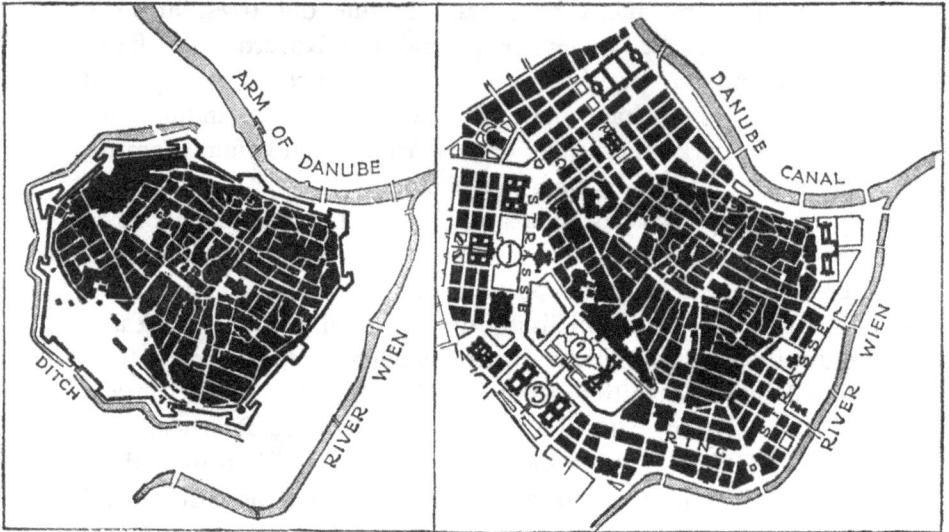

VIENNA

On the left the inner city before the removal of the fortifications (1857), on the right after their removal (1887). (1) The Town Hall, Houses of Parliament, and University; (2) the Imperial Palace; (3) Museums of Natural History and Fine Arts

From "Towns and Town Planning," by T. H. Hughes and E. A. Lamborn. By kind permission of the Clarendon Press

another, Karl Marx Hof, 5,000; and the latest, the Engelshof, when completed will contain 2,224 flats. Only 25 per cent of the total ground is used for buildings. The rest of the site is left for open courtyards and gardens. The blocks are so designed as to shorten the northern front and create as many sunny and airy balconies and verandas as possible. In the scheme are always included some shops, a public kitchen and laundry or two, as well as kindergartens, youth schools, and workshops. All these arrangements help to get over the drawbacks of the height of the buildings. Lifts are expensive and dangerous, especially for children. But by providing gardens, laundries, etc., there is a minimizing of the number of times stairs have to be climbed by those living high up. These schemes have been put through without adding to public debts—a most important point, and they have been financed to some extent by a tax on the owners of ground values.

Vienna had a population of 1,855,360 in 1928, which was more than 28 per cent of the total population of Austria. Its population increased by 13,000 between 1920 and 1928 but diminished by 175,000 between 1910 and 1928, and by even more than this figure since immediately before the war, when it was the capital of an Austria containing 52,000,000 persons against a present population of 6,500,000 persons.

Vienna has twenty-two municipal open-air baths for children of six to sixteen, besides some open-air swimming and sunning baths for adults. Herein it differs from many, in fact most, other places, where the vogue for enjoying these things making for better health is sometimes exploited by the fortunate owners of suitable ground and water. Happily, however, people are becoming wider awake both as to the desirability of indulging in air and sun baths and as to the best means for their provision. America and places on the Continent of Europe have been in front of England in these matters, partly perhaps because they get rather more sunshine. But English seaside resorts particularly are now alive to the advantages of providing bathing pools, etc. Skegness, Poole, and Hastings may be specially mentioned. The Municipality of Vienna owns 70 per cent of the shares of the timber firms and of the brickworks, and supplies nearly all the materials for municipal buildings and undertakings. On the other hand there is free competition amongst architects and contractors, etc., for the work.

Town-planners nowadays are giving constant attention to smoke abatement and planning for sunlight. The prevalent plan of always building dwellings with front aspects to the road of access, regardless of the points of the compass, is, at least in northern latitudes, a reprehensible one. It arises out of tradition and custom, and out of cramped site development. A good deal of mean, closely packed, sometimes back to back, house building was done last century. In the consequent reaction to-day many planners are shocked by anything, however decent, in the nature of "close" development. Yet placing buildings close together need not be barred so long as aspect and the lie of the land be considered sufficiently. In connection with planning for sunlight a reference may here be usefully made to a book published as long ago as 1912, but still of interest and value.[1] It is the difficulty of getting land on which to build in most purely rural districts in Great Britain which is often the obstacle to a better orientation of dwellings. In village after village one can find cottages very badly placed and crammed closely together when all around are plenty of eligible sites. The Liberal Land Committee, in its excellent shilling book, *Towns and the Land*,[2] states: "The average cost per acre of land acquired since the war for assisting housing schemes works out at £230 in urban areas and £127 in rural areas. It should be remembered with regard to urban areas that their housing sites have, generally speaking, been well on the outskirts of the towns, and with regard to rural areas that the best agricultural land is not taken, and that if building land in villages is sold at £50 an acre the transaction may be considered to be very satisfactory by the landowner. Examples given in the second chapter of this report show that despite powers of compulsory acquisition local authorities are frequently compelled to pay enormously high prices for the land they need."

In Sweden sunshine is not always too plentiful. Therefore it is fortunate that a good deal of attention has been given recently and successfully to this aspect of housing and town planning in that country. Mr. V. Lundberg[3] recently told an English audience that in Stockholm, where most people live in flats, the old-fashioned broad block of flats with a well-like courtyard is no longer being copied. Better planned blocks on the "Lamell" type are now being erected, not too high and with plenty of space between them. Each one is placed in the direction of north-south. All will now receive the same amount of sunshine, and the children will have sunlit gardens to play in.

[1] Wm. Atkinson's *The Orientation of Buildings; or Planning for Sunlight* (J. Wiley & Son, New York, and Chapman & Hall, London, 1912).

[2] *Towns and the Land*, p. 91 (Hodder & Stoughton, London).

[3] *The Times*, October 4, 1933.

CHAPTER XVIII

GROUND VALUES AND PROPERTY APPRAISALS

IN CHICAGO, NEW YORK, PITTSBURG, AND HOUSTON:
BOUNDARY DIFFICULTIES NEAR MANCHESTER

THE present generation is learning to appreciate the fact that nothing influences the growth and distribution of population so much as systems of land tenure and taxation. Hence a study, however brief, of some of the more exciting details about property assessments is called for. These things have a profound effect upon the way industries develop and upon the way people are herded together. The last two chapters have dealt with several aspects of the subjects of town-planning and the decentralization of industries. Before proceeding to the examination of a few concrete examples of the way in which property is appraised for taxes a few more observations on industry and occupation are desirable.

In 1921 rather over 17,000,000 persons were engaged in industry in England and Wales out of a total population of just under 38,000,000. Fewer than 50 per cent, the actual figures being 489 in every 1,000, were engaged in production, repair, and maintenance; 86 per 1,000 in transport and communication; 91 in commerce and finance; 39 in professional, 117 domestic; 58 draughtsmen or clerical; 20 warehousemen, storekeepers, and packers; 9 stationary engine-drivers; and there were 91 others, mainly labourers. The largest proportion of producers were in the primary industries of agriculture, mining, and quarrying. In the decade 1921–31 there was a great increase in the number claimed by the commercial and distributive occupations, by the professions, by the personal service, entertainments, and sports, and in a less degree by transport. The more strictly industrial occupations that have absorbed much new labour are building, painting and decorating, woodworking and furniture, and the newer electrical and chemical industries, the making of food, drink, and tobacco, and the trades connected with printing and publishing. At the same time agriculture, metal-working, and mining have declined, and textiles have remained stationary (for men). (See also tables on pp. 211 and 212.)

Now, as previous chapters in this book have emphasized, to attain a healthier distribution of population it is necessary for a bigger proportion of persons to be (*a*) producers, especially of food-stuffs, and (*b*) engaged in more than one occupation. This could be brought about if greater freedom of production could be achieved through overcoming the obstacles obstructing man from gaining ready access to nature's storehouse. This is so, despite the fact that we live in an age of specialization and mass production, and despite the advantages of such methods of industry. New inventions and greater specialization enable fewer persons working for a shorter time to produce the commodities necessary to satisfy human needs. Easier wealth production sends up land rent, as does also an increase in numbers. Professor H. P. Fairchild, in a discussion in June 1931 on a paper by Professor J. W. Gregory, read to the International Union for the Scientific Investigation of Population Problems, said: "He believed he was correct in saying that in the five years between 1923 and 1928 the industries of the United States actually employed about 800,000 fewer labourers; and the railways were employing 150,000 fewer labourers than they did sixty-five years ago." He went on to say that such facts represented a menacing feature of modern civilization; "as population was increased, a lesser demand for population was created." The last-quoted phrase seems to indicate false thinking. One wonders what is conceived in the mind when a "demand for population" is talked of. Is it not the phrase of one belonging to the master class who looks upon people as "hands" in a factory, or "recruits" for an army? If the inhabitants of this globe become increasingly clever at production, even to a much less extent than has been shown in previous pages of this book to be the case, why should increasing numbers be a menace? What is wrong with civilization? What really is the menace? Why, that many are poor, not because there are too many but because man finds obstacles hindering his productiveness, despite his inventiveness and ability. These obstacles are connected with land tenure and taxation and, incidentally, they prevent decentralization of industry. When they are comprehended and have been swept away, and when economic justice holds sway, then sound principles of town-planning will be practised.

A few people seem to look upon the private appropriation of publicly created site values as legitimate. They are getting so used to this misappropriation that they almost come to agree with the individual claiming them to-day, who generally considers they are due to his foresight. When efforts are made to alter the law, or to act under present laws so as to bring about a more equitable state of affairs, a combination of all the interested parties is sometimes too strong and success but short-lived. Moreover, efforts made in Australia, New Zealand, Johannes-burg, Vancouver, and other parts of Canada (Edmonton, for example), as in the United States at Houston, at San Diego, in New York and Chicago, besides being up against local vested interests, have all been partially spoilt by a stupid system of taxes, the federal import duties. In the British Dominions, despite "protection," however, considerable and lasting good has been accomplished. In Queensland, for nearly fifty years, not one penny in rates has been levied on "improvements" (i.e. buildings, etc.), and outside the Sugar Belt social conditions in that State are best in all Australia. Forty years ago Sydney had a high mortality rate. But to-day and for ten years it has had one of the lowest death rates of any important city in the world, and that can be ascribed partly to the fact that rates have been on unim-proved values alone since 1916. *The Times* not long ago mourned that the districts around the town were strewn with the wreckage of land companies, killed by the rating system. But their demise was all to the good of the people of Sydney. Though efforts have so far failed there to base sewerage and water supply charges on land value they have brought a stream of recruits from business men to support such a plan. Somewhat similar tales might be told about Johannesburg, Durban, Nairobi, Salisbury (Southern Rhodesia), Vancouver, and the Prairie Provinces of Canada. In the latter, however, in recent years many endeavours towards further advance have been sterilized through looking to the realtors for financial support of those politicians who have striven after progress. But to turn now to the affairs of those American cities above mentioned in the following order: Chicago, New York, Houston, and San Diego.

The City of Chicago is blessed by nature through being so placed as to be not far away from some of the finest land in the world for producing all the following raw materials and products of agriculture: coal, petroleum, wheat, maize, oats, pigs, and cattle; besides having a fine position for transporting such products to other parts of the world. With such advantages reflected in an enormous population which has increased with astonishing rapidity during the last twenty or thirty years, it might have been thought that the city authorities would have had no difficulties whatsoever in gathering a regular revenue amply sufficient to meet the cost of whatever public services the inhabitants of the city thought desirable. But what do we find? Chicago is filled with legions of unpaid municipal employees. Crime there is notoriously rife. Corruption, gambling, and blackmail are leading the city's name to be a by-word. The city's credit is at a low ebb: the reason being that its officers cannot collect its revenue. And whenever an effort, however strenuous and well supported, is made to straighten things out through overhauling the assessments, the interests vested in the private ownership of ground values find themselves able to bring the effort to naught. Study a few happenings there since the spring of 1926. That veritable dynamo of human energy, Miss Margaret Haley, business manager of the Chicago Teachers' Federation, and one of the outstanding figures in the political life of the city, began to stir things up in March 1926. As now, teachers and other municipal servants were in heavy arrears as to the payment of their salaries. But apart from this Miss Haley and others awoke to the scandal of the system of local taxation which held sway in Cook County, Illinois, in which Chicago and some seventy smaller towns and cities are located. About that time Cook County had as unequal and unfair a method of assessing estate for taxation as can possibly be imagined. As a result of the agitation inaugurated in the first half of 1926, three to four years later Cook County had practically completed the installation of as uniform and scientific a system of assessing real estate—both land and improvements, separately—as could be found anywhere on the face of the globe. This was done by help obtained from a study of Cleveland land-value maps, of John Zangerle's book on the *Principles of Real Estate Appraising*, and from consultation with and advice from Walter W. Pollock, President of the Manufacturers Appraisal Company of Philadelphia. But of what avail? Since 1929 the vested interests have been so clever and powerful as to see to it that the evaluation has not been used as a basis of assessment for gathering the taxes. Needless to say, the lawyers were brought in. While arguments continued as to whether the city could legally collect its taxes on the old valuation, the city got no tax revenue at all. The plight of the teachers and of all the employees of the council continues. So do corruption and crime.

The first stage of attempting to bring in just dealings in local taxation in Chicago required six months. It comprised the appraisal of the central business district, known as the "loop." The most glaring inequalities in assessments were uncovered—both with respect to land and improvements—and a total of more than $600,000,000 of property values was found to be escaping taxation. A wail of public indignation arose. So in October of the same year (1926), a resolution was introduced into the County Board to have all real estate in Chicago and Cook County appraised by the same methods as had been used in the "loop." The resolution passed and an appropriation of $450,000 was set aside by various governmental bodies to cover the cost of making such an appraisal. Owing, however, to powerful opposition the opportunity fell through and the money was never used. But this did not end the matter. Surveys were started by various private bodies to determine the extent of "tax-dodging," surveys that disclosed a shocking state of affairs. The fight now took a new turn. Under the driving power of Miss Haley, the Chicago Teachers' Federation got the ear of a body that no one ever seemed previously to have heard of—the State Tax Commission. This Commission began to hold hearings. The hearings showed the situation to be positively disgraceful and the State Tax Commission thereupon ordered the assessors to publish the tax lists for the whole county; a duty prescribed by law, but which had not been performed for twenty-nine years. The assessors declined to act!

In March of 1928 the Board of Review finished in its chaotic way the quadrennial assessment of 1927 and the people got their tax-bills—with a 50 per cent increase in taxes. A terrific hue and cry now arose. Deluged with complaints the State Tax Commission set its jaws, declared the 1927 assessment invalid and ordered the assessors to make a new assessment. The assessors, after getting an opinion from the Attorney-General of the State that the Commission's order was "premature and of no effect," again declined to act. But after a lot of turmoil the State Tax Commission got full legal power to enforce its orders and again called upon the assessors to publish the tax lists for the whole county. The assessors obeyed—the first time, as already stated, this had been done in twenty-nine years. Within two months 1,050,000 lists were mailed out, each list showing the value of each taxpayer's lands and buildings as compared with his neighbours. The disclosures were appalling. A continuous stream of photographs and comparisons were published in the newspapers and the people were stirred as never before.

The State Tax Commission, for the second time, next declared the 1927 quadrennial assessment invalid and again ordered a reassessment. More than that, taking the Somers' System as its model, the State Tax Commission laid down the rules and standards by which this new assessment was to be made. The assessors reluctantly obeyed. The sum of $850,000 dollars, to begin with, was appropriated for the work. In the face of innumerable obstacles, lawsuits, injunctions, and court decisions (one of which, for example, compelled the bankers of the city to come forward with a gift of $250,000 so the appraisers might be paid), the work of revaluation proceeded. Tentative land-value maps of the whole city were prepared and published in the newspapers, public meetings for discussion were held and the taxpayers urged to send in any complaints, all to the end that errors might be eliminated and a just and equitable assessment secured. But, as already stated, the new system has not yet become fully established in practice, much less a permanent system. The forces of private interests seem likely to go on prevailing over those making for the public welfare.[1] Moreover, a majority in Chicago are still unaware of the principles which

[1] Most of the above facts are to be found in Mr. Otto Cullman's paper (No. 13) contributed to an International Free Trade Conference held in Edinburgh, August 1929. Mr. Cullman is president of the Manufacturers' and Merchants' Federal Tax League of America.

should guide real estate property appraisals. When they awake to understanding that site values belong wholly to the community, then the muddle of the local taxes of Cook County will soon end; school teachers, still in mid-1934 ten months in arrears in their

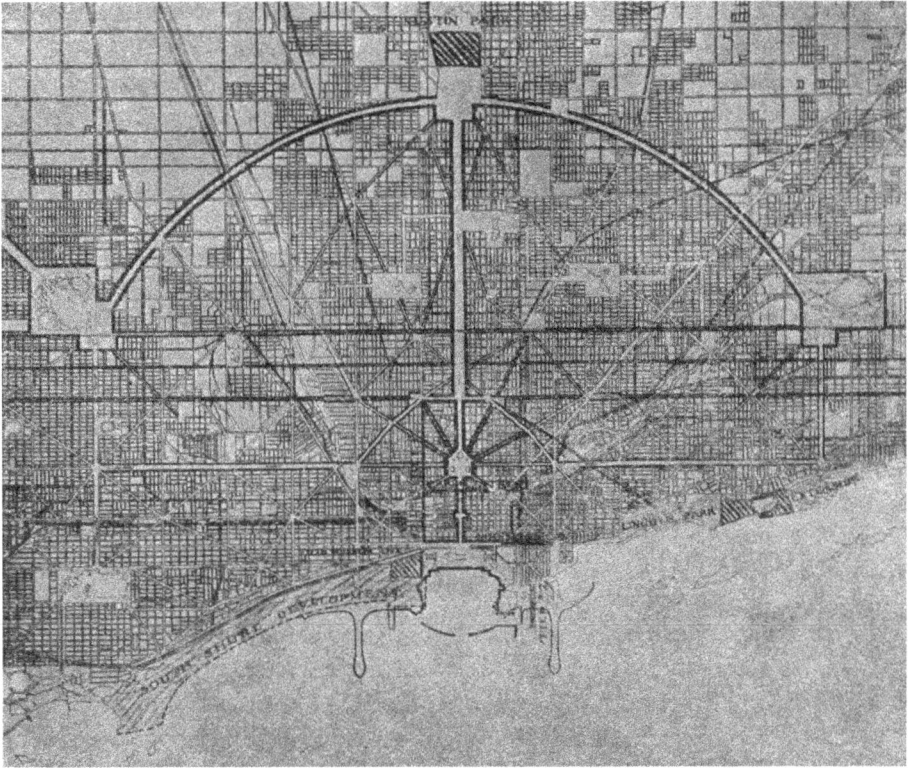

CHICAGO

Plan showing proposed improvements, indicated by thickened lines, and comprising better street systems, simplification of the railway system, and provision of parks, playgrounds, and forest preserves. The cost of the small portion of the work now completed or in hand is $90,000,000

By kind permission of E. Bennett and the Clarendon Press

salaries, may hope to be paid properly; and expensive legal fights in the courts will no longer be found necessary. The problems of tax arrears, of municipal debts, of rapid increase of the cost of public education will then find solutions. The taxes in arrears stood in May 1934 as follows: 1928 taxes, $34,286,211, or 7 per cent of the levy for that year; 1929, when the peak prices were reached in land values, 13 per cent; 1930, over $60,000,000, or 27 per cent of the levy; 1931, 25 per cent; and 1932, about 40 per cent. Since April 1933, when the Kerner-Skarda Act came into force, empowering the placing of property under a receivership until all taxes due shall have been paid, the flow of arrears has been quickened. But there is still, somewhat naturally, no market for Chicago Bonds. The teachers have about $30,000,000 owing to them. School expenses had increased three and a half times between 1916 and 1930, or ten and a half times as much as the increase in the population of Chicago in the same period.

Are things any better in New York? Somewhat; but still far from satisfactory. The men of the New York pay-roll are still getting their money. But compare New York with New York State. The latter has a far smaller revenue and on paper seems less strong financially. But at least its credit is still good, and it is hard to be sure that the city's is. Successive Governors have kept on calling for economy. But this is extremely difficult to bring about because, when times were good and money more plentiful, Tammany administration went on adding job to job and filling each newly created vacancy with its own followers. At a recent election Tammany, counting on the votes of these people, reckoned on a success they did not achieve. Nevertheless, these office-holders remain, a deadweight on the city budget. There are far too many of them. Hard by were recently to be found a million much-to-be-pitied unemployed. Somebody has to hold off starvation from these people. The remedy of borrowing is a poor one, even if lenders can be found. Yet there are a number of good features about the methods used to fill the public coffers of New York. For example, rather than let the fares, which are cheap, on the rapid transit lines bringing over 1,500,000 passengers daily into Manhattan rise too high, it is considered just to place some of the burden of the cost of providing and running these on ground owners who benefit by enhanced values, and on the public at large who benefit by increased prosperity and convenience. It is true this widening of the burden is not generally carried far enough, especially in respect of the landlords. Better is the system of special assessments for benefit received,

though in 1915 it brought in only $10,000,000. These special-
taxes are levied on the owners of a particular block of land which
gains advantage from public improvements. When streets are
paved and water, drains and sewers are laid down at the public
expense, most of the cost is apportioned amongst the owners of
the lands benefited, even though there are no buildings on the
land. Again, the special franchise taxes of New York collect for
public services some of the privileges of constructing and operating
rails, wires, pipes, etc., in, under, or above public highways or
places. Again, the method of raising taxes by the city government
is based as to a considerable extent on ground values. Unlike rates
in England and Wales the value on which assessments are based
is not made on a composite value which lumps land value and
the value of the building or other improvements together and on
the annual value—a rotten plan. But it is based on two valuations,
namely (a) of the land value of each piece of land and (b) of
the total or aggregate value of land plus improvements. This
separate valuation of capital values produces a more accurate
appraisement of the combined value than would otherwise be
achieved. This is one stage better than the English system, as
more in accordance with the facts of real estate property and as
preventing the owners of vacant land from escaping taxation.
Local taxes are levied by the several Boroughs of the City and
vary a little. But on the average the levy is about $2·70 on each
$100 dollars of capital value. In 1928 the tax on realty brought
in $433,000,000; and it is reckoned that of this about $200,000,000
is collected from the owners of land values. Theoretically real
estate is assessed at its full market value. In practice it is found
that the assessment averages only 70 per cent of such value. In
1925 the real estate of New York City was valued for taxation
purposes at $11,901,348,553, that is, almost 12 billions. About half
of this, $5,561,718,975 consisted of land value. A dozen years
before this date two-thirds of the assessment of real estate in New
York City consisted of land values and only one-third of building
values. The revenues derived from the ordinary land values of
the City in 1915 was approximately 41 per cent of the City
budget. The great activity in the building market since November
1918 (Armistice Day), coupled with the high cost of labour and
materials and with the higher rate of taxation on land values,

brought building values to a parity with land values. In 1930 the assessed selling value of the land on which the City of New York stands was over £1,500,000,000, as already stated (see p. 285). Unfortunately, besides being so foolish as to tax buildings, New York still taxes thrift and industry also by taxing mortgages, machinery, etc., and still imposes those class nuisance taxes called licences. In this last and in some other respects certain other American cities are ahead of New York. Pittsburg, for instance, is far in advance. She raises all her revenue from real estate and the greater part of that by taking a large slice of the economic rent of land. In Portland, Oregon, a few years ago two-thirds of the revenue was derived from land values, and in Houston, Texas; while in San Diego, California, in 1919 at least, the assessment figures were as follows: personal property, 9,000,000; buildings, 6,000,000; land values, 72,000,000.

Pittsburg at one time had one of the most inequitable systems of taxation in the country. But from 1910 onwards for a few years a concerted agitation from various boards of trade, chambers of commerce, teachers' associations, etc., brought about great reforms. A brief account of this struggle is given on pages 62 to 65 of the *Single Tax Year Book* (edited by J. D. Miller, New York, 1917).

The story of the fight for justice to get possession of the annual revenues belonging to the inhabitants of Houston in Texas is an exciting one. It began in April 1911, when the late Mr. J. J. Pastoriza was elected Houston's Finance and Tax Commissioner under the commission form of government adopted for that city a short time before. He introduced the separate assessment of land and improvements, and started to tax the franchise corporations of Houston, previously untaxed. From 1912 to 1915 he exempted from taxation all personal property, stocks, bonds, mortgages, and cash in banks, and assessed land at 70 per cent of its full value and improvements on land at only 25 per cent of their value. His system was popular, and the city prospered as never before. He was twice re-elected. During 1912–13 building increased 55 per cent, bank deposits increased $7,000,000, and the population increased 25,000. A reversal of the system, brought about by a few dissatisfied land speculators with the aid of the law, soon checked these advances. Pastoriza took a postal vote and got 99 per cent to ask for a return to the system he had introduced. He was able to arrange, for one year (1916) only, as follows: Improvements were assessed at 50 per cent of their value and land at 100 per cent. This plan, combined with foolish Federal taxes oppressing the people, left enough of the rental values to serve as a basis for speculation in land, and some of the results of the reforms were neutralized. Since those times, too, unfortunately, Pastoriza has died and the landlord influences have compelled Houston "to go back to the law." Town planning in Houston and the city development has been successful to a considerable extent and the people of Houston and neighbourhood have succeeded in the past, and to a less extent are succeeding to-day, in arresting the private appropriation of publicly created values. How much greater, then, would have been prosperity there if it had been possible to collect all the community ground values for the public use and to have abolished all taxes, and how much more beauty of structure and arrangement would, in those circumstances, have been displayed by this wonderful city.

Certain it is that nature gave the location of Houston peculiar attractions and many advantages. These, when population once became possible in those parts, but not before, gave value to the land, which grew as population increased. In 1850 there were but 2,396 persons in Houston; in 1880, 16,513; in 1900, 44,633; in 1910, 78,800; in 1920, 154,000; and in 1930, 292,352. The area of the city was doubled between 1910 and 1920, and it has increased more since 1920. It covers about 40 square miles. It was not the landlords who gave the ground its value, though they sometimes were responsible for adding to improvement values, and although they often scooped in a big proportion of the rents, giving nothing in return. It is worth enumerating a few of the advantages and attractions of this fine city and a few of the public improvements which, made largely at the expense of the public, helped to add fresh increases to the ground values. Houston is but 50 miles from the Gulf of Mexico. It is surrounded by producing oil-fields. It is also peculiarly well placed for exporting cotton (rather over 2,000,000 bales of cotton were exported in 1927). By widening and deepening the river-bed, the city has been made directly accessible to shipping on the Gulf of Mexico. Because it is blessed in having a lesser range of tides, as compared with some places (Liverpool, for example), it can dispense with dock gates. In this respect it is comparable to New York, Glasgow, Southampton. All this illustrates once more the importance of accessibility and ease of communications. Its climate is such that it can grow ripe strawberries in February and roses to bloom all the year round. Houston was the second city in the United States to be organized on the particular form of government it possesses. Its commission form of government was adopted in 1905. The municipality owns the port facilities, the Harbour Belt Railway, the water-works, the public market, and an auditorium seating 4,500. The parks have an area of 2,500 acres. The assessed valuation of property in 1927 was $279,504,510. It possesses a fine university founded and endowed by William Marsh Rice. The endowment of $10,000,000 had grown to $14,000,000 by 1920. Tuition in the university is free. The Federal Government and the citizens of the Harris County Navigation district had spent $24,000,000 dollars by 1928 on improving the channel and the harbour facilities of the port. The rapid development of Houston since the World War was accomplished by tremendous improvements in paving and widening streets, constructing sewers and bridges, building drive-ways along the bayous, and by adding parks and beautiful buildings such as the auditorium, outdoor theatre, new library, and art museum.

By looking at the progress of a few sample cities which have grown quickly in the last half century, the law that human progress, natural and numerical, entails the use of progressively smaller areas of land can be observed as readily as by looking at progress in more rural districts and amongst more primitive people. But such inspection reveals, perhaps even better than the latter, the means by which the less renumerative use of land can be replaced by the more renumerative without social dislocation or mishap. The means rests upon a recognition of the rights of property which presupposes a recognition of the inappropriateness of private-ownership in land. Possession for use, private or public, must replace ownership for exploitation or for restricting use to gain profits out of monopoly values. Due compensation to those who are displaced or superseded when the more renumerative use of smaller areas comes about can only be accomplished by the communal provision of such common services as may be of use to both parties out of the community-created fund, and by the wholesale cheapening of goods through specialization in production and through widened markets. The collection of common value for common needs is the lubricant which makes the changes occurring as population density increases smooth and beneficial. Hence the importance of a proper valuation and assessment of real property if the changes associated with increase of population are to produce general satisfaction.

The connections are intimate between ground values and property appraisals and a sound distribution of population. They are also intimate between property taxation assessments and town planning. For obsolete and wrong methods of taxing people hold up improved systems of transport, whether by road or rail. The claims and privileges of private owners of land frequently form obstacles to good planning and to improved lines of communication, even though such betterments appeal to the cupidity of owners. The principle of "ability to pay," a bad one, as a basis for taxes should be replaced by that of "benefits received." The site- or ground-value is always a true measure of the benefits received by a holder of the plot. Again, once establish that better system of collecting for the public services the values the public create and leaving to the individual without deduction the products of his own exertions, and those multifarious difficulties which arise around the question of boundaries would dissolve into thin air.

From time to time great difficulties arise over the question of boundaries between different local governing bodies. Big squabbles and serious obstacles to arranging satisfactory and economical public services spring up. Despite such obstacles local authorities have been compelled, voluntarily in most instances, to act in collaboration. Joint committees, district commissions, and regional planning boards have been set up. Many of these bodies were formed some time before the central government advised or compelled their formation. Most of the discussions connected with these matters revolve around finance, around the varying assessments for taxes, the varying weight of the rates, and the varying costliness of the necessary public activities in different areas. Once a system were adopted which ensured that no one paid rates or taxes but only contributed into the common pool according to the benefits he received, once the private and the common interests ceased to conflict, then collaboration between the authorities governing adjoining areas would be arranged easily, almost automatically. Sentiments centring round local history, local traditions, names, and government, precious and justifiable in their right place would not be found conflicting with common sense. To take a few examples of what happens to-day.

No better illustration of the sort of difficulties which arise over questions of boundaries could be given than the study of an assortment of the problems which have arisen during the last few decades at Manchester. As is well known, that city of 766,000 inhabitants is closely contiguous to Salford with a population of 223,500. The boundary between them is purely artificial, except in so far as the narrow River Irwell must be called a natural one. Within 25 miles of the centre of Manchester there is a population of 4,000,000, or more than 200,000 to the square mile. This constitutes the most densely populated area of similar extent in England. Within a radius of 100 miles of Manchester there is a population (about 18,500,000) equal in numbers to three times the population of Australia, nearly equal to one-fifth of the population of the United States, and equal to the total white population of the British Empire outside the British Isles. Within a few miles of the centre of Manchester are such towns as the following: Bolton, Oldham, Stockport, Rochdale, and Bury, with populations in 1931 of 178,683; 140,300; 125,500; 90,278; and 63,163 respectively; besides many other somewhat smaller towns, and other bigger ones rather further afield. Manchester has but seldom extended its boundaries in the last sixty years. In 1838 its area was about 4,320 acres and its population slightly over 200,000 persons. Its present area is 21,690 acres. From time to time since before the end of last century, the idea of amalgamating Salford with Manchester has been put forward. Committees have been appointed, and have met, but seldom have they issued any report. Generally Salford was opposed to the amalgamation. But about 1921 this feeling changed to a considerable extent coincident with excessively high rates in Salford. On various occasions, too, Manchester has sought powers to extend its boundaries in this direction or in that. As soon, however, as any concrete proposal is made (for example for the absorption of Heaton Norris between Manchester and Stockport in 1912 and of Cheadle and Gatley in 1934), the people of a jealous neighbouring town (Stockport in this instance) also desire to see their city grow in area, population, and importance. Both promulgate Bills before Parliament. Legal expenses mount up. The district with few poor residents will generally try to avoid amalgamation with a poor district, which will certainly have higher rates. Bribes are offered. The ratepayers of the smaller town are offered a favourable differential rate for a number of years and a disproportionately large number of representatives on the Manchester Council. But in the end nothing happens as a rule, except a unanimous decision that competition of neighbouring boroughs for the absorption of urban and rural districts is undignified, expensive, and usually haphazard and unsatisfactory.

The inhabitants of rural districts, under rural districts or county councils, in the proximity of large towns nearly always oppose absorption into the city area, however strong the arguments for their absorption are; and they do so nearly always because they object to paying higher rates, i.e. local taxes. This is natural. County councils object to curtailment of their areas, again because of decrease of persons from whom they can collect the local rates. For example, the County Council of the West Riding (of Yorkshire) feared such loss a few years back and pointed out that the proposals for the extension of the borough boundaries recently formulated or projected in the West Riding threatened the County with a loss of 187,734 acres, a population of 409,249, and an assessable value of £2,082,541. Some members of the County Council also emphasized another disturbing element in all these schemes, namely that there was no finality about them. Immediately an extension was authorized, new conditions of contiguity arose and led to further applications. None the less, renewed discussions are going on merrily in the West Riding as I write.

It was estimated in 1927 that 250,000 persons working in Manchester resided outside its precincts. Many of these enjoyed the advantages of Manchester City's expenditure, yet so far as their place of residence was concerned they escaped very lightly as to their local taxes. Manchester Corporation contributed heavily towards the early losses on the Manchester Ship Canal, opened by Queen Victoria in 1894. It lent £5,000,000 towards the initial cost, too. The independent borough of Stretford, a pleasant residential area for the richer workers in Manchester, with very few slums and therefore light rates, has always strenuously opposed absorption by Manchester. Yet in the past, when Manchester levied a rate of over one shilling in the pound to make up the loss on the Ship Canal, Stretford contributed nothing, but benefited probably more than any other district by the better trade brought by the Canal. There is only one easy way of measuring what are the benefits individuals in any district receive from public expenditure in that district and its neighbourhood and that is by appraisal of "site-values." That should be done and no public revenue should be raised except by collecting the annual rent from the holders of these. All would then discern the common advantage of carrying out sensible improvements of one sort and another. All would soon come to agree how best to arrange the services now generally provided by public authorities, whether transport, electricity, or water supply, education, or what-not. Co-operation over wide districts for such services seem desirable; while such matters as paving, lighting, and certain public health matters might perhaps be supervised by the servants of smaller local bodies. But sure it is that all these present difficulties over boundaries and differential and differing rates would disappear without the imposition of compulsion by Parliament or other authority. To show how ill-arranged some of these public services are to-day in the Manchester district, it is worth mentioning that in 1926, when the Manchester and District Joint Town Planning Advisory Committee issued a report on its regional scheme, 104 local authorities were concerned, and there were 26 statutory authorities operating for the supply of water, 53 for the supply of gas, 42 for the supply of electricity, and 97 for main drainage and sewage disposal. The state of affairs to-day is not much better, with the exception of electricity.

Another good example of present-day conservatism in reform is illustrated by quoting the following from the pen of E. D.

Simon. This comes from the Liberal Land Committee's book.[1] "There is a large amount of traffic in cotton goods from Oldham to Bolton. This goes by motor lorry and has to go right into the centre of Manchester and out again, simply because a direct road from Oldham to Bolton would pass through the areas of several local authorities, and it has been nobody's business to press for such a road, or even to think of the possibility of constructing it. This heavy traffic adds to the congestion of central Manchester, wears the Manchester roads unnecessarily, and the extra distance and delay increase the cost of transport. But it is a doubtful advantage to the districts between Bolton and Oldham to build a by-pass road for the sake of reducing the costs of Oldham spinners and of Manchester ratepayers."

Where these boundary problems do not arise the control of town and country planning and the expansion of cities is decidedly easier even though hampered by conservative ways of arranging taxes and land tenure. The position of certain "free towns" in Germany, for example, Hamburg and Bremen, gives to their governing authorities a largely unhampered control over the whole of the surrounding land. This is a great advantage compared to the more circumscribed English municipalities surrounded with innumerable lesser municipal bodies. In any case most German towns possess more autocratic powers than English ones, and can dispense with the parliamentary proceedings and sanctions which in England are found so costly.

Another way in which private ownership of land and bad systems of taxes interfere with efficient road or rail development is through the lien landlordism has on the materials coming from the land which are used to make the roads. Combines and cartels raise the price of cement, for example, or hold up the supplies of granite. Furthermore, such monopolies enable graft and corruption to creep in in many instances in Europe, in America, in Australia, and elsewhere. The history of Australian railway development illustrates this well. One of the most notorious of road-construction cases occurred a few years ago in Texas, where "Ma" Ferguson and family, with some contractors, were shown up so effectively by Mr. Attorney-General, Dan

---

[1] *Towns and the Land*, Urban Report of the Liberal Land Committee, 1923–25, p. 175 (Hodder & Stoughton, London. 1s.).

Moody, that the company employed to surface 1,050 miles of highway were compelled, by a verdict in the courts, to refund some hundreds of thousands of dollars to the State Treasury.

Nearly all peoples in the world recognize the principle that community-created values should be collected for the community. Earlier chapters of this book brought out how the principle is applied by many primitive races. This chapter cannot close without indicating once again how it has won increasing recognition amongst the people of progressive nations, especially since the rebirth in recent decades of town and regional planning. In America it is not only New York that has introduced a special assessment tax falling upon landholders benefiting by a public improvement. Other cities on that side of the globe have likewise brought in betterment, increment, special assessment, and site-value taxes, all of which aim to get for the community what the community creates. In Holland, Switzerland, Denmark, France, and Germany, in several places in Africa and Asia, particularly under British rule, similar efforts are being made. In England the Liberal Land Committee and subsequent Governments, both Conservative and Labour, have put forward measures with the same object. But in practice such measures seem, when dispassionately reviewed, to have accomplished little of that after which they strive. If these plans had been combined with a straight tax on all holders of land values would they have proved more successful? But this also has been tried in Australia, New Zealand, Denmark, and in some other places and it has not produced the results expected. What has been tried is not radical enough. Some think good results would have been accomplished if such measures had been reinforced by new laws to attack the leasehold system. An Act to make leasehold enfranchisement compulsory, by which it is meant that a landlord should be compelled to sell his ground if the lessee wishes to purchase, is unfair. It would bring a fresh crop of difficulties and a fresh overgrowth of lawyers' fees. Furthermore, such measures do not give any adequate stimulus to alteration in the structure of local government where that structure is obsolete and inelastic. The establishment of vested interests in this or that quarter are for ever proving too strong to get even satisfactory, much less quick reforms, accomplished. Justice so as to let public and private interests coincide is the only way of true reform. Justice demands that community values should *all* flow into the public coffers and that the only way to spend such revenues equitably to all is to let them finance all the public services. Then, or before long, every kind of tax could be swept away. Every attempt at half measures has failed. Measures for "de-rating" have proved a fraud, the taxation of land values sometimes worse than useless and increment value duties have simply kept politicians and lawyers busy. Betterment taxes have generally been evaded.

In some quarters people who have studied these things puzzle their heads as to who constitute the community. They seem to think the collection of the community's own revenue will somehow or other be upsetting, rather than a reform bringing real progress. They imagine difficulties over assessments and over apportioning the incoming land rent equitably between various bodies, local and central. That there would be no difficult details to adjust is not to be imagined. But they would be as nothing compared with the hardships and the intricate perplexities to-day. A reign of justice cannot produce injustice. If, in sweeping away hundreds of hardships, one or two arise, tribunals could easily be set up to dispense compassionate allowances, for example to ex-landlords who were found to be unemployables. Many of the qualms which arise in the breasts of those who oppose this essential and far-reaching reform are undoubtedly due to misunderstandings. The proposal is in essence quite simple. But complications are dragged in. Misconceptions and contentions arise because a clear distinction is not made at the outset between "improvement" value and the value attaching to the ground itself. The former is produced by the exertions and expenditure of an individual or individuals. It is made by man. The latter comes about from natural influences due to position, climate, the general well-being of the community, etc. The former begins to fall as soon as ever the improvement is completed. The latter generally rises with the increase of population, and with the steadily increasing efficiency of an advancing people due largely to the progress of invention and expenditure on public services. If a landowner develops his own estate, constructs roads, plants curbs and sewers, and sets out gardens, etc., he is entitled to all that it cost him, including something justly measuring his own time and even something for advertising his productions if such monies have been expended. But all those expenditures can be easily ascertained. When the improvement is finished they begin to depreciate and they cost money to keep up to the pristine state. Hence it is easy as a fact to distinguish their value from the site values, which may rise steadily. Yet so used have landholders got to looking upon all appreciations in value as rightly their property that they sometimes become indignant if not allowed to pocket all rises in value. Custom has permitted them to do this and they pride themselves on their clever foresight.

The politicians of some camps have suggested that special assessments should be made to try and get the unearned values from land holders, that reversion duties and increment taxes should be imposed. But unless all are treated alike and the principle of abolishing taxes and collecting the community's land rent from holders of every piece of land which possesses any "site-value" be adopted, difficulties arise. It is impossible to classify land, for example, into agricultural (or cultivable) and building (or site) land. Also the results achieved by partial, piecemeal legislation are thoroughly unsatisfactory. The speculative value of sites, hampering land users (namely, producers and commerce), is not eliminated unless a straight and "whole-hogging" reform is inaugurated. When this is done it becomes impossible for land holders to pass on the levy made on them. Hence land holders become synonymous everywhere with land users and with occupiers. Also these levies at once are seen to be no tax, no burden on industry, because it quickly becomes apparent that they are ground dues (i.e. rent due for exclusive possession of ground), which return in public services to the payer all that he pays. Not long after this most fundamental reform has been introduced everyone will find themselves taking interest in good planning. As J. S. Nettlefold says, in front of the introduction to his book, *Practical Town-Planning* :[1] "A strong economic incentive in the right direction is far more effective for reform than all the rules and regulations that were ever framed."

[1] St. Catherine Press, London, 1914, p. xii.

CHAPTER XIX

TRAFFIC TROUBLES

TRAFFIC troubles naturally group themselves under three headings, viz.: (*a*) The handicaps and hardships which produce loss of time and energy, as well as physical and mental strain. These occur for the most part on railways of various kinds, and on roads, and in public conveyances. (*b*) The bodily injuries and deaths occuring mostly on the roads. (*c*) Congestion arising from the transport of goods. All these troubles are affected by the density and distribution of population and have much to do with the concentration of people in the cities. They have to be considered by town and country planners. They have only become distressing and acute during this century. They have to do with modern inventions facilitating transport, principally applications of steam and electrical power and of the internal combustion engine. They are a necessary accompaniment of the greater speed at which people move nowadays and the greater amount of business encompassed. The three groups overlap to some extent. For example, on the New York quick-transit railways, on which each inhabitant of that great city makes on an average about 500 journeys a year, the physical and mental strain is the chief trouble. In 1927 rather over 20,000 people received bodily injuries on these railways, a low proportion considering the total amount of traffic. A graphic description of a journey on one of New York's tubes during the rush hour is given by a contributor to the New York *Evening Telegraph*. It is not an exaggeration and, although written six years ago conditions to-day have not improved. Though new tubes have been constructed so have higher sky-scrapers. The saturation point is being ever maintained. A tall building, well short of the tallest skyscrapers, in New York can accommodate 15 to 20,000 workers, and this number fills a good many trains. In fact, it requires roughly the whole capacity of a rapid transit line for twenty minutes morning and evening. It can be seen, therefore, that despite the desire of landowners to exploit their sites as fully as possible, enough rapid transit lines cannot be supplied to

NEW YORK ENVIRONS, SHOWING RAILWAY SYSTEM

By kind permission of the Garden Cities and Town Planning Association

enable every owner to develop his land to such a degree as to make the average height of all buildings in Manhattan even as high as eleven storeys. Here is an extract from the account of the return home on a New York tube during the rush hour, a journey taken by the writer (a woman) six days a week:

"34th Street.—A shouting, shoving, surly mass of humans climbing the steps against a bigger, surlier mass moving down. Punches, shoves, hurts, faint outcries! Incredibly, an opening and—entirely apart from our own volition—we are catapulted up the steps, across the platform—God knows how!—into the car, and with the hard-boiled guard's cruel fist in the small of my back somehow the door oozes shut behind me.

"Times Square.—The surging, seething mass moves me a fraction of an inch, and I lean, and heavily too, on the breast of a negro. He dislikes it. I do too. Twenty-seven bodies in the vestibule, not counting the arms, shoulders, and hips protruding over the line from inside.

"22nd Street.—Agony again. My hands shield my chest. I could not lower them if I tried. A jab from a bony knee in the region of my appendix. Two more now in our crowded, stinking cubicle. Right under my nose a poor chap's bandaged hand reeking of iodoform. Now the negro's arm is around my back. But that is better than jamming against the bar, as he keeps me from going down under the squirming, worming mass, girding themselves for battles at the next stop.

"96th Street.—Ah, they will get off here and then relief. But no! A sea of faces on the platform—angry, hungry faces—each trying to be the first through that slowly opening door.

"110th Street.—An onslaught of students, with football muscles and football tactics. They may laugh; they haven't been in the Turkish sweat as long as we have.

"116th Street.—I will get off; I am slipping, and there is no room to faint! I'm a second too late, the surge is against me and I am chained to my negro.

"125th Street.—Can I stick for two more stops? No choice! Like the rising centre of a prairie twister (cyclone), out come the vanguard of those who have been inside. Where can we go but through the glass? Can humanity contract any more? A miracle once more! The door opens; they do get off. Why, both my arms function! The negro gently, carefully, disengages himself and is gone.

"135th Street.—A foot more of room. Oh, what a boon! Only twenty-three now left of us. What heavenly space and freedom! Both my feet are on the floor. They weren't before.

M

"Mott Avenue.—I have lasted through. My knees wobble, water is streaming from my face. I do not recall coming through the door or around the corridor, but I am on the stairs."

It is estimated that, at the present rate of growth, the population in the New York area will be 21,000,000 by 1965, and that about 9,000,000 people may be entering Manhattan daily. Rapid transit lines, which by 1925 were 590 miles in extent within the limits of the city, many of them four tracks, are increasing steadily. They will soon be double the extent reached in 1925, and according to estimates, by 1965 should reach a mileage of 2,200. The area which is ultimately expected to be served by these lines extends to about 15 miles from the centre of the city. The traffic and transport problems of New York are comprehensively dealt with and future developments are surveyed in the fourth and fifth volumes of the *Regional Survey of New York and its Environs*, published about six years ago. There is no other form of locomotion comparable for efficiency and capacity with rapid transit lines. In the New York district they are financed by municipal funds. But the more facilities of transport given the greater seem the incentives to concentration of population in or near the biggest cities in the world. Whenever a new line is opened the land is quickly developed, generally by the building of dwelling houses acting largely as dormitories for those who work in the adjoining city.

It has been said one may judge the civilization of any country by the efficiency of its systems of transport, and that the stage of civilization reached can be measured from this efficiency taken in conjunction with the power resources of the country. The civilization of the present day continues to bring ugly "conurbations," where more and more persons fight daily to get into the centres to find, if they possibly can, jobs in commerce and the secondary industries. Already the evils of such a civilization are making themselves abundantly manifest. Many are the sorrows and privations which have arisen. Upheavals and revolutions multiply. What will be the end? Throughout all these developments the natural instincts of man dimly peep. When better facilities of travel are produced the workers of the world who labour in the cities daily travel centrifugally, if they can afford it, to get to those places where they can see green things growing, and where the amenities and advantages of more rural surroundings are to be found. The centres of cities lose population, except during the working hours of the day. For example, in London the total population within a 5-mile radius of the centre of the city fell by 250,000 to a total of 4,333,000 in the thirty years ending 1931. In the same period, however, the population outside this 5-mile radius increased by 1,750,000 to a total of 3,750,000. Since 1931 this process has continued more rapidly than ever.

London's "underground" system is now controlled by the Passenger Transport Board referred to in an earlier chapter of this book (see pp. 165-167). It now has less than half its lines in tube or tunnel. The northern extension of the Piccadilly Tube, completed on July 31, 1933, allows a through run of 25 miles from Hounslow in the south-west to the new terminus at Cockfosters in the north-east. The construction of these tubes is expensive. In London a route mile of tube railway, i.e. two tracks each in a single tube, costs £750,000 to construct and equip fully. During the 2½ years to July 1933 the London Underground Railways spent £11,000,000 in extensions. But it is not long before they earn well. For example, the extension of the City and South London line in 1926 from Clapham Common to Morden, a distance of 5¼ miles, for three-quarters of its length through a dense traffic area, was earning its operating costs and interest charges within two years of its completion. In 1929 over 30,000,000 passengers were using the extension annually, to-day about 40,000,000. Lord Ashfield, the accomplished head of the London Traffic Combine, now Chairman of the London Transport Board, advocated early in 1933 the electrification of all London surburban passenger railway lines as soon as possible, and later he prophesied the necessity for a completely new underground line extending from West London to Ilford. At present London's passengers are carried, as to 48 per cent by the omnibuses (mostly for short journeys near the centre), 26 per cent by trams, and most of the rest by railways.

Transport systems of whatever kind and wheresoever plying have always been intimately affected by taxation, central and local, of one kind and another, special franchises, licences, rates (i.e. local taxes), petrol taxes, income taxes, etc. For example, the London Traffic Combine (Buses, Tubes, etc.), paid £600,000 in rates in 1921, and just double this in 1930; and though its revenue had increased in the same period by 23 per cent the Government tolls had increased 100 per cent. In 1932 the Combine's Omnibus and Coach Companies paid in licensed vehicle duties and in petrol tax £1,745,000, equivalent to 1·85d. for each mile run. This is said to be distinctly above the share of the cost of the road upkeep used by the buses and coaches. But if this be so, as seems likely, the companies were able to get some counterbalancing redress through governmental aid given them in other directions, e.g. through guarantees under the Trade Facilities and the Development (Loans, Guarantees, and Grants) Acts. Successive Governments in various countries have usually been kind to monopoly owners and big combines. Some monopolies are necessary and advantageous, especially perhaps for some kinds of transport. But national planning and marketing schemes of recent years in various socialistically inclined countries, designed to make industry more profitable and efficient, have often fostered inefficiency and have despoiled the many for the gain of the few.

The same things as are happening in and around London and New York are happening in the neighbourhood of other big cities, in Paris for example. Paris, in spite of some good planning in Napoleon's time giving a number of fine broad roads and open spaces near the centre of the city, and despite a good underground railway system, is said to be one of the worst cities in the world for congestion of traffic.

The passenger transport systems of to-day, though skilfully organized, produce handicaps and hardships for crowds of city workers. The question is: will these traffic troubles be minimized howsoever cleverly the systems be planned in the future? The answer is in the negative. Something more radical is essential. To strike at the root of things, the suck to the towns must be stopped. A different outlook on the rights of property and the duties of the State must arise. Drastic alterations in the attractions, capacities, and openings for men and women to enter various kinds of occupations must come about. All these reforms will distribute industries and population more evenly over the land. The means whereby such changes can be accomplished have already been given in previous chapters of this book; but a further study of traffic troubles must be pursued.

When the second group of troubles, the toll of the roads in death and injury is considered it is seldom that the question of a better distribution of population is mentioned. It is true that the increased number of motor users is an indication of the increase of population, the increase in the standard of living, and the cheapening of production through greater knowledge, skill, and specialization. Yet roughly speaking, more congestion of population generally spells more accidents. It is obvious that a collision is primarily a matter of space. Two objects collide through the accident of occupying the same space. True it is that more space at a corner, in a congested city street, or elsewhere, does not necessarily mean no collisions. Other factors are of great importance, chief of which are carelessness and faulty judgment in using the roads. Nevertheless, this question of space, again obviously a land question, is important, and is more important in trying to reduce the number of deaths on the road, than attention to speed and to penalties and punishments.

The increase in the use of motor road vehicles has been rapid in the last thirty years. But roads users of every kind have not cultivated the necessary reactions and judgment at the same rate. As recently as 1911 60 per cent of wheeled vehicles in Great Britain were horse drawn, but in about eleven years from that date this percentage was reduced to under 10. In 1922 there were rather under 1,000,000 motor vehicles licensed in Great Britain, and four years later only one motor to every 45 persons. In 1932 there were 2,219,200. In 1933 the increase of motors had led to 1 person in 33 in Great Britain, and 1 in 6 in the United States of America having a motor vehicle of one sort or another. The car density per mile of road increased seven times in the thirteen years to 1926 in Great Britain. It is estimated that in the United States of America where there are 24,000,000 motors with a population of 123,000,000, as in Great Britain with rather over 2,000,000 motors amongst 43,000,000 population, there is one motor vehicle for every 7 miles of highway. The number of deaths from motor accidents in New York in 1899 was one, in 1926 it was 1,069. In 1929 in the United States 26,500 persons were killed in accidents involving motors. In 1933 the total number of persons killed on the roads of Great Britain was 6,924 (19 a day), and of injured 191,829; in 1932 the injured numbered 206,410 (565 a day). During 1930, the worst year, the number of killed was a little over 7,000, and of injured 220,000. The number of accidents and of fatalities has increased roughly in direct proportion to the increase in the number of vehicles in use. Thus the percentage increase, as compared with 1921 (as Colonel Pickard has shown), in the number of motor vehicles licensed in Great Britain and in street accidents is as follows:

				Vehicles	Accidents
1922	..	..	..	12	12
1924	..	..	..	53	57
1926	..	..	..	98	99
1928	..	..	..	134	135

But when the greater mileage, and heavier weight of motor traffic is taken into account, it can be said that matters are improving. This is due without doubt to the many efforts made at prevention, one of the most important of which is education. The generation of persons who were too old to acquire a road sense, particularly as pedestrians, is being superseded by a new generation, many of whom even when quite young have had the kind of instruction suggested by the Safety First Association. Another piece of education having effect is that which is gradually being absorbed by the motor drivers who are acquiring a better understanding of the situation. A knowledge of the facts is of some help; such facts, for example, as that 85 per cent of the fatal accidents were due to human failure; that pedestrians and cyclists (pedal and motor) furnish 9 out of 10 fatalities; that cyclists are usually between the ages of 14 and 22; that pedestrians are generally under 8 or over 50. By degrees all road users are learning that the highways exist for the common good and that the right to their lawful use imposes an equal obligation to respect the rights and safety of others. Many pedestrians, however, have yet to learn and practise the fundamental strategy of movement, as laid down by Colonel Mervyn O'Gorman of the Royal Automobile Club. He says: "For safety we need a universal recognition of the law of 'show your intention,' and the law of 'heed the intention of others,' and the law of 'move orderly.' " He does not advocate pedestrian hand signals, but "no jay-crossing," more footways on which the rule should be (in England) "keep to the left."

In 1933 the National Safety First Association published a map of England showing where all the fatal accidents happened in the months July to December 1932. From this it is clear that accidents occur most frequently in the areas where population is most concentrated. Out of a total of fatalities Greater London accounted for 689, Birmingham for 71, and Manchester for 56; and if the other places with 30 or more fatal accidents (Leeds 33, Liverpool 33, Sheffield 30, Newcastle 30) be added to these, it is apparent that the areas of seven cities account for 942 out of 3,029 fatal accidents, roughly a third. If the immediate neighbourhood of these seven towns be also included and a comparatively few additional urbanized districts (such as Bradford, Hull, Derby, Leicester, Leeds, Nottingham, and Bristol), then the proportion of fatal injuries on the roads occurring in these urban districts would be higher still. The rest occur more or less evenly scattered over the country. But the investigations carried out by this association and by the Ministry of Transport go to prove that fatal accidents do not happen so much as might be anticipated in streets where most crowded traffic is found. In the most congested traffic not only has the pace of vehicles to slow down a good deal, but everyone is more vigilant and more precautions to avoid accidents are taken. Thus of the 3,029 fatal accidents investigated by the Safety First Association, the proportion is shown to be 46·6 per cent in towns, 28 per cent in built-over districts, and 25 per cent in open country. The Ministry of Transport, too, in a report dealing with Fatal Road Accidents occurring in the six months to June 30, 1933, reports that only six such accidents happened in the confines of the City of London against 566 in the Metropolitan Police Area of London.

So far nothing has been said about the third group under which traffic troubles can be classified, those due to congestion of traffic connected with the transport of goods. Many improvements have been made in this form of transport. The use of roads and railways at night or at such other times as passengers are not travelling relieves congestion. The mechanical equipment of handling goods, especially in bulk, has improved enormously in recent decades. More sense and better arrangements are being made in marketing goods. None the less, the concentration of people into cities, especially the intense concentration at the centres during working hours where people have to be fed during these hours, has produced a whole crop of difficulties which have not as yet by any manner of means been surmounted. The opening of fresh market places in suburbs of big towns is constantly suggested, but not so constantly being carried out. Goods, and quantities of them perishable foodstuffs, still pour into central market places only to pour back again for suburban distribution. The clash and conflict of interests, canal company versus the railways, railway companies versus road carriers, etc., do not always, or indeed, often under the social system of to-day, conduce to the orderly arrangement of these things. When improvements are merely suggested, especially if public money is to be spent, up go the demands of the private owners of land; and what is more natural under the customs and usages permitted by society as organized to-day? Quite often, too, initiative in constructing betterments of one sort or another is foiled by the methods of taxing at present adopted, or by legal restrictions. Governmental action frequently prevents friendly co-operation between apparently rival organizations, railways and road-way carriers, for example, and when belated action is taken does much to encourage monopoly combines whose chief efforts are directed towards profits. Then Socialists of varied complexions come along to try their hand at State collectivism, only to find at the start a heavy incubus, namely the weight of the over-capitalization established, and subsequently absorbed by the monopolists. Besides this burden there is all too often a further incubus in the shape of the inexperience, red tape, and place-hunting sometimes inseparable from bureaucratic supervision.

In the wonderful plans for future developments in New York and its environs much attention and skill has been directed towards freight transport—see 4th and 5th vols. of the Survey already referred to. The planners see hopes by developing available foreshore for the establishment of industries and port facilities, by the building of belt lines of various kinds, and by boring small tunnels not requiring artificial ventilation for carrying goods. It is stated that four times as much land has been zoned as is likely to be required by 1965. It is as well, however, that Mr. Thomas Adams in his Foreword to the Survey says: "The only way to promote decentralization is by a properly balanced distribution of both industries and population over wider areas, with a lessening of the necessity of travel between the place of work and the home." But examine the map on page 362 illustrating what room there is for decentralization in one—the tobacco—industry alone, and how slowly it takes place. Moreover there seems doubt as to whether even this great man appreciates what are the greatest obstacles to the realization of this hope. At all events, he does not generally say much about the overweighted proportion employed in secondary industries, commerce, and transport, etc.; nor about private individuals' lien on land values; nor about the evils of taxation and of public debts; nor about the poverty of the masses.

Traffic troubles are due to a variety of causes. A rough idea of some of these causes has been given in the preceding pages. A connection between such troubles and the growth of population and its greater concentration into cities has been shown. Indications have been given that this connection produces more disabling and unbusinesslike loss of energy, time, and temper than actual bodily injury and death. The remedies which are being applied to overcome these troubles are all in their nature matters which have to do with the distribution of population, with town and country planning, with the education of the people, with the use of land, and with the rights of property. What are they? Most mean the finding of more space. Yet the world is large. There are plenty of eligible sites. Land is fertile. Human brains ingenious. Why does population so congregate in a few regions that these traffic troubles arise? An answer to this question has been surveyed in the previous pages and to some extent elaborated. Time will bring reforms; but how long will it be before the peaceful revolution outlined in this book takes place? And what turmoil, travail, and suffering may not be endured before people see the light? Meanwhile improvements to ameliorate and minimize present hardships and handicaps must continue; they are, indeed, desirable and necessary in any

M*

case. But we must see to it that all these improvements are so made that their construction and operation direct men's eyes to the bigger concepts, to the more far-reaching reforms.

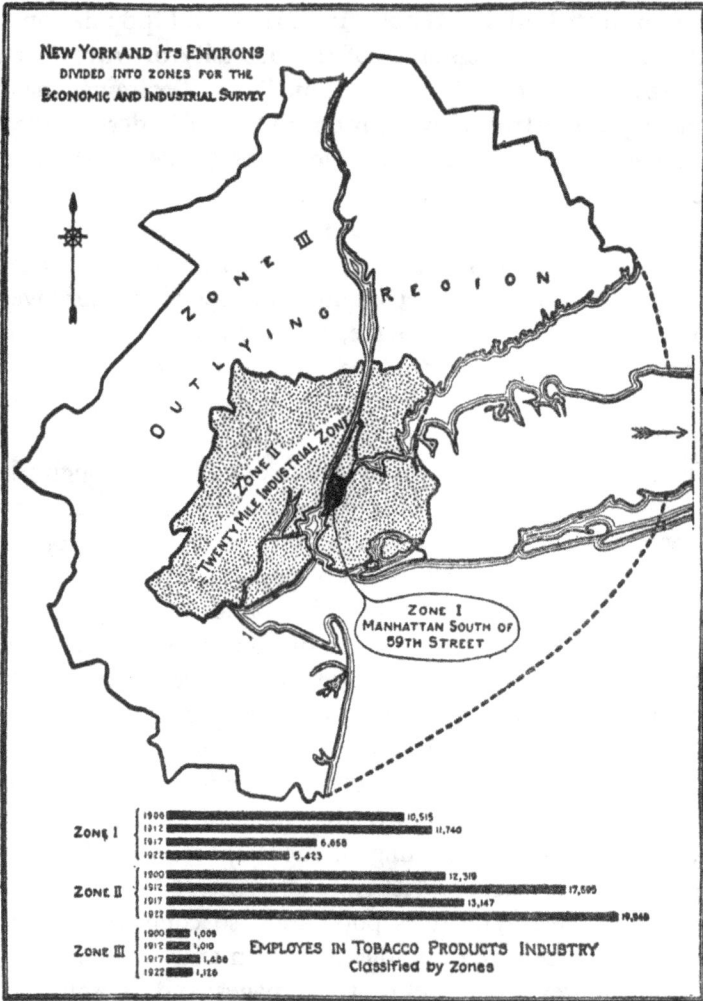

NEW YORK AND ITS ENVIRONS
DIVIDED INTO ZONES FOR THE
ECONOMIC AND INDUSTRIAL SURVEY

ZONE III

OUTLYING REGION

ZONE II
TWENTY MILE INDUSTRIAL ZONE

ZONE I
MANHATTAN SOUTH OF
59TH STREET

Zone I	1900	10,515
	1912	11,740
	1917	6,058
	1922	5,423
Zone II	1900	12,319
	1912	17,595
	1917	13,147
	1922	19,949
Zone III	1900	1,009
	1912	1,010
	1917	1,486
	1922	1,116

EMPLOYES IN TOBACCO PRODUCTS INDUSTRY
Classified by Zones

ZONING IN NEW YORK; THE TOBACCO INDUSTRY
By kind permission of the Garden Cities and Town Planning Association

Injuries to man's business capacity, to his health of body and mind by traffic congestion and accidents are being overcome firstly by education and better traffic regulation, and secondly by gaining more space. A "road sense" is being developed in most countries where there is much motor traffic, by careless pedestrians even, as well as by the much abused motorists. Even a capacity for the better endurance of the trials of travelling underground in rush hours is being acquired, though in the future psychologists may tell us how big the cost is. We are instituting, or have already introduced: one-way traffic streets; "round-abouts" at certain important road junctions (which incidentally increase the mileage now run by London omnibuses by 3,500 miles a day); automatic signals; white lines and other signs on the roads themselves; heavier penalties for those whose acuteness of senses is dulled by alcohol; a more sensible, broader, yet less harsh handling of offenders by judges and magistrates; mobile patrols; and improved arrangements for pedestrians' crossing places; better road surfaces; and better-lit roads. All these things are bringing about improvement. People are beginning to realize, too, that an increase of safety, and comfort in movement is one of the factors which send up the value of land and that such increments are not produced by landowners. But when all is said and done, despite the many ingenious ways in which the dangers of travelling in congested areas have been lessened, it is still safer to go lion hunting in Africa than it is to cross the street in London or New York.

Now about the gaining of more space. Would you widen a road; pare off a corner; cut down a bank; pull down a shed; construct a footpath or a special cycle track; build a bridge; acquire land for a car park, or for a playground to get the children off the streets, often the only place in the open air where they can play? Or do you wish to construct a new railway or special road for speedy motor traffic? Well, will you not, in nine cases out of ten, come up against landlordism? That is the experience in most countries. Seldom is the particular landlord at the same time far-seeing enough, capable (because like others, hard up) of immediate financial sacrifice, and public spirited enough to part with his plot on the easiest terms. Generally he is hostile; if not by direct opposition to the improvement, then by asking an extortionate price. The remaining pages of this book could easily be filled with well-authenticated examples of these statements. Yet all the time expenditure of other people's money (more likely than not of public money) on improvements which are urgent or desirable, together with the mere increase of population, sends up the value of sites regardless of how an individual may exert himself to better things. In fact, all the remedies so far suggested, all the burrowings and bridgings in contemplation will but add to the health, amenities, comfort, and efficiency of life in the already over-congested centres and will, therefore, send up land rent. This is becoming increasingly appreciated. Special assessments against holders of site-values which are sent up by the work of others, increment dues, betterment taxes, and even a straightforward taxation of the holders of land values are being proposed or actually being levied. These are directing people's thoughts to the fact that publicly created values belong to the public in their entirety, that taxes are unjust and oppressive, and that these half-measures—most of them are much less—leave a great deal of the speculative value of land in private hands and hence leave intact most of the evils associated with the term "land monopoly." They are only useful if they help to open people's eyes to demand drastic reform. A great agitation is necessary calling for that peaceful but far-reaching revolution which will do first things first and will bring about a better distribution of population. That alone can banish the perils and cure the troubles of traffic congestion.

CHAPTER XX

HOUSING

THE people who write about housing, slum clearances, town planning, etc., are generally people whose homes have a fairly ample space, not to say spaciousness both within and around. "House shortage" usually refers to houses for people who live more than two in a room, or more than 2½ persons per bedroom, whose homes are in cramped and squalid surrroundings. The proportion of persons in various countries in the world who live in deplorably overcrowded quarters is so great that the present task appears to be chiefly limited to slum clearances, the building of small parlour or non-parlour, two- or three-bedroom cottages, or of blocks of small tenements to house the working classes. Why is the larger vision, that of everyone living in ample space and comfort, apparently impossible? Is the world really so crowded? Take England, one of the most thickly populated countries in the world; it is easy to travel for miles in most parts and to see admirable building sites on every side in the midst of a beautiful countryside. But even if the population were not so concentrated into the towns, and even where it is most sparse, try, as a poor man, to get a site and to build a house for a small family and it is wellnigh impossible. Yet the materials and the willing hands are there, and the necessary skill does not take long years to acquire. There is something wrong in men's vision, because there is something wrong in the economic world.

One of the greatest English authorities on the provision of houses for the working classes, Sir Ernest Simon, said not long ago,[1] that although over 2,000,000 houses had been built in England and Wales since the war, "the pressure on the slums has not been reduced. The two troubles are that there are not enough houses yet and that the new houses are not cheap enough for working-class people." The 2,000,000 and more houses were quite inadequate to meet needs because the number of families had increased at a greater rate than the number of houses. Sir E. Simon calculates that to meet increase of population 1,500,000

[1] See *Manchester Guardian*, October 14, 1933.

new houses will be required by 1941, and nearly 1,700,000 by 1951. This is apart from those built in connection with slum-clearance schemes and apart from those for the replacement of any houses that were pulled down during the period.

What are the "homes" that must be demolished in order to get on with the great slum clearances so pitiably necessary? These are the kind of hovels; let me give only one or two illus-trations, which I could multiply without end:

(1) Not many years ago I went into a house in Portsmouth abutting the street, a rather narrow one. It had four rooms in it, and behind the house a tiny back-yard with a dripping tap and the remains of a dirty and leaky w.c. in it. The front room was the only habitable room, and its dimensions were such that most of it was taken up by the family bed. The family consisted of a man and wife and their two young children. The man's occupation was that of a costermonger who hawked vegetables for sale. The back room was originally a sort of kitchen-scullery and was used for storing the vegetables in between his rounds, though somewhat leaky drains were under its floor. The two bedrooms upstairs, one a very small one, were only habitable in dry weather because the roof leaked so badly. The window of one of them was tied to the roof to prevent its falling out. The rent was 5s. a week. Just round the corner of the street were some two-storied, small, newly built tenements one on each floor. The couple in the house, long ago condemned as unfit for human habitation, had put in repeated application for one of the tene-ments. But they were unable to obtain one for the following reasons: the number available was quite inadequate to supply the need of half the applicants; the couple were not considered suitable and eligible as being too dirty and unreliable; and even if these two reasons had not held, the pair could not have afforded to pay the higher rent for the tenement.

(2) In one of the famous back-to-back houses in Leeds which I was shown by the Medical Officer of Health of that city a year or two previous to my visit to Portsmouth there lived a couple of old cronies who paid 2s. 6d. a week for the two-roomed "villa," one room upstairs, one down. One of the old ladies had a pension from some source or other of 10s. a week. They supplemented this income by taking in washing. A "copper" had been put in

to their living room for which an extra 6d. a week rent was charged—and resented. There was no other place to hang out the washing except their own room, save for a small space immediately outside their door. But as this was only about 8 yards from a small range of privy middens which were only emptied about once a week, though they served about 20 persons, this was not a very nice place, even if it had not entailed constant bickerings with their numerous close neighbours.

Hundreds of such houses, or almost as bad, can still be found in use up and down the country, although condemned as unfit for human habitation sometimes years ago. Look round the smiling villages of England and poke into the courts of small market towns, and many a miserable pig-sty of a habitation can be found sheltering a family. Walk but a few steps only, as a general rule, from such spots in rural England and acres and acres of land can be seen at a glance which could be better utilized for houses than they are used at present.

In various parts of the world much less thickly populated than Great Britain the housing conditions of the workers is bad, often worse than in England and Scotland. Despite the strenuous efforts made by the Communist regime in Soviet Russia, and despite the numerous tenement blocks which have been erected in places like Moscow, there continues to be a terrible shortage of houses in Russia. The houses that are being built are in most places insufficient even for the natural increase of population. And in the towns whose inhabitants have swollen in numbers very rapidly in recent years it is, indeed, difficult to cope on the lowest standards with the needs of the people. Moscow's population increased from 1,800,000 before the revolution to 2,500,000 in 1928. The population of Kiev has increased from 500,000 before the revolution to about 1,000,000 in 1932, while that of Kharkov has grown in the same period from 260,000 to 800,000. Even in villages, too, there is often a housing shortage. Building material, tools, locks, etc., are so dear that the peasants prefer to live in the narrow quarters of their old huts.

In the Dutch East Indies, where only about 2 per cent of the total population live in towns or under urban conditions, the village housing conditions are indescribably bad. A result is that dysentery and hook-worm disease are very prevalent. In

Java at one time plague compelled attention to the insanitary state of the rat-infested houses.[1] In many of the large cities of the East the housing conditions and the state of overcrowding are appalling. In Bombay, for example, 70 per cent of the houses are one-roomed, and over 90 per cent of the working classes are accommodated in one-roomed tenements, some of them containing as many as 6 to 9 persons living in one room.

Truly has it been said that dogs, horses, cattle, and human slaves have often been and are often housed better. Some of the worst sort of homes have been referred to. But a majority of the working classes are not a great deal better off. In many towns houses built originally for one family have within living memory become, generally very incompletely, converted into "flats," each to house one or two families.

Since the armistice, up to June 30, 1934, 2,350,000 houses have been built in England and Wales, 1,192,944 with State assistance and 1,157,056 without. Of these, more than 300,000 have been erected within 15 miles of Charing Cross, that is, in the area of Greater London which contains a population of 8,250,000. Two-thirds of these houses in the London area were built by private enterprise. But considerably less than half the total of new houses are occupied by artisans. Censuses of housing in England and Scotland, published periodically, show that the percentage of overcrowding has not improved during this century. In London, according to a recent survey,[2] the percentage of persons living more than three in a room has risen from 3·1 in 1921 to 3·3 in 1931. Another striking but well-known feature of house rents is also brought out in this volume, viz. that the poorer the family the greater the proportion of their income which goes in rent and local taxes taken together. The 1931 census reveals the fact that there are 144,802 families in London living in one room, and 255,464 in two rooms; and the London County Medical Officer of Health has recently declared that 100,000 persons languish in 30,000 insanitary underground dwellings in London.

Throughout Scotland 2,000,000 people live in one- or two-

[1] See *The World's Health*, 1926, p. 441.
[2] *The New Survey of London Life and Labour*, Vol. III (P. S. King & Son, London, 1932. 17s. 6d.).

roomed apartment houses. At Stockton-on-Tees in Durham, a part of England where bad housing is especially prevalent, it was shown early in 1933 that the death-rate was sent up eight points through lack of food due to the increased rents which had to be met—they were up on the average from 4s. 7½d. to 8s. 10½d. —in a new housing estate compared with those ruling in the old slum. An ex-parliamentary secretary to the Ministry of Health, Susan Lawrence, suggested that this state of affairs should be met by feeding the children, anyway for two meals a day six days a week, out of public funds. So the burdened taxpayers are to meet unemployment pay, housing subsidy, and the cost of free meals, besides, of course, education, old-age pensions, etc. Is there any end to the vicious circle? Though 'tis true enough, as Miss Lawrence asserts, "hunger will not wait till the slums are cleared."

The New Statesman and Nation had a series of articles on housing in the first half of 1933. At the conclusion of these, which were from the pen of various experts (most of whom advocated public borrowing and action to build houses), the editor wrote[1] that "real and tragic conditions of overcrowding exist among the poor workers, undiminished by all the housing activities of the years since the war." Considering that the English justifiably pride themselves on being amongst the freest, most progressive, and politically enlightened people in the world, and that amelioration is so slow, are we really near to an eradication of these housing evils in our own country despite all the fuss? And what are the prospects of bettering conditions in some of the many other countries where they are bad? Unless the true causes of poverty and its concomitant, poor housing, are discovered and genuinely radical remedies are applied, prospects will continue to be gloomy.

Norwich Council has built many houses since the war. Four estates have been bought in or immediately outside the city and developed. There were not really big differences in the value of the land which had been purchased, but when a public authority comes into the market to buy land, inevitably up goes the price. These are the figures: The first estate was bought at £81 an acre, the second £101, the third £140, and for the fourth they had to pay £211 an acre. Always they paid scores of times the value of

[1] *The New Statesman and Nation*, March 18, 1933, p. 314.

the land if its value had been based on that on which it had previously been assessed for local taxes. For example, one estate of 147 acres bought for housing the people of Norwich cost 113 times its previous rating value. Innumerable similar examples from other places could be given. Here are a few more. These must suffice:

Acton U.D.C. paid £33,000 for 59 acres rated at £110
Bootle Corporation paid £13,100 for 28½ acres rated at   .. £213
Cardiff Corporation paid £31,399 for 204½ acres rated at   .. £304
London County Council paid £465,883 for 2,450 acres rated at £5,031

If land valued at £5,000 for paying taxes yet fetched nearly £500,000, there is something unfair here. What had any owner done to reap such sums? Yet most people acquiesce without serious outcry in these transactions. They go on being repeated from year to year. They multiply public debts and cause poverty and bad housing. For if any site (city or rural) or any other of the gifts of nature that exist independently of human action has a rental value, it is one which is created entirely by the needs, growth, and expenditure of the community. If such rentals were collected by the community, the true owners, then it would not be necessary to levy rates and taxes and thereby take away from producers certain wealth they have produced in order to let public servants spend it in "public schemes of work," such as house building, etc. Individuals could provide for their own needs if the old bad system were swept away.

Strenuous efforts to get rid of slums have been repeated periodically for a generation. They have been especially keen in the last decade or two. All the Governments of England and many of the municipalities have made honest efforts to grapple with this problem since the war. But are slums being banished? While some unfit houses are being demolished, all the time others are becoming unfit. A recent publication[1] demonstrates that even in towns where the population has gone down in the last ten years, there has usually been an increase in the number of families and an increased deficiency in the number of houses.

Some may think that better progress is being made in rural

[1] Sir E. D. Simon's *The Anti-Slum Campaign* (Longmans & Co., London, 1933. 2s. 6d. net).

districts. True it is that overcrowding in these districts is not so bad as in the cities. In the county of Norfolk, for example, the average number of rooms per dwelling in 1931 was 5·32 (in 1921 5·35), whereas in Norwich it is much lower, for the average number of persons per room in the city was 0·71 in 1931 (0·79 in 1921), and in the county 0·69 (0·75 in 1921).[1]

What are the remedies for housing shortage which are suggested in the Press, and in the writings and sayings elsewhere published? They all savour of the same ones which have been put forward almost from time immemorial. Take one of the latest and most fashionable: The creation of a National Housing Board "sufficiently influential to look at the problem as a whole and secure the co-ordination of all efforts whether they be municipal, public utility, or private" (Raymond Unwin). Most suggested remedies envisage public borrowing and subsidies in some shape or other. But no solution of the problem can be found along lines of action which lay an increasing burden upon the public purse, and which do nothing to diminish costs or to increase wages and the number of building operatives. An article on "The Housing Problem" in 1925,[2] states that the supply of building labour between 1901 and 1924 fell heavily. The total number of men in various occupations of house construction went down from 828,462 to 367,030. It also pointed out that there were not sufficient materials with which to build the houses urgently needed. To-day it is often the same if skilled and experienced bricklayers, masons, and plasterers, etc., are wanted. And more than once in the last year or two I have come across jobs being held up through inability to get bricks. Yet in recent years hundreds of thousands have suffered from unemployment, and leading economists and statesmen have declared that the recurrent "crises" which are causing the inhabitants of the world to suffer privation are due to a surplus of goods! The deficiency of skilled labourers is not entirely due to lack of opportunities for work produced by the obstacles of land monopoly and of taxation. Some of it is due to certain phases of trade-unionism. I have a friend whose son

[1] See also *Lancet*, 1927, I, p. 1041, where a summary of the census of housing taken at the 1921 census is given and comparisons between London Boroughs, and Rural Districts is made.

[2] *British Medical Journal*, March 28, 1925, p. 612.

soon became fairly expert as a bricklayer. He is now quite expert But for a long time he found it difficult to get jobs because he had trained without going through the usual channels and paying his apprenticeship dues, which, as a fact, his father could not afford.

It is freedom from restrictions and freedom from the burdens of taxation that is required, especially liberty of access without hindrance for labouring hands to the materials resident in the land. Where these conditions are to be found, or even some of them, there houses spring up to-day, and many of them are built, with a little help from others, by persons who have had no or very little previous experience of building. Once those combined conditions were found widely extended everywhere, there workers to build and goodly houses would appear in plenty. For this combination of circumstances also means diminished costs and increased "wages" (products of labour for him who produced). It is not a new batch of bureaucrats that is wanted but freedom to produce, freedom of access to land. Without freedom of opportunity to produce, without the removal of antiquated systems of local taxation, without a better education of the public there is no driving force behind the wish for better planned housing schemes and better planned towns. With this freedom, with abolition of taxation, and with better education that driving force will arise, and then the interest of the individual will be found to coincide with the interest of the community.

Over thirty years ago a Royal Commission on Local Taxation (appointed in 1896 by Mr. Balfour) reported: "Our present rates indisputably hamper building. Buildings are a necessary of life and a necessary of business of every kind. Now, the tendency of our present rates must be generally to discourage building—to make houses fewer, worse, and dearer" (Final Report, p. 167). Yet the basic principle of local taxation is the same to-day as then and any alterations in detail are rather for the worse than the better. Still assessments are based on two values which are totally different in origin and kind, the value of ground sites on the one hand and of building or "improvements" on the other. This antiquated system of local taxation is found in some other parts of the world besides in Great Britain, and in some of the British Colonies. But even if a better system is found elsewhere it is by no means an equitable one in most instances, and it is generally wedded to a vicious system of national taxes. So the same evil effects are produced on housing shortage, etc. It is a waste of time and money to appoint new commissions and boards.

After all, what are a majority of the houses built for the masses to-day like? It is true they have generally provided quarters which are far superior to those which many of the occupiers had to inhabit previously. But measure their capacity, inquire what is their rent, taking into account the expense of travelling to and from the place of work, examine the qualities they possess for enduring. Compare these little houses or flats—hundreds of them only three-roomed—and the materials used in them with some of the many small houses of Georgian or early Victorian days, or with little country cottages still in use, put up two or three hundred years ago. Ask any architect who has built for the well-to-do, and also participated in one of these schemes for housing the workers, what are his feelings on the cheese-paring, cost-cutting, cold and calculated restrictions which are imposed before they are erected, restrictions unfortunately necessary under present circumstances. Such comparisons force us to the conclusion that what are built to-day will be looked upon as meagre and mean within a generation. Mass production of the parts of a house and the quick erection of houses in large numbers through methods associated with the words "factory," "rationalization," and "technology" will not solve the difficulties of producing more houses, however much expense can be saved here and there in certain of the pieces and et ceteras required in houses. Houses of necessity have to be built rather slowly and on the site. Usually, not only local materials, but also local traditions and craftsmanship must be taken into account. Good craftsmanship was formerly, and is still, the basis of good building; and the best traditions in the various crafts meant once that these were adapted to the materials used. In one place houses were built in stone, in another in brick, in one place thatch was used, or tiles, in another slates. Though greatly increased facilities in transport make mobility of materials easier, the enhanced facilities of communication should not wipe out altogether the advantages attaching to previous habits.

Good houses are not dependent on whether they are built by private enterprise or out of public funds. That is a futile controversy for the reason that it generally assumes, what socialists are particularly inclined to assume, namely, that the public purse is bottomless. Most political parties to-day, wheresoever situated, and howsoever labelled are socialistic. They vary only in the degree in which they pile up taxes, and deal out ameliorative medicines to the poor. If local or national authorities should continue to build houses they ought not to do so without profit, or in other words without a due financial return for their labour and outlay. Carry taxation and social reform far enough, add housing and feeding and doctoring to education, to road and water-supplies and sanitation, and before long we shall be like the proverbial community which lived by taking in one another's washing. To socialism there is no end. But radicalism is dead in these days, for no one seems to think of striking at the roots of present-day evils.

Real progress in housing should meet the by-no-means-lordly aspirations of the workers of the world, and give them assurance in the unquestionably higher standard of living which by painfully slow degrees has now been attained. That higher standard is far behind what ought to have been reached if it was to be commensurate with the enhanced powers of production now possible through the increased knowledge and power of man. But such real progress cannot be attained so long as reformers will not recognize these two quite elementary facts, namely: (1) Houses are built by labour out of resources obtained from nature's storehouse; (2) When occupied the producers and users of houses are hit by the injustices and inequities of taxation, especially in some places the system of local taxes. To get better housing, therefore, demands first and foremost drastic reforms in methods of land tenure and of taxation. All else is of secondary importance. When taxes on production are abolished and the public coffers are filled only by collecting the ground values which belong to the community, "the housing question" will no longer be the nightmare it is to-day.

CHAPTER XXI

A GRACIOUS DISPOSITION

WHAT more admirable recommendations for insuring that a city develops on gracious lines could be propounded than the following drawn up by a committee of the Royal Institute of British Architects ten years ago:

1. Every town has an individuality and special features of its own which should be expressed in its plan.
2. Natural features of interest and beauty, such as hills, woods, important trees, streams, and pools, should not only be preserved, but their existence should be emphasized and they should be regarded as important determining factors in the making of the plan.
3. Main lines of transit should take the direction required, always with reference to the contours of the land.
4. The element of design—the art of combining many units in proper relation and proportion—is just as essential to success in planning a part of a town or suburb as it is in planning a large building: mere geometrical planning is insufficient.
5. Long, straight streets, when adopted, should have a definite objective.
6. Lines of sight should in general be restricted to what the eye can easily take in. All views should as far as possible be framed in a suitable setting.
7. The grouping and arrangement of the principle buildings and open spaces should be studied with a view to securing good architectural compositions, and no scheme of planning can be regarded as satisfactory unless there is a sufficiency of open spaces.

These rules for good planning are now generally accepted. There is a wholesome and sound taste abroad at all events amongst architects. The builders of this century have developed a new architecture. They use new methods of construction. They are gaining a dignity and a distinction in planning the disposition of buildings. They are showing a discrimination in their reverence for the best traditions of the past, and an intelligence in development which are perhaps greater than has ever been shown by past generations. But they have by no means solved all the problems modern constructional methods breed. Some of the modern means at the disposal of architects and planners are revolutionary in their effects. The rest of the century will probably see some striking changes in the adoption of modern methods. It behoves thinking men to ponder which of modern tendencies are the most admirable and to fathom the radical causes of social unrest. The terrible congestion of population into modern cities claims attention as never before. The town planner no less than the geographer has to-day to take far more notice of social economy, and of the use man is making of his buildings than he has of climate, contour, and soil. Even when it was rural economy that had to be catered for, the distribution of dwellings in the countryside varied according to the nature of the agriculture in the particular district. In past ages by a natural instinct and by the innate good taste of artificers who were good craftsmen using good native materials the proportions and disposition of buildings were generally dignified and satisfactory. The majority of houses and many of the other buildings of last century, on the contrary, put up in rapidly growing urban districts, are far from being well placed and well built. Rows upon rows of small houses eating up green fields and associated with the ruthless felling of trees showed a common disregard for decent planning, whether of house or town. Government authorities lacked soul and good sense. When such virtues rarely broke forth they were as a rule stifled by vested interests of one sort or another. Engineers have been busy conceiving, inventing, constructing. Atlantic liners, aeroplanes, motor vehicles, bridges, and barrages have been produced and made more perfect. But architects, until recently, have been asleep for a hundred years or more. The problem of the house, a machine in which to dwell has hardly been tackled in the same way as engineers have tackled the problems with which they have been grappling during the last fifty years. By very slow degrees are such important parts of the house machine as the following coming to be given proper attention in the light of modern inventions: baths; sun, light, ease of ventilation; hot-water, cold-water; warmth at will; conservation of food; ease and comfort for indoor eating, work, leisure or sleep; hygiene; beauty in the sense of good proportion. Utilitarian demands must be combined with a cultivated sense. There must be a gracious disposition of the pieces of a house and of the parts of a town. A good ground plan for house and town will produce well-proportioned lineaments of outward aspect, fine profiles, and contours, well set in beautiful surroundings. The plan is the basis of all. "Without plan there can be neither grandeur of aim and expression, nor rhythm, nor mass, nor coherence. Without plan we have the sensation of shapelessness, of poverty, of disorder, of wilfulness. . . . But the sense of the plan has been lost for the last hundred years. The great problems of to-morrow, dictated by collective necessities, based upon statistics and realized by mathematical calculation, once more revive the problem of the plan. When once the indispensable breadth of vision, which must be brought to town-planning, has been realized, we shall enter upon a period that no epoch has yet known."[1] Good planning, good architecture "proclaim the noble pomp of mathematics, the unassailable power of proportion, the sovereign eloquence of relationship."[2]

Le Corbusier in his *The City of To-morrow*[3] proposes startling arrangements of streets, buildings, and open spaces. He suggests central sky-scrapers of fifty or sixty storeys occupying only 5 to 10 per cent of the ground, each so planned that light and air gets to every office and workroom; surrounded by residential blocks about 125 feet high and occupying 15 to 20 per cent of the ground. A few straight arterial roads of two layers, the elevated road for one-way fast traffic. He holds that the centres of our towns have become like an engine which is seized, largely owing to our not realizing the functions of a street. These he defines as: a traffic way; a right of way to places; public way for water, gas, electricity, and drainage; the space which insures light and air to abutting buildings. He believes that solutions of traffic problems which ignore the other functions of a street are doomed. He considers the great mistake made in New York was that the sky-scrapers were not built in the parks. He looks upon this city as "a cataclysm,"and says that the critical condition of many cities to-day will lead to their becoming stifled and perishing unless they can quickly adapt themselves to the new conditions of modern life. If they do not adapt themselves other cities will take their place. Unfortunately sites for other cities are not so

[1] Le Corbusier's *Towards a New Architecture*, English translation by Fredk. Etchells, pp. 48 and 51 (J. Rodker, London, 1931. 25s.).   [2] Ibid., p. 161.
[3] English translation by Fredk. Etchells (J. Rodker, London, 1929).

good as those now occupied by the great cities of the present civilization, as has already been emphasized; and the causes obstructing rapid change to meet a freer life are hard to overcome. Le Corbusier is right to remind one of the Turkish proverb saying, "Where one builds, one plants trees"; and to desire "once more to cover with verdure the urban landscape and set Nature in the midst of our labour, so that our hearts might find some reassurance in the face of the dreadful menace of the great city which imprisons, stifles, and asphyxiates who are cast into it or who have to work in it."[1] He would de-congest the centres of cities in order to provide for the demands of traffic; increase the density of the centres to bring about the close contact demanded by business; increase the means whereby traffic can circulate; and increase the area of green and open spaces. He postulates (for a city of 3,000,000) the centre empty at night, but 500,000–800,000 there in the day. Half a million would reside round the centre, 2,500,000 in adjacent garden cities. He considers every great city should rebuild its centre along the lines he suggests, and should have but one central station with trains on three levels. Between the city and the garden cities should be a "protected zone" belonging to the municipality (bought up by it by degrees) on which no buildings should be allowed. The sky-scraper would be of steel and glass and would have garages for all in the angles of the arms. The possibility of engaging in sport would be open to every inhabitant of the city; and should take place at the very door of his dwelling. Every window in the residential blocks on every frontage should look on to open spaces.

To-day at the centre of big cities when great blocks of out-of-date and decayed buildings are demolished their sites are all too often used immediately for the erection of new buildings. Nobody interferes much despite town-planning control, not drastically at least. Interference would perchance prevent financially profitable transactions in the private appropriation of ground values which settle like a cancer round the heart of a city. Le Corbusier refers to the great improvements made by Haussmann in the centre of Paris in the time of Napoleon, and points out that he merely replaced six storey buildings by better ones of about the

---

[1] *The City of To-Morrow*, p. 78.

same height. He believes even so values were enhanced about five-fold, and that if the density of population were increased from 300 to 1,300 inhabitants per acre by the adoption of his own schemes ground values would be enhanced about twenty-fold. By taking such a course, if compensation to landlords were paid at the present-day highest market price it could soon be met out of the land values of the newly developed business centres. He would therefore simply issue a decree expropriating the centre of Paris from all present-day private owners at its present capital value.

But that is not the way things work in practice at all. To mention but four obstacles: (1) The decree would be stoutly resisted; (2) present values, under existing circumstances even, contain speculative monopoly values through present systems of land tenure and taxation and in anticipation of future rises; (3) public bodies, again because of present systems of taxation and land tenure, are poverty-stricken and cannot easily balance their budgets nor, consequently, raise money; (4) again, and for similar reasons, the users of the new buildings prospected would not find it easy to raise the money to pay the great cost of their erection.

However far-sighted and excellent Le Corbusier's schemes may be, and his ideas if somewhat revolutionary have many points in their favour, it seems unlikely that they can be put into force in their entirety. It is also doubtful if they were, whether when completed they would come to be considered a way of distributing the population which was without question conducive to the health and happiness of humanity. But supposing such schemes are the best possible, they cannot be successfully carried out so long as the financial profits accrue for the most part to a few individuals who lay claim to own the earth. Sometimes the suggestion is made that instead of the users of the new buildings providing their cost and the municipality buying out landlords, the national or local governmental authorities (or the two in combination) should find all the money for the demolition and improvement. But the result is much the same, land monopolists are fed and grow fat at the expense of the rest of the community.

Reference has been made above to certain proposed improvements in London, for example to the Charing Cross Bridge scheme. Another illustration follows to show how an actual development, carried out within recent years, affects site values and through them the public and private purses, and indirectly the distribution of population. A new bridge was built over the Thames in 1932 at Lambeth. It cost £839,000. Of this only £102,500 had to be spent beforehand in compensation for land, easements, etc. But the expenditure helped to increase the value of land afterwards, and this increment goes to a few fortunate ones who are allowed by the law of England to maintain private ownership of site values. One of these is the Duke of Westminster who just before this date received, according to the *Daily News*,[1] approximately £1,000,000 for 8 acres of the Grosvenor Estate on the main route between Victoria Station and the new Lambeth Bridge.

Improvements glaringly necessary are held up because the public and private interests are not made to coincide. This coincidence can only be brought about by discovering and bringing into force the instrument which encourages, when progress demands, one land user's displacement by another and the better use of the site without hurt to any party. When that comes about then planning and building can be handed over without qualms to those "who know best how to devise, order, and array a new town"—to quote the words of Edward I when he was devising Winchelsea at the end of the thirteenth century.[2] For then such persons can be found. To-day, under the existing schemes of things, sites are encumbered and actually depressed below their true value by bad planning and by the existence of obsolete buildings.

To refer to Westminster again: ever since my boyhood, getting on for half a century ago, when I first got a nodding acquaintanceship with Westminster, I have been conscious of how inappropriately much of the land there has been utilized. Within half a mile of Westminster Abbey and the Houses of Parliament are still to be found, though many have by degrees now disappeared, mean, narrow streets with tiny shops or little slum houses and courts. If public and private interests were the same the folly

[1] *Daily News*, March 20, 1930.
[2] T. H. Hughes and E. A. G. Lamborn's *Town and Town Planning; Ancient and Modern*, p. 71 (Oxford University Press, 1923).

of so using such sites would have forced betterments long years
ago. Yet it was only a few years ago that the Westminster Council
—to give but one instance—managed to do a deal with the Duke
of Westminster and his agents over some of this property, and
then only because the latter were astute enough to see clear
future gain in the transactions which were concluded. A former
Mayor of Westminster, wrote as follows to the *Evening Standard*[1]
a year or two afterwards boasting of what had been done by the
Council over which he then ruled:

"At Millbank we had 17 acres belonging to the Duke of Westminster. They were not slums: they had never been condemned,
but we wanted to clear them on account of age. The opportunity
came after the disastrous Thames floods some years ago. This
property was intersected by small streets, byways, and courts
which took up much space and also reduced the site into parcels
of land on which it was impossible to erect large buildings. These
streets and byways belonged to the Council. I, as Mayor, suggested
that if the site were cleared and most of the small streets and roads
thrown into it, the result would be a tremendous increase in the
value of the land; also that the clearance scheme we had in view
might benefit from the clearance. The Duke met us splendidly.
In return for the roadways added to his land he gave us 4½ acres
for our housing scheme and a gift of £120,000 to assist with the
rebuilding. He, in turn, will eventually profit from the rise in
ground rents that will result from the site being developed on
lines befitting the heart of London. Part of Thames House is
built on the site."

The suspicion arises that the Duke was more far-seeing than the
Council, and up to the present facts (so far as they can be ascertained—always a difficult matter), increase this suspicion. The
Duke need not have met the Council's wishes "splendidly," or
otherwise. He knew the value to himself of those small streets
once they were thrown into his land. The rise in site values,
already up and creeping rapidly higher, rose higher still from
the very moment it was *thought* that such a scheme was on
foot. History, one of these days, will relate how far the "gift of
£120,000 and the 4½ acres" falls short of the rich harvest of

[1] *Evening Standard*, November 28, 1933.

increased land rent which the Duke will be able to garner without much exertion and without any return in services to the payers.

A famous illustration of how the existence of an obsolete building, however well constructed and preserved, on a valuable site can detract from, instead of enhancing, the value of the site is the case of a copper king's (Senator Clark's) palace in New York. It is said that the purchasers of the site would willingly have given $100,000 more for it if it had been clear. And there was the Vanderbilt property on 57th Street and Fifth Avenue. This was sold to Mr. Heckscher for $7,000,000 (a figure virtually the same as the land value of the site as assessed for New York taxation), though the improvement value for the same purposes was assessed at $6,000,000.

"To devise, order, and array a new town"; to cultivate a new spirit in architecture; to learn quickly how to adopt new materials and new methods of constructing buildings so as to make them beautiful, dignified, and well set in their surroundings; all these things can only come about when people have learnt how to get over the obstructions which so frequently arise through the private ownership of land. The substitution of public ownership is not a suggestion—as some seem to think—for parcelling out land by government committees. To restore the land to the people does not mean that "authority" settles how the land is divided up for use. It is the rent of land which it is proposed to divide, and that plan can be adopted by a simple expedient whereby taxation is abolished. The plan is a reversal of much present-day practice. In so far as it is a reversal it is revolutionary, using the word in its strictest sense; but it can be brought about by orderly, constitutional means. The Government will not "take over" the land. Why should it? The Government should represent the people. It should collect the people's revenue from the holders of the public domain. The rent due will be willingly paid in the absence of taxes because the payers will agree that it is reasonable the people should get payment for what they do for the occupants of the land—supply public services. To understand how the plan would work a few more illustrations are necessary of how the opposite plan works. The present system of land tenure and taxation precludes a distribution of population along sound lines and prevents the buildings in towns and villages from being well disposed on the ground. By studying the evils of to-day it is possible to realize how a reversal of policy would act.

I know a small seaside resort with a population of 1,000 to 1,500, where a good part of the most important land in the village belongs to but a few people, half a dozen or so persons or bodies. In one or two instances the bodies represent the members of one family, or of a small syndicate of two or three persons. This little place is surrounded by, and indeed, has in its midst, purely agricultural land. More than 95 per cent of the approximately 700 acres of the parish is without buildings upon it. Yet access to sites for most purposes has nearly always been made difficult by the obstruction and extortions of landowners. When a small field for games and recreation was wanted the parish council after exhaustive inquiries were unable to find any other site than one standing outside the village in a most exposed and unsuitable position and it cost the tax- and rate-payers £430— for five acres. When sites for houses were urgently needed, especially for the workers, £250 an acre and more had to be paid. A public lavatory was badly wanted at a convenient site near the sea front and centre of the village. There was a handy acre lying empty and derelict. Fortunately its owner parted with it at a reasonable figure, £250. But over twenty years previously the former owner had asked £1,500 for the same plot, and refused £1,000 for it. Had he been told all such sites apart from "improvements" made or built by individuals (and there were none on this one) had a value which was not given to it by the legal "owner" and that, taken at his own lowest figure he ought to pay into the common pool £50 a year for exclusive possession of so valuable a piece of the community's property, he would doubtless have seen to it that the site was put to some suitable use long before the twenty-five or more years he had claimed possession of it. Furthermore that plan universally applied would have enabled the burden of rates and taxes to be swept away. Idle and derelict land means idle and poor men. That means job seekers, often drifting to the large towns and the secondary industries. It also means direct obstructions to healthy development, bad housing conditions, poor public buildings, and delay in the construction of what people should and do want both for

the satisfaction of their own and the public's needs. The development of a sound civic spirit is thwarted. So that the inspiration
for carrying out easily and smoothly and at the appropriate time
fine designs enhancing the dignity and augmenting the amenities
of villages and towns is obstructed in more ways than one.

About eight years ago a proposal was made that a town-
planning scheme should be applied to this particular village.
The district council actually sanctioned it on one occasion,
and the county council were said to be sympathetic. One of the
few far-seeing landowners, a man with large ideas and good
taste, approached a rich merchant very fond of visiting the village
to see if he would buy out the landlords of the most important
central plots and save the place from haphazard and mean
development. But neither plan came off. The merchant was
frightened by the high prices asked for land. The owner of the
important plots wanted money quickly. Before there was much
time to discuss larger ideas, and actually while the discussions
were going on, he had the foundations of half a dozen lock-up
shops along the beach road dug. Someone told the parish council
an architect would require a fee of £200 to make a plan for
decent development. The shops were built. The die was cast.
Near to them on the same owner's land there had already cropped
up some bungalows, each one on a plot but 90 by 50 feet, each
one therefore staring rudely into its neighbour's eyes. This out-
break of bungalitis and tripperitis has stamped the place and
spoilt it, probably for all time, like so many another similar
spot. If a more cultured generation arises which wants to undo
the deeds of this one there will be immense obstacles to surmount.

On the east side of the village is a hill somewhat awkwardly
approached from the main coast road. Instead of this being considered from the point of view of the general welfare and being
clothed with pine-trees, a sloping roadway has been prospected
and the inevitable notice-board, "eligible building plots for sale"
is exhibited. The village abounds with muddy paths and annoying
cul-de-sacs, partly due to various owners never making the opportunity to meet to discuss and forward the amenities and good
development of the place as a whole. A tee-shaped plot with a
long frontage on one road and a short one on another was sold
a few years ago, and the vendor commended it as having no less

than eleven building plots on it, four on the shorter frontage and seven on the longer and asked the higher price therefore. Yet the shorter one was only 64 feet long and actually one bungalow, with a long axis of 44 feet, and its surrounding garden, has taken up the whole of this piece. A neighbouring square field with good roads all round it, at that time unbuilt upon save for a small house at one corner belonged to a lawyer a few years ago. In 1909 and 1910 Lloyd George and others raised a great agitation about the people's right to their own site-values. An Act was passed after a threat to create 600 more peers was made by the Prime Minister, Asquith. This Act contained a little levy of a $\frac{1}{2}$d. in the £ (capital value), an "undeveloped land tax." Our lawyer friend knew well, as some of them do—it is one of their jobs, and who can blame them?—how to escape tax levies. He employed a man to dig a few holes in the ground and plant here and there some trees in his land. Though the trees soon died and the land remained unused for years it was no longer technically "undeveloped." By such means or by similar devices of one sort or another are complicated half measures to collect public dues for the use of the community frustrated every time! Straightforward declarations and actions are the only way.

No wonder population does not increase materially in such places. In many another similar resort along our coasts or inland the strangling grip of land-monopoly holds up development. Yet, it may be asked: How can an increase of population which has hardly occurred send up land values? The answer to this is given by asking the question: Is it not an increase of population in other centres which affects the seaside values? In the large towns weary workers abound and some of them, when they can afford it, want to visit the seaside for fresh air, sunshine, recreation, and rest. Besides which there are other factors sending up land values, the expenditure of public money on development. It is not possible to give a by any means complete list of the public's expenditure which has benefited the landlords of the particular place under consideration. Before attempting to enumerate some of them, however, it is well to mention that two great railway companies have expended big sums about thirty-five and twenty-five years ago respectively in railway construction to this village. That obviously sent up land values there and has

enabled landlords to reap where they have not sown. It has not
been so much in rent as in the pocketing of capital values that this
harvest has been gathered. But the question is, which is worst
for hampering industry, and holding up development, unduly
high rents or witholding land from use for speculative reasons?
There is probably little to choose. When the first of the two railway companies opened a line to this seaside village with a
palatial station landowners saw a chance. The land agents and
their myrmidons the lawyers soon got busy. By clever advertisement and an astute use of champagne at a luncheon before a
sale, and by the well-known methods of organizing a boom, a
number of gullibles were inveigled into purchasing various
plots in the parish. They were all on the get-rich-quick stunt,
even those who went away without realizing they had paid a
deposit on some ambiguously defined piece of mother earth. On
occasions like these the vendors get away with plenty of swag,
the ill-gotten gains which the sleeping public allow them to take
from them. But it is not the mugs who purchase who are the only
victims of such predatory, though wholly legalized acts. That is
not the worst of it by any manner of means. Many of the purchasers when they find out their mistake are, naturally enough,
loth to cut their losses. Hence they hang on in the hope that
time will bring a rise again to the value of the ground in which
they have speculated. Hence they come to be a break on progress,
and a hindrance to development. The land they hold is kept out
of use, or is under-used, perhaps merely to graze a few cattle or
horses on it for a short part of the year. The strongest wish of
many of them is to forget their folly. They may never go near
their holdings again, except perhaps very occasionally to see if
by luck someone has by mistake built a house on their site. They
will perhaps relegate their foolish bid which gained them the property to a clause in their wills in the hope that their descendants
may eventually reap the speculative value which may at long
last fructify. But by such processes the workers of the world
suffer, for the products of labour are less plentiful than they
should be through difficulty of access to land. A delay of many
decades, or even longer in some circumstances, is imposed upon
the march of events. The growth and distribution of population
are affected by these things and a gracious disposition of buildings,

of open spaces, of roads and paths in villages and towns are prevented. In the case of the particular English village mentioned, these effects are secondary to the tendencies of the last forty or fifty years regarding the distribution of population in England generally, and the peculiar position of health and recreation resorts. The seaside villages and towns have become more and more mere summer annexes to the large industrial and commercial centres. They have become more dependent on more visitors staying shorter periods. They have been affected by the financial slumps which have affected business and commerce. But apart from such considerations (which are dealt with in other pages of this book) a little examination of the details of land tenure will reveal how disastrous to a spontaneous and healthy growth of population private ownership of land, and the consequent taxation it involves, has been in this particularly pleasant and salubrious spot.

What are the details of public expenditure in this village? Public bodies have expended much on its development as the years have gone by. Over thirty years ago waterworks were constructed to supply the village out of public funds and the cost was over £5,000. Not long afterwards a drainage and sewerage system was carried out. About twenty years ago a sea wall was built with approaches at a cost of £1,500 and two groynes were erected at £1,300. Since then another £750 has been spent on improving the water supply, about £3,000 more on sewerage extensions and improvements. Besides which several thousand of pounds have been spent in the near neighbourhood on road widenings and improvements. All for a village with a normal population of about 1,000 inhabitants, and a summer season of only a few weeks. The incubus of landlordism, as elsewhere, is what has prevented the place developing despite such noble expenditures, coupled as that handicap always must be by the burdensome incidence of taxation. Under these twin obstacles population cannot grow normally and as it should, with more even distribution; nor can any village or town hope to attain a gracious disposition of its buildings, roads, etc. To sweep away these obstacles is far more important than is the passing of fresh town planning Acts, or the giving of more authority to controlling bureaucrats.

That is a tale of what happened in a small village in England. On a larger scale the same thing happens elsewhere. It is a far cry from an English coast village to San Diego in Southern California. But that place may be taken as another good illustration of the effects of rail communications and of public developments on land values and the successive waves of boom and depression which arise out of consequent land speculation. In 1885 the final achievement of a trans-continental railroad, the Santa Fé, was followed immediately by a real estate boom which was almost without equal anywhere. This boom collapsed and the rapid growth of the village was checked. In 1870 the population of San Diego was 2,300. In 1871 work was started on the Santa Fé railway. In 1872 the new city was incorporated. In 1890 the population was 16,519. Though the boom after 1885 collapsed the village had attained city consciousness and had developed a water supply, a street railway, and harbour improvements. Trying times ensued for a good many years after the collapse of the boom, but their true cause was not well appreciated. Certain speculators had raked off the cream, and the multitude of babes had to live on skimmed milk for years thereafter. No wonder they throve indifferently. In the year 1919 the San Diego and Arizona Railway (Southern Pacific Company) was completed. This again led to a boom in real estate lasting several years. The opening of branch lines, the development by the municipality of docks and warehouses all sent up the value of sites. Since 1911, when the tidelands were ceded to the city by the State, over $4,250,000 have been spent in improvements. The assessed value of property went up in the City of San Diego from $198,000,000 in 1927 to $392,836,000 only two years later. Over $100,000,000 building permits were issued during the years 1920–27 inclusive. Yet the tax-gatherer still collects taxes from owners of buildings. Though these may be comparatively light it would be better to exempt them and collect dues for public services appraised on assessment valuations of sites only, so that the holders of these paid the community values into the common pool and everyone escaped all taxation. Town developments take place. The natural advantages smiling nature has blessed certain sites with are bound to be used as the population of the world increases. Many places develop beauties of lay-out, of buildings, of parks despite the obstacles which have to be faced. But how much more gracious and good will be the cities of to-morrow when people have become alive to the means of abolishing all conflict between public and private interests.

CHAPTER XXII

EMIGRATION

PART I—ANCIENT TIMES; IRELAND, FRANCE, ITALY

THE causes of emigration are hunger and the love of adventure. Lack of opportunity to satisfy the primary wants is the chief cause of the movements of population. Political and religious animosities are for the most part the jealousies bred out of such lack of opportunity. This is so throughout the ages. Expulsions and restrictions on emigration have usually been injurious to the nations imposing them; and the objects aimed at by the people of those nations have seldom been achieved. To-day in civilized countries crude hunger is, fortunately, not frequent, and even partial starvation, though present, is seldom admitted by the prominent persons in such places. Nevertheless, how could Hitler and his Nazis, for example, in recent times have dared to re-inflame old prejudices had not unemployment, spelling privation, been abroad in the land? Similarly behind most of the "quota" restrictions, the anti-alien Acts, etc., of this century, the spectre of want lurks. It is hard for us in the twentieth century when religious tolerance has become more generally established to realize the condition of affairs in mediaeval times. Difficulties in satisfying the primary needs of life were, even in those days, probably the primary motive actuating emigration. But how far these difficulties were produced and mixed up with political and religious persecution is rather hard to estimate now. As has truly been said, the incentive to emigration will exist so long as the conditions of human life are, or are believed to be, less hard in one region than they are found to be in another. But oppression, persecution, exploitation, and a variety of other factors may condition the hardness of life rather than actual want and privation. Be it noted, however, nearly all of these come under the head of lack of equal opportunity.

Progress is often measured by the ability man shows to dominate the forces of nature. Progress is erratic, capricious, and irregular.

Invention and science have led to rapid progress through the discovery of nature's laws, through a wider knowledge about the physical materials and forces of nature. But despite such progress the advance of civilization is checked by inability to find out and use the natural laws which underlie the economic life of man. Hence, just when the science of production and of transport has reached such a wonderful state that there should no longer be any hunger anywhere in the world, a shortage of the necessities of life is by no means unknown. The poverty of many, consciously or sub-consciously admitted, is at the bottom of all the efforts various prominent persons are making to control population by this or the other restriction or regulation. But as E. B. Reuter has said,[1] "When population control has proved effective it has not always proved wise," and he instances Spain as a case in point. He writes: "Spain undertook, more systematically than most of the West European nations, to control the type of her population. The Moors, her industrious and prosperous but religiously and racially heterodox citizens, she expelled in the interests of racial and religious unity. The unde-signed result was the destruction of the possibility of industrial development. In the interests of religion and the redistribution of financial power, she expelled the Jews with results disastrous to her business and commercial prosperity. And, finally, and again in the interests of a decadent religious orthodoxy, she destroyed her intellectuals and thereby insured herself a long period of religious orthodoxy and intellectual stagnation."

It is rare for emigration seriously to diminish the population of the country from which exit has been made. The gaps are usually soon filled up. Often the death-rate falls and sometimes the birth-rate goes up. The amount of emigration does not necessarily depend upon the density of the population. For example, Holland and Belgium have a higher density of population than England, Italy, and Germany, yet very few Dutch and Belgians have emigrated compared to English, Italian, and Germans. Again, the density of population in the Scandinavian countries is low yet they have had an exceptionally high emigration rate. Some hold the opinion that even extensive migration into a country does not make much real difference in the long

[1] *Population Problems*, p. 10 (Lippincott, London and Chicago, 1933).

run to the total population in that country because it is thought that the immigrants interfere with the natural increase of the indigenous population. This theory is largely founded on observations made in the United States, which seem to show that increasing immigration and a declining birth-rate of the native stock go on side by side. (See E. B. Reuter, loc. cit., pp. 191–97.) But most of the writers who examine this theory pay but scant regard to that most important factor affecting immigration into America, the factor of "free land." In other words in these matters the questions of ready access to nature's storehouse and the allied question of freedom from burdensome taxation must be considered.

Human geography must ever be taking cognizance of climate. No well-known geographer has emphasized this more than Ellsworth Huntington. In his *The Human Habitat* and elsewhere he has drawn attention to the large cycles of climatic change which, it seems probable, have taken place in distant ages, and he has drawn interesting deductions from a study of these climatic pulsations. He brings forward good arguments to show how these changes have led to migration of people. The most famous emigrating horde in history was the trek of the Israelites out of Egypt into Palestine. This took place because of persecution and exploitation of the Israelites by their Egyptian taskmasters. But there is also evidence to show that another factor was the extraordinary low state of the Nile. And E. Huntington states that in addition to this migration many others are recorded as taking place about this time, 1200 or 1300 B.C. They are just the sort of thing that normally occurs during great periods of drought. From a study of the rings of the big trees, which are 1,000 to 4,000 years old, deductions as to climatic change can be made. Historical research has brought forward other evidence, too, in recent years supporting these ideas. It seems as if a period of cooler weather and of heavy rains increasing the bearing powers of the soil also occurred at a later period than about 1300 B.C. If that is a correct view it helps to account for the high level of progress during those times in Babylonia, Assyria, Syria, Palestine, Egypt, and finally Greece. "Ultimately, however, a new period of drought, migration, war, and misery set in after the days of Alexander the Great" (writes Huntington in

Chapter XI of *The Human Habitat*). "Trouble seems to have prevailed almost everywhere about 200 B.C., at the very time a period of rapid decline in growth is recorded in the big trees."

Early migration had much to do with climatic conditions. These had a big influence on the means of livelihood. Obviously agriculture cannot flourish where the land is perpetually ice-bound on the one hand, or in a dry desert on the other. Migrations

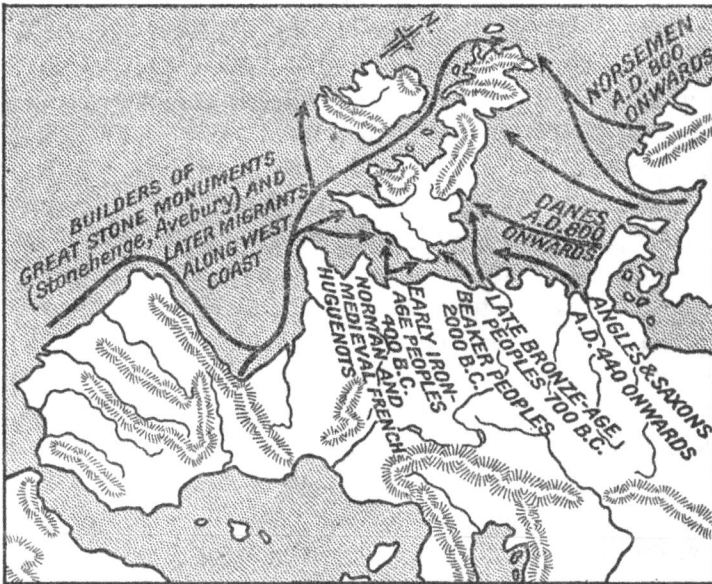

MAP SHOWING WAVES OF IMMIGRATION INTO THE BRITISH ISLES
By kind permission of the B.B.C. and "The Listener".

affect a mixture of races, and with their causes they produce an elimination of the least fit. There are many pieces of evidence to indicate that 10,000 years ago much of North-western Europe was either uninhabitable because too cold or else so stormy and inclement that few people could live there. With amelioration of the climate, tribe after tribe moved in. They were still moving in vigorously in the early part of the Christian Era. Their migrations were voluntary and unassisted. They were in many instances over the seas, in the case of the British Isles, of course, entirely so, and therefore by races who, amongst other pursuits requiring vigour and determination, were capable sailors and fishermen.

N*

Readers are referred to Chapter XIV, "The Civilization of Europe," in E. Huntington's *The Human Habitat*, to a discussion between Professor H. J. Fleure and Mr. A. Bryant, published in *The Listener* (October 18, 1933, p. 579) for a further study of these aspects of migrations.

Before leaving the subject of the influence of climate and climatic cycles in distant days on the growth and distribution of population, brief reference should be made to two parts of the world where once, ages ago, prehistoric civilizations existed, one the Sahara and the other Central America. There is no doubt that in both these regions during the times, many centuries ago, when what from ruins and other relics would appear to have been a comparatively advanced stage of progress existed, the climate was very different from what it is now. Furthermore, it was a climate which permitted grain growing, an art practised by the then inhabitants of those parts, an art afterwards lost or, at all events, not practised for some reason or other. The decline and departure of Empires in the Sahara and the Soudan, in cities such as Wargla, Gao, and Timbuktu are generally ascribed solely to political causes. After the death, for example, of the Great Askia of Songhai warrior bands of Moors driven out of Spain are supposed to have sacked these ancient cities. Peoples fled, lands became uncultivated, and irrigation channels fell into decay. But, as is usual in historical records, it is battles and the doings of rulers that are set down. It may be that climate and even methods of taxation and wrong systems of land tenure had more to do with the decline of former civilizations than anything else. Sure it is that further research is wanted in these directions, and it would seem probable that it would be rewarded by interesting discoveries if more can be found out about such points. In British Honduras and in Guatemala the relics of the Old Maya Empire indicate that there were cities of nearly 250,000 inhabitants existing probably about 350 A.D. Almost certainly these peoples knew a great deal not only about grain culture, but also about intensive cultivation and the rotation of crops. E. Huntington has several interesting pages on these topics.[1]

[1] E. Huntington's *The Human Habitat*, pp. 132, 151, 237-40 (Chapman & Hall, London, 1928).

THE CONNECTION BETWEEN EMIGRATION AND WAR has frequently been discussed by other writers. Generally, however, too little attention has been given to the friction preceding wars which makes them inevitable; not the squabbles of statesmen, but the restrictions of Governments to freedom of production and exchange, and the cover they give to the exploitation of natural resources. These cause apprehensions, poverty, and strife. The opening up of opportunities, the duties and burdens of colonization, the pacifying influences of civilization, and the penetration of a higher culture amongst primitive races, all these things are over-much in the hands of the privileged few who are behind Governments. They generally have distinct influence on the movement of peoples from one country to another. Arguments amongst diplomats and discussions about armaments, sometimes labelled "disarmament," under the aegis of Holy Alliances, Concerts of Europe, or Leagues of Nations go on from generation to generation. The meetings of statesmen which ensue give newspapers and radio announcers something to talk about; and that keeps up the prestige of the statesmen. All the while the old games of bluff, called diplomacy, go on. In secret concession hunters, the masters of the diplomats, and statesmen, out to annex the earth where it is worth grabbing at home and abroad, are arranging their "coups." All the migrations which take place before, during, and after war arise in reality from a denial of equality of opportunity to life, wealth, and the pursuit of happiness. No one could be persuaded to cross a line, the border between one country and another, shouldering lethal weapons for the purpose of killing fellow human beings if he knew his own and his fellow-countrymen's happiness and welfare were equally secure whichever side of the line he lived and worked. It is because, in the condition of present-day society, such security for happiness and material well-being seldom exists that jealousies arise and hindrances to the free movement of persons of different nationalities are imposed. Professor J. W. Gregory of Glasgow seems alive to some of these causes of conflicting national aspirations and racial jealousies in his interesting book, *Human Migration and the Future*.[1] There is really no other reason but the insecurity of low wages and unemployment that leads people to

[1] Seeley Service, 1928. 12s. 6d.

acquiesce in the increasing regulation by Governments in the movements of population. The spirit of adventure is always sufficiently checked by the stay-at-home instincts of the majority to preclude wholesale and inconvenient migrations of people, so long as conditions of life at home are tolerable. Sometimes it would be better if those suffering from bad conditions would try to discover the causes of insecurity and poverty, instead of becoming just selfish discontents whose one aim in life is to desert the home conditions which they find so hard. The conditions might be mended the quicker, and the unoccupied areas of their home country could become colonized. That kind of migration would do more than any other to produce commodities and a demand for more commodities. By such means would the vicious circle of poverty and unemployment be broken. It is only because the eyes of so many concentrate on the "great wens" of the city agglomerations of population, and because we are so used to things as they are, that people are blind to the innumerable areas in any country where the land could be more productively used. So many readers of the last line will be town dwellers that immediately the words "land" and "productive" are used, up will spring the idea of agricultural production. It seems desirable therefore to add: There are innumerable sites other than those suitable for agriculture which could be better utilized than they are to-day. But confining attention, for the moment, to food production alone and to the land of Scotland, my friend the late William Wright, M.P., for Rutherglen, than whom none knew better, stated that all the unemployed in Scotland could easily be absorbed in their own country if there were ready access to land. He wrote:[1] "In Scotland 1,000,000 acres could be used to provide 50,000 crofters and small-holders with 20-acre farms each. If combined with fishing, poultry keeping, goats, and bees, there would be work all the year round, and a vast increase of food from Scottish soil and waters. Many would prefer such a life to emigration, dwelling in their native land, amidst the associations of childhood; their native hills, straths, and glens, and where their forefathers rest in peace."

The shameful way in which natives were driven from the land of their forefathers by landlordism in Scotland and Ireland is a

[1] *Blantyre Gazette*, May 17, 1930.

well-known story. Similar expulsions from England are but a shade less glaring, Mr. Wright states in the same journal[1] that: "The greatest exodus was from Ireland; the total number of emigrants from that country between May 1851, and December 1910 was 4,187,443." And "The emigrants from England, unable to gain a livelihood at home, have been 8,500,000 during the last sixty years."

It was in 1870 that Gladstone passed his Irish Land Laws, forcing through the House of Lords an Act to give tenants a right to repayment for their own improvements before they could be evicted. Under the laws of eviction over 200,000 homes were destroyed in Ireland during the life-time of Queen Victoria, or were rendered tenantless for the recovery of civil debts or to clear the inmates off the land to make room for cattle. Families were flung on the bogs and mountain sides to die of starvation, cold, and from broken hearts. All this by direct sanction of England's Parliament. Gladstone's Act was passed to mitigate these horrors; but it was not as successful as anticipated. Consequently the Irish Land League gained renewed vigour, and by 1881 it had become the *de facto* Government of Ireland, and religious differences ceased to divide the people when the land question was raised. (Would that a similar agitation could arise to save Ireland from faction fights and hollow political and constitutional issues to-day!) When Michael Davitt, one of the most prominent Nationalists, came North his meeting was presided over by the Master of an Orange Lodge.[2] English politicians' artfulness and the artlessness of the Irish a year or two later, however, concentrated action upon political Home Rule. Since agrarian and clear-cut economic issues were abandoned about that time, barren results have met the agitation for freedom. Such results, too, come from depending on force and land purchase. The march of the Irish has been deflected from the straight path leading to national freedom, social justice, and industrial prosperity; and to-day they seem deeper in the slough than ever.

The Purchase Acts released no fresh lands for use in Ireland. They did nothing to open up the ranches. Nor have they saved the town population from being herded in slums and cellars. The inevitable tragedy of poverty continues in Ireland and will

[1] *Blantyre Gazette*, June 21, 1930.
[2] See Dalta's *An Irish Commonwealth* (Fisher Unwin, London, 1920. 6s.).

continue until the Irish once again follow the advice given them by former leaders such as Parnell and Lalor. The former referred in 1880 to "The eternal truth that the land of a country, the air of a country, and the water of a country, belong to no man. They were not made by any man, and they belong to all." And Lalor preached that "rents for land should be paid to the people themselves for public services." Overcrowding in slums and hovels, shortage of food, scarcity of raw materials, want of employment, retaliative and oppressing taxes, in a country like Ireland are not inevitable tragedies. They are criminal wrongs founded upon lack of recognition of the fact that the chief function of the public authorities should be to secure to all, on terms fair to the rest of the community, the opportunities for livelihood provided by nature. When such wrongs are righted the people of Ireland, whose emigration to other countries has contributed so nobly to the advancement of mankind in past generations, can remain, if they will, in their own country to live healthily and happily. But if any of them continue to wish to emigrate to other climes, then there need be no clash of colour, conflict of creed, nor race antagonisms when that liberty reigns which is alone limited for each by the equal liberty of all.

Shortly after the Great War large numbers of French peasantry abandoned the soil in favour of the higher wages of the towns. Many able-bodied men had been killed; yet for several years there was considerable development of French industries. This migration from rural districts was an accentuation of a movement of population which had been going on for many years. A scarcity of native labour arose in the fields. Italians having poorly developed agricultural resources and an insufficiency of raw materials for their industries were attracted into France. Italy's population was increasing rapidly; France's was stationary. So great was the influx, at first natural and unchecked as well as unresented, that the foreign population of France increased by nearly 1,000,000 between January 1, 1922 and January 1, 1925, and a majority of these were Italians.[1] But presently immigration movements into France became a factor in national policy. The politicians and diplomats were compelled to study the matter and interfere,

[1] M. Paon's *L'Immigration en France*, with a Preface by M. Albert Thomas (Payot, Paris, 1926).

but only because real wages began to fall and employment to wane. The political conjurers of France, reshuffling the pack (namely themselves) into the seats of office every two or three months, vainly try to balance budgets. Even before the war her national debt was the largest *per capita* in Europe.[1] Their edifice is built upon a bad electoral system and upon ill-omened finance. Is this because the French are such strong supporters of peasant proprietorship? This form of private land ownership is not in essence better than any other; and it is a form which leads very definitely to conservatism. It is only in Denmark that a majority of landowners are opposed to ownership of land; and that is because they are small-holders well versed in the doctrines of Henry George. Would that the French, too, could learn something of these doctrines! Then might their anxieties over the growth and distribution of population be dispelled as well as their anxieties over immigration. In Italy, on the other hand, where population increases at the rate of over 600,000 a year, their powerful dictator says, "The Versailles Treaty cannot stop the sun," and he looks across his frontiers for territories to people. He says, "It is difficult to find unoccupied lands." Hence strife brews; diplomats are employed; armies furnished with weapons; and meetings of an international trade union of taxing authorities, the League, are held. (Would that the costly new palace at Geneva—there's one already at The Hague—was for a real league of nations!) Territories could be peopled by foreigners quite easily if good systems of land tenure and taxation prevailed. There are plenty of unoccupied lands to be found. People could emigrate freely under systems giving equality of opportunity to all. Then the disparities in population and in soil fertility, etc., between one country and another would not matter very much, and the pattern and colours of flags would command less attention. I went to a music hall in the East End of London thirty years ago. There the most vociferous cheers were given to ultra-patriotic songs and sentiments by an audience whose English, if they had any, was not always easy to understand. In those days immigration officers were rare and passports hardly ever used. Emigration becomes a difficult question to handle when colonies spell prestige for journalists and arm-chair politicians; when they

[1] Lothrop Stoddart's *Racial Realities in Europe*, p. 86 (Scribner, 1924).

produce a fine harvest of salaries and bonuses for civil and military bureaucrats at the expense of taxpayers; and when they are rich in natural resources which Governments grant as concessions to a few monopolists to exploit. Italy from an arable point of view is poor compared to France, because it is smaller (about half the size, with roughly the same number of inhabitants) and has more mountainous areas and, in Southern Italy, much land uncultivable on account of drought and malaria. Yet for fifty years before the war, during which period the population increased by more than one-third, the condition of Italians improved by peace and labour. They imported from abroad corn, iron, coal, cotton, copper, and petrol—all the essential raw materials. She paid for these materials by exporting Italian products, and to a less extent by the sale of Italian products to visitors from abroad and by the work of her emigrants who sent back money to their families. To-day Italians can truthfully say, "the Governments of other countries are trying hard to exclude our emigrants and our goods." Ethnologists are being called in to give countenance to the statesmen. They try to prove that admixture by marriage of different races (I do not here allude to whites and coloured) has had bad effects, and that the climatic conditions of a country are suitable alone for one kind of stock. There is, for example, the cry in the United States of America that only "Nordics" should be admitted, and in Germany that that country must be only for the Aryans. Racial prejudices are easily flattered and the politicians welcome pseudo-scientific support for their actions. Yet history gives little support to such notions and the work of Dr. Frederick Hertz[1] and others have shown clearly that what, not many years ago, was ascribed to heredity and inherent racial qualities, is to be attributed to environment, tradition, and history.

From time to time for many years scares have been raised amongst white peoples that they would presently become swamped by the nations with different coloured skins. Even years ago when civilizations were beginning to totter fears of "barbarians" were conjured up by the rulers who called soldiers to the flag. About a generation ago there appeared *The Yellow Peril*, if I

[1] *Race and Civilization*, translated by A. S. Levetus and W. Entz (Kegan Paul & Co., London, 1928. 18s.).

remember rightly, written by my distinguished namesake Karl
Pearson. More recently we have had *The Rising Tide of Colour*;[1]
The Clash of Colour;[2] and *The Peril of the White*.[3] The second of
these differs from the others in seeing no peril, nor necessity for
clash. Even that wise and wonderful writer, Havelock Ellis, has
got much fright aboard. He writes under the heading of "Migration,"[4] in reviewing Stoddard's book just cited: "The White
labourer can nowhere, absolutely nowhere compete with the
coloured labourer. The more we approach to Democracy, to
Directorate of the Proletariat, the more inevitable are we
rendering the Dictatorship of the coloured man and his right
to settle where he will. Yet" (quoting Stoddard) "such migrations
upset standards, sterilize better stocks, increase low types, and
compromise national futures more than war, revolutions, or
native deterioration." He seems to agree with Stoddard that the
world is drifting into a gigantic race-war unless Asiatics forgo
all idea of migrations to Africa and Latin America, and the
White world abandon tacit assumption of permanent domination
over Asia. [A new alignment of world forces possibly more perilous
to peace, and more conducive to a worse war than that possibility
predicted by Stoddard, has already come about in the few years
since that was written. More sinister forces for strife are leavening
society to-day!] But he is more frightened apparently of rapid
population increase than of anything else, and agrees with Dr.
Stoddard that "it is not the eagle of pride or the vulture of greed,
but the stork which is the real enemy of the dove of peace." He
desires to see procreation of the species homo checked by deliberate birth-control, and welcomes any sign he can find of the use
of contraceptives amongst India's or China's poverty-stricken
millions (see p. 96, Chap. V above). International Labour
Federations, too, follow the lead given elsewhere. At a conference held in London in June 1926 this federation handled a
report (of 325 pages!) on *World Migration and Labour*. This gave
many details, amongst others those dealing with the restrictions,
regulations, and organizations imposed upon immigrants, and

[1] Lothrop Stoddard (New York, 1919).
[2] Basil Matthews (Church Missionary Society, London, 1924–28, etc. 2s.).
[3] Sir Leo Chiozza Money (W. Collins & Co., Sydney, 1925).
[4] See Havelock Ellis's *Views and Reviews*, Second Series, 1920–32, p. 29
(D. Harmsworth, London, 1933).

somewhat diffidently approved of most of them. The tendency of such organizations is to absorb too readily the views that other bodies promulgate, for example, that the following four alternatives are inescapable: (1) Over-population with a fall in the standard of living; (2) Mass emigration; (3) War; (4) Restriction of population.

The purport of this book, or one of them, is to show that neither over-population, nor mass emigration, nor war, nor restriction of population need be feared once a reign of true justice giving equality of opportunity to all comes into force. Equality of opportunity to all is not communism. It does not mean sharing everything. It does not mean a dull level. Persons differ in capacities, in desires, in needs. Peoples differ in temperament, in upbringing, in traditions, in culture. Many parts of the world must obviously be peopled by races of different origin. The white man, with technical training and modern scientific knowledge, can train and direct the coloured man. But there need be no clashing when each learns to play his part and when no unfair exploitation by or of anyone occurs. If a state of society could be inaugurated when no one, whether black or white, was able to reap where he had not sown, where everyone was entitled to the products of his own labour (without deduction through taxes), of what moment would it be supposing the white-skinned ones forming one-third of the total population were increasing only half as fast as the darker skinned races? Basil Matthews in the book referred to on the previous page insists that there is no real colour problem but a vital one of wage competition; and he quotes three dominion Prime Ministers, Mr. Bruce (Australia in 1923), Mr. Massey (New Zealand), and Mr. MacKenzie King (Canada, 1921–26) to this effect.[1] He emphasizes that Africans and American negroes do but make common cause with every people in the cry for self-determination; and that all race-differences can be extinguished by joining together in a real fight against the common enemy, the greed that exploits the weak.

Reference has already been made in previous chapters by allusion or directly to some aspects of this question in regard to the peoples of India, Japan, and China. These races are

[1] Basil Matthews, *The Clash of Colour*, p. 54.

increasing every ten years from 6 to 10 per cent, or even more rapidly. Japan is not much bigger in area than Great Britain and Ireland, 162,655 to 121,742 square miles. The growth of population in the latter countries since 1872 has been from 31,800,000 to 48,000,000, whereas in Japan it has been from 33,100,000 to 60,800,000. The future welfare of Japan, according to Iwao F. Ayusawa,[1] and he is probably largely right, is through an increase of her industrial capacity. Comparing Japan with Australia, enormously greater in area, and judging by the present growth of population in the two places, by 1950 Japan will have a population of 80,000,000, while Australia will number 9,000,000 to 10,000,000.

PART II—AUSTRALIA

MENTION of Australia brings up several points, all of which have bearings on emigration. Amongst them are: (1) The question of "a white Australia"; (2) that of Empire settlement; (3) wrong methods of developing natural resources and national industries. Taking these in order: The sole reason, at bottom, why Australians will not tolerate the idea of coloured immigration is the certainty, under present circumstances, of wage-competition. The Chinaman and the Jap, accustomed and able to live on less than the white man, would swiftly undercut and eliminate the white artisan by sheer pressure of economic law. Yet where the white man sees a way of employing cheap coloured labour without undue risk of this kind he is not slow to do it. And there are parts of Australia, in the north, wherein people from Asia, and possibly from Africa could thrive, parts whose climate is largely intolerable to whites. When access on fair terms to suitable users of land is possible, means for opening up such places will be forthcoming; production will increase. Asiatics will then be welcomed in Australia and suitable outlets will be found for them. By that time the untrammelled influence of natural forces will hold sway. These have operated in race-migrations in past history. They carried the Angles and Saxons into Britain; the Goths and Vandals into Rome; and Europeans into America. Transport was much more difficult in those early days; but access to

[1] *Industrial Conditions and Labour Legislation in Japan* (Geneva I.L.O., and London, P. S. King, 1926. 2s.).

mother earth was much easier. Already pressure is being brought
to bear on Australia for the northern parts of Western Australia
and Queensland to be thrown in with the Northern Territory;
and some who know about these things consider that the Tamils
of Southern India would prove even more suitable inhabitants of
these regions than the Australian aboriginals now consigned to
them. Communication and water difficulties would be overcome
by modern engineers.

For more than twenty years efforts at Empire Settlement,
including aided schemes of migration into Australia, have
cropped up periodically. Many of them have been grandiose.
Many of them have been ill-planned and ill-fated. Yet on the
face of it Australia wants more population and there would
appear to be room for many more inhabitants. Despite the dire
results of and the scandals associated with one of these schemes
fairly recently, another one is now being launched. In February
1934, for example, the Empire Development and Settlement
Research Committee issued a report which put forth a plan
for the redistribution of the population of the British Empire
under a chartered company to be backed, it was hoped, by the
financial guarantee of the British Government. The report says:
"Since 1914 net emigration has totalled 1,246,000. Had the
average rate of the five years prior to the war been maintained
the number of emigrants would have been greater by some
3,000,000. When it is remembered that the number of unemployed at the end of September 1933 was 2,300,000 the lesson is
most striking." As if other parts of the British Dominions had no
unemployed! The scheme, recognizing the uncontrollable suck
to the towns, proposes to plant 160,000 emigrants in out-of-
the-way, at present undeveloped regions, "where, at any rate
for a period of years, the settlers are not likely to stray into the
cities and compete with present Dominion citizens." The same
forces underlie this, the latest scheme, and the same doom waits
it as brought to worse than naught the effort to settle a group of
British settlers in Victoria a few years ago. The dire hardships and
the financial chicanery and injustices which occurred in connection with that scheme have not even yet been finally cleared
up. Brief but vivid (signed) accounts of the experience of two
of these settlers were published in some English newspapers

towards the end of 1933.[1] Even more lurid details of the graft which went on upon a big scale is to be found in the little London weekly *The Commonweal*.[2] Governments, British and Australian, found millions of pounds out of taxpayers pockets to finance these ill-fated schemes. But very few settlers benefited. If more people settle in a place that sends up the value of the land and the rents flow generally into the private pockets of the few. Frequently the land users cannot make ends meet. Sometimes more money is got out of taxpayers pockets to compensate or repatriate them. In the State of Victoria most of the public land has been alienated from common ownership within the lifetime of a single generation. Land sold not many years ago by the State at £1 an acre, but never used, has been bought back at £7 10s. an acre and then has been found so unproductive as to be unsuitable for the immigrants planted upon it under the Government's supervision. More than ten years ago, referring to one of these schemes, the *Sydney Bulletin*[3] wrote: "The New South Wales Government has spent fourteen borrowed millions in putting returned soldiers 'on the land,' and already £5,000,000 is considered lost. In addition to the costly settlement on repurchased land, other people were put last year on 1,200,867 acres of State land, which is about an ordinary year's work. And with all this industry which has been in progress for a century, the cultivated area was reported in 1921 as 4,465,143 acres—a falling-off as compared with five years earlier, and about equal to three years' 'settlement.' Yet the Government . . . want to borrow millions more to keep the dismal procession moving on to the land and off the land, and on again and off again." A few years later, as reported in a London newspaper,[4] the Australian Minister for Lands and Water Supply (H. S. Bailey), announced that "of 9,221 ex-soldiers settled on the land in Victoria 2,126 have not met any of their liabilities, 2,681 have paid under half, and only 990 have met their liabilities in full. . . . Many millions of pounds have been irretrievably lost. The Commonwealth Government advanced £35,000,000 for this purpose to the State Govern-

[1] Vide the *Manchester Guardian*, December 5, 1933.
[2] Vide *The Commonweal*, July 1, 1933; November 4, 1933; and March 10, 1923. Vide also the *Melbourne Herald*, April 29, 1929.
[3] March 8, 1923.   [4] *Daily Telegraph*, February 15, 1928.

ments, which themselves found considerable additional funds. In most cases inefficiency had been displayed in dealing with the problem. Unsuitable land had been chosen."

It is the throttling effects of private ownership of natural resources, and the pocketing by individuals of the values which the public create which is at the bottom of the failure of settling people on the land in Australia. Perhaps Australia affords a better illustration of these phenomena than most places; and it is certainly true to say that Australia, with its wide fertile but unpeopled acres, illustrates better than most countries the way in which the people drift to the towns. The land monopolist is waiting for the settler, the taxpayers at home shell out to pay his passage, on which the shipowners make their profits. The taxpayers in the Commonwealth and at home pay up to build railways, having as their chief result the enhancement of the land values which the public permit the monopolist to annex. They pay, too, interest on much money borrowed for such purposes as well as the loss on running the railways. Poor taxpayers; how long suffering they are! Yet many of them listen with respect to Prime Ministers or Agent Generals when they talk about "Australia's assets." These potentates declare that the public debts of Australians are assets because less of them have been incurred in paying for wars than is usual (only about 27 per cent), and because much of the money borrowed has been spent in railway construction, water, and sewerage works, etc. But have those developments and advantages inured to the mass of the people? Assuredly not. The assets have not become those of all Australians, but have to a large extent inured to a few, the landlords and a small group of manufacturers. No wonder that it is men of these classes who are found on the platforms of Ministers and Agents when they plead for more population. Sir Sidney Kidman, for example, the "Cattle King," it seems is a great believer in Australia's need for population. This is natural since he is "a man who owns probably more land than anyone else in the British Empire," and his 60,000 square miles (exceeding the area of England) would be valueless without population.

Here are some details about the way things have gone at three places on the railway line in New South Wales, namely Molong, Condobolin, and Forbes. The population to-day of these three places is only 1,513, 1,469, and 4,300, though the last named place contains a meat-freezing works and a wool-scouring factory. And the populations in the localities around these towns have increased comparatively little in recent decades. Mr. Huie of Sydney wrote in *The Standard* as follows about these places:[1]

"It is nearly twenty years since my first visit to Molong. It has grown very little during that time. At present the Government is constructing a line of railway from Molong to Dubbo. That has given the place a temporary fillip, which, of course, will pass when the line is opened for traffic. Molong has a good climate and rainfall. The soil is good, the possibilities are enormous. There are also valuable limestone and marble deposits. What is wrong with Molong? The place is land-locked. The big estates are choking it. Four big estates in the vicinity of the town monopolize about 40,000 acres. The land should support about 100 farmers. It is said that railways are constructed to open up the country. That is the pleasant fiction of the party politician. But it is not true. Their real purpose is to enhance the value of privately-owned land, chiefly that held in large estates. The Dubbo railway will enable the large landowners along the route to work their land cheaper and to make more money out of it, while the railway will probably be run at a loss. Thus the effect of the railway is to lessen the employment of labour in the district served. The remedy for this state of affairs is plain. Charge the interest on the cost of the railway to the value of the land, and thus impose upon land-owners a financial guarantee that they will provide the traffic to make the land pay.

"Off and on for 26 or 27 years I have visited Condobolin. For a number of years it has practically stood still. There is no progress. There is a dull hopelessness about the place which is depressing. There is general agreement among the townspeople as to the cause of the trouble. The land is held in big estates. The future of the town mainly depends upon the effective occupation and use of the rich land on the south side of the river. Here you will see very clearly the abject failure of the Labour Party's graduated land tax. One big estate on the south side, Borambil, is growing bigger, adjoining smaller areas being added to it.

[1] *The Commonweal*, Vol. IV, No. 14, April 21, 1923, p. 3.

It now comprises some 60,000 acres, room for, say, 60 farmers. Further down the river are two estates formerly held by separate owners now monopolized by one family, but so held that the graduated land tax is neatly evaded. Here is room for another 40 or 50 farmers. The young people drift to Sydney, not so much from choice as from necessity. The open spaces of the country languish for lack of men, the towns are mostly cramped, business is dull, and employment scarce. The Fuller Government's land policy arouses no enthusiasm at Condobolin. The Trida railway line to the west does not pay, and it is proposed to build another south to Wyalong, also for the benefit of big estate owners; and, of course, it will not pay either.

"The town of Forbes has increased its population barely 2 per cent in twenty years. In the same time the population of Sydney has increased nearly 82 per cent. The situation of Forbes is good. Climate, soil, and rainfall are good, and the river assures a permanent water supply. What ails the place? Land-locked. It is the same story. The big estates monopolize the bulk of the land in the district. Again, the chief trouble is on the south side of the river. In fact, the land is so held that for a hundred miles down the river it is only at odd places where a man can get access to it for a drink of water. Here and there are small reserves, sometimes as much as 12 miles apart, where you can get a drink from the only natural permanent water supply. The valley of the Lachlan is remarkably fertile, and it is well fitted to become a great series of highly productive districts. Forbes is dying. New work fails to keep pace with depreciation. The same dullness so noticeable at Molong and Condobolin was apparent, but the position at Forbes is distinctly worse. A new cross-country railway to Stockinbingal has recently been opened for traffic. Of course, it does not pay. The land along it is all right, but the line was built to give the big estate owners unearned increment."

The following advertisements from an Australian newspaper (*The Standard*, Sydney, April 4, 1928) indicate a warning to those who think all will be well when Socialism is in force and the railways are all Government owned: "There is no factor which has greater influence on land values than construction of railways. Immense profits have been made by people who have purchased land in the vicinity of an approved or newly constructed line."

And: "Your opportunity is now—the railway just started—land still cheap. . . . A rise in values will be swift and sure. Buy before the mass of the people realize what is happening."

The growth and distribution of population in Australia has not proceeded as it might have done because the wrong methods of developing natural resources and national industries have been followed. In the last seventy years the growth of the population in Australia has been, roughly, 75 per cent of it due to natural increase and 25 per cent by immigration.[1] Australians increase at about 2 per cent per annum, while the English increase at only 0·8 per cent per annum. The staple industries of Australia, wool and wheat, were built up before the days of the unholy alliance between the protected manufacturers and the Government, whether of labour or other complexion. The proportion of people living in cities in 1921 was 62 per cent, and 43 per cent lived in the six capital cities. By 1928 it was 48 per cent who were living in the six capital cities. Half a century ago 44 per cent of Australian bread-winners were working on the land; by 1921 this figure had fallen to 25 per cent and it is now lower still. The cities are spacious, Greater Melbourne, for example, will within measurable time cover an area equal to that of Greater London. One reason why Sydney is spacious and healthy (it has the lowest death-rate of any like place in the world) is because, according to the "Sydney rating system," no householder as such has any local tax levied upon him. But what can one say about the fact that one-third of the total population of Australia is living in two cities? The causes of this are political and economic.

Not many years ago a Labour meeting in East Ham, in the East End of London, passed a strong resolution condemning the snares which were being set to entice English boys to emigrate to Australia, "not only to earn a comfortable livelihood, but to become a capitalist on his own account." They were to become primary producers, agriculturists. They were to swell the population of the Commonwealth. But they would be swindled and ground down by the bad system of taxation there which interferes

[1] P. D. Phillips and G. L. Wood's *The Peopling of Australia* (Melbourne, 1928).

with the natural development of a country to swell the profits of landowners and manufacturers. This scheme was got up by the British Empire Producers' Organization, to which were attached the following bodies: the Associated Chamber of Manufacturers of Australia, the Australian Meat Industry, the Australian Sugar Producers' Association, the British Empire Sugar Machinery Manufacturers, the Dominion Wine Merchants' Association, the Empire Tobacco Committee, etc. These bodies immediately demanded more favourable, preferential import duties on meat, wheat, sugar, wine, tobacco, etc. Favourable—not to the worker, not to the consumer! Preferential—yes, to a handful of manufacturers! The fruit-growers wanted the duty on currants raised fifty times and on other fruits ten times. Who will get away with a large share of the tribute extracted from British housewives? Why, the merchants banded together into the Australian Fruit Trust in the first place. In the second place, when the fruit-grower proceeds to spend the money in Australia in the purchase of machinery, boots, clothes, sugar, etc., he will be robbed by the local trust of manufacturers operating behind the tariff wall. They alone will be winners. That is why they are behind the emigration ramp. The more primary producers, the more plunder for the tariff boodlers of Australia.

When the transported boy arrives in Australia to become a "capitalist" in the land flowing with milk and honey, he will be surprised not to find jam upon the table of his master, despite the glut of fruit. This is the reason. Australia produces sugar. The sugar-cane is sold to a sugar-refining Trust. The Government has imposed an import duty on sugar which secures to the sugar Trust gigantic profits, and which has raised the price of cane land to over £120 per acre. But this duty so increases the price of jam as to limit its consumption. One of the chief jam manufacturers is Sir Henry Jones, of Hobart, familiarly known as "Jam Jones." This is from a report of his wail in 1923: "Householders could not afford to pay 1s. 2d. a lb. for jam which before the war cost 6d. to 8d., and it was essential if production was to go on that the price should be brought down to near the pre-war figure. With sugar at 5d. a lb. this is a difficult proposition. His firm had on hand 3,000 tons of last year's pulp. . . . This month Australia would produce enough apricots to last for two years.

. . . Australian Governments were to blame for promoting irrigation schemes and putting returned soldiers on the land to grow fruit."

Here, then, we see the fraud that is being[1] perpetrated on those who are being induced to go to Australia and embark on fruit-growing. They will be beggared by the tariff and be told their only hope lies in Britain further beggaring her own people on their behalf by levying a preferential tariff on dried fruits.

A few years later the Town and Country Union of Australia, as reported in *Progress*,[2] was "doing good work in directing public attention to, and demanding the removal of, the sugar embargo which, to serve the interests of a few, holds all Australia in bondage. . . . Housewives pay 4½d. a pound for sugar instead of 2d. a pound. If the embargo were removed, Java white sugar could be landed in Australia to-day at £10 10s. a ton. Australia A 1 white sugar is sold for household use at £36 10s. a ton, and for use in the making of jams, canned fruits, sweets, etc., at £30 10s. a ton. Manufacturers of jams, etc., are compelled to pass on the increased price to the consumers, and they suffer a diminuation of trade in consequence. Before the imposition of the embargo Java sugar was bought largely for manufacturing purposes, and it was also bought and appreciated by housewives. Estimating the consumption of sugar in Australia at 300,000 tons, and allowing a rebate to manufacturers at £6 a ton on 40,000 tons, the additional cost to consumers is £7,560,000."

Import duties, embargoes, subsidies are all subversive to prosperity and to a healthy growth and proper distribution of population. Take Queensland and the northern part of the continent. Virtually the only effort on the part of the Australian Commonwealth to develop the northern portion of Australia has been its experiment in the sugar industry—trying to establish it by virtue of taxation which cost in 1933 over £6,000,000. Says an authority writing on this subject:[3] "Many think that the sugar industry is responsible for Queensland's small population—less than 1,000,000 —although Professor Gilruth-Taylor says that this State is the

---

[1] *The Commonweal*, Vol. IV, No. 8, March 10, 1923, p. 2.

[2] Melbourne, September 1, 1929.

[3] R. H. Webster (of Ariah Park, New South Wales), in *Manchester Guardian*, September 6, 1933.

richest of all in natural resources. . . . The policy of Queensland is to withhold her rich lands from the people of the land-hungry south, meanwhile making a living out of sugar and other industries established by taxing the people of the Commonwealth. Within a generation it is safe to prophesy that this State will have the biggest population of any, and will be the most productive—and her products probably will not include sugar.''

It would be too long a diversion to enter into a variety of knotty problems connected with Australian Federalism. Suffice it here to point out that bad systems of taxation and land development and tenure bring internecine as well as other kinds of war, and to give a reference to excellent articles in *The New Statesman* and the *Manchester Guardian* on this subject.[1] These articles demonstrate that Western Australia is especially badly hit by the difficulties Governments have created, and that States with large areas but small populations cannot pursue a policy of development nor absorb new migrants.

By pursuing wrong policies Governments may attempt emigration schemes to redistribute population along better lines, but they will not meet with success. They cramp developments in population's growth and distribution by imposing barriers to the free exchange of commodities, and by attempting to force trade in special directions through rotten taxes. The obvious expansions which the overseas trade of Australians would naturally take would lead to more business dealings with Chinamen, Japs, and the peoples of Eastern Europe. In this connection the facts and figures published in Mrs. N. Windett's book[2] are worth studying. Would that those in high places, with a clique of vested interests behind them, could be deposed and their interferences stopped!

A sound growth and a healthy distribution of population demand not only the open door but also ready access to land. When such policies reigned in various parts of the world there were no cramping restrictions, no carping criticisms, no conflicting interests, and there was no overweighting of the secondary industries. The open-door policy in the United States of America

---

[1] *The New Statesman* (London, May 26, 1928), *Problems of Australian Federalism*, and the *Manchester Guardian*, June 2, 1934.

[2] *Australia as Producer and Trader*, 1920–32 (London, Humphrey Milford, 1933. 15s.).

produced great developments in agriculture and primary production. These were accompanied by unprecedented industrial expansion and a rise in the standard of living. According to the Report of the Oversea Settlement Committee for 1927,[1] during the thirty years 1891 to 1921 the population of Canada increased by 80 per cent and the *per capita* value of external trade increased more than six times. New Zealand's population nearly doubled and her external trade increased almost three times. Australia's population increased by 70 per cent and her external trade by 116 per cent. The report makes these two observations amongst others: "Dominion Statesmen are not forcibly reminded that their policy of discouragement of emigration of all except agricultural and domestic workers is a contributory cause of the rapidly declining birth-rate in the mother country. . . . The resurgent coloured peoples of the world have legitimate cause for complaint if they are arbitrarily denied access to empty and potentially fertile lands in British possession."

Some indication has already been given of the way in which public debts have been piled up and how the burden of these has cramped the natural growth of population through free immigration in the British Dominions and its better distribution in primary industries and away from overlarge cities. But it is necessary to enlarge a little further on these topics. Continuing to take Australia as an illustration—it is a good one—reference may be made to the fact that under the constitution it is a duty for the States to develop lands and provide social services. But instead of this being done out of the people's true revenue, the community created values, it is done out of burdensome and throttling taxation and the heaping up of uneconomic debts and deficits. The very railways which ought to have increased prosperity and aided production have been hampering to true progress. A country may be opened up too rapidly. That is when railways are built and landlords reap most of the benefits, population does not follow the development. Stagnation and slumps follow. The States of the Commonwealth are finding the railways a very serious financial burden. The total losses for the ten years preceding 1929–30 were about £38,000,000, despite the fact that the primary industries were complaining of high freight

[1] H.M. Government Publication [Cmd. No. 3088] (1928, 9d.).

rates. The reason why this statement is correct, despite the fact that official returns state the railways of Australia pay £9,000,000 or £10,000,000 profit yearly, is because the railway accounts as presented for ordinary consumption are misleading and not in accordance with the facts as usually set forth in a business concern. Australians had a rude awakening when the high world prices and the ease with which they were able to borrow came to an end. In the three years immediately preceding 1928–29 Australians had added to their overseas indebtedness by about £106,000,000, whereas in 1928–29 and 1929–30 their added borrowings (apart from short-dated indebtedness) amounted to only about £1,700,000 per annum. Necessity compelled them to reorder their doings; and in the last year or two they have been able to readjust many of their loans so as to save about £2,000,000 a year in interest charges.

When loans are issued and spent on, for example, railways built before they are required, the British capital which finances them leaves partly in the form of railway material. Tariffs may tend to block the entry of these materials, and employment at both ends wanes. For this reason and through lack of attraction to new population from causes already mentioned, the borrowers find their speculation is not turning out as anticipated. Meanwhile the primary producers in the new country find themselves less well off. Burdens of taxation and of debts become increasingly heavy. Further loans are apt to be issued from England. But instead of all of these going out in goods produced, a lesser quantity of goods is exported because those overseas owe interest. Production generally is damped down. Debtors and creditors alike are all too often persuaded to seek a remedy in tariffs. But that only makes matters worse, creating fresh impediments to trade and fresh imposts on production. And so the vicious circle goes on.

The interest on overseas debts can be paid best, one might say almost only, by the £50,000,000 to £70,000,000 worth of wool and wheat produced annually, for the other primary industries (butter, sugar, fruits, etc.) and the secondaries largely exist only by virtue of direct and indirect taxation borne by producers of wool and wheat. These two form about 60 per cent of Australia's exports. Yet there are periods when the producers of wool and wheat only keep going through Government relief, doles, or bounty, and by the grace of their creditors. The combined debts of the Federal and the States' Governments amount now to over £1,000,000,000, or more than £180 per head of the population. Yet the people of Australia seem far from waking up to the defects and mistakes which keep these shackles upon them, even though once upon a time they were foremost amongst the nations demanding the "taxation of land values," and some of them imagine they have accomplished big strides in this direction. Experience there seems clearly to point to the failure of demanding, and getting to a certain extent, a tax on land values. Abolition of all taxes and the collection of the public's revenue should be the cry.

Mr. E. J. Craigie, of Adelaide, has spoken and written wisely and well on the blighting influence of the tariff in Australia, e.g. before an International Conference at Edinburgh to Promote Free Trade and Land Value Taxation, in 1929. He shows how the tendency of the tariff has been to concentrate secondary production in two of the States and bring about centralization. In his paper before the conference he states that: "In the year 1916–17 the number of persons engaged in rural pursuits was 477,308. Ten years later, instead of there being a greater number employed, as there should have been, the number had fallen to 425,187." Similarly, the quantities of copper and gold mined fell deplorably. The number of persons per 10,000 employed in Australia in the four primary industries, agriculture, pastoral, dairying, and mining, had dropped from 1,795 in 1907 to 1,575 in 1917, to 1,535 in 1927. Meanwhile heavier and heavier tariffs were imposed upon more and more articles more economically made elsewhere than in Australia. These not only burdened primary producers but sent up prices for all and depressed trade (the exchange of goods) and production. Chiozza Money gives[1] the following figures about the increase of urban population in Australia and relative decrease of primary producers: "The rural in the ten years 1911–21 increased by only 163,419 or 8·75 per cent. On the other hand the population of the capital cities increased by 643,750, or nearly 38 per cent. . . . The Australian 'primary producers' in 1921 numbered 598,604 (wives

[1] *The Peril of the White*, pp. 52, 53 (Collins, London, 1925. 10s. 6d.).

and other non-earning dependents not included), an increase of only 12,456 in the ten years. The pastoral producers actually decreased in the period by nearly 10,000; the miners also fell by over 39,000. On the other hand, the industrial workers increased by 161,189 and the professional, domestic, and commercial classes by 133,635." Yet to-day modern discoveries and inventions could make life in the bush more tolerable than ever before. Wise development and a sane distribution of population need not spell the isolation and boredom of former days. One of the most striking parts of Mr. Craigie's paper is that compiled from the official figures of twelve protected industries employing a total of 72,021 persons. He shows from an examination of the figures that the added cost of the commodities produced by reason of the tariff taxes was £26,500,000, and that the wages paid to those employed in the twelve industries was £12,500,000. The consumers could therefore have pensioned the 72,021 workers engaged in those industries to the extent of the wages they received, secured the goods (or most probably better ones) under Free Trade conditions, and would then have saved over £12,000,000 on the year's purchase. He adds: "Is it any wonder there is stagnation and misery whilst such a policy is allowed to operate?"

The growth of population in another British Dominion, Newfoundland, and what claims it has for attracting fresh immigrants, have been even more grossly interfered with by national rulers than in the case of Australia. Only in this instance, even more than holds good for Australia, the private appropriation of the public domain has been more bare-faced. It is indeed astounding how it comes about that a God-fearing, honest, hardworking set of electors can allow such glaring legalized theft of land and such devastating public finance and taxation to occur. The incubus of public debt in Newfoundland is not actually so heavy as it is in Australia, but considering the greater poverty of most of the inhabitants in the former place it is relatively heavier. The recently published report (December 1933) of the Royal Commission (Lord Amulree's) contains an amazing story of land speculation and financial mismanagement, and brings to light many of the scandals. In 1893 and 1898, e.g., contracts for building railways, which since construction have never paid working expenses, were entered into with Mr., afterwards Sir, Robert

Reid. The first contract provided that the contractor should receive 5,000 acres of land for each mile of line operated. The contracts were not simple, but the 1893 contract and similar ones made later resulted in over 4,000,000 acres being assigned to the contractor, including some coal-bearing land near Grand Lake. The Governor nearly refused his consent to the necessary legislation and the Colonial Secretary, Joseph Chamberlain, protested strongly, ending his protest with these words: "Such an abdication by a Government of some of its most important functions is without parallel." The report of the Royal Commission also condemned the reckless borrowing and the "seriously oppressive" custom and excise duties which hit the fishermen and other poor hardworking people so hard. Of Newfoundland's total area of 42,000 square miles, nearly two-thirds of its forest lands, about 15,000 square miles, is to-day either owned by or leased to the two paper companies; and the balance is mostly held by private individuals, very little of it for use. The Anglo-Newfoundland Development Company (one of the two paper companies), which was promoted by Messrs. Harmsworth, of London, enjoys freedom from taxation on its land and buildings. The report says: "The concessions granted to such companies have deprived the Exchequer of a valuable source of revenue." In the Labrador similar conditions have arisen. Ask Sir Wilfred Grenfell. The Commission recommend that under certain conditions "the land should revert to the Crown."

The financial transactions which have taken place in times gone by in another British Dominion, Canada, not to mention the disgraces associated recently with the Ottawa Conference, will not bear inspection and space forbids fishing out some of the facts from this dirty water. Suffice it here to mention the financial state of the Canadian National Railways and to quote the opinion that "more than any other single factor Canada's transport problems are retarding her recovery from the economic depression."[1] Not since 1928 have the Canadian National Railways balanced their budgets. The year 1933 closed with an operating profit of about $7,500,000, but left a balance of close on $50,000,000 required for interest charges to be found by the people of Canada.

[1] Special correspondent's report, the *Manchester Guardian Commercial*, January 6, 1934.

CHAPTER XXIII

CO-OPERATION FOR THE COMMONWEAL

DISCUSSIONS on the rights of man are unending. Many perorations drag in the words liberty, equality, brotherhood. It is nonsense to assert that all men are born equal. But there is an inherent feeling in the human breast that all should have an equal opportunity. It is nonsense to say all men are born free into the society of to-day. But there is a sentiment in the human heart which is very widespread that each should enjoy liberty, limited only by an equal liberty for others. When the millionaire, whether a great financier or an oil king, writes an article for popular consumption he usually lets it be assumed, especially if he himself started in a lowly position, that any poor lad can rise to the position he has reached. But examine the origin of his fortune and nearly always it can be traced to the legal appropriation of the earth, to the pocketing of public values, or to the exploitations of monopoly. Political and industrial magnates usually dilate upon the wisdom of co-operation and the joy of working for the commonweal. They toil and sweat to attain this wisdom and joy for themselves and for others, but, knowing not the foundations on which to build, their endeavours are fruitless.

To seek opportunities for self-development is natural. All are for liberty and home rule. At no time have intelligence and knowledge been higher than at the present time. To labour side by side with one's neighbours in friendliness and efficiency is the mark of a progressive society. "He that is void of wisdom despiseth his neighbour." At no time in the history of the world have so many persons lived in close proximity with their neighbours and at no time has labour been so productive. Yet the wisdom upon which to establish the love of one's neighbour, the wisdom which will eliminate all sources of conflict with him, the wisdom which permits a sound growth and distribution of population is rare. The instrument which would banish despite of a neighbour because bringing about equality of opportunity for all is in the hands of many primitive peoples (all the Moslem world, for example). Crowds in advanced civilizations are groping after it with ever-increasing enlightenment. It consists in the abolition of private property in land, so that all taxes can be swept away and only the community's own revenue, the rent of site values, be used to finance public services. Those who held the most valuable sites in their possession, secure in them because tenants of the community, would willingly pay for the much greater services they received compared with their neighbours; they would automatically and naturally use their superior positions 1ully. All land would come to be well developed according to the needs of the people. No land user would be afflicted by any tax. No able-bodied worker would suffer from involuntary idleness since difficulty of access to land would vanish. Public works would contribute really and equitably to the service of the people. No one could establish a monopoly or special privilege to exploit others. Then a true co-operation for the commonweal would have become established.

Jefferson has said : "The land belongs by usufruct to the living." The word usufruct is a fine one. *The fruit of use.* Land which is never used is really without value in a well-ordered society. But to-day, in many places, because this principle is not accepted and private individuals are allowed to claim property in what they never made, the earth, a few can hold land out of use and can find it profitable so to do. This is what gives power to landlordism. It enables all the monopolies and special privileges to be erected. It enslaves the many. It sets employee against employer. It brings public and private interests into conflict. But usufruct means more than just the fruit of use. It comprises in its meaning temporary *use for profit.* Land should be held *temporarily* and for a purpose. In the interest of the holder *and of his neighbours* it must be put to that purpose. Yet the ownership of it is *inalienable*; that meaning is also conveyed by this word. "Not capable of being transferred" because vested in the people. The possession of land for use, with "improvements" upon it, can be transferred; yes, but not the land. Land is in a fixed place. It belongs to no man. It belongs *to the living.* The child born to-day, claiming usufruct through his parents or guardians, has as big a claim to it as the aged multimillionaire about to die to-morrow. Obviously such claims can only be met in practice through the rent; and in practice the only sure way of being fair to all claimants is to spend the revenue for the general good. By such an arrangement the construction of roads and other means of transport out of this fund would be quite sound. The benefits accruing could not pass to private individuals as such but to the members of the community. Every facility to produce profitably from the soil, from a site, and every increased facility of transport would enhance the value of communal property and increase the rent return. If this became greater than was wanted to meet the communal services it could be reduced or distributed amongst all the people.

Governments which carried out their first duty, that of collecting the public revenue, might be of very great service to the workers, and these services might include the giving of advice by real experts. To-day Government officials set up sometimes as experts, but more frequently they are purely bureaucrats interfering with the production and distribution of commodities. This state of affairs exists because most politicians, belonging to various parties, subscribe to the theory (Socialism it is best labelled) that men can be compelled to behave themselves, can be compelled to produce wealth and compelled to turn that wealth over to the Government for distribution. This is an erroneous theory. The rent of land being public property, is the only thing that can be socialized. Though many public services are best run socially, this is preferably *after* the socialization of land rent.

Ownership of land by all the people and the use of a site by a temporary holder give the best security of tenure. To-day the scramble for plots is greater than it would be under the just system because much land is held out of use by landlords, and the landlords of many more plots are able to exact unduly high rents which, with taxes, burden producers. Under the just system of public ownership of rent there could be no scramble. As population grew, as inventions multiplied and made production easier, the more intensive use of land would occur. Yet any adjustments between users, or between individuals and the use of land for public services of one sort or another, would automatically be made. Such changes as came about would not push people into huddled crowds because the economic causes underlying overcrowding would have disappeared.

The use of land has generally been looked upon as a privilege carrying duties. The question of land ownership, when studied by Lord Coke, Sir Henry Maine, Blackstone, and other builders of legal concepts, has involved profound historical study. Sir Henry Maine[1] has shown that in primitive society it is inconceivable for land to be treated as capable of belonging to an individual, even to a king. Its ownership was vested in the office of the king. A chief or king held it only by virtue of his office in trust for the tribe. In ancient times disobedience to an award of the village council, on these and other matters, brought universal disapprobation. Generally no punishment was meted out; disapprobation was enough. Consequently customary law was practically synonymous with morality; the separation of the two ideas "legal" and "moral" is modern. To-day these matters of land tenure and taxation are coming again to be viewed more and more as moral rather than fiscal and legal. We are learning again not only from fresh experience but from the ancients.

The question of Federal revenue from site values will come to the fore in the United States of America. In practice absolute ownership ("allodial" titles), i.e. titles to land free from rent or service (as opposed to feudal holding for services), seems to be established in the United States. But legally it is arguable whether even in the United States absolute ownership of land exists. In England legal authorities are in agreement that there is no absolute ownership under the law. Freehold titles are of the king, not the owner of his domains but the trustee of the dominions for the people. Sir William Blackstone writes: "By the law nature and reason he who first began to use the land acquired therein a kind of transient possession that lasted as long as he was using it and no longer. . . . But there is no foundation . . . why a set of words upon parchment should convey the dominion of land." And Sir F. Pollock says,[2] "No absolute ownership of land is recognized in our law books, except in the Crown. All lands are supposed to be held immediately or mediately of the Crown, though no rent or service may be payable and no grant from the Crown on record." Now, at all events, in the original thirteen States, all titles to land in the United States have some direct legal connection with English law. The king as trustee could never diminish his right to the land value, though he could suspend its collection. Since the States at the time of the American Revolution

---

[1] *Ancient Law* and *Village Communities*.   [2] *The Land Laws.*

could not acquire by revolt from the king any right he did not have, they could not legally give away land, or sell it away in private ownership. Private ownership arose in the United States neither by cession of land (west of the Alleghanies) to a Federal agency, nor by its grants of titles to settlers. These titles were vested at the Revolution in the sovereign States and not in holders of crown grants. But the courts have been dominated in the United States since their inception by the rent repudiating free-holders who in 1642 devised customs and excise to be paid by others in lieu of their duty to the public trustee. This subject is more fully dealt with by J. Edwards Jones in *Land and Freedom* (150 Nassau Street), New York, February issue, 1934.

Co-operation for the commonweal cannot be accomplished properly until equality of opportunity to life, liberty, and the pursuit of happiness is acquired by all. But those greatly desiring freedom frequently forget that nations are not kept in thrall by either oligarchies or tyrants. In the last resort it is ignorance which alone is responsible for the perpetuation of slaveries. But until the captives learn that the door opens inwardly they will continue to use force to push it outwards. Governments to-day represent the reaction which results from the employment of wrongful means to obtain liberty. Governments based upon force are devised to restrain indiscriminate anarchy, and become more ruthless the more tumultuous the subject nations become. They have a forlorn hope that law and order may be thus preserved. Tranquillity and good government can go hand in hand when Governments recognize that their first duty is to collect their own revenue and cease from the robbery of taxation. Individuals can easily measure the desirability of living within the jurisdiction of such Governments by assessing the economic rent of land. The measure of government is the difference between the social value of living in solitude and the value of living in society and it mani-fests itself in site value. By aggregating land rent into a balancing fund or common pool it can be returned in equal portions to all members of the nation by devoting it to common needs. Useful public enterprises, not the piling up of debts and the making of wars, are thus encouraged, while the abolition of taxes shatters the causes of niggardly production and unfair exchange.

Great activity has been exerted during recent generations

towards securing the liberty of the individual. Attempts to restrict that liberty have been exposed and frustrated. Yet little interest is displayed in the question of all others which most fundamentally affects that liberty. The powers of one man to influence the destinies of another have been continually curtailed when that power has taken the shape of readily recognizable personages such as kings, barons, or priests; yet daily submission is tolerated to an ever increasing extent to a far more drastic control exerted by one individual over another through the institution of free-hold in land. We are ready to clamour against the least increase in taxation, which we impose on ourselves through the recognized medium of laws framed in accordance with the wishes of the majority, but we accept quite readily, as though it were a natural phenomenon, the collection of a tax, which we all contribute to pay, of an uncertain almost unascertainable amount in the form of a ground rent, which is levied upon the majority by a minority. People imagine sometimes that economics and political science are abstruse subjects. This is because their professors make them so. The science which treats of the nature of wealth and the laws of its production and distribution is instinctively understood by a majority of people. It is the science of getting a living. But the economists befog their own and other people's minds by lack of a grasp of fundamentals. A chaos of discordant opinions is what issues from these teachers. He who seeks guidance must not rely on authority but seek it by the use of his own reason in an honest search for truth. Then he may hope to reach firm and clear conclusions untrammelled by the schools and hosts of vested interests. For, as Henry George[1] has written, "If political economy be the one science that cannot safely be left to specialists, the one science of which it is needful for all to know something, it is also the science which the ordinary man may most easily study. It requires no tools, no apparatus, no special learning. The phenomena which it investigates need not be sought for in laboratories or libraries; they lie about us, and are constantly thrust upon us. The principles on which it builds are truths of which we are all conscious, and on which in everyday matters we constantly base our reasoning and our actions. And its processes, which consist

[1] *The Science of Political Economy*, General Introduction, p. xxxv (Fels Edition, Doubleday, Page & Co., 1897).

mainly in analysis, require only care in distinguishing what is essential from what is merely accidental.

"We all have some sort of political economy. Men may honestly confess an ignorance of astronomy, of chemistry, of geology, of philology, and really feel their ignorance. But few men honestly confess an ignorance of political economy. Though they may admit or even proclaim ignorance, they do not really feel it. There are many who say they know nothing of political economy —many indeed who do not know what the term means. Yet these very men hold at the same time and with the utmost confidence opinions upon matters that belong to political economy, such as the causes which effect wages and prices and profits, the effects of tariffs, the influence of labour-saving machinery, the function and proper substance of money, the reason of 'hard times' or 'good times,' and so on. For men living in society, which is the natural way for men to live, must have some sort of politico-economic theories, good or bad, right or wrong. The way to make sure that these theories are correct, or if they are not correct, to supplant them by true theories, is by careful and systematic thinking."

Into what morasses have the false guides in political economy led statesmen and people? Let us examine a few. The inhabitants of this globe, abounding in ability and intelligence, are told that recovery from the ills they endure can be brought about by lessening production and by making things dearer. Needless to say they do not believe it. Yet actually schemes have already been put into force for destroying grain food, pigs, tea, etc., or for limiting their future production, while statesmen vie with one another in devising plans for raising prices. Meanwhile elections are fought here, there, and everywhere—pitiable to relate—on the question as to how much more this candidate will promise compared with his opponent towards a "dole," a wage on "relief" work, or an "allowance" of some sort or other. Class is set against class, and party against party. New "leaders" are sought. Despite it all, allegiance to party persists, generally because of the inequities brought about by the system of election, and the direction of men's minds is diverted from a study of fundamental principles. Seats in Parliament are not at all in proportion to the votes cast in support of this or that party or proposal. Wittingly or unwittingly politicians place themselves at the service of private interests. One consequence of all this is that the younger generation tends to think the whole Parliamentary system hopelessly corrupt, and to believe in other and anti-democratic methods instead.

Producers have a natural inclination to regard overflowing harvests as the best barometer of prosperity, and so also have consumers. They are apt to exhibit impatience with those who prescribe the destruction of wealth in order to create income. They only applaud subsidies when they can see direct financial gain to their own particular group. North American wheat-growers contracted their sowings for the year 1934 by nearly 10,000,000 acres, though the crop harvested in 1933 was one of the smallest for decades, due partly to the fact that the carry-over from the year 1932 was about 50 per cent of the crop against a normal one of about 15 per cent. The United States wheat subsidy will cost the American consumer over $100,000,000 annually. The United States Government has advanced over $2,000,000,000 in loans through various agricultural credit agencies since July 1929, not including $360,000,000 lost by the defunct Federal Farm Board. A higher standard of living in many parts of the world has led humans to eat relatively less cereal foodstuffs and more meat, fish, poultry, and dairy produce. About 11,000,000 fewer horses are used in industry and agriculture than was the case a decade or two ago owing to motor traction and more machinery. Yet in various places in the world are to be found millions of people who would be only too thankful to be able to buy cereal food abundantly and cheaply. A greater number of buyers would in itself help producers by tending to send up prices. Similar remarks apply to pigs and other commodities. An American professor complained recently that 5,000,000 pigs and 200,000 sows were to be slaughtered to restore national prosperity; and it appears that Danes are having to turn many of their pigs into soap, because new British laws have limited their market for bacon. Meanwhile the retail price of bacon in England went up about 6d. a pound, and cotton operatives suffered unemployment because the Danes retorted by imposing quotas on English cotton exports. The English Pig Marketing Board first underestimated the British pig supply and the curers had

o*

to face a loss of £160,000. Next they made a miscalculation and overestimated the supply. Fresh burdens on taxpayers or consumers, or both, are usually a consequence of such bureaucratic interferences with trade. Yet despite strenuous efforts towards better co-operation, reorganization, and efficiency in production and distribution, there is hardly ever any commensurate improvement in these directions.

In connection with the production and distribution of milk similar difficulties are arising. Space forbids giving any details. But a few brief remarks on the theoretical side of these matters is necessary because of the influence such things have upon co-operation for the commonweal and upon the distribution of population. The system of private ownership of businesses and industries run for private profit is widely accepted by the community as a sound method of production and distribution so long as there is a free and open market in which producers and distributors compete. The reasons for this are: Firstly, in an open competitive market the benefit of all improvements in methods of production and distribution are ultimately automatically distributed to the whole community; and secondly, competition stimulates invention and compels efficiency. The theories of socialism, generally rather ill-defined, are not well supported by arguments to show how under that regime the community would be so well served. But now come along semi-socialists, who seek the best of both worlds. They banish internal and external competition, the former by marketing Acts and such like legislation, the latter by quotas and tariffs. Subsidies and the fixing of prices are also brought in, indeed seem to be well-nigh inevitable *sequelae*.

All these schemes fall heavily in the long run upon consumers and taxpayers. Wealth becomes more unevenly distributed than ever; the poor are made poorer; and a natural and healthy growth and distribution of people on the surface of the earth are hindered. State treasuries become difficult to fill because prosperous production is hampered. Debts grow. These schemes require more money out of public coffers to finance them, and they breed conflicts and wars. Nation distrusts nation. Armament industries are stimulated. Diplomats talk. Those that lay claim to the earth, especially where minerals exist, keep in the background but take care that they are not ousted from their "spheres of influence." The harassed statesmen cease to balance the public accounts and start circulating uncovered promises to pay. Currency questions baffle them. Unemployment continues. Then the statesmen and economists hold council together and decide that the people must lift themselves up by hauling at their own bootlaces. A great impetus comes from the big-wigs at the centre. They attempt to boost up production by much advertised schemes of organization. They think thereby to provide the income to meet the inflationary I.O.U.s they have created. But all the time they fail to grasp the fundamental truths, that the commodities upon which all live are produced by the application of labour to land and its inherent resources, and that taxes hinder production. Meanwhile the rise in prices, which hit the poorest most, set the economists inventing new words for "inflation," new explanations of the trouble. Would that all could escape from that prevalent error of confusing money (seldom defined) with wealth! If all would think in terms of goods, would realize that all trade is exchange, and that people live largely "from hand to mouth," most of these subjects would be more easily and clearly understood. Then it would immediately become clear that it is folly to cry for reparation payments and at the same time to set up tariff barriers against goods, and that the hoarding of gold in bank cellars was not without its drawbacks. Currency wars will not cease and the stabilization of prices be achieved until a return is made to basic principles, and until these are better understood. Prosperity cannot be attained until taxes and, above all, the worst kind of taxes, tariffs, are lowered or, better, removed altogether, and until man is free to produce by ready access to Nature's storehouse. It certainly will never become established by patent "social credit" schemes which set out to make all rich by advancing them credit on the strength of their human capacities for producing. Money is not synonymous with wealth. Nothing is easier than to manufacture certain kinds of money. In this sense any potentate in a position of authority, given a little paper, can easily "make pots of money." But wealth requires something more than human labour. Man's brain and muscle have to be applied to the resources of nature to produce wealth. This is where the land question comes in. Give man credit by all means for his powers of wealth production. But give him, too, easy access to the inexhaustible storehouse.

Many of the points made in the preceding paragraphs are closely connected with the causes of war. This side of the subject has been dealt with fully by John E. Grant,[1] to whose book reference has already been made. But since wars have a great influence upon the growth and distribution of population brief reference to the subject is called for before this book is ended. References have been made to some of the aftermaths of war, viz. debts, reparations, unbalanced budgets, retrograde taxation schemes, currency difficulties, etc. There is not often a sufficient appreciation of the differences and the interactions between internal and external debts. Again, when State Treasuries are in deep waters and new issues of currency notes, intrinsically valueless, are being made, the statesmen are generally more concerned by the exigencies of the State as borrower than by the requirements of the subject as trader.[2] Throughout the ages it has been the common practice of potentates in difficulties to debase the currency. It is labelled with more highfalutin designations nowadays. A further observation of the greatest importance is: debt payments (internal and external) and reparation arrangements are manipulated as a means to alter the ownership and the enjoyment of the earth, e.g. steelworks in the Ruhr, iron-fields in Lorraine, coal mines in Silesia, oil wells in Canada.[3] Yet many persons who call themselves "Left Wingers" would attack the banks and are blind to the evils of land monopoly and taxation. Walton Newbold has ably elaborated some of these things in his *Democracy, Debts, and Disarmament*. He shows that the vested interests used war and diplomacy around the year 1814 to affect property rights and business development dependent partly upon Saar coal fields. He writes:[4] "Silesia and the neighbouring coal field of Wilnowitz-Ostrava were not put under three different and antagonistic regimes, for the first time by the treaties made at

[1] *The Problem of War and Its Solution* (Allen & Unwin, 1922. 12s. 6d.).

[2] Burke describes paper money as "not a measure of the trade of a nation, but of the necessities of its government," quoted by William Cobbett in his *Paper against Gold*, 1828, p. 75.

[3] Not yet being worked (at Athabaska, e.g.).

[4] Walton Newbold's *Democracy, Debts, and Disarmament*, p. 91 (Methuen & Co., London, 1933. 8s. 6d.).

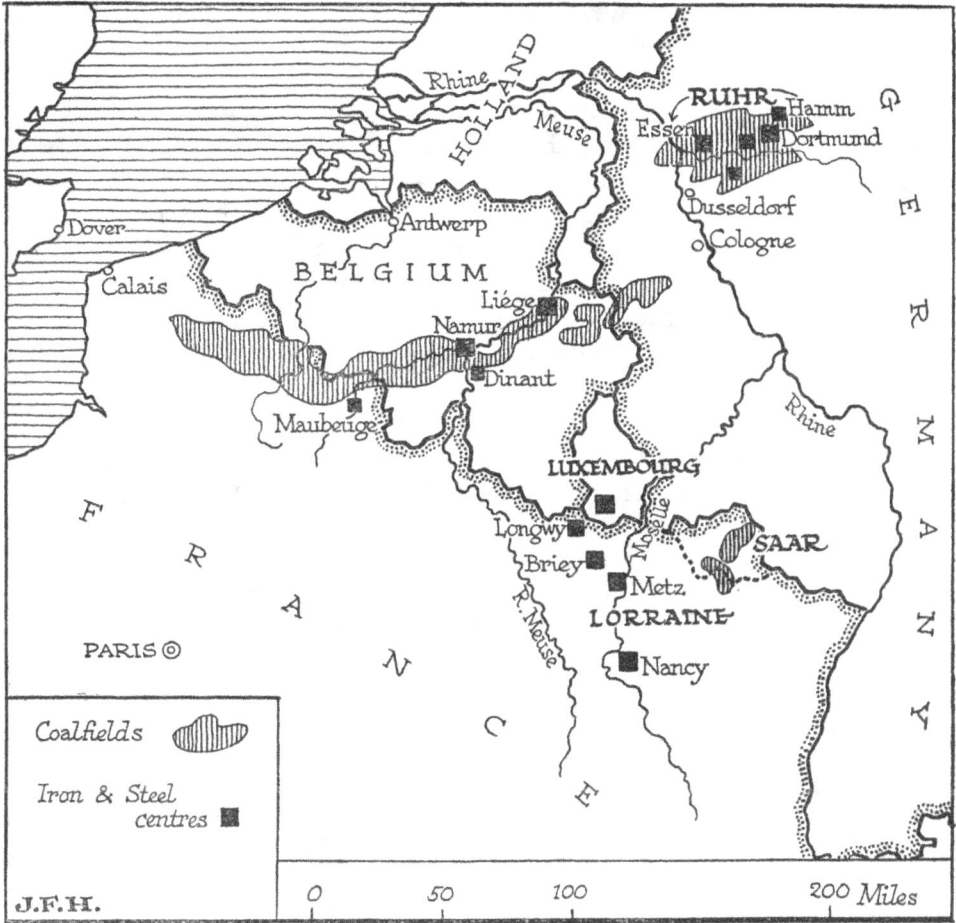

SAAR AND RUHR DISTRICTS

Conflict breaks out when private interests appropriate natural resources.
Exploitation and poverty produce a maldistribution of population even
when the interests are "consolidated" by international capital, as in the
case of the European Steel Trust which governs the coal- and iron-fields
shown in the above map

Plebs Atlas

Versailles. . . . Only those who know nothing of history (and seem
to care less) harbour the childish illusion that wrongs in those
quarters date simply from the time of Clemenceau and the Comité
des Forges de France."[1]

[1] See also the *Week-End Review*, London, January 23, 1932, p. 93.

Normal demand will throw land into use. The ballyhoo of real-estate dealers is not required. The growth and distribution of population along natural lines direct the way land is used. But Government restrictions and taxes on the one hand and the grip of landlordism on the other curb and warp the growth and pervert and corrupt the distribution. If land booms occur, speculation throws marginal land into use sooner than necessary, forces unneeded improvements, and results finally in a collapse as population refuses or is unable to sustain these artificially swollen land values. It is the interference of statesmen, the machinations of armament makers (busier than ever, it appears to-day), and of land monopolists which explain the aggressiveness of warring peoples. A case in point is the Japanese, who are led into aggression and war through causes that are not understood by most of them. They have not equality of opportunity to life and liberty in their own country. Internal economic depression and shrinkage of overseas trade alike have the same origins as elsewhere. The Japanese suffer from heavy taxation, from land-lordism, and from tariff and Chinese boycotting barriers to trade, etc. Consequently Japan's development is lopsided, masses of her people are poor, her industrial workers are underpaid. So there is no well-ordered co-operation for the commonweal, and her politicians can cry about the pressure of population and lead her men to the shambles. It has been stated that over 50 per cent of the annual rice crop in Japan is taken by landlords as rent for letting their fellow-countrymen work. This class and their followers it is who urge their fellow-countrymen to look abroad for that territory which the growing population seems to require. But it will not be the growing population who will get those lands abroad, but the imperialist landlords.

Economic pressure is constantly forcing square pegs into round holes, forcing numbers of people to abandon even partial touch with the soil, forcing an undue preponderance of workers into secondary industries, forcing crowds citywards, and forcing masses of workers the world over to a mere subsistence level. When this pressure ceases through returning, by an easy and equitable method, to the age-long outlook on property rights which regards land as belonging to all, then population can grow naturally and become more sanely distributed. It may be said,

"But the people have consented to the system which has now come into vogue." This is not true. The people were never consulted. Apart from the undemocratic methods of consulting the people which in some degree are still extant in many countries, it is true to say there is not a single "law" on the Statute Book affecting the tenure and holding of land which was first submitted to the people for approval or otherwise. That is exactly the sort of thing the politicians say little about beforehand. So far from consenting, history relates revolts and uprisings of the people to protest when their freedom was encroached upon, and in former times at least the connection between liberty and the land was well understood. Wat Tyler and his men in 1381 answered Richard II when he asked them what they wanted by saying: "We will that ye free us, us and our lands; and that we no more be held any man's slaves." And Robert Kett, at the head of his Norfolk peasants, protested in 1549 that: "The common pastures . . . are taken away. The lands . . . are ditched and hedged in . . . and we are shut out. We desire liberty, and an equal use of all things. This we will have. Otherwise these tumults and our lives shall only be ended together." Again, it is sometimes said: "But how would the community fix rents; and what would prevent rich people obtaining unfair advantages through their bigger means?" How are rents fixed to-day? Landlords get all they can, and wealth is maldistributed. Economic pressure affects the many. It is the rich who are few. To-day competition for the use of land is over-stimulated by valuable sites and soils being held out of use or under-used. Under the new regime it would not pay such holders (who, like every other holder, would have to pay their contributions into the common pool) to let the land continue to be under-used. Sites of all kinds would be easier, therefore, to acquire; and riches would not gravitate to the few. Under the new regime periodic offering of sites at public auction would help to settle rents. The Crown lands in Regent Street, London, now bring in nearly £500,000 annually. The rentals were fixed by the tenants. To test values the Crown Land Commissioners caused several sites to be offered at public auction a few years ago just when the old leases were coming to an end. The rents obtained were found to be higher than the values placed upon the frontages by their own surveyors. When a year or two later some of the tenants found business slumping from causes they ill-understood, they complained against rents but said little condemning rates, taxes, and the causes which sent down the purchasing powers of their customers. Under the new regime purchasing power would go up, business would be brisker all round, yet the competition for sites everywhere would be lessened.

Easier access to land for users of all kinds under the new regime of land restoration and tax abolition, in other words lessened competition for sites, means far more secure tenure than under the regime of to-day. Complete security of tenure is, in fact, ensured to all holders capable and willing of continuing to use their holdings well. Experience in use of a particular site gives advantage to present holders. Growth of population and increase of public services in the neighbourhood of sites with high rents will lead the tax-free user to be willing to pay such rents. If he has to bid against others his advantages are great, as already indicated, compared to the position of such users to-day. Furthermore, he knows he is secure in the possession of his own improvements whether he wishes to remain or go. There is no blackmailing landlord to steal his goodwill or annex his buildings. If he cannot see his way to continue as holder of a site no man will feel aggrieved in relinquishing it when private property in the rent of land has been abolished. He may be old and weary, for example, and be quite ready to step aside to let another pay the rent or a higher one. He would feel well content in the recognition of the fact that his capabilities had not grown so as to enable him to afford to continue to pay rent and utilize the site. He would give place to another and realize it will suit him and his fellow-countrymen better to seek a new site. Thus when the magical instrument is discovered and applied the growth of population necessitating the use of smaller areas will cause no troubles and the well-ordered distribution of population will produce no difficulties. That instrument, that lubricant for changes in population density, consists in the confiscation of common value for common needs. To-day common values are confiscated by those who do not create them, and the common needs have to be met by taking from a man (by means of taxes) his own rightful property, the products of his own labour. The community requires payment for what it does for land holders, and the holders will willingly pay for what they get in public services. All will be satisfied. Human inventiveness, as well as growth in numbers, leads, too, to smaller areas being sufficient, for it enables more products to be grown or made from equal quantities of land. Human beings can make more of natural opportunity through advances in knowledge. Under the new regime to use land, *whether the user be a private body or a public authority*, less remuneratively than it could be used will not be tolerated, for an enlightened age will realize the stupidity of any such plan. Hence the less remunerative use of land will be discontinued in suitable localities quite voluntarily. Those who find it best to give place to more skilled and advanced workers will receive due compensation, and this again will contribute to their willingness to step aside and retire to another site. That compensation will be twofold. The higher rent which a better use can pay will flow into the communal coffers to provide better public services benefiting both parties; and by more specialization and a better grouping of people, goods will be cheapened. These principles apply throughout society to primitive tillers of the soil advancing slowly in their methods of cultivation and in their means of communication, or at the other end of the scale, to the workers in factory, shop, and office.

As has already been shown, the principles set forth in this book are widely accepted already, amongst others, by primitive folk, Moslem nations, Henry Georgists, and all those persons, in many lands, who are striving after tax relief. It remains for a great majority to awake and proclaim the truth that communal values must be for the common need. This should come about most readily in civilized countries where human intelligence and knowledge have advanced by such big strides in recent generations. The essential simplicity of the method is too much for the wiseheads and the professors. It is for the people, the mass of the poverty-stricken, to arise and insist on common sense. Then will human geography enter into a new era. Then will the science of man's relationship to his environment be recognized as being based not only on climate, contour, and accessibility, but also upon social justice and the play of economic factors.

The wide acceptance of the principle (sometimes called

"Physiocracy") that direct taxation from holders of land according to the value of their holding is the only proper source of the
revenue of society, has been dwelt upon in the previous chapters
of this book. Much has been said to show that a levy of this kind
is no tax as the word is ordinarily understood. Several chapters
have enlarged upon the condition and outlook of the peasants,
some of whom were our ancestors. They originally belonged to a
pacifist Neolithic culture which is in our blood and bones. This
culture still exists in purity in Polynesia and, incidentally, almost
intact in the Protectorate Kingdom of Tonga. Similar customs
as to land tenure are extant in many places where dark-skinned
races are under the suzerainty of the British. Under British rule,
in various parts of the world, the customs of the native races in
regard to land (as to much else) have been respected under
various "Codes"; witness the Lugard Code in Northern Nigeria,
the MacGregor Code in Malaya, going back to 1886, the Byatt
Code of 1923 in Tanganyika, and in Somaliland. Under such
systems the thing to note is that poverty and exploitation are
utterly unknown. It may be mentioned in passing that the
Slavonic Mir is not remote from the ideals of those under which
these primitive races and the Neolithic Aryans have or have had
their being.

The great numbers of persons here and there, in many lands,
who desire to bring about relief from taxes, are not, as a rule,
under the influence of the most direct descendants of the Physiocrats, the Henry Georgists, or, as they used to be called in America,
the "Single-Taxers." Most of them are practical men, often municipal leaders, who would scorn being classed with any of the foregoing groups. An account of the actions of some of these persons has been given in previous pages, especially in the chapter
on "Ground Values and Property Appraisals." They are men
and women with no particular philosophy, who are moved by
the pressure of the conditions of society around them. Striking
examples of members of this group, not hitherto mentioned, are:
Kitchener, who abolished rates on houses in the Transvaal; Lord
Mayor Meagher, of Sydney; and the great physiocrat, Rivadavia,
who revived the Asiatic-Roman law of Emphyteusis in 1826 in
Argentina. Similarly, the members of the Wellington Harbour
Board, New Zealand, let reclaimed land on indefinite leases with

frequent revisions of site value. All these, vaguely or clearly, have seen how to diminish conflict between public and private welfare and how to introduce the means of attaining a better co-operation for the commonweal. Governments are ever trying to help the governed, and are succeeding well along certain lines even when in other directions they are hindering. Guidance and advice have done marvels in aiding backward nations and the development of tropical countries. The economic expansion of Africa, to give one example, has advanced wonderfully, but often at a heavy cost to Africans. Education, especially the patient propaganda encouraging an improved agriculture, and the scientific attack against disease (maladies due to malaria, hook-worm, and tsetse fly especially) have already done wonders. In all these cases the initiative and hard work have originally come from Governments foreign to the soil. Where these things have been done without introducing the burdens of new taxes and without upsetting the co-partnership and tribal basis of land tenures which have ruled for hundreds, nay thousands, of years, there peace and prosperity have reigned. Where the opposite is true, many troubles and checks to progress have arisen.

In the countries of the advanced, so-called Western and civilized nations, Governments also have done much of great service to the workers. But how much more might have been accomplished if Governments had not also retarded progress and undermined development by spending most of their exertions in wrong acts! The direct result of their misdeeds, all too often backed by a majority of the workers, it is true, is war. Wars would not occur when a true co-operative commonwealth had been established by all, producing equality of opportunity to life, liberty, and the pursuit of happiness; and that can only be brought about by restoring the land to the people. The use of this expression, however, is all very well only if it is understood in all its meaning and effects. But too often, addressing town dwellers, as is the rule nowadays, expressions of this kind are coupled with such phrases as "people are poor because land has been fenced in." So the meaning and effects of socializing land *rent*, the only property that can be socialized, are obscured, and people are puzzled to understand how by such means equality of opportunity can be brought about and strife and wars eradicated.

It is also true that landowners to-day succeed to some extent in keeping secret their conveyances. Title deeds are not for the eyes of the uninitiated. Domesday Books have only been published twice in a thousand years in England. But when the morrow of a new era dawns there will soon be a new Domesday Book. The people will then know the vast revenue to which they are entitled. Moreover the conveyance of their rent can then be accomplished by the use of parliamentary machinery. It is the unchallengeable power that the House of Commons has over finance which will enable the people to bring about this bloodless revolution without interference from the Lords or the Crown. It is even possible that Conservatism may itself be enlisted for the restoration of the ancient rights of the English people.

Land rent, unlike goods and income, is essentially something which cannot be hidden, and it is easily assessed. Smuggling and deceit over public revenue will vanish when taxes are abolished. Corruption and theft will disappear when human nature, instinctively virtuous and humane, attains true liberty of expression. Furthermore, when Governments attend to their main duty and collect the public revenue, no longer will nations exist where one in every ten workers is a servant of the authorities and lives, drone-like, on the work of the producers. With the disappearance of armaments, war debts, and too big a crowd of bureaucrats (vainly attempting to alleviate poverty but doing nothing to eradicate it), less revenue for public "services" than the present day's requirements will be amply sufficient. Probably therefore a good deal less than half of what Governments now collect will be more than enough. Land rent to-day can be shown to be quite equal to meeting such requirements. If it is more than enough, the surplus can be returned to individuals on a *per capita* basis. It has already been mentioned that the ground rents from Crown property in Regent Street, London, comprising more than three-quarters but not the whole of the street, amount annually to nearly £500,000, and that the annual land values of New York come to $675,000,000. This gives some idea of the land rents which exist. Another can be got by mentioning the ascertained fact that the selling value of the land of New Zealand (apart from buildings and improvements) was £318,000,000 about the year 1930, equivalent to £218 per head of the population. The selling value of the land of Great Britain is not likely to be less. If the total population of Great Britain is multiplied by £218 the result is just over £10,000,000,000, only about seven times as much as the ground value of Greater London. This selling value gives an annual one of £500,000,000. But this estimated value is that of to-day, when the occupier of each piece is subject to existing rates and taxes. It represents therefore only that part of the value which the landowners are able to put into their own pockets. It is clear, then, that there is enough communal income to supply all necessary public services. The community will see to it that this is so, for the amounts made payable and the expenditure are adjustable.

National necessity demands the establishment of the claim of the community to that which by right belongs to the community. Let us hope this just claim will be confirmed before another devastating war drifts along. For after wars injustice strikes deeper roots, reaction triumphs, and beloved ones, who have been "called to the colours" as crusaders for righteousness and liberty, will return no more. We do not want the horror of the proof of the fruitlessness of their sacrifice to be added to the sting of death. Yet if new wars break out and the lips of ghosts could speak, the dead might rise from a million graves and say, "We have died in vain." Before that day, to prevent such sacrifice let us learn the manner in which liberty can be achieved. The result of war is death and destruction. Furthest from war is liberty, which gives life and love in their fulness. One by one the States which have not been based on justice have fallen. To fulfil the purpose of existence, liberty founded on justice must reign. Then can nations flourish together in amity, and individuals within a nation live in friendly co-operation and prosperity. Justice within a nation must precede that justice between nations upon which alone peace can be founded. And justice within a nation can have no sure foundation unless based upon liberty and mutual respect. These are not to be found in the courts of law. The law upon which liberty is based is—the equal rights of all to the free gifts of nature.

The courts of law administer legal enactments, often faulty, complicated, and biased. In 1927 two Italian fish-hawkers were electrocuted in Massachusetts. They were arrested over seven years previously on a charge of murder and kept in prison throughout the seven years. These two, Sacco and Vanzetti, were proved innocent. But their views were heretical at that time to the class who tried them, and the courts of law would not admit a mistake. They did not ask for mercy but for justice. Justice is a spirit, the law is a convention. These two peace-loving, non-revolutionary, philosophical anarchists triumphed over death.[1] They died without flinching, in the knowledge that their death could do more for tolerance and justice than all their street-corner oratory. Vanzetti's farewell to his friends runs as follows: "If it had not been for this I might have lived out my life, talking at street corners to scorning men. I might have died. Now we are not a failure. This is our career and our triumph. Never in our full life could we hope to do such work for tolerance, for justice, for man's understanding of man, as now we do by an accident. Our words, our lives, our pains—*nothing*. The taking of our lives—*all*! This last moment belongs to us. This agony our triumph." And the noble-hearted Sacco wrote the following good-bye to his son: "My son, do not cry. Be strong to comfort your mother. Take her for walks in the quiet country, gathering wild flowers, resting beneath shady trees, and visiting the streams and the gentle tranquillity of Mother Nature. Do not seek happiness just for yourself. Step down to help the weak ones who cry for help. Help the persecuted, because they are your better friends. They are your comrades who fight and fall, as your father and Barto fought and fell, to conquer joy and freedom for all the poor workers."

This pair had denounced American civilization on the grounds that it exploited the worker and denied justice to the ignorant and the poor. But they denounced with equal vehemence revolution by violence, and the new tyrannies, Russian Bolshevism, as roundly as Italian Fascism. They desired only "to collaborate to raise all humanity to the dignity of free men." The injustice they suffered through their execution for a murder they never committed was actuated by the unconscious fear of the privileged classes. These do not hate the truth, in fact they strive to learn it, but their prejudices all too often blind them, and their fears at times make beasts of them. Justice for such poor, ill-understood

[1] Anarchy in this sense means a minimum of government and a maximum of individualism.

eel-pedlars in the courts of law can only follow a reign of justice in the State at large; and the first thing society must see to is to stop that "continuing offence" which robs the community of her due revenue, the community-created values attaching to land. That great robbery must stop; and when it is ended the second great robbery comprised in taxation can cease too. Then can individuals, and committees of individuals chosen to exercise certain authority for the common good, co-operate for the commonweal without detriment to their own interests. Then can population grow without artificial constraints on life and love. Then can the inhabitants of the earth people its surface in such a way as to fulfil the purpose of existence. Opportunities for the satisfaction of each one's desires, differing from another's and executed by unequal powers and abilities, will be open and free. The horrors of overcrowding and poverty, leading to erroneous notions of over-population, need no longer be seen.

Justice knows no qualifications. It recognizes no class distinctions. Insurgence against wrong can be hotter in the heart and on the lips of a fish-pedlar than in the heart and on the lips of a high court judge. "Out of the mouths of babes and sucklings" wisdom may come. The crowd dimly sees the chief cause of injustice and exploitation. The day of full enlightenment may be nearer at hand than some imagine.

The vague irritability which is one of the characteristics of modern life can be cured by re-establishing contact with nature, not alone through the senses, but through the mind. Nicolo Sacco, in his beautiful good-bye to his son, realized this. The path to that contact has been shown in this book. When that path is followed, the workers of the world can at last reach a happy contentment because they will then feel they have attained the satisfaction of being able to exercise aright their own powers. Fulfilment of function breeds contentment and peace. They will realize that they are using to further their own purposes the vast forces to which they owe their being and that in helping the fulfilment of their own beings they do nothing of hurt to the rest of the community. People will then, more than ever before, feel conscious that their efforts are rooted in something greater than themselves. To be in tune with nature and at peace with one's neighbour are the greatest things in life.

INDEX

For Product Safety Concerns and Information please contact our EU
representative GPSR@taylorandfrancis.com
Taylor & Francis Verlag GmbH, Kaufingerstraße 24, 80331 München, Germany